Nationalism and Communism in
MACEDONIA

PUBLISHED UNDER THE AUSPICES OF
THE SPEROS B. VRYONIS CENTER FOR THE STUDY OF HELLENISM
Sacramento, California

This work is the twelfth volume in the series
————————————Hellenism
Ancient, Mediæval, Modern

General Editors
Christos P. Ioannides, Stylianos Spyridakis, Speros Vryonis, Jr.

Nationalism and Communism in
MACEDONIA
Civil Conflict, Politics of Mutation,
National Identity

Evangelos Kofos

Aristide D. Caratzas, Publisher
New Rochelle, New York
1993

For Anna

Aristide D. Caratzas, Publisher
30 Church Street, P.O. Box 210
New Rochelle, N.Y. 10802
Tel: 914-632-8487 • Fax: 914-632-3650

ISBN 0-89241-540-1

Manufactured in the United States of America

The essays in the Appendix have been published
previously as indicated below,
and have been reprinted
by permission:

THE IMPACT OF THE MACEDONIAN QUESTION
ON THE CIVIL CONFLICT IN GREECE (1943-1949),
Hellenic Foundation for Defense and Foreign Policy,
"Occasional Papers," no. 3, 1989.

THE MACEDONIAN QUESTION: THE POLITICS OF MUTATION
Balkan Studies, vol. 27, 1986.

NATIONAL HERITAGE AND NATIONAL IDENTITY
IN NINETEENTH- AND TWENTIETH-CENTURY MACEDONIA,
European History Quarterly, vol. 19, 1989.

Cosmos Publishing Co., Inc.
262 Rivervale Road
River Vale, N.J. 07675-6252
Phone: 201-664-3494

"The Source for Greek Literature"
"Η Πηγή του Ελληνικού Βιβλίου"

PUBLISHER'S FOREWORD

Nationalism and Communism in Macedonia is probably the most quoted book on the post-World War II Macedonian issue. Initially published in 1964, the book has survived the test of time. Historians and analysts of the Balkan scene have appreciated the mature approach to a complex and delicate problem of an unusually young author. The book's value was augmented by the use of hitherto inaccessible historical documents, as the the author had been given access to the archives of the Greek Ministry of Foreign Affairs for the period 1940–1950. Incidentally, these archives still remain closed for that period.

Almost three decades later, the new crisis in the Balkans and the re-emergence of the Macedonian problem have prompted a reprint of the 1964 edition without any changes.

In consultation with the author and with his permission, the publisher has included three essays on Macedonian issues written more recently by Evangelos Kofos. All of them were published in the late 1980s. They provide a fresh look at an old issue and have profited from a wealth of new documentary and secondary sources as well as the author's thirty-year experience with Balkan politics.

"The Impact of the Macedonian Question on Civil Conflict in Greece (1943–1949)" was initially presented at the Copenhagen conference "Greece during the Civil War" (3–5 June 1987), which was sponsored by the Lehrman Institute of New York. It was published by the Hellenic Foundation for Defense and Foreign Policy as No. 3 in its series "Occasional Papers" (Athens, 1989).

"The Macedonian Question: The Politics of Mutation" was read in an early version during a symposium jointly held in Thessalonike and sponsored by the Institute for Balkan Studies of Thessalonike and the Südosteuropa Gessellschaft of Munich (7–9 March 1985). It was published in *Balkan Studies*, vol. 27, 1986.

"National Heritage and National Identity in Nineteenth- and Twentieth-Century Macedonia" was first published in *European History Quarterly* (SAGE, London, Newbury Park and New Delhi), vol. 19, 1989. It was reprinted independently by ELIAMEP (Athens, 1991).

Nationalism and Communism in Macedonia. Civil Conflict, Politics of Mutation, National Identity, consisting then of the original 1964 edition and approximately one hundred pages of additional material, offers readers the opportunity to judge for themselves not only how a controversial and complex international problem has evolved over three decades, but also how a now mature expert on the subject perceives this evolution today. Perhaps more importantly, it is the only work published recently that provides a historical context for the crisis emerging after the implosion of Yugoslavia.

ACKNOWLEDGEMENTS

Initially introduced to Macedonian history through childhood stories, I became seriously interested in the subject during my graduate studies at Georgetown University, Washington, D.C. The distortions and inaccuracies of most relevant secondary sources, and the scarcity of well-documented up-to-date works, convinced me, at the time, of the need for undertaking the writing of this book.

With a grant by the Institute for Balkan Studies and the encouragement of Mr. Basil Laourdas, Director of the Institute, I conducted research in Thessaloniki and Athens which complemented my work in the United States.

I am particularly thankful for permission to study the archives of the Royal Ministry of Foreign Affairs for the years 1940-1950. These included part of the archives of the Nazi-imposed Athens Government (1941-1944) and the archives of the Government in exile (1941-1944). Although not all documents of that critical period can yet be made public, sufficient material is being used here for the first time to allow a more intelligent appraisal of events connected with Macedonia. Of great value to me were the published Bulgarian and Yugoslav material found in the archives of the Ministry.

I was also fortunate to have access to Greek communist published documents — most of them not easily accessible in the West.

The archives of the Institute for Balkan Studies were found to contain important unpublished documents of the period prior to the Balkan Wars, as well as useful material of more recent origin.

Many qualified persons assisted me with wise counsel, valuable data and material and all-round support. I am especially indebted to

Mr. Philippos Dragoumis, Mr. George Themelis and Mr. Basil Laourdas. I want to express my deepest thanks to the Board of Scholars of the Institute for Balkan Studies for offering me the grant and for undertaking the publication of this book. Yet, the responsibility for the opinions expressed herein and the conclusions reached is entirely mine.

Much appreciation is reserved for the assistance rendered by Mr. Const. Hadjithomas, director of the Historical Archives of the Royal Ministry of Foreign Affairs, Mr. A. Provatas, director of the Library of the Parliament and Dr. Howard W. Johnston, President of Anatolia College, Thessaloniki, whose generous understanding offered me valuable time to continue my work.

Loving gratitude is expressed to my sister, Mrs. Ninetta Godis who typed an early draft of the manuscript; to Mrs. Janet Lugo who, on another occasion, selflessly spent time and intelligent effort in the collection of important material in the United States; to Mr. Theodore Adam for assisting in the drawing of the maps, and last but not least to my parents for their constant moral support.

TABLE OF CONTENTS

PART TWO

BALKAN COMMUNISTS AND THE MACEDONIAN QUESTION

APPENDICES

MAPS

GLOSSARY OF TERMS AND ABBREVIATIONS

A.F.Z. Women's Anti-Fascist Front; NOF's section for women.

"Aegean Macedonia." Term used for Greek Macedonia by the advocates of a unified Macedonian state.

"Autonomous Macedonia." Slogan adopted by IMRO "Centralists" aiming at the establishment of a Bulgarian-inclined, unified Macedonian State, as a first step to its incorporation to Bulgaria.

B.C.F. Balkan Communist Federation. Balkan section of the Comintern composed of all Balkan parties (Inter war).

Balkan federation. Political objective of the B.C.F. A unified Macedonian state—ostensibly Bulgarian-affiliated—would be a *bona fide* member of the federation. Following the Tito-Cominform break in 1948, and until Stalin's death in 1953, the P.R. of Bulgaria reverted to the same slogan.

Central Macedonia. The central part of Greek Macedonia between the Strymon river and a line west of the Axios (Vardar) river.

"Centralists." IMRO's wing espousing the slogan for an "Autonomous Macedonia."

Comitadjis. IMRO's guerrillas notorious for their atrocities during the Macedonian Struggle.

C.P.B. Communist Party of Bulgaria. (Refers to all variations of the title of the Bulgarian party).

C.P.S.U. Communist Party of the Soviet Union.

C.P.Y. Communist Party of Yugoslavia (Refers to all variations of the title of the Yugoslav party, including the "League of Yugoslav Communists" which is the official name since 1952).

"Democratic Army of Greece." The military establishment of the Greek communist guerrillas (1947-1949).

E.A.M. National Liberation Front. Communist-dominated, political front organization in occupied Greece.

Eastern Macedonia. The part of Greek Macedonia between the Nestos and Strymon rivers.

E.L.A.S. Greek People's Liberation Army. Communist-controlled military organization in occupied Greece.

"Exarchists." Slavophone inhabitants of Ottoman-ruled Macedonia, followers of the Bulgarian Church (Exarchate), who severed their ties with the Ecumenical Patriarchate and Hellenism.

"Federalists." Left-wing followers of IMRO (inter-war) adhering to the slogan of the Balkan federation.

"Grecomans." Term used by the Bulgarians to distinguish the Slavophone inhabitants of Ottoman-ruled Macedonia who were actively oriented to Hellenism.

Historic Macedonia. The region of the Macedonian-Greek state of ancient times.

I.M.R.O. Internal Macedonian Revolutionary Organization. Bulgarian Macedonian terrorist organization.

K.K.E. Greek Communist Party.

K.O.A.M. Communist Organization of Aegean Macedonia. Short-lived organization founded in 1949 by the KKE for its "Slav-Macedonian" followers.

Macedonia. A vague and contested geographic region in central Balkans.

Macedonian Bulgarians. Inhabitants of Macedonia of Bulgarian nationality.

Macedonian Greeks. Inhabitants of Macedonia of Greek nationality.

"Macedonian" language. A Bulgarian dialect—mixture of Slavonic, Greek, Turkish, Albanian, Vlach e.t.c.— spoken by the Slavs of northern Macedonia. In recent years an attempt is being made to reshape it into a unique, independent Slavonic language.

"Macedonian" nation. (see "Macedonians").

Macedonians. In ancient times the name of a Hellenic people. Now it has retained only its geographical concept. It is used to denote the inhabitants of Macedonia irrespective of their nationality (Greeks, Serbs, Bulgarians e.t.c.)

"Macedonians." The name given by the Yugoslavs to the Slav inhabitants of upper Macedonia, in the attempt to invest them with a new national identity.

"Megali Idea." Great Idea. The goal of the Greeks since their independence (1830) to liberate the hellenic regions under Ottoman rule. Abandoned in 1930.

"Monarcho-fascists." Name given by the communist guerrillas to the lawfully constituted Greek Government and the Greek armed forces.

"New Lands." The Greek and Yugoslav regions occupied by the Bulgarians during World War II and incorporated to Bulgaria for the duration of the war.

N.O.F. National Liberation Front. Organization of the "Slav-Macedonians" cooperating with the Greek communist guerrillas for the overthrow of the Greek Government (1948-1949) and the incorporation of Greek Macedonia to the P.R. of Macedonia.

"Ohrana" battalions. Terrorist bands of Bulgarian sympathisers in occupied (World War II) Greek Macedonia, armed and organized by Bulgarian officers.

"Patriarchists." Greek or Slav-speaking inhabitants in Ottoman-ruled Macedonia who remained loyal to the Ecumenical Patriarchate and to Hellenism and actively opposed the Exarchist Bulgarians.

P.F.R. of Yugoslavia. People's Federal Republic of Yugoslavia. (Since 1963 it has been renamed Socialist Federal Republic of Yugoslavia),

P.R. of Macedonia. People's Republic of Macedonia. One of Yugoslavia's six federative republics. (Since 1963 it has been renamed Socialist Republic of Macedonia).

"Pirin" Macedonia. Name used for the Macedonian region of Bulgaria by the proponents of a unified Macedonian state.

"Slav-Macedonians." Slavophones of Greek Macedonia who exhibited anti-hellenic attitude during the occupation and the Guerrilla war by espousing now the Bulgarian now the Yugoslav Macedonian views. Since 1949, they live scattered in the P.R.of Yugoslavia and the other people's republics where they escaped following the crushing of the Guerrilla war.

Slavophones. Slav-speaking, or bilingual, inhabitants of Greek Macedonia having a Greek national consciousness.

S.N.O.F. Slav-Macedonian Liberation Front. War-time partisan organization of the "Slav-Macedonians," known for its affiliation with the Yugoslav partisans.

South-Slav federation. Federation envisioned by Tito and Dimitrov, with Yugoslavia playing apparently the leading role. It failed on account of Soviet opposition.

Supreme Committee. IMRO's wing espousing the direct annexation of Ottoman-ruled Macedonia to Bulgaria.

Supremists or Verhovists. Followers of the Supreme Committee.

"United IMPO." Short-lived, left-wing of IMRO (inter-war).

"United and Independent Macedonia." Slogan promoted initially by the B.C.F. and later by all Balkan communists and the Comintern (inter-war). Following the Tito-Cominform break in 1948, it was readopted by the Greek and Bulgarian communist parties. It was abandoned quietly following the change of Soviet international tactics in 1954-1955.

"Vardar" Macedonia. The Yugoslav part of a purposed unified Macedonian state.

Verhovists. (See Supremists).

Western Macedonia. The Western part of Greek Macedonia comprising the prefectures of Pella (Edessa), Florina and Kastoria.

Western Thrace. The Greek part of Thrace.

"Western regions." Parts of Bulgaria annexed by Yugoslavia following World War I.

"Yugoslavism." The recent policy of the Belgrade Government for the gradual integration of the numerous nationalities of the country and the establishment of a Yugoslav national consciousness.

THE BALKANS AND MACEDONIA TODAY

— · — State frontiers
——— Boundaries of Macedonian provinces
▲ State capitals
● Macedonian capitals
▨ Greek Macedonia
▨ Yugoslav Macedonia
▰ Bulgarian Macedonia

Map 1

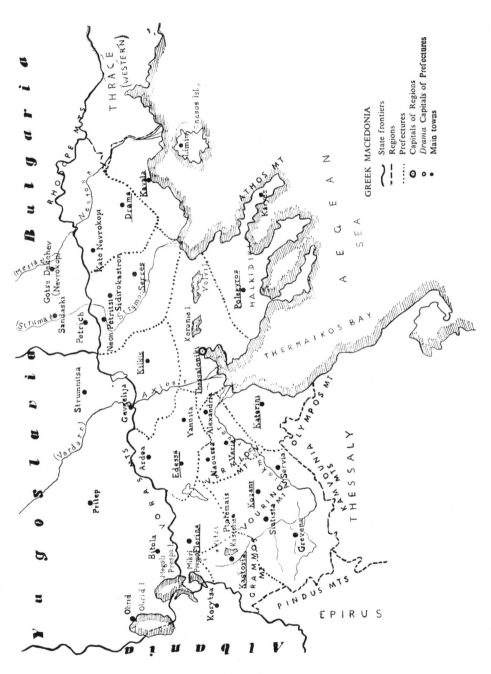

Map 2

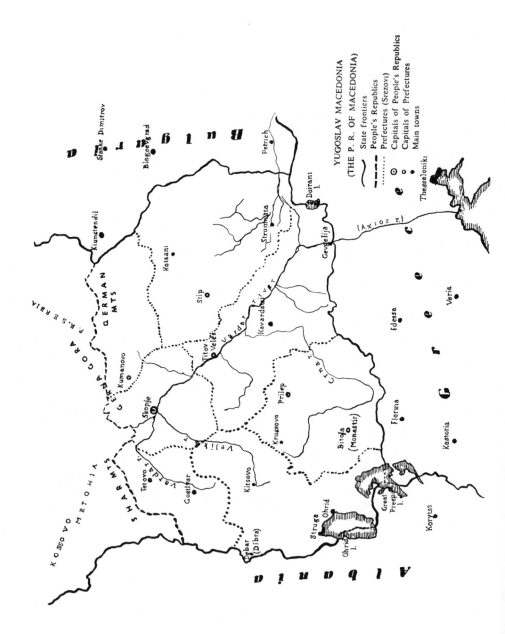

Map 3

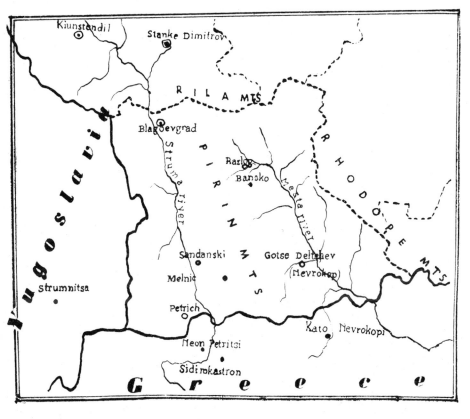

BULGARIAN MACEDONIA (REGION OF BLAGOEVGRAD)

〜　　State frontiers
－－－　Prefectures
ⵔ　　Capitals of Prefectures
○　　Capitals of Districts
●　　Town-Districts

Map 4

INTRODUCTION

For almost a century, the Macedonian Question has occupied a unique position in Balkan politics, unique because it is the most controversial issue keeping the Balkan peoples apart.

In Macedonia, as in most highly disputed lands, one hardly feels confident when trying to untangle the strings of confusion. In the endless game of politics, propaganda has been elevated to the rank of scholarship; hopes and national aspirations have assumed the form of rightful demands. A serious student of the problem, or a conscientious diplomat in the field, experiences uncertainty as to what constitutes a fact and what a myth in the Macedonian paradox.

Macedonia has suffered from far too extensive a bibliography, one tending to obscure rather than clarify the real issues. Few have been the true scholarly works. Most of the books, brochures, pamphlets and articles have been written in the heat of passion, prompted by the urge to defend or to project one side over the other. The geographic boundaries of the region, for instance, have been exposed to numerous interpretations and have caused many a scholar and propagandist to devote time and energy arguing on end over seemingly insignificant points. History, always a convenient means for converting past glories into contemporary political claims, has been twisted and recast a hundred times in order to justify individual national views. Worse yet, the analysis of the ethnological structure of Macedonia has been subjected to a savage treatment at the hands of the respective national propagandas, since it was felt, that whoever appeared to command the loyalties of the majority, enjoyed a greater chance of seeing his views enforced.

Today, however, marks a period of relative calm. The revolutionaries — known either as chauvinist *comitadjis* or communist guerrillas — have been withdrawn from the scene. Though propaganda war is still on, it is now strong and aggressive, now gentle and couched in diplomatic undertones. In such a tranquil respite this study was undertaken hoping to shed a little more light on a complex issue; weigh a little more soberly the events which shook this part of the world in recent years, and draw — if possible — the proper conclusions in order to better comprehend the

1*

elements and motivations which tend to bring the Macedonian issue constantly to the foreground.

* * *

The Macedonian Question has been a combination of age-old national antagonisms, messianic ambitions, Great Power politics, racial suspicions, economic considerations and, more recently, conflicting socio-political ideologies.

Initially, it commenced as a typical example of a national awakening of neighboring peoples, only it soon manifested itself in an unbridled urge for territorial expansion, sometimes justified, more often not. At the same time, the geopolitical value of the region attracted the attention of the Great Powers who tended to complicate the issue and accentuate local antagonisms by espousing now one, now the other of the Balkan peoples.

The peace treaties which ended the Balkan wars and the First World War, settled the issue juridically. The population transfers of the first two decades of the 20th century, reduced, to some extend, the importance of the ethnological aspect of the problem. Yet, other considerations continued to keep it alive. Among them were economic interests, as expressed in Bulgarian efforts for a territorial outlet in the Aegean Sea; group pressures, like the case of the Bulgarian Macedonian refugees in Bulgaria agitating for return to their native villages in Greek and Yugoslav Macedonia; and irresponsible actions by the various dictators who had come to power in the Balkan states during the inter-war period and who tended to act impulsively on whatever concerned Macedonia. Finally, the emergence of communism in the Balkans was instrumental in reviving and accentuating the old controversy.

* * *

Before anyone proceeds with a study of this problem, it is important that certain bacic facts are well taken into consideration.

Macedonia is neither a geographical nor a national entity. For the past fifty years it has remained, above all, a political problem which from time to time, emerges with varied degrees of acuteness. A land of high mountains and fertile plains, traversed by wide but unnavigable rivers which follow a general southerly direction, it occupies the most important economic and strategic location in Southeastern Europe. Its natural and confortable harbors of Thessaloniki and Kavala, on the Aegean, can stimulate the trade of the entire peninsula; they can also provide excellent access to the interior of the Balkans for military operations and, indeed, they have. Its plains which cut the monotony of southern Balkan mountain ranges constitute the granary not only for Macedonia but for the surrounding regions as well; yet, these same plains have been over the ages the main gateways for invaders coming to pillage and conquer. Valuable commercial routes traverse Macedonia linking Greece with Central Europe and the Orient with the West; but, again, these same routes have been an endless temptation to old and new imperialist-minded powers. In the present international situation, Macedonia constitutes the most tempting — and vulnerable — region in the North Atlantic defense complex. In the event of a major confrontation between the two blocs it bars a descent of the Soviets toward the Mediterranean, at the same time remaining a valuable forward base for the Western Alliance. Thus, since Macedonia excels in paradoxes, it is no surprise that whatever appears to be a God-sent gift, is frequently an unwarranted anathema.

Today the commonly accepted boundaries of Macedonia follow the administrative divisions of the respective Macedonian provinces in Greece, Yugoslavia and, to some extent, in Bulgaria. In the north, they follow the direction of the Shar Mountains and the hills north of Skopje; in the east they move along the Rila and Rhodope Mountain ranges and, inside Greece, along the Nestos River. The southern limits begin at the mouth of the Nestos, and follow the coastline to the slopes of Mount Olympus and thence, to the edge of the Pindus range. There, they take a sharp northerly direction, forming the western boundary with the lakes of Prespa and Ohrid as focal points.

The periphery of Macedonia crosses four national boundaries entering only briefly into Albania in the region of the lakes. Greek Macedonia occupies 51.56 per cent of the area, or 34,602,5 square kilometers; Yugoslav Macedonia 38.32 per cent or 25,713 square kilometers and Bulgarian Macedonia 10.12 per cent or 6,789,2 square kilometers.[1]

It is fruitless to trace the boundaries of Macedonia throughout the ages. Yugoslavs and Bulgarians generally agree on the delimitation as presented above, although at times, for political reasons, they tend to exclude certain districts of southern Greek Macedonia. The Greeks, on the other hand, do not accept the northern demarcation, contending that it was

---

1. Figures for the Greek and Bulgarian Macedonian regions are taken from Christopher S. Christides, *The Macedonian Camouflage in the Light of Facts and Figures* (Athens: The Hellenic Publishing Company, 1949), p. 53, and for Yugoslav Macedonia from *Petit Manuel de la Yougoslavie, 1962* (Belgrade: Federal Institute of Statistics, 1962), p. 20.

4

drawn arbitrarily on the basis of Ottoman administrative divisions rather, than on historical tradition. Instead, they limit the geographical region of Macedonia to the confines of the old Macedonian state of classical times. According to their view, present-day Greek Macedonia, and only certain narrow belts north of the border in Yugoslavia and Bulgaria, can be rightly referred to by the name ''Macedonia.'' Consequently, when the Yugoslavs talk of a ''Macedonian'' state in their country — for that matter, a ''Macedonian'' state of Slavs — the Greeks feel that their neighbors are manipulating arbitrarily a name and a state which rightfully belongs to their own classical heritage.

Today, Greek Macedonia is divided into three geographical regions, i.e. Eastern Macedonia, comprising the towns of Serres, Drama and the port of Kavala, Central Macedonia with Thessaloniki, and Western Macedonia whose major towns are Kastoria, Florina, Kozani and Edessa. Administratively, it is divided into twelve *nomoi* or prefectures, each with a prefect appointed by the Government. Thessaloniki is the capital of Macedonia and the seat of the Minister of Northern Greece who has the rank of a full cabinet minister and whose jurisdiction extends over Thrace as well as Macedonia.

Since 1944, Yugoslav Macedonia has been known as the People's Republic of Macedonia,[2] one of the six federative republics of the People's Federal Republic of Yugoslavia. Skopje, a city of approximately 170,000[3] inhabitants, is the capital of the region and the seat of the local government and assembly. Administratively it is composed of seven departments,i.e. Bitola (Monastir), Kumanovo, Ohrid, Skopje, Stip, Tetovo and Titov Veles.

At present, the regions which comprise what was traditionally known as Bulgarian ''Pirin'' Macedonia, are the Prefecture of Blagoevgrad and the district of Kiunstendil in the new (1959) Prefecture of Stanke Dimitrov. The Prefecture of Blagoevgrad comprises six administrative districts: Blagoevgrad, Goče Delčev, Petrić, Razlog and Sandaski. In addition there are the town-districts of Bansko and Melnik.

The Macedonian provinces in Greece and Bulgaria are fully integrated in the respective countries with no separate status. Only Yugoslav Macedonia, for reasons which will be analyzed in due course, has a type of autonomy as a federated component of Yugoslavia. There is no communion

4

2. In April 1963, Yugoslavia and her republics replaced the ''People's Republic'' by the ''Socialist Republic.'' Since the present book deals with events prior to this change, the old name will be retained.
3. *Petit Manuel de la Yougoslavie, 1962, op. cit.,* p. 121.

between the three parts of Macedonia. In fact, there is more dividing them than uniting them, the only exception being the relationship between Bulgarian and Yugoslav Macedonia whose common historical past and racial kinship tend to bring them together. Yet, even in their case, political considerations influence their orientation more effectively than historical ties.

Today, Greek and Bulgarian Macedonia are ethnically homogeneous regions. In Greek Macedonia, according to the latest official figures, there are 1,700,835 inhabitants of whom 41,017 are classified as Slav-speaking. In Bulgarian Macedonia (Prefecture of Blagoevgrad only), according to the 1956 census there were 281,015 inhabitants of whom 187,789 were classified as ethnic ''Macedonians.'' At present, although the results of the 1961-1962 census have not been published, all inhabitants are considered as ethnic Bulgarians. Yugoslav Macedonia is a different case. Since 1944, a ''Macedonian'' nationality has been recognized by the communist regime, and all the inhabitants of the region — known until that time as Serbs or Bulgarians — are termed ''Macedonians.'' According to 1961 official estimates, the population of Yugoslav Macedonia is 1,404,000.[4]

It is not for this introductory section to try to examine in detail the merits of the argument over the question of the existence of a ''Macedonian'' nationality. It is only hoped that in subsequent pages this point — as well as a score of others — will emerge a little more clearly.

---

4. *Ibid.*, p. 20. The 1953 official statistics gave a more detail breakdown for the population of the '' P.R. of Macedonia : ''

''Macedonians''	861,000
Turks	204,000
Skipitars (Albanians)	163,000
Serbs	35,000
Gypsies	20,000
Vlachs	9,000
Croats	3,000
Montenegrins	3,000
Yugoslavs (various)	2,000
Greeks	1,000
Bulgarians	1,000
Slovenians	1,000
Russians	1,000
Undesignated	1,000
Total	1,305,000

Source : Federal Statistical Institute : *Statistical Year-book of Yugoslavia, 1959* (Belgrade, April 1959), p. 23.

* * *

The present book is divided into two parts. Part One, which is based on secondary sources, has been included mostly as an introduction for the uninitiated reader and as a basis for allowing for intelligent comparisons. Briefly, it reviews the ''old'' Macedonian Question, as it developed from the time of its 19th century awakening of nationalities to the Second World War when Bulgaria, allied to Nazi Germany, appeared to have come close to realizing her century-old aspirations of occupying the entire region. Part Two, which is far more extensive and brings to light previously unpublished data, deals with the role of communism in the shaping of the ''new'' Macedonian Question. It begins with a return to the first decades of this century, when the Bolsheviks began to consider the potentialities of the Macedonian issue for the advancement of their own objectives in the Balkans; it ends at the time of this writing when tensions are considerably low on all sides.

PART ONE

NATIONALIST STRUGGLES
FOR MACEDONIA

CHAPTER I

THE STRUGGLE FOR OTTOMAN - HELD MACEDONIA

THE HISTORICAL ROOTS OF THE CONTROVERSY

.1. *The Macedonian Greeks in the War of Independence*

At the turn of the 19th century, Macedonia, as all other Balkan lands, lay in the lethargy of four centuries of despotic Ottoman rule. The call to liberty sounded by the republicans of the French Revolution could scarcely reach the masses of illiterate peasants. And even if it had, it is questionable whether it would have made any significant impression on the docile *rayahs*.

Yet, a strong current of resentment against Turkish arbitrary measures was traversing the Peninsula. The excesses of the pashas, the beys, and the *janissaries*, as well as the heavy tribute paid to the Sublime Porte and to the local chieftains, had set in the Balkan peoples the mood for revolt. In 1804, the Serbs under Karageorge revolted and after a long and interrupted struggle obtained in 1820, a form of territorial autonomy. One year later, the Greeks raised the banner of their war of independence, and in 1830 a small, but fully sovereign and independent Greek state emerged. Its boundaries, however, which extended south of Thessaly included only a segment of the Hellenic people. Among those outside were the Macedonian Greeks who had taken an active part in the War of Independence and had, subsequently, agitated for the inclusion of their land in the new state.[1] The Great Powers refused to endorse their petition, a fact which had serious political repercussions fifty years later when Macedonia became the most coveted Ottoman land, both by the Balkan peoples and the Great Powers.

The Macedonian Greeks expected their liberation as compensation for their services in the War of Independence under the enthusiastic but

---

1. During the Fourth National Assembly held in Argos in 1829, the fighters and refugees from Macedonia petitioned President Capodistrias to ask the Protecting Powers for the incorporation of Macedonia in the newly founded Greek State. I. K. Vasdravellis, *Οἱ Μακεδόνες εἰς τοὺς ὑπὲρ τῆς ᾿Ανεξαρτησίας ᾿Αγῶνας, 1796-1832* [The Macedonians in the Struggles for Independence, 1796-1832] Second Edition, (Thessaloniki : Society for Macedonian Studies, 1950), p. 179, footnote 1.

inexperienced leadership of Emmanuel Papas, a member of Philiki Hetairia. The Greeks of Chalkidiki had taken the arms in May 1821, and, for a moment, threatened to seize the vital port of Thessaloniki. Inexperience proved a more determining factor than enthusiasm as the Turks massed against the insurgents superior forces. By November of the same year, the revolt was crushed. The countryside was ravaged and the Greek population of Thessaloniki massacred. In the face of such severe reprisals the other towns remained docile, including Serres on whose support Papas depended much for the success of his plans.

The second round of the revolt in Macedonia began in February 1822 when the *klefts* and *armatoloi* of the Olympus and Vermion Mountains joined the Greeks of Naoussa and the surrounding villages and succeeded in virtually declaring that town free. The Turkish military authorities were compelled to employ against the insurgents the thousands of troops they had assembled from Asia Minor and Constantinople to subdue the revolt in Southern Greece. Under the able military leadership of Ebu Loubou, they succeeded in defeating the Naoussa defenders by April, thus, putting an end to the revolt in Macedonia. Naoussa was completely destroyed, the men were killed and the women and children were taken as slaves. After this, many Macedonian fighters fled to Southern Greece to continue fighting alongside the Peloponnesians, the Rumeliotes and other Greeks.

The failure of the first uprising in Macedonia should be attributed to the lack of coordination between the various revolting regions, and to the fact that Macedonia, being much closer to Constantinople and Asia Minor, could easily and quickly be reached by a large number of Ottoman troops.

Although the revolt of the Macedonian Greeks failed to free Macedonia, it, nevertheless, offered invaluable service to the Southern Greeks by tying the Turkish forces in the North, thus allowing the South to consolidate its initial successes.

The heavy toll paid by the Macedonian Greeks bended their determination to continue the struggle in their land. The formerly flourishing Greek community of Thessaloniki was almost completely strangled financially, and for many years to come, the Jews took over the leading position among the multi-racial population of the city.[2] With the exception

---

2. On the basis of Turkish tax catalogues Vasdravellis has concluded that following the Revolt in Macedonia, the Greek population of Thessaloniki was reduced from 24,000 to 8,000. *Ibid.*, p. 149, footnote 2.

of the men who escaped to Southern Greece to continue the fighting, Macedonia was pacified under stern Turkish measures.

For close to twenty-five years, no revolutionary movements were noted in Macedonia. It was only during the Crimean War that the Greeks tried, once again, to begin an uprising in Thessaly, Epirus and Macedonia. A few thousand *emigrés*, Macedonian Greeks from independent Greece, crossed the Greek-Turkish frontier. Their lines of communication from the sea, however, were cut off by French and British warships whose countries were at that time allied with the Ottoman Empire against Russia. Suspecting the Greek insurrection as a Russian diversive scheme, the two Great Powers brought about its collapse.[3] Not until 1878 did the Macedonian Greeks attempt again to achieve their union with the motherland. In the meantime, however, new perplexities were rapidly appearing in the Macedonian horizon as the Slavs of the Balkans began to be aware of their own national identity.

B. The National Awakening of the Slavs

Until the Crimean War the Slavic population of the Southern Balkans, i.e. the region of present-day Southern Bulgaria, Southern Yugoslavia and Northern Greece, was neglected by most foreign travelers and diplomats. By a strange coincidence, the appearance of the Slavic factor in Balkan political developments followed Russia's defeat in the Crimean War and paralleled her search for new supporters of her political objectives in the Peninsula. At that time, the Panslav movement was gaining among influencial leaders in Russia as well as all Slavic lands. First Serbia and then Bulgaria caught the attention of Russian diplomats as possible carriers of Russian imperialist designs. Although Russian policy underwent many changes, its basic, primary motivations were conditioned by three major considerations: avoidance of diplomatic isolation, security at the Straits, and maintenance of a strong position in Bulgaria.[4] The last of

3. John A. Tozis, «'Αμερικανικαὶ καὶ 'Αγγλικαὶ πληροφορίαι περὶ τῆς 'Επαναστάσεως τοῦ 1854 ἐν Μακεδονίᾳ» [American and British Sources for the Revolt of 1854 in Macedonia], Μακεδονικά, Vol. III, 1953-1955, (Thessaloniki: Society for Macedonian Studies, 1956), pp. 142-207. Tozis describes in detail the efforts of the Greeks throughout the world to raise money and support for their compatriots in Macedonia and the strong opposition they encountered from Great Britain and France.
4. Charles Jelavich, *Tsarist Russia and Balkan Nationalism; Russian Influence in the Internal Affairs of Bulgaria and Serbia; 1879-1886* (Berkeley: University of California Press, 1958), p. 1.

the three considerations prompted her interest in the national awakening of the Bulgarians.

It is true that the national awakening of the Bulgarians was a belated one as compared to that of the Greeks and the Serbs. Yet, once nationalism took possession of the leaders and the masses, its expansionist features brought them in direct conflict with their neighbors, particularly in regions inhabited by mixed populations; and such was the case in Macedonia.

Until the middle of the 19th century, Macedonia was generally regarded primarily as a Hellenic region and there was good reason for this. During four centuries of backward Ottoman rule, the national consciousness of the illiterate peasants, with the sole exception of the Greeks, had receded to a point near non existence. Only the common Orthodox Christian heritage acted as a link between the Balkan peoples and set them apart from the Mohammedan Turks. The Church was in the hands of the Greeks and the Greek language was a characteristic of social and cultural superiority to such an extent that even the Bulgarian elite, in order to raise itself from the masses, had to learn it. However, when the religious authority of the Greeks was challenged — especially after the establishment of the Bulgarian Church in 1870 — the Slavic national consciousness emerged. This led to the fallacy that the Church, next to the Ottoman civil oppresion, exerted a spiritual oppression of its own, over its non-Greek speaking folk.

The Slavic element which lived in rather compact groups in the northern half of Macedonia — approximately coinciding to present-day Yugoslav and Bulgarian Macedonia — was generally regarded as Bulgarian, because of its Slavic vernacular. Yet, a significant number lacked a Bulgarian national consciousness, and there is convincing evidence that many considered themselves Greek. Indicative of this situation was a report prepared in 1885 by the Secretary-General of the Bulgarian Exarchate which described the situation in Macedonia as follows:

It is a sad fact but we must admit that the largest part of the Bulgarian population of Macedonia does not have a Bulgarian national consciousness ... If Europe were to demand today that the Macedonian people decide on their fate and say to which nationality they belong, we are certain that the largest part of the Macedonian people and of Macedonia would slip away from our hands. If we exclude two or three regions of Northern Macedonia, the inhabitants of the other regions are ready to declare that they are Greeks ... If the Great Powers were to intervene and demand a plebiscite to solve the Macedonian problem, the Greeks would come out as winners.[5]

The Bulgarians had realized much earlier that if they were to strengthen their position in Ottoman-held Macedonia, they would have to combat neither the Serb nor the Turkish influence but the Greek. As many travelers who journeyed throughout Macedonia during the latter part of the 19th century have attested, in addition to the Greek-speaking element which predominated in the southern part of Macedonia a large portion of the Slav-speaking — Slavophone — inhabitants considered themselves Greek, even though they spoke but a few words of Greek.[6]

During the fifty years which followed the establishment of the Bulgarian Exarchate at Constantinople, until the final political settlement at the end of the First World War, the Bulgarians attributed the Hellenic sentiments of the Slavophones to the intensive Hellenization of the Greek clergy.[7] Indeed, the clergy was instrumental in keeping Greek consciousness alive in the Hellenic inhabitants of Macedonia, even though these Greeks tended to adopt the slavonic vernacular of their illiterate neighbors.

MACEDONIA: A CONTEST PRIZE FOR DIPLOMACY

A. The Religious coup: The Establishment of the Exarchate (1870) and its Consequences

It was precisely the strong hold of the Greek Church on the peoples of Macedonia which prompted the nationalist Bulgarians to focus their

5. D. Missev-Obreikov, ''Report on the Present Situation of Bulgarism in Macedonia,'' as quoted in D. Vogazlis; ʿΗ Μακεδονία: ʿΙστορική, ʾΕθνολονική καὶ Νομικὴ Συγκριτικὴ Μελέτη [Macedonia, A Comparative Historical, Ethnological and Legal Study] (unpublished) (Athens, 1962), p. 131.

6. Djoko Slijepcević, *The Macedonian Question; The Struggle for Southern Serbia*, (Chicago: The American Institute for Balkan Affairs, 1958), p. 87. The author quotes the following description from James Baker's book *Die Turken in Europa* (Stutgard, 1878), pp. 19-20: ''I asked some Bulgarian peasants in Macedonia about their nationality, and they immediately replied 'Rum' which, indeed, is the name peculiar to the Greek population of Asia Minor. They insisted that they were Greeks. 'If this is so', I told them, 'why do you speak Bulgarian at home?' 'Because our forefathers did so', was their reply. 'We have had to suffer a great deal for being called Bulgars, although we are Greeks'.''

7. James D. Bourchier, ''The Balkan States. Their Attitude towards the Macedonian Question;'' in Luigi Villari (ed.), *The Balkan Question: The Present Condition of the Balkans and of European Responsibilities* (London: John Murray, 1905), p. 51.

attention on combatting the Greek influence rather than directing their efforts against the ruling Ottomans.[8] Ecclesiastical autonomy was considered as the first step toward Bulgarian nationalism.

Initially, they petitioned the Ecumenical Patriarchate to allow them a form of spiritual autonomy which would eventually have led to a complete religious independence. On its part, the Patriarchate was prepared to make a number of concessions, such as appointing Bulgarian Metropolitans to all dioceses in Bulgaria proper and permitting the Bulgarian liturgical language to be used.[9] It refused, however, to authorize Bulgarian Metropolitans in the dioceses of Macedonia where the population was a mixture of Greeks and Slavs, pleading that Canon Law did not permit more than one Orthodox Metropolitan in a diocese.[10]

For a moment, the Bulgarians flirted with the idea of shifting their allegiance to the Catholic Church.[11] However, the latter's centralist authority and Russian objections canceled these plans. From that moment, the Bulgarians agitated for an independent Church. Their demands were finally accepted on February 28, 1870 when the Sultan permitted the establishment of the Bulgarian Exarchate, which, as he rightly forsaw, was bound to raise a permanent barrier between the Christian subjects of the Empire.[12] Instrumental in the establishment of the Exarchate was the Russian Ambassador in Constantinople, Count Ignatiev, an ardent Panslavist who viewed the Bulgarian Church as a major step towards attracting the Bulgarians to Russian objectives in the Balkans. Initially, the creation of the Exarchate was welcomed by the Serbian Government, which believed that the new Church would further the solidarity of the Balkan Slavs.[13] Soon, however, they were disillusioned by the Exarchate's role as the laboratory of Bulgarian nationalism.

Thus, the stage was set for the ensuing struggle between the Balkan peoples. If in the beginning the conflict had the appearance of a religious

8. H. R. Wilkinson, *Maps and Politics: A Review of the Ethnographic Cartography of Macedonia* (Liverpool: University Press, 1951), p. 59.

9. M. Th. Laskaris, Τὸ ᾿Ανατολικὸν Ζήτημα, 1800 - 1923 [The Eastern Question, 1800-1923] (Thessaloniki, 1948) Vol. I, p. 265.

10. *Ibid., op. cit.* 273. Also Ch. Fragistas in: "The Balkan Wars: Their Meaning in the History of Greece," *Balkan Studies*, vol. III, no. 2 (1962) pp. 247-248.

11. Mihailo D. Stojanović, *The Great Powers and the Balkans, 1875 - 1878* (Cambridge, University Press, 1939), pp. 3-4.

12. Bourchier, "The Balkan States" in Villari, *op. cit.*, p. 54.

13. Slijepcević, *op. cit.*, p. 106.

controversy, it was due to the fact that the national affiliation of the people was still mostly determined by their religious loyalties. When, years later, they matured ethnically, their antagonisms developed into purely agressive nationalistic conflicts.

In 1872, the Ecumenical Patriarchate declared the Bulgarian Exarchate schismatic. The Bulgar Exarch, undaunted by the excommunication, set his See at Constantinople. Once the Orthodox Church rule that no two prelates could exercise religious jurisdiction over the same region was violated, the Exarchate initiated a wide-ranged program to detach the Slav-speaking peasants who inhabited the European Ottoman provinces from the politico-religious authority of the Patriarchate.

The steady disintegration of the Ottoman Empire was promptly sensed by the Balkan states who began to promote their claims in the contested Ottoman provinces, lest an outside suitor among the Great Powers attempt to take the place of the Ottoman ruler. The Bulgarians, under the Exarch and with the invaluable assistance of the Panslavs of Petrograd, were already making significant progress in that direction. Although it is a myth that the Russian Government pursued at that time a purely Panslavist foreign policy, it is certain that the advocates of Panslavism exerted a considerable influence on the Russian Court and political leaders to adopt a pro-Bulgarian attitude. Moreover, Russian diplomats in the Ottoman Empire, initiated in the Panslavist movement, were acting with sufficient independence, but their actions did not accurately portray the leanings of Russian foreign policy.

Russia's espousal of the Bulgarian cause in the sixties and seventies had deeper meanings. Ever since the Crimean War and the admittance of the Ottoman Empire to the European System, Russia had come to realize that she could no more deal with Turkey as she pleased. She was now faced with the need for reverting to more subtle ways to undermine her southern neighbor. At the time it appeared the best solution was to secure a loyal Balkan *protegé* who could be properly projected as heir to the Ottoman Empire in the Balkans and the Aegean. Rumania was already turning to Western Europe. Moldavia and Wallachia had united in 1862, not with the help of the Tsar of Russia but with the assistance of the Emperor of France. The traditionally pro-Russian Ecumenical Patriarchate had become less eager to follow blindly Russian directives, and Greece had shown signs that she was little inclined to let her foreign policy be molded subservient to Russia.[14] Indicative of this attitude was the question of the

---

14. Valentine Chival, "The Attitude of the Powers" in Villari, *op. cit.*, p. 236.

succession to the Greek throne raised in 1863 with the dethronement of King Otho. Following long diplomatic negotiations, the question was solved contrary to Russian interests. The Russians were finally convinced that only in the Balkan Slavs, and more particularly in the Bulgarians, they could find the supporters they were seeking.[15] As for Serbia, Great Power politics had already abandoned her to the Austrian sphere of interest.

Thus, if the Russians had flirted for a time with the idea of satisfying both the Bulgarians and the Greeks in their ecclesiastical dispute, by 1870 they had decided to throw their full weight behind the Bulgarians.[16]

B. The Diplomatic coup: The Treaty of San Stefano (1878) and its Legacy

In the mid-seventies, the primary concern of the Bulgarian politicians, the Bulgarian Exarchate and the Russian Panslavists was the establishment of a large, independent Bulgarian state.

In December 1876 at a conference held in Constantinople, a plan was introduced by the European Powers which provided for the reorganization of the Bulgarian provinces of the Ottoman Empire into two vilayets under Christian governors to be aided by popular assemblies. The Eastern vilayet with Tirnovo as its capital would have included all the sanjaks of Eastern Rumelia, plus three kazas of the vilayet of Adrianople. The Western vilayet with Sofia as its capital would have comprised the sanjaks of Vidin, Nish, Skopje, Monastir (except for the two southern kazas), the three northern kazas of Serres, and the kazas of Strumnitsa, Tikvesh, Veles and Kastoria.[17]

The Turkish Government was adamant against the plan and the Conference finally dropped it. Yet, the Bulgarians regarded it as a document which justly delineated the ethnological boundaries of new Bulgaria. Only the Treaty of San Stefano, concluded between Russia and Turkey two years later, treating even more liberally Bulgaria's ethnological claims, substituted the Constantinople proposal as the *Magna Carta* of Bulgaria's ''manifest destiny.''

The collapse of the Conference led to the Russian-Turkish War of

15. Barbara Jelavich, ''Russia, Bavaria and the Greek Revolution of 1862-1863'' *Balkan Studies*, Vol. II, No. 1, (Thessaloniki: Institute for Balkan Studies, 1962), p. 134.

16. Charles Jelavich, *op. cit.*, p. 11.

17. Villari, *op. cit.*, p. 57.

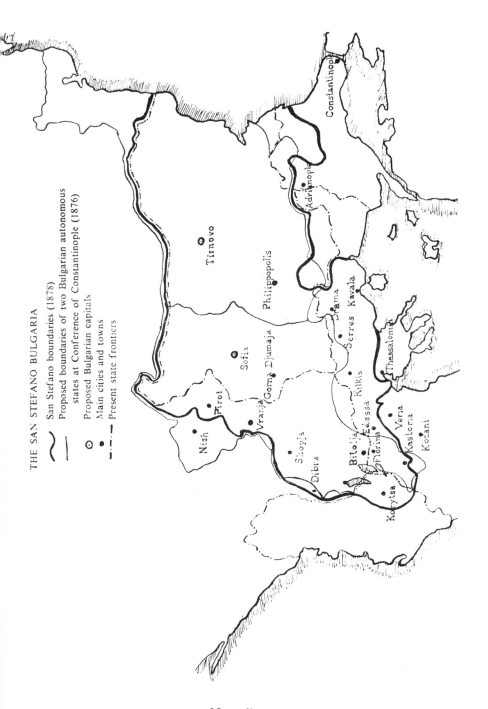

THE SAN STEFANO BULGARIA

∿ San Stefano boundaries (1878)

⎯ Proposed boundaries of two Bulgarian autonomous
states at Conference of Constantinople (1876)

⊙ Proposed Bulgarian capitals

• Main cities and towns

-·-·- Present state frontiers

Constantinople

Adrianople

Tirnovo

Philippopolis

Drama

Kavala

Serres

Sofia

Kilkis

Gorna Djumaja

Thessaloniki

Vranja

Pirot

Edessa

Veria

Nish

Skopja

Bitolja

Kastoria

Florina

Kozani

Dibra

Korytsa

Map 5

1877-1878 which ended with the victory of the Russian Army and the Treaty of San Stefano. Negotiated by Russian Ambassador Ignatiev, the treaty provided for a large Bulgarian state which would include Bulgaria proper, Eastern Rumelia, the whole of Macedonia to the very gates of Thessaloniki, and which would stretch as far to the west as the Shar Mountains, Dibra and Koritsa. Even the most ardent Bulgarian nationalists were pleasantly surprised. The Treaty was the work of a Panslavist. Yet, it was purely an expression of Russia's own imperialist designs which were placed far ahead of the interests of a united Slavdom.[18]

The Bulgarians rejoiced, but the Serbs and the Greeks reacted strongly against its provisions which were considered as ceding to the Bulgarians the Serbian and Greek districts in Macedonia inhabited by mixed populations. The concern of the Greeks was such that they even fomented an uprising in Macedonia by dispatching armed bands to join with the indegenous population in a major insurrection. Rapid international developments, however, halted their plans.

For their own political considerations, the European Powers objected to the unilateral Russian settlement of the "Eastern Question." Britain, in particular, suspected that the Treaty concluded at San Stefano was a Russian maneuver to seize Constantinople by means of a Bulgarian puppet state. Austria-Hungary, desiring the Bosnian province for herself, looked with displeasure on Bulgaria's expansion into Macedonia as baring her own eventual descent in the direction of Thessaloniki.

Russia, not willing to risk a war against the European Powers, accepted an invitation by Germany's Bismark for a congress to settle the outstanding differences.[19] The Congress of Berlin, held June 13 to July 13, 1878, confined Bulgaria to almost half its present size. Eastern Rumelia and Bulgaria were recognized as two separate autonomous principalities. Macedonia remained under Ottoman rule.

The time had not yet come for Macedonia to change hands. The religious *coup* of 1870-1872 had opened the road for the gradual Bulgarization of Macedonia, but had failed to bring about any sudden major changes. The diplomatic *coup*, attempted in 1878 through the Treaty of San Stefano, was jeopardized by the combined opposition of the European Powers. It was time for a military *coup* to try to gain for Bulgaria what other means had not accomplished.

18. Charles Jelavich, *op. cit.*, p. 5.
19. R. W. Seton-Watson, *The Rise of Nationality in the Balkans* (London: Constable and Co., Ltd., 1917), pp. 108-109.

18

C. *The Military Coup: The Annexation of Eastern Rumelia (1885)* *and its Significance for Macedonian Developments*

The new treaty brought a temporary *détente* over the Balkans. Russia accepted the Austro-Hungarian demand for a free hand in Serbian affairs, receiving in turn Austria's support for her political intervention in Bulgaria. Thus, a pro-Russian Prince, Alexander of Battenberg, was chosen for Bulgaria, while Milan of Serbia, thoroughly dissappointed with the much talked about "solidarity of the Slavs," oriented his country's foreign policy toward Austria-Hungary. Greece, the third Christian Balkan state, was under severe restrictions by the European Powers to restrain her irredentism.

Though all three Balkan states were under semi-tutelage by the Great Powers, the dynamics of Balkan politics were steadily creating a boiling situation in the Peninsula, particularly in the provinces of Eastern Rumelia and Macedonia. Two major political developments were mostly instrumental for projecting Macedonia as the final and most critical problem whose solution was bound to create world-wide repercussions. One had to do with Serbia, the other with Bulgaria.

At the Congress of Berlin, the Slav territories of Bosnia and Hercegovina had been assigned to Austria-Hungary. Prince Milan, realizing that he could not acquire the coveted Austrian lands inhabited by Slavs, sought Vienna's support to direct his country southwards, toward Macedonia. In an agreement signed between the two countries on June 16, 1881, Austria-Hungary agreed to support the Serbian objectives in Macedonia provided "future circumstances should permit such a development."[20] The Austrian promise was in conformity with the terms of the *Dreikaiserbund*, the agreement signed between the German Emperor, the Austrian Emperor and the Russian Tsar ten days before the Austrian promise to the Serbs. It is interesting to note that before the signing of the Pact, Austria had demanded of the Russians that all Bulgarian propaganda in Macedonia aiming at the eventual restoration of San Stefano Bulgaria should cease.[21] Serbia interpreted the Austrian attitude as a signal to move in the direction of Macedonia.

The second major development affecting Macedonian politics, was Bulgaria's successful *coup d'état* in Eastern Rumelia in September 1885.

20. Nikolaos V. Vlahos, *Τὸ Μακεδονικὸν ὡς Φάσις τοῦ Ἀνατολικοῦ Ζητήματος 1878-1908* [The Macedonian Question as a Phase of the Eastern Question: 1878-1908], (Athens: Petroudes and Christou, Printers, 1935), p. 29.
21. Charles Jelavich, *op. cit.*, p. 24.

Over the opposition of the Russians who feared that potential enemies, such as Austria-Hungary, Serbia and Greece, might demand territorial compensations,[22] the Bulgarians declared the union of the region to Bulgaria. Their move was bound to disturb the Balkan balance of power established at the Congress of Berlin and bring Bulgaria in direct proximity to Macedonia.

The first reaction of the members of the *Dreikaiserbund* was to declare themselves against the annexation and in favor of the *status quo ante*. Britain, however, acting on the supposition that a united Bulgaria opposed by Russia would be a Russophobe Bulgaria, came to her assistance. Thus, thanks to British benevolent intervention which neutralized an imminent hostile intervention on the part of the three Emperors and Turkey, the annexation of Eastern Rumelia was consolidated. Turkey threatened to intervene militarily but was duly advised by the British that any action on her part could precipitate an attack by Serbia and Greece on Ottoman European possessions.[23]

Serbia did not wait for Turkey's initiative. Disappointed with Great Power politics which seemed to work constantly to her disadvantage, and fearing that Eastern Rumelia's annexation would open the way to Bulgaria's advance into Macedonia, she did not hesitate to declare war on her Slav neighbor. Though the odds favored the Serbs, the Bulgarians were able to defeat them and to solidify their hold on Eastern Rumelia. Greece protested strongly against the Bulgarian seizure of a region which was inhabited by a large and prosperous Greek minority. Yet, she was incapable of actively intervening on account of Britain's opposition. The Union of Rumelia and Bulgaria was finally ratified on April 5, 1886 by the Convention of Top-Khané.

* * *

Less than a decade after the Treaty of San Stefano and the Congress of Berlin, the conflict over Macedonia began to concretize as a triangular nationalist contest between Greece, Bulgaria and Serbia; a contest which, in one form or another, was destined to prevail until our times. By 1886, Serbia had come to realize that her own "manifest destiny" lay southwards. Bulgaria could better than ever remain confident that, having acquired physical proximity to the coveted region, her chances for grasping Macedonia had considerably increased. Greece, though slowly awakening to the history-making developments in her North, began to orient herself

---

22. *Ibid.*, p. 222.
23. *Ibid.*, p. 226.

toward the adoption of more drastic measures to safeguard her vital national interests.

Of all three contenders, it was Bulgaria which succeeded for a considerable time, in maintaining the initiative in Macedonian developments. Having prepared the ground through religious, diplomatic and military *coups*, she was better qualified to enter the final stage of directly cultivating the annexation of the coveted region. If one may adopt military terminology, the phase of maneuvering for positions had ended, with Bulgaria as the winner. The phase of shelling the enemy territory was about to commence.

MACEDONIA : A CONTEST PRIZE FOR UNDERGROUND ACTIVITIES

A. Penetration by the Exarchate : 1885 - 1893

Despite Petrograd's official opposition to Prince Alexander's policies, Russian representatives in Rumelia and Macedonia — guided by Panslavic considerations — constantly and unswervingly maintained a pro- Bulgarian attitude.[24] At times, as in the preparation of the Eastern Rumelian *coup*, Russian agents had even misguided the Bulgarians by falsely attributing to the Tsar their own initiatives and promises. A similar situation was now cultivated by Russian agents *vis-à-vis* Bulgarian aspirations in Macedonia.

The Exarchate's efforts at proselytism of all Slav-speaking inhabitants of Macedonia met from the first moment with the moral and even the material support of the Russians. In short, the Russians appeared to advocate the unification of all the San Stefano Macedonian lands under the Exarch, thus, recreating Greater Bulgaria through a religious if not a political union.[25]

Yet, what followed in Macedonia was not necessarily the making of the Russians. It is true that they were instrumental in establishing the Exarchate and offering it valuable assistance. Their backing had doubtlessly encouraged even the conservative Bulgarian elements to espouse a policy of adventurism in Macedonia. From that point, however, Bulgaria's policy in Macedonia was purely and clearly a Bulgarian undertaking initially directed by the Exarchate in Constantinople and, later, by the Bulgarian Government and the various Bulgarian-Macedonian revolutionary organizations in Sofia and Macedonia.

---

24. Valentine Chival, "The Attitude of the Powers" in Villari, *op. cit.*, p. 247.
25. Charles Jelavich, *op. cit.*, p. 162.

Following the annexation of Eastern Rumelia, the Bulgarians turned their full attention to Macedonia, particularly to those northern regions which were inhabited by more compact Slav populations. The Bulgarian-claimed region comprised vaguely the area north of the mouth of the Aliakmon river on Thermaikos Bay and south of Veria and Kastoria, up to the Grammos Mountain.

Naturally, such extensive claims came into direct opposition with those of the Greeks who projected their own as far north as the cities of Nevrokop, Melenikon, Strumnitsa and Monastir. On their part, the Serbs extended theirs south almost to the line claimed by the Greeks, and, as was the case at Florina, Strumnitsa and Monastir,[26] they overlapped. Briefly, Bulgarian and Greek claims conflicted in Central Macedonia and Bulgarian and Serbian in both Central and Northern Macedonia.

The tactics adopted by the Exarchate in the six or seven years following the annexation of Eastern Rumelia, concentrated on increasing significantly the number of Exarchist Slavophones in each Macedonian village and town so that Bulgarian priests might take over the local church. Once this was accomplished, Bulgarian teachers, paid directly by the Exarchate or by the Bulgarian Government, were dispatched to cultivate further the Bulgarian national consciousness of the inhabitants. Thus, while under the terms of the decree of 1870, which established the Exarchate, the Bulgarian Church was allowed to found bishoprics only in pure Bulgarian provinces, i.e. in Bulgaria proper, by 1890 it was granted a *berat* by the Sublime Porte to appoint Bulgarian prelates in the Macedonian cities of Ohrid and Skopje. Four years later, in 1894, it was successful in doing the same in Nevrokop and Veles.[27]

The political and religious successes of the Bulgarians are attributable to many reasons. First, the majority of Slav-speaking inhabitants of Northern and Central Macedonia felt a natural kinship to the Bulgarians which, when properly cultivated by the teachers and priests, was easily turned into a Bulgarian nationalist sentiment. Secondly, the Serbs had not, as yet, been fully engaged in a major proselytizing program of their own. Thirdly, a very determining factor was the attitude of the Ecumenical Patriarchate and its prelates in Macedonia. The establishment of the Exarchate was a nationalistic manifestation and should have been dealt with as such since it appeared to project its nationalist character more than its religious. Yet, the Ecumenical Patriarchate faced with the dilemma of

---

26. Vlahos, *op. cit.*, pp. 29-30.
27. James D. Bourchier, "The Balkan States," in Villari, *op. cit.*, pp. 67-68.

pursuing a national Greek policy, as prodded by the Greek Government, or maintaining solely spiritual authority over all the Orthodox, even at the expense of Hellenic national aspirations, tended more often than not to adopt the latter course.[28] Thus, the Greek position was seriously imperiled since the Church was in fact the only bearer of Greek national ideals during this period. In addition to the official policy of the Patriarchate, the quality of the prelates in the Macedonian cities was far below the requirements of the moment. Most of them showed an astonishing incompetence to grasp the changes occurring in their midst. Others tended to be concerned with safeguarding their own privileges, paying little attention to the national interests of their folk. Repeatedly the Greek Government, through its Ambassador to Constantinople, asked the Patriarch to transfer the incompetent prelates, even threatening to reconsider its relations with the Ecumenical Patriarchate.[29]

Two more factors should be mentioned regarding Bulgaria's initial successes with the Slavophones of Northern and Central Macedonia. One was the friendly overtures of the Bulgarian government under Stamboloff[30] toward the Sublime Porte, a fact which won for the Bulgarians the benevolent attitude of the Ottomans.[31] The other, was the failure of the Greek Government to take serious measures — since the Patriarchate was unwilling to do so — to finance a major program of national education and indocrination which, among other things, would have strengthened the determination of the native populations to remain firm to their Hellenic traditions and consciousness.[32]

B. The Impact of Propaganda on the Peoples of Macedonia

Since the interested countries, as a first step towards supporting their influence over the region, concentrated in fomenting among the inhabitants of Macedonia the national consciousness of their choice, it is necessary to turn to an investigation of the population structure of the disputed area. Population statistics for this period are scant and thoroughly unreliable,

28. Vlahos, op. cit., p. 233.
29. Ibid., p. 128.
30. Prince Alexander was forced by the Russians to abdicate. He was succeeded in June 1887 by Prince Ferdinand of Saxe-Coburg Gotha.
31. Bourchier, "The Balkan States" in Villari, op. cit., p. 88.
32. For the failure of the Greek Government to provide adequate funds to the Greek schools in the contested region, see Greek consular reports quoted in Vlahos, op. cit., pp. 128-130.

either compiled to project specific national claims, or, as with certain foreign census-takers, based on insufficient or intentionally distorted facts and sources.

It is, however, commonly accepted that prior to the Crimean War, with the exception of the purely Greek element inhabiting Southern Macedonia and to a lesser extent Central Macedonia, a large segment of the Slav-speaking inhabitants was thought to be Greek since its loyalties were a blend of Orthodoxy and Hellenism.[33] Only when the Exarchate, established in 1870, introduced its program of national and religious proselytism, were these masses faced with a clear question of a national, as distinguished from a religious, affiliation. Since they lacked a formulated national consciousness, the appeal of the Exarchists was necessarily a combined religious and nationalist one. The Slav-speaking peasants of Macedonia were confused and divided and though many chose to remain loyal to the Patriarchate, a Bulgarian nationality gradually began to take root. By the end of this period — roughly around 1890 — the Exarchists could take pride in the fact that due to their efforts, the name ʽʽBulgarˮˮ came to be distinguished from ʽʽGreekˮˮ in the Ottoman Empire.[34]

In conclusion, neither the work of the Exarchists nor the atrocities committed by the armed *comitadjis* who appeared on the scene after 1894, were sufficient to instill a definite Bulgarian national consciousness in all the Slavophones of Macedonia. This is evidenced by the fact that members of the same family divided their allegiance between the Bulgarian Exarchate and the Greek Patriarchate.[35] The following gives a vivid, though probably somewhat exaggerated picture of the prevailing situation :

> Children became a valuable commodity for which the rival agitators paid in hard cash and enterprising fathers have been known to distribute their favours equally among the rival propagandas, with the result that it is by no means uncommon to find three brothers in a single family professing three different nationalities. Numerous instances could be given of men who have changed their names from Vlach to Greek, from Greek to Bulgar and from Bulgar to Serb...[36]

---

33. Serbian historian Cvijić wrote that the Slav Macedonians did not have a well-defined national consciousness because they lacked an historic past of their own or a literary language. Jovan Cvijić, *Remarques sur l'ethnographie de la Macédoine*. Second Edition augmented (Paris : G. Roustan, 1907), p. 5.

34. S. P. Ladas, *The Exchange of Minorities : Bulgaria, Greece and Turkey* (New York : MacMillan, 1932), p. 7.

35. S. P. Ladas, *op. cit.*, passim.

36. R. W. Seton-Watson, *op. cit.*, pp. 129-130.

In the late 1880's and early 1890's, the situation in Macedonia had developed to such an extent that various population belts could be distinguished. In the north, the Slav element predominated though its degree of inclination toward Bulgaria could not be fully ascertained; in the extreme west, most populous was the Albanian nationality; in the south, the Greeks constituted the overwhelming majority. Between and within the Greek and the Slavonic belts there was a mixture of nationalities, mostly multilingual, which could not be definitely classified with either group, since there was no patriotism developed other than local patriotism.[37] Macartney, an expert on minorities, probably best described this situation when he wrote:

> In Macedonia, Turks, Greeks, Bulgars, Serbs, Vlachs, Albanians, Circassians, Jews, Gagauz, Armenians and others beside lived in a glorious *olla podrida*. No clear delimitation of national boundaries was possible; worse still, even national feeling was hopelessly capricious. Centuries of mixed marriages had resulted in bilingual or polyglot families . . .

> Although certain areas were predominantly occupied by one group there was a large intermediary zone in which the population was not merely mixed, but actually, to a large extent, of uncertain nationality. A man would probably go, quite easily and quite sincerely, where his sympathies led him; and those sumpathies would not be rooted in the past, but would be swayed by considerations often material, of the present and the future,..

> ...Obviously in such a situation, almost any party would be able to put forward a reasonable claim for the debatable territory, and equally obviously the different national claims would conflict.[38]

The Bulgarians, though partially successful due to the work of the Exarchate, could not restrain their impatience with the slow progress of their Church. The success of their *coup* in Eastern Rumelia had encouraged extremist elements in Bulgaria and Macedonia to favor the solution of more drastic methods. Thus, a new round to conquer the allegiance of the peoples of Macedonia and to substantiate individual national claims began to take shape. This time it was not to be restricted to peaceful propaganda alone, but to expand into an endless bloody conflict.

---

37. John Mavrocordato, *Modern Greece*, (London: MacMillan Co., 1931), pp. 77-78.
38. C. A. Macartney, *National States and National Minorities* (London: Oxford University Press, 1934), pp. 136-137.

C. The Birth of the I.M.R.O. and its Objectives; 1893-1902

By the early 1890's small groups advocating a more vigorous, revolutionary program in Macedonia had made their appearance in Bulgaria. Most important of all was the Internal Macedonian Revolutionary Organization — better known by its initials I.M.R.O. Among its founders in 1893, were Gotse Deltchev, Damjan Grujev, Pere Tochev, Petar Pop Arsov and other Bulgarians from Bulgaria as well as from Macedonia, who formed its Central Committee.[39] According to the Statute the aims of the Organization were to "gather into one entity all discontented elements in Macedonia and the area of the Aegean, regardless of nationality, in order to achieve, by means of revolution, complete political autonomy for these areas."

From the very beginning, the Organization came into direct opposition with the Bulgarian Church and the most chauvinist Bulgarians over the methods to be employed for annexing Macedonia to Bulgaria. While the Church had succeeded over the years in cultivating a Bulgarian consciousness among a significant segment of the Slav-speaking inhabitants of Macedonia, the I.M.R.O. adhered to the view that only revolutionary means would bring the hoped for results. The Exarchate's opposition to the I.M.R.O. was apparently prompted by the fear that a premature revolutionary movement would awaken the Greeks and the Serbs to the direct threat which Bulgarian activities posed to their own national interests and would force them to reciprocate by sending their own agents and bands into Macedonia. The circles of the Exarchate feared that an uprising by the Bulgarians in Macedonia would provide an excuse for the Great Powers to intervene there before the Bulgarian position could be fully secured. In this case the Macedonian Question ran the risk of being solved according to alien interests.

Yet, the I.M.R.O. appeared to be little disturbed by the Exarchate's opposition. Despite its initially proclaimed intention to accept into its ranks all subject nationalities, it tended to depend only on Bulgarian Exarchists, limiting its operations, in the beginning, to areas controlled by the Exarchate. It had no confidence in the Slav-speaking inhabitants who remained loyal to the Patriarchate, let alone in the Greeks, Albanians, Vlachs, Serbs and other nationalities living in Macedonia.[40] Later, however, in order to allay the suspicion that its activities were simply a manifestation

39. Slijepcević, op cit., p. 120.
40. Dimitar Vlahov, Iz Istorije Makedonskog Naroda [From the History of the Macedonian People] (Belgrade, 1950), p. 34.

of Greater Bulgarian chauvinism, it sought — though without much success — to enlist followers from among other nationalities, claiming that its
struggle was the struggle of all Macedonian peoples for an autonomous
state.[41] It is, indeed, a fact that some of the leaders of the I.M.R.O.
seriously favored an autonomous solution for Macedonia. They did not hide
their Bulgarian identity and viewed the establishment of an autonomous
Macedonia as simply another Bulgarian state.[42]

In the summer of 1895, the Organization dispatched from Bulgaria
armed bands which attempted to foment a large-scale uprising in Macedonia. Their appeal made no mention of Bulgaria, but merely called on
the peoples of Macedonia to overthrow the oppressive Ottoman rule. With a
few minor exceptions, the people failed to be roused by such slogans and in
a relatively short time, the Ottoman Army was able to destroy the bands.[48]

At this moment, the Bulgarian Government and Court, officials of
the Exarchate and nationalist Bulgarians from Bulgaria and Macedonia,
including followers of the I.M.R.O., reached the conclusion that although
the I.M.R.O.'s revolutionary tactics appeared to be useful to their cause,
an autonomous Macedonia did not coincide with their plans for the outright annexation of the region to Bulgaria. To bring the I.M.R.O. under
their own control, a new organization — the Macedonian-Andrianople Revolutionary Organization — was set up in Sofia in 1894, operating under a
Supreme Committee.[44]

41. Cvijić, op. cit., p. 13.
42. Dimitar Kosev, "Revizionističeski Falsifikacii na Bulgarska Istorija u
Skopskite Istorici," [The Revisionist Falsifications of Bulgarian History and the
Historians of Skopje] Istorιčeski Pregled. Vol. I, (Sofia, 1959), p. 28.
43. Vlahos, op. cit., pp. 136 - 137.
44. Dimitar I. Vlahov, Makedonija : Momenti od Istorιjata na Makedonskiot
Narod [Macedonia : Moments in the History of the Macedonian People] (Skopje :
Državno Knigoisdatelstvo na Makedonija, 1950), p. 93 (from a Greek mimeographed
translation). Vlahov says that the Supreme Committee was in the service of the
Bulgarian Government and Court. The late Dimitar Vlahov was an old I.M.R.O.
activist since its first days. Following the Young Turks Revolt in 1908, he was elected
to Turkish Parliament as a Bulgarian delegate. During the interwar period he formed
the short-lived leftist United I.M.R.O. and after the war he emerged as a Yugoslav -
style "Macedonian," and was appointed first Premier of Yugoslavia's People's
Republic of Macedonia.
A similar view was expressed by Christ Anastasoff, The Tragic Peninsula :
A History of the Macedonian Movement for Independence Since 1878 (St. Louis,
Mo. : Blackwell Weilandy Co., 1938), pp. 63-64. Christ Anastasoff is one of the
chief spokesmen of Bulgarian Macedonians in the United States who adhere to the
illusions of a San Stefano Greater Bulgaria.

The Statute of the new organization spoke similarly, though in vague terms, of the need for political autonomy for the people of Macedonia and the Vilayet of Adrianople (i.e. Thrace). From the subsequent clauses of the Statute, however, it was clear that the primary aim of the new revolutionary group was to promote the Bulgarian cause in Macedonia. Among its cardinal objectives was the union of all Macedonian Slavs, be they in Macedonia, Bulgaria or abroad, as well as all those who viewed sympathetically their cause;[45] and the cultivation of a favorable world opinion by means of writings, propaganda and meetings. In the cource of its work it could "utilize such other means and actions as might be dictated by circumstances." All existing Macedonian-Andrianople associations in Bulgaria and other countries were to be united in one body which would be governed by the Supreme Commitee established in Sofia.[46]

The two factions, the "Centralists" of the initial I.M.R.O. and the "Supremists" — or "Verhovists" — found themselves at odds from the very beginning. Although there were certain differences of principle, the feud was to a considerable degree due to the individual ambitions of the leaders. As personalities succeeded each other at the top, so changed the relations between them. In 1898, Boris Sarafov, the new ruthless chief of the Supreme Committee, succeeded temporarily in uniting the two groups under his leadership.[47]

Under Sarafov, the Supreme Committee received the whole-hearted support of the Bulgarian Government. Collectors were allowed to pass through the Army on pay-day to collect money for the "cause." A "patriotic loan" was issued, and Sarafov's emissaries enforced subscription by threats and even murder.[48] It was not difficult for the Bulgarians of Bulgaria proper to support either leadership because they believed that even an autonomous, independent Macedonia would ultimately become part of Bulgaria, precisely as had Eastern Rumelia.[49]

The Turks found it necessary to adopt certain measures in Macedonia so that the Great Powers might not use the disturbances as a pretext to interfere with the internal affairs of the Empire. Thus, in 1896, they put forward a reform plan — thoroughly inadequate — which provided that all

---

45. By one account, toward the end of 1890, there were more than 100,000 Macedonian Slavs in Bulgaria. Anastasoff, *op. cit.*, p. 56.

46. Text of Statute in Frederic Moore, "The Macedonian Committees and the Insurrection," in Villari, *op. cit.*, pp. 187-188.

47. Slijepcević, *op. cit.*, p. 124.

48. Moore, "The Macedonian Committees..." in Villari, *op. cit.*, p. 195.

49. Wilkinson, *op. cit.*, p. 151.

Christians could participate in the Administration and the Gendarmerie; that each Governor would be assisted by a Christian assessor, and that Christian inspectors would supervise and report on the execution of justice and the collection of taxes. In fact, all these "administrators" and "advisers" had no real authority and no protection in the face of intimidation and even murder. The situation which followed the introduction of the reforms was probably best described by Miss Victoria Buxton, an ardent Bulgarophile, who remarked: "The Macedonian Revolutionary Committees retaliated with violence and Europe left her consular reports unread."[50]

Retaliation by the I.M.R.O. took the form of a ruthless murdering of all those who opposed its program, particularly the Patriarchist Greek and Slav speaking Macedonians. But at the turn of the century, these a-trocities of the I.M.R.O. guerrillas — popularly known as *comitadjis* — pro-voked the protest of the European Powers who demanded that the Bulgar·ian Government disband them. Bulgaria refused and Premier Danev, speaking before the Sobranje in 1902, explained the measure of inter-dependence between the Government and the I.M.R.O. as follows:

> Should the Government proceed to dissolve the revolutionary organ-izations, not only it would provoke their hostility, but it would also run the risk to lose its popularity in the country. The exist-ence of the revolutionary organizations has been widely tolerated and their activities on account of the patriotic objectives they pursue, have been viewed sympathetically by all the strata of our society.[51]

D. Serbian Activities from 1887 - 1902

The Serbs had nothing similar to the I.M.R.O. in the field. They had only lately awakened to the possibility of claiming as Serbian the regions south of Nish, and then only as an afterthought.[52] Even the continuous struggle to assimilate the Slav-speaking masses could not arouse the emotions of the Serbs as did the struggle for the unredeemed Serbian lands

---

50. Victoria Buxton, "A History of Turkish Reforms since the Treaty of Berlin" in Villari, *op. cit.*, p. 111.

51. Quoted in Christopher Naltsas, Τὸ Μακεδονικὸν Ζήτημα καὶ ἡ Σοβιετικὴ Πολιτικὴ [The Macedonian Question and the Soviet Policy], (Thessaloniki, Institute for Balkan Studies, 1954), p. 58, (translated from the Greek).

52. It is interesting to note that in 1873, after the Bulgarians had already begun their propaganda in Macedonia, a member of the Serbian Royal Academy who argued that Macedonia was Serbian and not Bulgarian was repudiated by his colleagues. Wilkinson, *op. cit.*, pp. 93-94.

which lay within Austria-Hungary.[53] Nevertheless, following Austria's implied consent to Serbia's expansion in the direction of Macedonia, preparations were made by certain Serbian groups and the Skupstina secretly allocated funds for educational purposes and for agitation in Macedonia.[54] In the field, Serbian consular agents began to lay dawn the foundations of a Serbian Macedonian policy. By 1887, they had taken steps to establish Serbian schools, to distribute textbooks free and to provide salaries for teachers. They also advanced a proposal for establishing a Macedonian propaganda section in the Ministry of Foreign Affairs which would attempt to organize the Serbian refugees from Macedonia into brotherhoods (bratstva) under a central leadership.[55]

Thus, the Serbs entered the Greco-Bulgarian feud in Macedonia. At first they concentrated primarily on the Slavs of Northern Macedonia. Gradually, however, despite assurances given to the Greek Government that they would not oppose Greek national claims in Macedonia they expanded southwards toward Thessaloniki.[56]

When the Serbs began to send their own priests and, thus, enter the religious as well as the national phase of the controversy, the Ecumenical Patriarchate tended to adopt a milder attitude toward them than toward the Bulgarians on the theory that since the Serbs paid allegiance to the Patriarchate it did not matter much if they agitated for the conversion of the inhabitants to Serbian nationality. Such an attitude was strongly protested by the Greek Government which notified the Patriarchate that it viewed the Serbian actions as unfavorable to Greek national policy.[57]

In the closing years of the century, Serbian propaganda faced a major counter-offensive by the Bulgarian propaganda, the latter assisted by armed I.M.R.O. guerrillas. Failing to attain a significant following among the inhabitants of Macedonia, the Serbs were forced to withdraw some of their agents and to close a number of schools in Southern and even Central Macedonia.

Thus, the first phase of Serbian intervention in Macedonia resulted in a gradual awakening of the interest of Serbian people and Government to the idea of expanding southwards. How deeply rooted this interest became in the course of succeeding years is evidenced by Serbia's partici-

53. Charles Jelavich, op. cit., p. 174.
54. Wilkinson, op. cit., p. 93.
55. Wayne S. Vucinich, Serbia between East and West; the Events of 1903-1908 (Stanford, California : Stanford University Press, 1954) p. 26.
56. Vlahos, op. cit., p. 169.
57. Ibid., p. 183.

pation in the Balkan Wars; by her desire for further expansion during the inter-war period, and, finally, by the irredentist propaganda which followed the establishment of a communist regime in Yugoslavia in 1944.

E. Greek Reactions: 1893-1902

The Greek Government's primary concern during the last quarter of the 19th century was the struggle of the Cretans to unite their island with Greece. Though Macedonia was considered a Hellenic land, developments there were unknown to the Greeks, except for a small group of dedicated patriots and diplomats in the field. With one cabinet replacing the other in rapid succession, the finances of the country in a deplorable state and the Cretan Question absorbing all the energy of the Foreign Ministry, little time was left to delineate a firm, long-range policy for Macedonia and the other regions of the Ottoman Empire inhabited by large Greek populations. Thus, vital national questions were allowed to pass to private organizations and societies which, at times, tended to act irresponsibly.

Two main tendencies were apparent among those Greeks who concerned themselves with the national issues : one preached the idea of Panhellenism, or the "Great Idea," which disregarded the rights and the interests of the other Balkan peoples; the other, more conservative in outlook, favored the active promotion of Greek national interests though taking into account the justified needs and claims of the other Balkan States.[58]

The atrocities of the first Bulgarian *comitadji* bands in Macedonia and the continued inactivity of the Greek Government, prompted a number of young officers in Athens to form in 1894 the National Society. The aims of the Society, as outlined in its secret Statute, were to assist the subject Greek populations of the Ottoman provinces in retaining their Greek consciousness, and to prepare them — and Greece — for the eventuality of a war against Turkey.[59] In 1896 and early 1897 the Society sent two armed bands into Macedonia to raise the morale of the hard-pressed Greeks. They were soon, however, defeated by the Turkish Army.

Greece's first major attempt to solve definitely the Macedonian problem came in the form of a declaration of war on Turkey in 1897. This ended ingloriously in defeat. Thoroughly unorganized the undertaking

58. *Ibid.*, p. 22.
59. Following the Greco-Turkish War of 1897, the Council of the National Society included Professor S. Lambros as chairman, Professor N. Politis, Dion. Stefanou (Cabinet Minister), Gennadis (Captain), Fikionis (Captain), Lambrides (Journalist), L. Matesis (attorney at law), C. Mazarakis (Lieutenant) and Pavlos Melas (Lieutenant) as members.

resulted from an impulse of some extreme nationalist enthusiasts in Athens who forced the nation to an unfortunate adventure because their demands for liberating Crete had been denied by the Great Powers. Humiliated, Greece was finally saved by the intervention of the Powers. As for Macedonia, the Greek cause suffered a serious setback. Completely defenseless, the Macedonian Greeks were severely punished by the Turks, both during and after the war. To avoid persecution, whole villages which until that moment had maintained their allegiance to the Greek Church and Hellenism, shifted overnight to the Bulgarian Exarchate.[60] The Turks now tended to favor the Bulgarians over the Greeks in their daily disputes. Thus, the Bulgarians found themselves unopposed in preparing the ground for the final *coup* which would give the region to them. In their activities they were indirectly assisted by the complete incapability of the Greek state to render any worthwhile assistance to the Macedonian Greeks. The political instability and the financial chaos at Athens had an adverse impact on the morale of the Greek populations. Particularly damaging was the decision of the Greek Government to cut sharply the grants which it provided to the Greek schools.[61] Moreover, the Greek Government, in its postwar conciliatory spirit toward Turkey, ordered the dissolution of the National Society and instructed its consular representatives in Macedonia to discourage any armed activity on the part of the local population, even in self-defense against the activities of the Bulgarian *comitadjis*.[62]

The only real defense against Bulgarian propaganda and terror was organized by dedicated individuals, teachers and priests. The Greek schools which had been established in Macedonia as early as the 18th century, became the cradles of Hellenism. They were chiefly maintained by the communities and by Macedonian Greeks living abroad.

However, as the activities of the *comitadjis* increased, and more and more villagers were converted to Bulgarism in fear of their lives, it became evident that neither the schools, nor the Church would suffice to save the Greeks and Macedonia. The hour was rapidly approaching for an all-out armed effort in which the Greeks of free Greece and the Greeks of Macedonia would join to stem off the Bulgarian advance. What followed, has come to be known as the "Macedonian Struggle."

60. Bourchier, "The Balkan States..." in Villari, *op. cit.*, p. 76.
61. Vlahos, *op. cit.*, pp. 128-129.
62. Informative of the prevailing situation is the personal account of the wife of a Greek official serving in Thessaloniki from 1898 - 1903. See : Melpomeni Avgerinou, Μακεδονικὰ ᾽Απομνημονεύματα καὶ Διπλωματικὰ Παρασκήνια [Macedonian Memoirs and Diplomatic Backstage], (Athens : "To Kratos," 1914), pp. 9-10.

CHAPTER II

WARS FOR MACEDONIA

THE MACEDONIAN STRUGGLE : 1903-1908

By the spring of 1903, the Bulgarians were sufficiently prepared to attempt a major *coup* in Macedonia. The situation was generally favorable. In northern and central Macedonia, particularly, most of the peasantry appeared to follow the Exarchate, either by conviction or by coercion. The remaining Greek villages, were completely terrorized. The governments of Greece and Serbia had entrusted their co-nationals in the Macedonian provinces to the protection of the Ottoman administration, a rather inadequate and unrealistic confrontation. They were apparently motivated by hopes that a program of administrative reforms introduced early in 1903 at the insistence of Austria and Russia, could be sufficient under the circumstances to curtail Bulgarian excesses against the Greek and Serbian element.[1] The Bulgarians were, furthermore, assisted by a favorable international opinion, which they had successfully cultivated over the years. Particularly in Britain there was a number of humanitarian-minded societies and individuals who tended to regard Bulgarian atrocities as heroic deeds of an oppressed people against the rule of a despot. In the meantime, the *comitadjis* had been able to assemble in Macedonia large quantities of arms thus turning Exarchist villages to fully-equipped armories.

The first signal was given in Thessaloniki in April of 1903. I.M.R.O. terrorists blew up the French steamship *Quadalquivir* and the Ottoman

---

1. In December 1902, the foreign ministers of Russia and Austria-Hungary met at Vienna and decided on a program of administrative reforms to be introduced in the vilayets of Kossovo, Monastir and Thessaloniki. In February 1903, the Sublime Porte accepted the proposals which included the reorganization of the Gendarmerie and the dispatch to Macedonia of European officers to assist in the reorganization and execution of the law. Vlahos, *Τὸ Μακεδονικὸν ὡς Φάσις τοῦ Ἀνατολικοῦ Ζητήματος 1878 - 1908* [The Maeedonian Question as a Phase of the Eastern Question, 1878-1908] (Athens : Petroudes and Christou, Printers, 1935), pp. 253-256; also Douglas Dakin, "The Greek Proposals for an Alliance with France and Great Britain : June - July 1907," *Balkan Studies*, Vol. III, No. 1, 1962, p. 46, footnotes 10 and 11.

MACEDONIA UNDER THE OTTOMANS (XIX CENTURY)

Boundaries of Vilayets
Present state frontiers
Present Macedonian provinces
Capitals of Vilayets
Capitals of Sanjaks
Main towns

Map 6

Bank, while bombs were thrown against foreign schools and institutions. Immediately, the fire spread to the countryside where railroads and bridges were blown, wire services disrupted and complete villages set on fire.[2]

The culmination of the Bulgarian activities came in August, when the I.M.R.O. instigated a large-scale uprising in the vilayets of Monastir and Andrianople. The "Iliden revolution" — as it has been termed by the Bulgarians and recently by the Skopje "Macedonians" — lasted barely three weeks before it was crushed by the Ottoman Army. Yet, in that short time, the Bulgarians were in a position to ascertain that significant progress had been made in Macedonia. Thousands of peasants, either because they believed in the Bulgarian assurances that the defeat of the Ottomans was possible, or because they were threatened by reprisals, followed the *comitadjis* to the mountains.[3] The town of Krusovo, near Skopje, mostly inhabited by Greeks, was seized by the insurgents, and the "Krusovo Republic" was proclaimed. Twelve days later, the town lay in ruins as the *comitadjis* retreated before the Imperial Army, abandoning the Greek population to the vengeance of the Turks.[4]

The Bulgarian insurrection had significant repercussions, disproportionate to its achievements in the field. The measures adopted by the Ottomans against the native population created a stormy indignation in public opinion abroad. More important, however, was the fact that the events finally awakened the Greek nation. Mass demonstrations in Athens followed the announcement of the destruction of Krusovo and the murder of many Greeks who refused to become instruments of Bulgarian aspirations. The Greek Government clearly realised that Macedonia was in danger of being lost by default to the Bulgarians, and that neither the Great Powers nor the Ottomans could be trusted to safeguard the rights of the Greeks in the region. The moment had riped for the Greek counter-offensive to take a concrete form.

Thus, the crushing of the "Iliden" uprising ushered in the "Macedonian Struggle," which in turn prepared the way for the liberation of Macedonia ten years later.

* * *

Prior to the launching of the Greek offensive, there were only a few discerning minds in the Greek Kingdom and in Macedonia who had been

2. Vlahos, *op. cit.*, p. 262.
3. *Ibid.*
4. The events at Krusovo have been recounted by the teacher of Krusovo, Nikolas Ballas, in his book, Ἱστορία τοῦ Κρουσόβου [History of Krusovo] (Thessaloniki: Institute for Balkan Studies, 1962).

34

able to grasp the significance of Bulgarian activities for Hellenism in Macedonia.[5] The first encouraging sign for the Greek cause came at the turn of the century with the appointment to many Macedonian dioceses of younger, more energetic religious leaders determined to protect the faithful — the "Greek Patriarchists" — against the terror of the "Bulgarian Exarchists." The most capable of them all was Germanos Karavangelis, who was appointed bishop of Kastoria in 1900, at the age of 34.[6] One of his first successful undertakings was the formation of Slavophone Greek bands to protect the villages of his diocese against the *comitadjis*.[7]

The prelates in Monastir, Kastoria, Serres, Nevrokop and elsewhere tried to encourage the submissive peasants to resist Bulgarian pressure.[8] At the same time, they flooded the Patriarchate at Constantinople with reports of the weak position of Hellenism in Macedonia. Meanwhile, Greek consuls in Macedonian cities sent similar reports to the Government at Athens. Among the most dedicated was the then young secretary of the consulate at Monastir, Ion Dragoumis — son of the later Prime Minister of Greece Stefanos Dragoumis — whose brilliant mind and noble idealism aroused the interest of influencial Greeks of Athens in the fate of Macedonia.[9]

The "Iliden" uprising, however, succeeded where the reports of the bishops and the consuls had failed. Early in 1904, four young Greek officers, including Pavlos Melas — "the Byron of the Macedonian Struggle," [10] whose early death impressed on all the worthiness and necessity of the crusade — secretly visited Macedonia and reported back to Athens that time was rapidly running short for the Greek cause. The only solution was to detail armed bands from free Greece and to arm the natives.

A Macedonian Committee was formed in Athens under Dimitrios

5. Dakin, *op. cit.*, p. 44.
6. Germanos Karavangelis, 'Ο Μακεδονικὸς 'Αγὼν — 'Απομνημονεύματα [The Macedonian Struggle - Memoirs]. Second Edition. Edited by Vasilios Laourdas. (Thessaloniki: Institute for Balkan Studies, 1959).
7. *Ibid*, pp. 9-10.
8. The reaction of certain Greek prelates to Bulgarian tactics is vividly shown in Vasilios Laourdas (ed), 'Η Μητρόπολις Νευροκοπίου: 1900-1907. 'Εκθέσεις τῶν Μητροπολιτῶν Νικοδήμου καὶ Θεοδωρήτου [The Metropolis of Nevrokop: 1900-1907 — Reports of the Metropolitans Nikodemos and Theodoritos], (Thessaloniki: Institute for Balkan Studies, 1961), p. xiii.
9. Idas (Ion Dragoumis), 'Ηρώων καὶ Μαρτύρων Αἷμα [The Blood of Heroes and Martyrs], Second Edition, (Athens, 1914).
10. Douglas Dakin, "British Sources Concerning the Greek Struggle in Macedonia: 1901-1909", *Balkan Studies*, Vol. II, No. 1, 1961, p. 83.

Kalapothakis, publisher of the newspaper "Ethnos," which undertook to organize and direct the struggle. Ostensibly a private society, the Macedonian Committee was invested with the moral and material support of the Greek Government.[11] In Thessaloniki, the Greek Consulate under the new Consul-General Lambros Koromilas — later Greek Foreign Minister — became the headquarters of the armed struggle against the Bulgarian *comitadjis*, and later against Rumanian and Albanian propaganda and subversion.[12]

The first Greek band led by Melas, entered Macedonia in September 1904. Already bands of native Greek and Slav-speaking Macedonians were in the field.[13] Melas was ambushed and killed by the Turkish Army before he could even reach Kastoria. His death caused a sensation in Athens which reacted in anger sending numerous bands to Macedonia to combat the Bulgarians.

The Macedonian Struggle was a relentless underground war in a region occupied by Turks whose interest was not its subduance, but, rather, its perpetuation, since it tended to divide the subject Christian nationalities. When the Serbs and the Rumanian oriented Kutso-Vlachs began to form their own bands, the situation became utterly confused. The European Powers attempted to improve it by presenting the Ottoman Empire with a new program of reforms — the Mürzsteg Program — which aimed at bettering the measures of the Vienna reforms. European officers were dispatched to the region, but they rather increased the confusion by acts and reports tending to project their own individual preferences and prejudices.

Terrorism in Macedonia was the culmination of a quarter of a century of conflicting nationalist propagandas in a region whose peoples had, more or less, no formulated national consciousness, but were guided by the expediency of the moment and the instinct for self-preservation.

Since the underground fighting did not aim at overthrowing the Ottoman ruler, the successes and losses on both sides cannot be appraised in terms of territorial gains. The only safe conclusion is that the Greeks, in the course of four years, were successful in containing the Bulgarian advance in central Macedonia and even reverting its course by reconverting to Hellenism and the Patriarchate tens of villages which had under Bulgar-

11. Vlahos, *op. cit.*, pp. 348-349.
12. For the role of the Greek Consulate of Thessaloniki in the Macedonian Struggle, see Vasilios Laourdas, Τὸ Ἑλληνικὸν Γενικὸν Προξενεῖον Θεσσαλονίκης 1903 - 1908 [The Greek General Consulate of Thessaloniki, 1903-1908], (Thessaloniki, Institute for Balkan Studies, 1961).
13. Karavangelis, *op. cit.*, p. 17.

ian pressure declared themselves Bulgarian and Exarchist. The result was that the Bulgarians could not justly claim that Macedonia was mostly inhabited by Bulgarians. By the eve of the Balkan Wars of 1912-1913 the Greek element — Greek and Slav-speaking — predominated over the Bulgarian in southern and central Macedonia.

In 1908, the Young Turks' revolt and the amnesty given to the guerrillas ended the Macedonian Struggle. Initial hopes for an improvement of the situation soon ended in disillusionment, as the Young Turks began to exhibit an oppresive nationalistic attitude towards the various nationalities. The moment was approaching for the Christian states of the Balkans to try to solve the Macedonian Question in a definite and final way.

THE BALKAN WARS

Thirty years of proselytism, indoctrination, terror, uprisings and guerrilla warfare by the Balkan pretenders had failed to uproot the Turks from Macedonia. Gradually, it was becoming clear that only a concerted effort by all the Christian states could end Ottoman rule in the European provinces of the Empire.

Mutual hatreds and suspicions still constituted the main obstacle to a working rapprochement. The Bulgarians feared, not without justification, that a joint war undertaken against the Turks would require the denouncement of their claims over Macedonia as a whole. There were still many Bulgarians who preferred an autonomous Macedonia under Turkish suzerainty rather than an independent Macedonia partitioned between the three Christian Balkan states.[14] Yet, in a sparse moment of enlightenment, the leaders of Sofia, Belgrade and Athens succeeded in drawing their countries together in a combined effort to force the Turks out of their European possessions.

A. Diplomatic negotiations

Long diplomatic negotiations preceded the declaration of war against Turkey in October 1912. Two opposing views prevailed initially. The one, shared by the Greeks and the Serbs, thought of the eventual solution of the Macedonian problem by means of partition; the other, held by the

---

14. Report by the Carnegie Commission of Inquiry as quoted by Anastassof, *The Tragic Peninsula: A History of the Macedonian Movement for Independence Since 1878* (St. Louis: Blackwell Weilandy Co., 1938), p. 169.

Bulgarians, aimed at keeping Macedonia as an entity to be united eventually to one of the Balkan states, i.e. to Bulgaria.[15]

In the beginning, the Bulgarians and the Serbs conducted talks at the exclusion of the Greeks. On February 29, 1912, they reached agreement by signing at Sofia a treaty of friendship and alliance which included a secret annex and a military convention outlining the military cooperation of the two allies against Turkey.

Under article 2 of the secret annex, the signatories agreed that the territories which would fall into their possession during their common action against the Turks would be considered as falling under the joint occupation of both states. Their future would be determined in less than three months after the conclusion of peace, under the following terms: Serbia would recognize Bulgaria's right to annex the territories east of the Rhodope Mountains and the Strymon River. Bulgaria, on her part, would recognize Serbia's right over the territories north and west of the Shar Mountains. As for the territories between the Shar Mountains, the Rhodope Mountains, the Aegean Sea and Lake Ohrid — the geographical region commonly referred to as Macedonia — the secret annex stipulated that, should the establishment of an autonomous Macedonia not be realized for various reasons, Serbia would not raise any claims over the territories beyond a straight line from Golen Mountain to the east coast of Lake Ohrid.[16] Thus, Serbia was denouncing any claim that she might have had over the Macedonian cities of Veles, Prilep, Ohrid, Monastir, Florina, Edessa, Kozani and Thessaloniki. Skopje and Dibra were allocated to Serbia, while Kastoria and Siatista were left entirely out of both the Serbian and the Bulgarian spheres. Bulgaria was willing to abide by this demarcation line, provided the Russian Tsar, who was to act as the final arbiter, would pronounce himself in favor of the agreement.[17]

The Serbo-Bulgarian agreement, although allocating the most generous portion of Macedonia to Bulgaria, was a retreat — though a minor one — for the Bulgarians who had long favored the establishment of a unified autonomous Macedonia to be united eventually to the Bulgarian Fatherland, exactly as Eastern Rumelia had been 30 years before. The Bulgarian Government was compelled to concede to this solution fearing that a prolongation of the negotiations with the Serbs might bring Greece and

---

15. Assen Iv. Krainikowsky, *La Question de Macédoine et la Diplomatie Européenne*, (Paris : Librairie Rivière & Cie, 1938), p. 239.

16. Iv. E. Guechoff, *L'Alliance Balkanique* (Paris : Librairie Hachette et Cie, 1915), pp. 198-199.

17. Text and map of treaty and secret annex in Guechoff, *op. cit.*, pp. 196-200.

Serbia together to conclude an agreement to the detriment of Bulgaria. An attack by the two Christian neighbors and, of course, by Turkey could prove disastrous to Bulgarian aspirations in Macedonia.[18]

While the Serbo-Bulgarian negotiations were proceeding toward an agreement, the Greek Government indicated that it was willing to begin discussions with the Bulgarians over an eventual cooperation between the two countries. As early as the spring of 1911, the recently appointed Premier Venizelos sounded the Bulgarians about such a possibility and found them receptive.[19] Despite the fact that the Bulgarians were simultaneously negotiating the partition of Macedonia with the Serbs at the exclusion of the Greeks, the Greco-Bulgarian talks proceeded satisfactorily. Initially, the Bulgarians attempted to secure Greece's consent to include in the treaty a clause that Greece would not oppose any eventual Bulgarian demand for an administrative autonomy in Macedonia and the Vilayet of Andrianople (Thrace) with equal rights safeguarded for all nationalities. However, in the face of stern Greek opposition, Bulgaria withdrew her proposal and the treaty was signed on May 29, 1912. In September 1912, the two countries also signed a military convention providing for cooperation during the war.

The Greco-Bulgarian treaty did not attempt to draw the lines of the future territorial settlement in Macedonia, as was the case with the Serbo - Bulgarian treaty, though the Greek Government repeatedly attempted to convince the Bulgarians to partition Macedonia before the outbreak of the war.[20] The Bulgarians, successful in eliminating the Serbs with only a few concessions in the north-western Macedonian districts, apparently felt confident that their military strength was sufficient to assure the realization of their objectives in Macedonia. Thus, the treaty between Greece and Bulgaria was confined to two major items, namely, the obligation to assist each other in the event of an attack by Turkey (article 1), and the obligation to use their influence among their co-nationals in Turkey to cooperate with each other (article 2).[21] By the military convention signed on September 12, Greece further assumed the obligation to deploy in the front at least 120,000 men, as compared to Bulgaria's 300,000, and to attempt the neutralization of Turkish sea communications with her fleet. According to the Convention, Bulgaria was obliged to assign the largest

---

18. Letter published by former Bulgarian Premier Al. Chankov in *Makedonska Tribuna* (Indianapolis, Ind., U.S.A.), September 18, 1952.

19. Alexis Ad. Kyrou, Οἱ Βαλκανικοὶ γείτονές μας [Our Balkan Neighbors], (Athens 1962), p. 94.

20. *Ibid.*, p. 95.

21. Text of treaty in Guechoff, *op. cit.*, pp. 223-228.

part of her Army to the vilayets of Kossovo, Monastir and Thessaloniki. In the event Serbia were to participate in the war, Bulgaria could transfer all her forces to the Thracian front assuming the obligation toward Greece to see that Serbian forces put pressure on the Turks from the direction of northern Macedonia.[22]

B. Wins and Losses in the Wars

The war declared on the Ottoman Empire by Bulgaria, Serbia, Greece and Montenegro early in October 1912, was conducted in a way which adhered little to the provisions of the treaty; and the settlement which followed resembled even less the expectations of the framers of the treaties, particularly the expectations of the Bulgarians.

The Bulgarian Army moved victorious toward the Thracian front. To consolidate its victories and open the way to Constantinople, it asked for Serbian assistance. In the meantime, however, a Bulgarian Division was assigned to move in a south, south-westerly direction to capture Thessaloniki before the Greek Army could reach the city.[23] As it turned out, the Greek Army was able to capture the capital of Macedonia just hours before the Bulgarians arrived.

On the Serbian front, developments, likewise, proceeded in a way not envisioned by the treaty. Austria-Hungary and Italy, not wishing the expansion of Serbia toward the Adriatic littoral and Albanian regions, prohibited the westerly march of the Serbian Army. Thus, the Serbs diverted their advance in a southerly direction and reached Monastir, deep inside the zone assigned to Bulgaria by the Serbo-Bulgarian treaty.

The war ended with Turkey defeated and limited to a narrow belt around Constantinople. Immediately, however, the Balkan allies began to quarrel over the spoils of their victory.

On May 25, 1912, the Serb Prime Minister sent to Sofia a list of proposals aiming at revising the treaty. The Serbian note claimed that the Bulgarians had failed to provide the Serbs with the assistance they had promised, while the Serbs had fulfilled their obligations, even sending troops to Eastern Thrace to assist the Bulgarians in the siege of Andrian-

---

22. Text of the convention in Guechoff, *op. cit.*, pp. 228-234.
23. The secret diversion of a significant part of the Bulgarian Army toward Thessaloniki is vividly told by Souliotis Nikolaides who was attached as a liaison officer by the Greek Military General Staff to Bulgarian Army Headquarters. See: Athanasios Souliotis - Nikolaides, Ἡμερολόγιον τοῦ πρώτου Βαλκανικοῦ πολέμου [Diary of the First Balkan War], (Thessaloniki: Institute for Balkan Studies, 1962).

ople. In view of the denial of Austria-Hungary and Italy to a Serbian advance toward the Adriatic, the Serbs asked the Bulgarians to consent to a revision of the treaty which would allow them to keep the newly acquired districts of Central Macedonia, especially since the Bulgarians had expanded in the direction of Thrace.[24]

* * *

As expected, the Bulgarians rejected the Serbian proposals. In the meantime, they tried to enforce a *de facto* condominium in Thessaloniki where certain Bulgarian units were allowed to be quartered by the commander-in-chief of the Greek Army. Realizing that long talks and indirect methods could not bring about the expected results, the Bulgarians attacked the Greeks and the Serbs on June 16, 1913. Soon, however, they began to lose much of the ground they had gained in Macedonia, a fact which forced them to conclude a treaty.

The Second Balkan War proved disastrous to Bulgarian aspirations in Macedonia.[25] The Treaty of Bucharest, concluded on August 10, 1913, limited Bulgaria's possessions in Macedonia to an outlet in the Aegean between the Nestos River and a line just a few kilometers west of Kavala.

The peace settlement left the Bulgarians in deep disillusionment. Despite the moderate tone of the Greek delegation in Bucharest,[26] it was evident that the Bulgarians would try to overrule the treaty of peace. The most opportune moment appeared at the outbreak of the World War.

THE WORLD WAR AND THE PEACE SETTLEMENT

A. The Bulgarian Occupation of Macedonia

The outbreak of World War in 1914 provided Bulgaria with the opportunity to regain Macedonia. Both blocs tried to elicit her participation

---

24. Dotation Carnegie pour la Paix Internationale. *Enquête dans les Balkans : rapport présenté aux directeurs de la Dotation par les membres de la Commission d'Enquête*, (Paris : 1914) p. 44.

25. Two former Bulgarian premiers have called the attack on the allies ''criminal stupidity'' : Al. Chankov in his letter to *Makedonska Tribuna* (September 18, 1952) and Iv. Guechoff, in his book *La Folie criminelle et l'enquête parlementaire* (Sofia, 1914) as quoted by V. Colocotronis, *La Macédoine et l'Hellénisme : Etude historique et ethnologique*, (Paris : Berger - Levrault, 1919), p. 407.

26. Eleftherios Venizelos, representing Greece at the peace conference worked hard to smoothen the scars of the war and to prepare the ground for a firmer, lasting Balkan peace, V. Colocotronis, *op. cit.*, p. 409.

in the war on their side by making generous offers for territorial compensation in Macedonia.[27]

Bulgaria succeeded in drawing the promise of the Central Powers to acquire that part of Macedonia occupied by the Serbs as well as certain areas in possession of the Greeks, in exchange for a benevolent neutrality.[28] A little later (September 13, 1915), the Entente Powers promised to cease the Macedonian territories corresponding to the boundaries drawn on the map annexed to the Serbo-Bulgarian Treaty of 1912. This was done on condition that Bulgaria would conclude a military alliance with them and declare war on Turkey immediately.[29]

The Sofia Government finally favored the side of the Central Powers. The Bulgarian army took possession of the entire region of Serbian Macedonia and the eastern section of Greek Macedonia. Civilian administrators were dispatched from Bulgaria and assigned the task of converting the annexed regions into provinces of the Bulgarian state. Their authority included the adoption of severe punitive measures against local populations objecting to such integration.

It appears that a great share of the blame for the happenings during the three years of Bulgarian occupation should be attributed to the irredentist I.M.R.O. followers. They not only exerted pressure on the Bulgarian Government to decide in favor of the Central Powers and occupy Macedonia, but were also directly involved in the atrocities committed against the Greek and Serbian populations. Indeed, many Bulgarian-Macedonians joined the Bulgarian Army of occupation and some of them were even appointed civilian officers in the occupied regions.[30] As Elizabeth Barker described the situation in Greek Macedonia:

> The Bulgarian occupation authorities in Greek eastern Macedonia had behaved towards the Greek population with brutality singularly inappropriate in supposed liberators. An Inter-Allied Commission in 1919 reported that 94 villages had been entirely demolished, that 30,000 people had died of hunger, blows, and disease during the occupation, that 42,000 had been deported to Bulgaria, and that 16,000 had fled to Greece.[31]

---

27. Vasil Radoslavoff's *Bulgarien und die Weltkrise* (Berlin, 1923), pp. 144-170, as quoted in Slijepcević, *op. cit.*, pp. 172-175.

28. Slijepcević, *op. cit.*, p. 173; Radoslavoff, *op. cit.*, pp. 156-157.

29. Slijepcević, *op. cit.*, p. 174; Radoslavoff, *op. cit.*, p. 159.

30. Elizabeth Barker, *Macedonia; Its Place in Balkan Power Politics* (London: The Royal Institute of International Affairs, 1950), pp. 19-20.

31. *Ibid.*, pp. 29-30.

The defeat of Germany brought the short-lived Bulgarian occupation to its end. While retreating, the Bulgarians devastated the region, a fact instrumental in accentuating age-old hatreds between the neighboring peoples.

B. The Treaty of Neuilly and the Exchange of Minorities

The Treaty of Neuilly which ended the state of war between Bulgaria and her adversaries, also marked the final stage of one of the most critical eras of the Macedonian Question. Bulgaria lost to Greece the entire Aegean littoral, including the Thracian regions which she had seized from Turkey. To Serbia she lost even certain districts which were *bona fide* areas of Bulgaria proper.

The treaty provided, moreover, for the voluntary exchange of minorities between Greece and Bulgaria. This stipulation merely facilitated a process begun earlier during the Balkan Wars. Bulgarians living in areas occupied by the Greek Army, and Greeks living in areas which had passed under the control of the Bulgarian Army, fled to their respective national homelands. The exodus of the Greeks assumed greater proportions after the Treaty of Bucharest of 1913. Similarly, many Greeks left their homes in Serbian Macedonia and settled in Greek Macedonia along with the refugees from Bulgaria.[32]

During the Bulgarian occupation of Greek Macedonia (1915-1918), the local Bulgarians had closely collaborated with the Bulgarian authorities in the persecution of the Greeks, a fact which made them liable to Greek punitive measures. Precisely to avert maltreatment of the alien element in both countries and to reduce the possibility of seditious activity on the part of the minorities, a convention for voluntary exchange was concluded at Neuilly between Greece and Bulgaria entering force on August 9, 1920. The contracting parties recognized the right of those of their citizens belonging to racial, religious or linguistic minorities to emigrate freely to their respective territories. They also agreed not to place any restrictions on this right of emigration.[33] The emphasis was on its voluntary character, though there was no provision against compelling national minorities to emigrate.[34]

The Internal Macedonian Revolutionary Organization immediately

32. Pallis, *Macedonia and the Macedonians: A Historical Study* (London: Greek Information Service, 1949), p. 7.
33. Stephen Ladas, *The Exchange of Minorities: Bulgaria, Greece and Turkey* (New York: MacMillan, 1932), p. 41.
34. *Ibid.*, p. 42.

reacted against the implementation of the exchange of populations.[35] The leaders of the Organization issued orders for Bulgarians not to take advantage of the Convention presumably fearing that the exchange would seriously weaken Bulgaria's ethnological claim to Greek Macedonia.[36] It seems that a substantial number of Slavs who had expressed a desire to emigrate to Bulgaria chose, as a result, to remain in Greece. Soon, thereafter, the 1922 defeat of the Greek Army in Asia Minor and the influx of hundreds of thousands of Greeks from Turkey forced most of the Bulgarian-oriented Slav-speaking inhabitants of Greek Macedonia to flee to Bulgaria.[37] In fact, the minority emigrations on both sides assumed the form of compulsory transfers.

Approximately 30,000 Greeks left Bulgaria while 53,000 Bulgarians departed Greece. To these figures one should add 16,000 Greeks and 39,000 Bulgarians who had fled to their respective homelands during the war.[38]

The Greco-Bulgarian exchange of populations was by no means the only one. Following the defeat of the Greek Army in Asia Minor in 1922 and the compulsory exchange of Greeks and Turks, over a million of Greeks from Turkey fled to Greece. Under the convention concerning the compulsory exchange of Greek and Turkish minorities signed between the two countries at Lausanne in 1923, only the Greek minority in Constantinople and the Moslem minority in Western Thrace remained in the lands of their birth. Most of the Greek refugees were settled in Macedonia.[39]

Following the war treaties and the transfer of minorities, the Macedonian Question appeared to have been definitely solved. The Greek and Bulgarian parts of Macedonia attained a high degree of national homogeneity and were easily integrated into the body politic of the mother country. The situation was different — and more complicated — in Serbian Macedonia where the majority of the Slavic population was considered Bulgarian.

In terms of numbers the territorial settlement in Macedonia after the War treaties assumed the following picture:[40]

35. Wilkinson, *Maps and Politics: A Review of the Ethnographic Cartography of Macedonia* (Liverpool: University Press, 1951), p. 262.
36. Barker, *op. cit.*, p. 30.
37. Ladas, *op. cit.*, p. 105.
38. *Ibid.*, pp. 122-123.
39. An excellent contribution in this respect is the recent book by Dimitri Pentzopoulos, *The Balkan Exchange of Minorities and its Impact upon Greece* (Paris: Meuton Co., 1963).
40. Christopher Christides, *The Macedonian Camouflage in the Light of Facts and Figures* (Athens: Hellenic Publishing Company, 1949), p. 53.

Greek Macedonia	34,602.5	sq. km.	51.5%
Yugoslav Macedonia	25,774.0	»	38.4
Bulgarian Macedonia	6,789.2	»	10.1
Total:	67,165.7	sq. km.	100.0%

The most significant fact, not revealed by numbers, was the elimination of Bulgaria from the Aegean littoral, and the existence of a large irredentist number of Bulgarian Macedonians in Bulgaria who agitated for their return to Greek and Serbian Macedonia. Both affected considerably Bulgarian foreign — and even domestic — policy during the interwar period.

CHAPTER III

THE INTER-WAR YEARS

Of the three Balkan neighbors, only Serbia and Greece emerged from a decade of war adequately compensated in Macedonia. Bulgaria remained dangerously resentful of her military and diplomatic defeats. Thus, the pattern of international relations between the Balkan states during the inter-war period was set. Greece, following her defeat in Asia Minor, abandoned her policy of *Megali Idea* and, along with Serbia, proclaimed a policy of *status quo*. They were soon joined by Turkey who, under the leadership of Kemal Ataturk, renounced, in the Treaty of Lausanne,[1] all rights to the territories she had lost.

On the home front, the Balkan states were faced with a multiple of economic and social problems inherited along with the new territories. On the international front, they maneuvered — with the exception of Bulgaria — to prepare the ground for a more durable peace with their neighbors.

In the late twenties and early thirties, a series of unofficial and semi-official talks took place among statesmen of the Balkan countries in the hope of establishing closer Balkan cooperation. For four years negotiations aimed at concluding a Balkan Pact.[2] Finally when the Pact was signed in Athens, on February 9, 1934, the Bulgarians remained outside it. One of the basic reasons for Bulgaria's nonparticipation was her dispute with the Greeks and Yugoslavs on minority and territorial issues.[3]

The value of the Pact should not be overemphasized, since the

1. *Treaty of Peace with Turkey and Other Instruments Signed at Lausanne on July 24, 1923, Together with Agreements between Greece and Turkey Signed on January 30, 1923 and Subsidiary Documents Forming Part of the Turkish Peace Settlement* (with maps). Great Britain, Foreign Office, "Treaty Series," No. 16 [1923]. (London : H. M. Stationery Office, 1923), Art. XVI.

2. For the attitude of Greece towards the Balkan Pact, see : Panayotis N. Pipinelis, Ἱστορία τῆς Ἐξωτερικῆς Πολιτικῆς τῆς Ἑλλάδος : 1923 - 1941 [History of the Greek Foreign Policy : 1933-1941], (Athens : Saliveros Co., 1948), Part II, pp. 149-192· A good, contemporary account is given in R. J. Kerner and H. N. Howard, *The Balkan Conferences and the Balkan Entente, 1930 - 1935*, (Berkeley : University of California Press, 1936).

3. Barker, *Macedonia; Its Place in Balkan Power Politics* (London : The Royal Institute of International Affairs, 1950), p. 33.

Balkan states tended to conduct their international relations in the light of individual interests and orientations rather, than with a sense of Balkan solidarity. Yet, the Pact and a number of other treaties and agreements bound them together — except for Bulgaria — and tended to reduce tensions and antagonisms in this part of the world.

Life in the Balkans would have developed in an orderly, peaceful way, were it not for Bulgaria's irredentism to secure the lands she had coveted for half a century and which, it appeared, she had definitely lost.

THE "MACEDONIAN QUESTION" IN YUGOSLAVIA AND GREECE

A. The Case for Southern Serbia

During the inter-war period, the successive Yugoslav governments publicly treated the Macedonian Question as non-existent, and appeared to be satisfied with the acquisition of a large portion of Macedonia. Their main concern remained the conversion of the inhabitants of the region into Serbs. Understandably, this was not an easy task.

During Ottoman rule, the most dedicated champions of Bulgarian nationalism in Macedonia were natives of the region alloted to Serbia by the Treaty during Bucharest. Although Bulgarian conduct during the short-lived occupation of the First World War had caused a number of inhabitants to resent them, it is certain that the loyalties of the majority of the population did not belong to the Government in Belgrade, especially since the latter began to apply a policy of forceful national assimilation. Reaction against Serbian oppression, hidden Bulgarian sympathies and continuous agitation by I.M.R.O. activists inside Yugoslav Macedonia had invigorated the resistance of the inhabitants to the central government. The situation tended to become worse as Belgrade increased the pressure, and as foreign interests — Fascist Italy and Nazi Germany in particular — attempted to profit from the internal instability by supporting the revolutionary and separatist tendencies of the extremist elements.

During the inter-war period, the Slavs of Yugoslav Macedonia were never accorded the status of a national minority, despite Bulgarian protests that they constituted a Bulgarian minority eligible to receive the benefits of the minority treaties of the League of Nations. The Yugoslav Government's response was that there could be no question of allocating to the inhabitants of Yugoslav Macedonia the status of an ethnic minority protected by the League of Nations especially since the Bulgarian Government aspired at employing them as an instrument of its views against Serbian lands. Apparently, the Yugoslav Government was motivated by the principle that a minority could expect to be accorded minority rights only if it exhibited a scrupulous loyalty to the state of which it formed a part. And that was not the case with the inhabitants of Yugoslav Macedonia.

For the Belgrade Government, the people of Macedonia were Serbs. The name Macedonia was dropped and replaced by the administrative distinction of Vardar Banovina. Pro-Bulgarian leaders and members of the Bulgarophile intelligentsia were deported or imprisoned. At the same time, thousands of Serbs were settled in the region to assist in the assimilation of the native Slavs. If methods of peaceful integration and assimilation were abandoned in favor of compulsory means, it must be attributed to the fact that the Belgrade Government was, at the time, in the hands of a dictatorial leadership by nature inclined toward drastic solutions. Yet, arbitrary measures tended to increase the pro-Bulgarian sentiment of the inhabitants who began to look nostalgically toward Bulgaria as the endeared motherland which could relieve them eventually from an intolerable regime.

B. Greek Macedonia and the Slavophones

Greece emerged from ten years of war with a shattered economy, a badly defeated Army and almost a million refugees. Yet, despite the reverses in Asia Minor, she could still measure her war experience with adequate satisfaction. On the whole, the military and diplomatic battles she had fought, had resulted in the incorporation of most of the Macedonian regions ·previously claimed as Greek. Indeed, Greece had never claimed the entire geographical region of Macedonia.

The population exchanges between Greece on the one hand, and Turkey and Bulgaria on the other, had almost eliminated the alien elements, and rendered Greece the most homogeneous state of the Balkans, if not of the entire Eastern Europe. The statistics compiled by the League of Nations, for the ethnological composition of Greek Macedonia in 1912 and 1926 give a vivid picture of the changes which occurred during the wars.[4]

	1912 Population	%	1926 Population	%
Greeks	513,000	42.6	1,341,000	88.8
Moslems	475,000	39.4	2,000	0.1
Bulgarians	119,000	9.9	77,000	5.1
Miscellaneous	98,000	8.1	91,000	6.0
	1,205,000	100.0	1,511,000	100.0

4. League of Nations, *Greek Refugee Settlement* (Geneva, 1926), annex.

48

The official Greek census of 1928 corroborated the findings of the League of Nations indicating that out of a population of 6,032,761, there were only 81,984 Slavophones.[5]

The above tables probably explain why Greek Macedonia — along with the other ''new lands'' — was able to integrate itself smoothly into the body politic of ''Old Greece.''

The only remnant of the old, acute struggle for Macedonia in Greece, was the existence of the 80,000 Slav-speaking inhabitants who remained in Western Macedonia. Greece classified them officially as Greeks who spoke a Slavonic dialect and refused to place them under the minority treaties of the League of Nations. Yet, a large number of them continued to have a Bulgarian consciousness. If they did not avail themselves of the provisions of the Greco-Bulgarian exchange agreement and emigrate to Bulgaria, it was due either to pressure exerted by the I.M.R.O., the natural attachment of the peasant to his land, or the attitude of certain Greek Macedonian politicians who, in the hope of winning Slavophone votes, prevented their emigration to Bulgaria.[6]

* * *

Next to the exchange of minorities, the most significant political development concerning Greek Macedonia was the conclusion in September 1924, of a Greco-Bulgarian agreement, known as the Kalfov-Politis Protocol.[7] The Greek Government appeared to accept the view that the Slavophones of Western Macedonia were Bulgarians, a fact which would entitle them to the protection envisioned by the League of Nations minority treaties.[8] Soon it was realized that the agreement was a blunder, since it tended to classify as Bulgarians thousands of Slavophones who had actively proven themselves to be loyal Greeks.

The Protocol had also a serious impact on Greco-Serbian relations. The Serbs, fearing to set a precedent which might affect their own citizens in Macedonia, reacted strongly against the initiatives of the Greek Government. Their foreign minister, Marigović, expressed to the Greek Ambassador in Belgrade his country's disapproval in these words:

---

5. *Annuaire Statistique de la Grèce* (Athens : National Printing Office, 1928).

6. Kostas Bramos, Σλαβοκομμουνιστικαὶ 'Οργανώσεις ἐν Μακεδονίᾳ. Προπαγάνδα καὶ ἐπαναστατικὴ δρᾶσις. [Slav-Communist Organizations in Macedonia : Propaganda and Revolutionary Activities], (Thessaloniki, 1960), Second Edition, p. 74.

7. For the text of the Protocol, see Macartney, *National States and National Minorities* (London : Oxford University Press, 1934), pp. 367-368.

8. Barker *op. cit.*, p. 31.

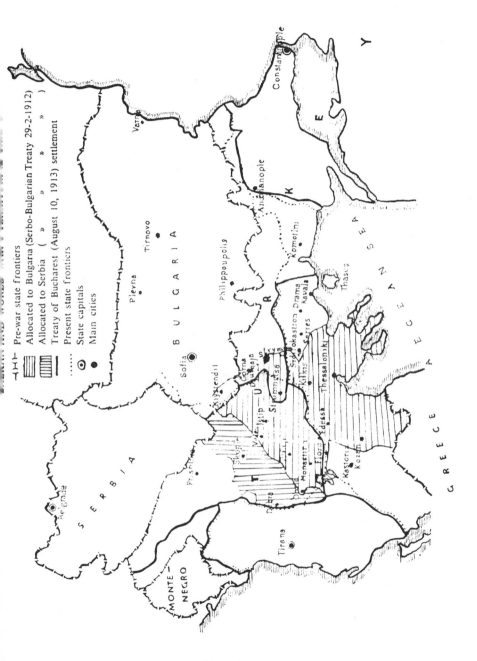

Key (legend):

- ⊣H⊢ Pre-war state frontiers
- ▥ Allocated to Bulgaria (Serbo-Bulgarian Treaty 29-2-1912)
- ▦ Allocated to Serbia (» » »)
- ⋯⋯ Treaty of Bucharest (August 10, 1913) settlement
- ⋯⋯ Present state frontiers
- ◉ State capitals
- ● Main cities

MONTE-NEGRO

SERBIA
Belgrade
Pr. shtina

BULGARIA
Sofia
Pleven
Tirnovo
Kyustendil
Gorna Dzhumaja
Vardar
Skopje
Strumitsa
Philippoupolis

Tirana

Debra
Veles
Shtip
Monastir
Florina
Kostoria
Kozhani
Edessa
Kilkis
Seres
Thessaloniki
Drama
Kavala
Nevrokastron
Komotini
Thasos
Andrianople
Varna

Constantinople

TURKEY

GREECE

AEGEAN SEA

Map 7

We do not wish nor can we wish to rely on arms alone for the defense of Serb Macedonia. For us it is essential that no third party should be able to dispute the Serb character of that territory; therefore, the dogma that the Slav inhabitants of Macedonia are Serbs is the basis of our policy. We cannot possibly accept that north of the frontier the Slavs are Serbs while beyond that frontier these same people are Bulgarians. To recognize that the Slavs of Edhessa and Florina are Bulgarians would be to destroy the very foundation of our policy in regard to Serbian Macedonia. That is the basis of our policy and should Greece be unwilling to back us up on this question then we shall regretfully be compelled to change this basis and seek an agreement with Bulgaria by dividing up Greek Macedonia into spheres of influence.[9]

In the meantime the Greek people and political parties had agreed in opposing the Protocol. In its February 3, 1925 meeting, the Parliament refused to ratify it. Foreign Minister Roussos was forced to resign. Venizelos was summoned from Paris to Geneva to explain before the Council of the League of Nations why the terms of the Protocol could not be implemented. Finally, on March 14, the Council of the League relieved Greece of her responsibilities under the Protocol.[10] Meanwhile, the Serbian Government had denounced the Greco-Serbian Treaty of 1913 on the grounds that the Protocol had violated both the letter and the spirit of the treaty.

The Greek Government made one more attempt to find a conciliatory solution by declaring the Slavophones "Macedono-Slavs," i.e. a national minority which could even have schools in its own language. But, the project failed primarily because it met with the objections of the Bulgarians who demanded the use of the Bulgarian language, and the protests of the Serbs who insisted that Serbo-Croatian should be the language of the schools.[11] Ever since, Greece has treated her Slav-speaking inhabitants as "Slavophones," i.e. Slav-speaking Greeks who enjoy the same rights as all other citizens of the state.

During subsequent years the Greek authorities tried to integrate peacefully the alien elements among the Slavophones. The settlement of thousands of Greek refugees from Asia Minor in Macedonia helped gradu-

9. Pipinelis, *op. cit.*, p. 28.
10. *Ibid.*, p. 27.
11. D. Vogazlis, Φυλετικὲς καὶ Ἐθνικὲς μειονότητες στὴν Ἑλλάδα καὶ τὴ Βουλγαρία [Racial and National Minorities in Greece and Bulgaria], (Athens: Society for Thracian Studies, 1954), p. 12.

4*

ally to establish Greek influence, particularly among the younger generation, which was becoming familiar with the Greek way of life.[12]

While this peaceful assimilation was winning to Hellenism even the formerly outspoken pro-Bulgarians, the sudden establishment of a dictatorial regime in 1936 under General Metaxas adopted a policy of forced assimilation. In a series of administrative measures, the Slavophones were forbidden to speak their Slavonic dialect in public, and deportations to the islands assumed a nondiscriminatory character. The result was that such unwarranted measures tended to revive in some Bulgarophiles, a strong opposition and resentment against the country in which they lived. In retrospect, the policy of the Metaxas' dictatorship towards the Slavophones appeares to have cultivated enough resentment so that when the opportunity was given — with the German invasion — it erupted with disastrous consequenses for Greek Macedonia.

THE I.M.R.O. AND THE MACEDONIAN QUESTION IN BULGARIA

While in Greece the Macedonian Question for all practical purposes had been eliminated with the exchanges of populations, and in Yugoslavia had been reduced to an internal, though still a serious problem of an uneasy minority, in Bulgaria it assumed such wide proportions, on account of the irredentist mentality of the Bulgarian governments and the agitation of the I.M.R.O. that, at times, it conditioned the internal political life of the country as well as its international alignments.

Following the end of the World War, the Bulgarian Macedonians who had joined the Bulgarian Army and been its most ruthless agents in the occupied parts of Serbian and Greek Macedonia, were demobilized and returned to Bulgaria.[13] Their immediate concern was to regroup and strengthen the I.M.R.O. so that it could both put pressure on the framers of the peace treaties and maintain contact with the ""enslaved brethren"" in Serbian and Greek Macedonia. They were more successful in the latter task.

It has already been mentioned that according to the terms of the Greco-Bulgarian agreement on the voluntary exchange of minorities, those of the Slav-speaking inhabitants of Greek Macedonia who con-

---

12. William Hardy McNeil, *The Greek Dilemma: War and Aftermath*, (Philadelphia: J. B. Lippincott Co., 1947), pp. 261 - 262.

13. Ivan Mihailoff, *Macedonia: A Switzerland of the Balkans* (St. Louis, Mo., Pearlston Publishing Company, 1950), pp. 88 - 89.

sidered themselves Bulgarians could apply to the League of Nations Mixed Commission, entrusted to supervise the population exchange, in order to emigrate to the country of their national origin. The I.M.R.O., realizing that a mass exodus of the remaining Bulgarians in Greece would sharply weaken Bulgaria's bargaining power to reclaim the Greek Macedonian territories, launched a major campaign to stop it. Through propaganda and coercion, it succeeded in convincing many to withdraw their application.[14] Only later, when Greece was faced with the unprecedented task of settling approximately one million refugees, did the Greek government press the Bulgarians to flee to Bulgaria, since most of the Greeks in that country had already been compelled to emigrate to Greece.

Failing in Greece,[15] the I.M.R.O. focused its subversive and propaganda activities on Serbian Macedonia where most of its leaders were born. Thus, Bulgarian nationalism was accentuated by home-town nostalgia. I.M.R.O. bands began to rove over Serbian Macedonia, committing acts of terrorism and inciting the population against the Belgrade government. In late 1922, Todor Alexandrov, leader of the right-wing I.M.R.O., went as far as to ask Stjepan Radić, who was pursuing an anti-Serbian policy with his Croatian Republican Peasant Party, to join hands in order to bring about the collapse of Serbian rule.[16] Radić's reply called for a moderate policy and was rejected by the I.M.R.O.

On the home front in Bulgaria, the I.M.R.O. was not very successful at first. The Government of the Agrarian leader Stambuliski, who had ascended to power immediately after the war, tried to curtail the I.M.R.O.'s irredentist manifestations.[17] Indeed, Premier Stambuliski adopted an uncompromising attitude against I.M.R.O. extremists even arresting in 1919, the two chiefs of the Organization, Todor Alexandrov and General Protogerov, although both later escaped. In May 1923, the Bulgarian Premier signed an agreement with the Serbs to coordinate the measures of the two governments against the I.M.R.O. terrorists.[18] Finding itself persecuted, the I.M.R.O. conspired with the Officers' League under Colonel Vulkov in the successful *coup* of June 1923, which ended with Stambuliski's murder and Alexander Chankov's appointment as Premier of the new government.

---

14. Bramos, [Second Edition], *op. cit.*, p. 74.

15. Barker, *op. cit.*, p. 33.

16. Slijepcević, *The Macedonian Question : The Struggle for Southern Serbia* (Chicago : The American Institute for Balkan Affairs, 1958), p. 180.

17. Pipinelis, *op. cit.*, p. 76.

18. *Ibid.*

Vulkov kept the influential Ministry of War and, for over ten years, proved himself an invaluable ally, if not the true leader, of the I.M.R.O.[19] From 1923 to 1934, the I.M.R.O. was allowed to grow into a powerful armed organization. The Government tolerated its activities and even permitted it to conduct fund raising campaigns. In fact, the I.M.R.O. ruled over the Petrich Department, i.e. Bulgarian Macedonia. Gradually, however, it degenerated into an organization of bandits and criminals. Elizabeth Barker points out that the I.M.R.O. had ceased to be genuinely revolutionary in the twenties and had become more of a financial racket. Emigrants from Greek and Serbian Macedonia, as well as the inhabitants of Bulgarian Macedonia, were compelled to buy immunity from economic blackmail and terrorization through "voluntary" patriotic subscriptions or "taxes."[20]

Since the I.M.R.O.'s original objective to create a "free" Macedonia designed to become a province of Bulgaria or an autonomous state dependant on Bulgaria had no hope of realization, it was natural that the organization was eventually bound to be reduced to a state where the personal ambitions and vendettas of its leaders counted more than patriotism. Inevitably it split into various factions, each pursuing its own policy. In fact, when one talks of the I.M.R.O. during the inter-war period, actually refers to numerous factions which many times were at odds and, occasionally, in open war against each other.

As previously seen, even before the turn of the century, the I.M.R.O. was divided between the "Supremists" favoring a clearly nationalist Bulgarian policy, and the "Centralists" who viewed the autonomy of Macedonia as the easiest solution able to be realized. In the years 1916-1918, when the Bulgarian Army occupied Serbia and a great part of Greek Macedonia, all factions of I.M.R.O. were dissolved and their members joined the Bulgarian Army. Bulgaria's defeat brought the Organization once again into prominence. The leaders of the old "Supremists," Todor Alexandrov and Alexander Protogerov, emerged in control of the Organization whose orientation was definitely nationalistic Bulgarian. A little later, in 1921, a closter of old I.M.R.O. men referring to themselves as "federalists," formed another group. Among its leading members were Philip Athanasov, Todor Panitsa, Dimitar Vlahov and Dimo Hadji-Dimov, representing the "Centralist" tradition of the earlier I.M.R.O.[21] Their purpose was the establish-

19. Barker, op. cit., p. 25.
20. Joseph Swire, Bulgarian Conspiracy (London : R. Hale, Ltd., 1939), p. 50, 287, as quoted in Barker, op. cit., p. 37.
21. Barker, op. cit., p. 40.

ment of an autonomous Macedonian state which would join a federation of the Balkan states. It is interesting to note that their program was almost identical to that of the communists as outlined in the decisions of the Comintern.[22] Most of the leaders of this group were in fact, either communists (Hadji-Dimov) or leftists who later became communists (Vlahov). Thence the similarity in their respective objectives. The "federalists," following the example of the right-wing I.M.R.O., organized and dispatched armed bands to Serbia, ostensibly to promote their views with the local population, but, more frequently, to fight Alexandrov's rival I.M.R.O. bands.

For a short moment in 1924, the right-wing I.M.R.O., the "federalists" and the communists, joined forces. They signed a Manifesto which accused the governments of Greece, Bulgaria and Serbia of having partitioned Macedonia, and demanded the establishment of an autonomous Macedonia within a Balkan federation. The Manifesto was a major affront of the right-wing I.M.R.O. leaders who depended on the support of the Bulgarian Government. Alexandrov was murdered on August 31, 1924 and Protogerov took over the leadership of the Organization. In less than one year the leaders of the leftist Macedonian movement, Hadji-Dimov and Panitsa were similarly murdered.

The "federalists" split, with one group joining Protogerov's I.M.R.O., and the other under Vlahov forming, in 1925, the "United I.M.R.O.," a new organization advocating a united and independent Macedonia within a Balkan Federation, a policy which was identical to the line pursued by the Comintern. The "United I.M.R.O." never attracted many followers. Its only contribution to the confusion of Macedonian politics was that it provided shelter to those revolutionary elements who accepted in principle the Comintern's views but did not wish, as yet, to be openly asssociated with the communist movement. Finally in 1936, Vlahov dissolved the "United I.M.R.O." and departed for Moscow.[23] He returned in 1943 as one of the most influential of the Yugoslav "Macedonian" leaders to build the People's Republic of Macedonia.

As for the original I.M.R.O., it continued for a time to dominate Bulgarian Macedonia's politics though it was nothing more than a group of extortionists and killers. In 1928, Protogerov was murdered by Ivan Mihailov's men who assumed the leadership of the Organization and

22. For the inter-war cooperation between the communists and the leftist I.M.R.O. followers: *Infra* Chapter IV.
23. Barker, *op. cit.*, p. 42.

continued to monopolize the Macedonian movement until 1934 when the revolt of the Military League and the Zveno group overthrew the government and disbanded the Organization.

* * *

The first phase of the Macedonian Question — the phase of "Nationalist Struggles for Macedonia" — was rapidly approaching its climax at the outbreak of the Second World War. The emergence of communist power in the Balkan states during the Occupation was bound to alter significantly its form.

To comprehend better the tactics and objectives of the Balkan communists in regard to Macedonia, it is important to turn, at this point, to the beginning of the century when the first leftist, socialist movements began to take interest in Macedonian developments and lay down certain principles destined to affect profoundly the shape of the old dispute in the years to come.

PART TWO

BALKAN COMMUNISTS
AND THE
MACEDONIAN QUESTION

CHAPTER IV

THE YEARS OF PREPARATION

THE FORMATION OF COMMUNIST PARTIES
AND THE MACEDONIAN QUESTION

The thunder of the October Revolution had hardly subsided in Russia when the leaders of the international communist movement began to show a lively interest in the Macedonian Question and its inherent revolutionary potentialities. Even prior to the revolution, Bolshevik leaders had been impressed with the complexities and paradoxes of Balkan politics. Lenin had remarked that the class struggle in the Balkans took the form of a religious and national struggle because the big landowners were Moslem Turks while the oppressed farmers were Christian Slavs. Even the Balkan war, which Serbia, Greece and Bulgaria had fought primarily for the purpose of liberating their enslaved brethren, was viewed by Lenin as a rising of oppressed peasants against their domineering Turkish overlords.[1]

Once the Bolsheviks of Russia had taken the reigns of government into their own hands they tried to spread their social theories utilizing the enormous social, political and economic problems of post-war Europe which had been further accentuated by national antagonisms. Macedonia presented probably one of the most suitable cases for communism to thrive on. From the beginning, Russian Bolsheviks found the Bulgarian view close to their own objectives and hastened to espouse it. Their attitude was prompted by a thorough knowledge of history as well as a calculated appraisal of the revolutionary potentialities of the Bulgarian position.

Of the three contenders for Macedonia, only among the Bulgarians could the Bolsheviks find a significant number of active followers to share their ideology and have a close and sincere sentiment for the great Slav nation of the North. The communist theory of "national self-determination" could have a strong appeal to a large segment of the Bulgarian revolution-

---

1. Lazar Mojsov, *The Bulgarian Workers'Party [Communist] and the Macedonian Question* (Belgrade : Borba, 1948), quoted in Elizabeth Barker, *Macedonia : Its Place in Balkan Power Politics* (London : Royal Institute of International Affairs, 1950), pp. 45-46.

aries in Macedonia who genuinely despised the direct central control of Sofia and preferred a kind of an autonomous Macedono-Bulgarian state. Neither the Greeks, nor the few Serbs of North Western Macedonia could be enticed by such a slogan since their political yearning to be united with their respective fatherlands had, more or less, at the end of the wars, been fulfilled. Consequently, if the Bolsheviks hoped for an early uprising in the Balkans, and more precisely in Macedonia, they had to take into serious consideration the frustrating resentment of the Bulgarians and the Bulgarian Macedonians against the Balkan and World War peace settlements. By 1919, Serbs and Greeks alike had become champions of a *status quo* policy in the Balkans and, consequently, they were of limited use to any immediate initiatives the Bolsheviks might wish to undertake in the Peninsula.

This point will be the subject of a more thorough analysis in subsequent pages. At this juncture it becomes necessary to turn back a few years to review the conduct of certain organizations in Macedonia and examine their political orientations, since it was from such organizations that the communist movement drew its cadres when it decided to enter actively Macedonian politics.

A. The Macedonian Struggle

The Internal Macedonian Revolutionary Organization, which so actively pursued the Bulgarian cause during the Macedonian Struggle (1903-1908), provided also the training ground for a significant number of Slav Macedonian communists who were to carry, in the years to come, the banner of an autonomous, communist Macedonian state. Dimitar Vlahov, emerging in 1943 as a prominent member of Marshal Tito's new regime in Yugoslavia and top historian for the People's Republic of Macedonia, interpreted the policies and conduct of the Centralist wing of the I.M.R.O. as a class struggle of oppressed land workers against the oppressive Ottoman landowners.[2] He attacked the Supremist wing as an instrument of the Bulgarian Government and Court which disregarded the genuine, autochthonous movement aimed at the self-determination of the ""Macedonians.""[3]

---

2. Dimitar I. Vlahov, *Makedonija; Momenti od Istorijata na Makedonskiot Narod* [Macedonia; Moments in the History of the Macedonian People] (Skopje : Drzavne Knigoindateletve na H.R. Makedonija, 1950), pp. 91-92. (*Note:* The page references are from a Greek translation of Vlahov's book).

3. *Ibid.*, pp. 95-96. In recent years Yugoslav, as well as Bulgarian writers,

Although dating is hazy since the true objectives of the various movements in Macedonia were ambiguous and at best overlapping, it can be said that the first socialist movement in Macedonia made its appearance as early as 1893. Initiated by Basil Glavinov from Veles, this group was actually formed just before the I.M.R.O. and independent of the Social Democratic and Labor Party of Bulgaria. Among its more well-known figures were Nikola Karev (later leader of the short-lived "Krusovo Republic"), Vele Markov and Nikola Rusenski.[4] Few in number, it did not long enjoy independent status, primarily on account of opposition from the Bulgarian Socialist Party which would not tolerate a similar group in a region claimed as Bulgarian, though still under Ottoman rule. Consequently, the group was dissolved and its leaders joined the I.M.R.O. where they formed its left wing.[5]

---

have attempted a major reconsideration of historical events in conformity with communist practice. Ostensibly, this major effort, which at present has reached unprecedented proportions for this part of the Balkans, was undertaken to shed light on the historical past of Yugoslavia's newly-founded People's Republic of Macedonia. In fact, the objective is easily detected; a would-be scholarly effort to substantiate the attempt of the Yugoslav communists to build a "Macedonian" nation and to instill a "Macedonian" national consciousness in the backward peasants of Yugoslav Macedonia who, over the years, have shown a closer attachment to the Bulgarians than to the Serbs. In their attempt, the authors of the historical past of Yugoslav Macedonia, have inevitably fallen victims to their own pretentions and have magnified well out of proportion the role of certain persons and groups who participated in the Macedonian Struggle, whom they considered as the forerunners of communist ideology and Yugoslav-styled "Macedonian" nationhood. Consequently, it is with caution that one should evaluate their theories and interpretations of historical events.

4. Wayne S. Vucinich, *Serbia Between East and West; The Events of 1903-1908* (Stanford : Stanford University Press, 1954), p. 28.

In the main editorial of the first issue of their paper *Revolucija*, they declared themselves in favor of an independent Macedonia: "The liberation of Macedonia lies in an internal rising. Whoever thinks to liberate Macedonia in any other way, lies to himself and to others ... In our systematic struggle we shall also pupularize the idea of creating an independent republic ... The people ... should free themselves for ever not only from the sultan and his satellites but also from every Prince and King ... " (May Day Proclamation of 1896 quoted by Lazar Mojsov, "The National Resurgence of the Macedonian People", *Macedonia* (Belgrade : "Jugoslavia," 1957), p. 14. Of course, such slogans at a time when the winds of extreme nationalism, fostered by Bulgaria, Greece and Serbia, were sweeping the region, could barely make an impression on the masses. They simply serve today as historical footnotes which are emphasized, de-emphasized or twisted according to the political expediency of the moment.

5. Speech by Lazar Kulishevski before the First Congress of the Communist

The Iliden uprising of 1903, has long been viewed as the turning point of the Bulgarian struggle to win Macedonia. Now, the advocates of a "Macedonian" nationality have raised claims as to the revolt's parenthood. Vlahov has claimed that since measures of social justice were proclaimed during the "Krusovo Republic," and since its leader, Nikola Karev was a declared social revolutionist, the "Republic," was, in essence, a socialist, democratic minute Macedonian state, in fact, a predecessor of the People's Republic of Macedonia. It is a fact that in a manifesto which the revolutionaries issued at Krusovo, they called for social justice. They even attempted to give it an all-national character, calling upon the Moslem workers to join the struggle against the common oppressor, the big Turkish land-owner. But they failed. They failed as socialists because there were only a handful of them who were imbued with socialist ideas and viewed their cause as a socialist uprising.[6] The masses and probably the majority of the leaders were ignorant of such theories. Their motivations were conditioned by their Bulgarian nationalism. Ever since, experience has shown repeatedly that Bulgarian nationalism in Macedonia can successfully utilize socialism in carrying out its own objectives, while socialism can only hope to place in its service the dynamics of Bulgarian nationalism. Vlahov has attributed the failure of the Iliden uprising to the Supremists who rose prematurely. He contends that the most "progressive" elements of the I.M.R.O. were disheartened by the failure, and consequently lost initiative to the Supremists.[7]

It took two years for these "progressive" elements to begin to make their existence felt again within the I.M.R.O. In a congress held at the Rila monastery in September 1905, the right wing, composed mostly of nationalist Bulgarians headed by Boris Sarafov, Lazar Tomov, Peter Kusev and Georgi Pop-Hristov, fought the left wing under Yanne Sandaski who challenged the former's control of the organization. The left wingers advocated the establishment of an autonomous Macedonia. Regionally, the "rightists" claimed control of the organizational apparatus in the Mona-

Party of Macedonia, held at Skopje, December 19-24, 1948. (Hereafter quoted as Kulishevski, *1948 Congress Speech*). *Greek Foreign Ministry Archives* (hereafter GFM) A/19630/Γ2/1949.

6. Many Bulgarian "Narrow" socialists [the left wing of the Party] and Serbian socialists were cool toward the uprising in fear that it might be a machination of Austria-Hungary. Joseph Rothschild, *The Communist Party of Bulgaria; Origins and Foundations: 1883-1936* (New York: Columbia University Press, 1959), pp. 214-215.

7. Vlahov, *Makedonija, op. cit.*, p. 111; also Vucinich, *op. cit.*, p. 124.

stir and Ohrid regions while the "leftists" were in charge of the bands in the districts of Serres, Thessaloniki and Strumnitsa.[8] The congress failed to satisfy the demands of the left wing, and the conflict came into the open with murders committed by both sides. Macedonia, already the battleground of Greek, Bulgarian, Serb, Albanian and Vlach bands, as well as the Turkish Army, had become also an arena for inter-Bulgarian armed clashes.[9]

B. The Revolt of the Young Turks

In 1908, the Young Turks Revolt put an end to years of guerrilla war in Macedonia. The various nationalities, as well as the various factions within the national movements, could now openly propagate their national, political and social views for the future of Macedonia.

The left wing of the I.M.R.O. supported the revolt of the Young Turks and formed its own party, the National Federative Party. Its hard core was composed of I.M.R.O. followers from the Serres and Strumnitsa regions, but others joined as well. Among them were Dimo Hadji-Dimov, D. Daskalov and Dimitar Vlahov.[10] The platform of the party, as outlined by Vlahov,[11] was in favor of the abolition of all national and class privileges; the right of each nationality to organize itself freely and independently; and, autonomy for the communities and large regions such as Macedonia, Albania, Armenia, etc. The party favored the establishment of an Eastern Federation based on the democratic union of all nationalities of the Ottoman Empire.[12] On August 3, 1909, the party held a congress at-

8. Vlahov, *Makedonija, op. cit.*, p. 111.

9. Ivan Mihailov, the ruthless leader of the I.M.R.O. during the interwar period, whom the communists regard as a fascist and instrument of Greater Bulgarian chauvinism, labeled the conflict a "fratricidal war," contending that it was actually a struggle between Bulgarians. Commenting on the theory that the "leftist" elements of the I.M.R.O. of certain regions should be credited with initiating certain alleged social reforms at the time, he took the view that the I.M.R.O. as a whole should be regarded as the initiator of these reforms. Ivan Mihailov, *Macedonia; A Switzerland of the Balkans* [Translated by Christ Anastasoff with an introduction by John Beleleus] (St. Louis: Pearlstone Publishing Co., 1950) pp. 69-70 and 73.

10. Vlahov *Makedonija, op. cit.*, p. 185.

11. *Ibid.*, p. 186.

12. Some influencial young Greek intellectuals and diplomats in Constantinople and Athens had envisioned a grandiose plan having certain similarities with the platform of the National Federative Party. They envisioned an Eastern Federation in which all nationalities would live in harmony, but in which the Greeks would, gradually, assume the leading role on account of their superior culture. In

tended by 33 representatives. The only contribution of the congress was that the delegates realized that their party had no appeal and no significant following. As Vlahov pointed out, its followers were mostly Bulgarian teachers of the countryside; the intelligentsia and the masses had not joined it. There could be little wonder for this development since in Macedonia the Slavs, in their greatest majority, felt themselves Bulgarians, exactly as the Greeks felt themselves Greeks, the Serbs, Serbs, and so on. Complex social theories and twisted national propaganda could hardly be understood, let alone attract the loyalties of the inhabitants of Macedonia. The left wing of the I.M.R.O., and later its offshoot, the National Federative Party, was far from being a communist or even a truly socialist group. From its ranks, however, grew the cadres of the later Slav communist movement in Macedonia.

It is interesting to note that at that time, the most genuine socialist movement in Macedonia was neither Bulgarian, nor Serbian, nor Greek, but Jewish. The "Socialist Federation," with headquarters in Thessaloniki, though listing among its members Greeks, Bulgarians and Turks, was mostly composed of Jews. It received wide recognition in 1909 when its membership was accepted by the International Socialist Federation.[13]

In conclusion, it may safely be said that prior to the Balkan Wars and the First World War, no serious, autochthonous social movement existed in Macedonia. Even labor disorders showed little evidence that

short, they envisioned the transformation of the Ottoman Empire into a predominantly Hellenic Empire on lines similar to the transformation of the Eastern Roman Empire into a Byzantine-Greek state. Athanasios Souliotis-Nikolaides Ἡμερολόγιον τοῦ Πρώτου Βαλκανικοῦ πολέμου [Dairy of the first Balkan War] (Thessaloniki: Institute for Balkan Studies, 1962), pp. 32 - 33. It is worth quoting in part the "Diary's" January 2, 1913 entry :

> I and [Ion] Dragoumis, while the various Greek Governments had no foreign policy plan in their minds, put forward the following double plan; either we Greeks will gradually govern Turkey along with the Turks, or we will unite all the Balkan states against Turkey and will solve the Eastern Question, by establishing a new political East, where we the Greeks will have the leading role ... In Constantinople [Note: after the Young Turks Revolt] I united under the Greeks and the Patriarchate all the other Christian nationalities (I even began to attract the Moslem nationalities). In this struggle, the leadership was in the hands of the Greeks because as a Nation they are superior in every aspect.
> (translated from Greek by the author).

See also D. Xanalatos, "The Greeks and the Turks on the Eve of the Balkan Wars," *Balkan Studies*, Vol. III, No 2, (1962), pp. 277-296.

13. Even after the liberation of Thessaloniki by the Greek Army in 1912, the Federation was the largest socialist group of the entire Greek state with approximately 2000 members of which 90 per cent were wealthy Jews.

they were motivated by any class-conscious theories. What really stirred the masses was the national aspirations of each ethnic entity. The Balkan Wars, and later the First World War, attested to this fact in the most dramatic way.

C. The Wars and the Balkan Socialists

At this point, a parenthesis should be opened to examine briefly the position of the socialist parties in the free Balkan states during the pre-World War I period. While their strength in the individual countries was quite weak and little considered by the politicians in power, they were able, in 1910, to join forces at a conference held in Belgrade to establish the Balkan Social Democratic Federation. The significance of this event was not realized at the time. Ten years later, however, this federation, renamed the Balkan Communist Federation, joined the Third International and played a major role in the shaping of the Macedonian Question.[14]

The World War created social unrest in many countries. The Balkans, and more precisely, Macedonia, had their share in these history-making upheavals.

In a Greece, enlarged by the liberation of the largest part of Macedonia, the Greek Social Party and the Socialist Federation of Thessaloniki merged. All splinter socialist groups finally joined forces during the First Socialist Congress held in November 1918 and a new political party called the Workers' Socialist Party of Greece emerged.[15] A year later it joined the Second Socialist International. In its majority report on Greek foreign policy, the Congress did not refer specifically to Macedonia but favored a Balkan democratic federation — whatever that meant — with autonomous vilayets, or provinces. Subsequently, all outstanding national and territorial questions could be settled by referenda.[16] Their naive program soon underwent major changes and the Party moved rapidly to the left. Early in March 1919 it made contact with the Third International and in 1920 joined it as a full member, changing its name to the Workers' Socialist (Communist) Party of Greece. It was in 1923 that it finally took its present name, the Communist Party of Greece (KKE).

---

14. Jane Degras, *The Communist International 1919-1943; Documents*, Vol. 1, 1919-1922; (London : Royal Institute of International Affairs, 1956), p. 85.

15. Christopher J. Chistides, *The Macedonian Camouflage in the Light of Facts and Figures* (Athens : Hellenic Publishing Co., Ltd., 1949), p. 118.

16. Κομμουνιστικὸν Κόμμα τῆς Ἑλλάδος [Communist Party of Greece). *Τὸ KKE ἀπὸ τὸ 1918 ἕως τὸ 1931*. Vol. I, (Athens : Central Committee KKE, 1947), pp. 4-6.

In Bulgaria, the socialists had the longest tradition of all socialist parties in the Balkans and commanded the respect of the international socialist movement. However, they were badly split between the moderate "Broad" wing and the extreme revolutionary "Narrow" wing.[17] The split became definite in 1903 and despite the efforts of prominent personalities of the Socialist International, no reconciliation was possible. Within the International the Bulgarian socialist parties —both wings were represented— were given an importance quite disproportionate to their number because of the increasing preoccupation of the International, after 1905, with the danger of war in the Balkans. The Narrow party usually stood on the left of the International, at times with a doctrinarism irritating even to Lenin.[18] When the war between the Balkan states finally broke over the Peninsula, the Balkan socialist parties and the International denounced it. The Narrow party objected to Bulgaria's entering the First World War and its leader, Blagoev, called on the Government to form an anti-war bloc through the federalization of the Peninsula.[19] On the other hand, Sakazov, leader of the Broad socialists, supported Bulgaria's right to keep and rule Macedonia though in theory he objected to the war.[20] The Bolshevik Revolution in 1917 and the end of the World War saw the Narrow socialists definitely casting their lot with the communists. Christian Rakovski, a Bulgarian who became a famed Soviet politician and diplomat, signed the founding document of the Comintern and represented the Narrow party at the first Comintern Congress in March 1919. In May, the Party changed its name to the Bulgarian Communist Party (CPB) and affiliated itself with the new International thus bringing to it the only mass party — apart from the Bolsheviks — which was of a truly "Russian" complexion.[21]

In that part of the Peninsula today constituting the People's Republic of Yugoslavia, social ideas and socialist groups made their appearance in the 1870's under quite different historical conditions according to each region of the country. Three distinct groups of provinces existed and consequently, three groups of workers' movements developed. First were the independent lands (Serbia and Montenegro); second were the lands under the Austro-Hungarian regime (Vojvodina, Croatia and Slavonia, Bosnia

17. Their original feud began over the abolition of private property. The "Narrow" wing advocated complete abolition "from the biggest machine to the tailor's needle." Rothschild, *op. cit.*, pp. 24 - 25.

18. *Ibid.*, p. 58.

19. *Ibid.*, p. 62.

20. *Ibid.*, pp. 70-71.

21. *Ibid.*, p. 73.

and Hercegovina, Dalmatia, Istria, Slovenia, with Gorizia and Trieste); third was Macedonia, a province under Turkish domination.²² The most important socialist party, the Serbian Social Democratic Party, was founded on July 20, 1903. The development of separate parties had as its consequence the development of separate approaches to the questions of concern to the socialists. Some of the major problems dividing the various regional parties were the peasant question, the position on war, the national question,²³ and finally the Bolshevik Revolution and the problem of relationship with the Third International.²⁴ Soon after the creation of the new Yugoslav state in 1918 the question of uniting the regional parties into a national one became of great importance. More important, however, was whether this national party would remain a social democratic party or be affiliated with the Third International. On August 20-23, 1919, a congress was held in Belgrade at the initiative of the Social Democratic Party of Serbia. At the "Congress of Unification" — as it was called — the old social democratic parties and the new communist groups merged under a common leadership into a common, revolutionary proletarian party, the Socialist Workers' Party of Yugoslavia (Communist). The Congress voted affiliation with the Comintern and accepted the principles of a proletarian state. But acceptance of these policies was far from unanimous,²⁵ a fact noticed later during the critical discussions over the national issue and particularly over the Question of Macedonia.

It is interesting to note that in Yugoslav Macedonia immediately after the incorporation of that region into Serbia in 1913, the existing small Slav Socialist Party lost its individual status and joined the Social Democratic Party of Serbia, exactly as the Socialist (Jewish) Federation of Thessaloniki had done with respect to the Socialist Party of Greece. The Macedonian socialists thus became Serbs, while the leftist elements, Bulgarians at heart and favoring an autonomous status for Macedonia, joined the ranks of the left wing of the I.M.R.O.²⁶ It was precisely the leaders of this group, men of the old revolutionary Serres and Strumnitsa groups,

22. U.S. Congress (Senate), Committee on the Judiciary, *Yugoslav Communism; A Critical Study* [author: Charles Zalar], (Washington: U.S. Government Printing Office, 1961), pp. 23-24. (Hereafter quoted as *Yugoslav Communism*).
23. To the specific question of the 1903 Iliden uprising, the Serb socialists lent their moral support and accepted the principle of Macedonian autonomy. *Ibid.*, p. 28.
24. *Ibid.*, p. 27.
25. *Ibid.*, p. 36-37.
26. Kulishevski, *1948 Congress Speech, op. cit.*

who were ready to espouse the communist slogan for a united and independent Macedonia at a time when the socialists were still passive.[27]

Late in 1918, the leaders of the left wing of I.M.R.O. published a
manifesto announcing a new policy toward the settlement of the Macedonian Question. Its four major points provided that Balkan brotherhood
should replace Balkan nationalism; that Macedonia should be restituted in
its geographical boundaries as a state including Thessaloniki, Skopje, Monastir and the Vardar valley; that the establishment of an independent
Macedonian state would be the benefit of all Balkan peoples helping them
to co-exist peacefully, and, finally, that Macedonia should adopt the administrative system of the cantons of Switzerland.[28]

INTERNATIONAL COMMUNISM
ADOPTS THE BULGARIAN VIEW; 1921 - 1935

A. The Ideological Setting

The Second Comintern Congress, held on July 28, 1920, passed a
resolution favoring encouragement of the bourgeois-democratic national
movements in backward countries on the hypothesis that they represented
in essence "national revolutionary" movements which could assist in promoting communism in the respective countries.[29] At the same time, the
Congress set forth Communism's major principles on the national issue.
This is of particular interest because it was precisely on acount of these
dogmatic prerequisites — as applied to the Macedonian Question — that the
Greek and Yugoslav communists found their own countries seriously compromised. Comintern ruled that each communist party "should specifically
distinguish the interests of the oppressed classes of the workers and the
exploited from the general concept of so called national interests, which
signify in fact the interests of the ruling class."[30] The interests of the proletarian struggle in one country ought to be subordinated to the interests
of the struggle on a world scale. Consequenty, in the event of a communist victory in one country, the communists were expected to "display the
capacity and readiness to make the greatest national sacrifices in order to

27. Dance Zografski, *Egejska Makedonija* [Aegean Macedonia] (Skopje:
"Iliden", 1951, p. 99). (Note: pages are quoted from Greek translation).

28. Vlahov, *Makedonija, op. cit.*, p. 230.

29. Degras, *op. cit.*, Vol. I, pp. 138-139.

30. *Ibid.*, p. 140.

overthrow international capitalism."[31] The Greek and Yugoslav communists were soon to discover how far these sacrifices could lead.

Before turning to a detailed examination of the formulation of Macedonian policy by the Comintern and individual communist parties in the Balkans, a note should be added to clarify the Soviet doctrine concerning the handling of the national and minority problems.[32] Communism's bible on the national and minority issues remains to this day Stalin's *Marxism and the National and Colonial Question*. Inspired by Lenin, the principles projected in this book were incorporated in the 1936 Constitution of the U.S.S.R. and have since been adopted by the constitutions of the people's democracies established in Eastern Europe. Stalin defined a nation as an historically formed community of people who are bound together by a common language, inhabit a common area, lead a common economic life and have a common national character expressed in a common culture.[33] Every national group thus conceived should, according to communist theorists, enjoy the right of "self-determination." In Lenin's words, this right may be employed "up to the point of separation" of the national group from the state in which it lives.[34]

In analyzing the communist nationality doctrine one is struck by the conflicting objectives it pursues. It appears that its central motivating element is to safeguard the "sacred" right of self-determination, the ultimate objective of all nationalities.[35] Yet, Lenin's attitude was essentially opportunistic in that he outlined a nationality theory for the purpose of combatting nationalism itself. This may sound absurd, yet it is a well-known fact that Lenin regarded nationalism as a sort of nuisance which diverted the masses' attention from their class struggle against the bourgeoisie and focused their interests instead on issues which brought them into conflict with neighboring nationalities. On national issues, Lenin observed, workers and capitalists tend to form a united front against an alien national element in the state in which they live, or against a neighboring nation

---

31. *Ibid.*, p. 143.

32. The following paragraphs were previously published by the author as part of "Balkan Minorities under Communist Regimes," *Balkan Studies*, Vol. II, No. 1, (Thessaloniki: Institute for Balkan Studies, June 1961), pp. 26-27.

33. Joseph Stalin, *Marxism and the National and Colonial Question* (Greek Translation). (Athens: Marxist Library No. 1/10, March 1933), p. 29.

34. Hugh Seton-Watson, *The Pattern of Communist Revolution: A Historical Analysis* (London: Methuen & Company, Ltd., 1953), p. 20.

35. Vladimir Ilich Lenin, *The Right of Nations to Self-determination; Selected Writings* (New York: International Publishers, 1951), pp. 19 and 28.

which oppresses a kin minority. This was both anathema and a hard obstacle in Lenin's road toward a "socialist society." To remove this obstacle, Lenin formulated his nationality doctrine. An authority in this field clarified this doctrine when he wrote:

> The proletariat of each nation must oppose the policy of its own bourgeoisie. Thus, since the Russian bourgeoisie had wished to keep the non-Russian peoples in subjection to Russia, the Russian proletariat must insist on the right of these peoples to independence; since the bourgeoisie of the non-Russian peoples had wished to create separate states under their own domination, the proletariat of those peoples must insist on the necessity of union with the Russian proletariat in one socialist state.[36]

Having thus established the rational basis for a new national theory, Lenin proceeded to advocate that nationalism in a capitalist society is a form of oppression of the masses. The total eclipse of national oppression becomes synonymous with the final elimination of the state following a delimitation of the state frontiers according to the "wish" of the people who have the right to opt even for secession.[37]

2. Bulgarian Efforts for an "Independent Macedonia;" 1920 - 1924

By 1920, the internal social and political situation in Greece had suddenly become favorable to the growth of communism. For eight years Greece had been involved in wars first against Turkey, than against Bulgaria and later against Bulgaria and Turkey together. The cream of her youth was in far away Anatolia pursuing an unrealistic political dream. In newly liberated Macedonia, labor disputes accentuated by socialist and Bolshevik agitation, were gradually producing communist cadres. Unexpectedly, at the November 1920 elections, the KKE found itself with a sizeable following not to be surpassed until the Second World War. Of course, most of the votes were cast by anti-Venizelists who voted for the KKE which campained under a "ban-the-war" slogan. Particularly heavy was the pro-communist vote in Macedonia, especially in the Drama and Kavala regions. Among those voting for the KKE were many Jews from Thessaloniki, and Turks and Gypsies of the villages north of Drama.[38] What

---

36. Seton-Watson, *op. cit.*, p. 85.
37. Lenin, *op. cit.*, p. 14.
38. Eleftherios A. Stavrides, *Τὰ Παρασκήνια τοῦ ΚΚΕ ἀπὸ τῆς Ἱδρύσεώς του μέχρι τοῦ Συμμοριτοπολέμου* [The Backstage of the KKE; from its founding to the guerrilla war], (Athens: 1953), pp. 38-39.

should be noticed, at this time, is that no distinct regional communist party existed in Greek Macedonia.[39] The communists in Greece had begun to accept as definite the new national borders of the country.

At the end of the war, the Greek socialists, apart from certain ambiguous slogans for a Balkan federation, had no distinct policy in respect to the Macedonian Question and tended to follow the national policy of their government. Similar was the position of the Yugoslavs. Only among the Bulgarian communists, in whose ranks the left wingers of I.M.R.O. were amply represented, was there active agitation favoring an independent Macedonia.

On January 15, 1920, representatives of all the Balkan communist parties met in Sofia at the invitation of the CPB to organize the Balkan Communist Federation (BCF). According to its Statute prepared at the Second Balkan Congress in the early summer of 1921, the Federation was considered as an association of the Balkan sections — Bulgarian, Greek and Serbian — of the Third International. The Albanian section could be admitted as soon as a communist party was formed in that country (Art. 2). To stress its unique structure, the Statute provided that each party be represented by five members but that each vote as an individual, not as a representative of a national party. The decisions of the Federation were binding on its members (Art. 5). Through its Executive Committee it could direct and control those activities of the individual Balkan Communist Parties related to the purposes and objectives of the BCF (Art. 12).[40] These objectives were further clarified in a declaration of the Federation which appealed to the Balkan working masses to join the communist movement in order to win their national and social freedom through the establishment of a Soviet dictatorship of the workers and the peasants of the Balkans.[41]

The BCF was not a novel invention. Lenin, commenting on the Balkan Wars, had stated much earlier that the true objective of the Balkan peoples should be the struggle for the establishment of a federation of Balkan republics which would free the peasants of the Peninsula — irrespective of their nationality — from the "oppressive local feudalists."[42]

Once the Federation was formed it became unavoidable that the Macedonian Question be placed as a major topic on the agenda of the

---

39. Barker, *op. cit.*. p. 47.

40. Text in Κομμουνιστικὴ 'Επιθεώρησις [Communist Review], theoretical journal of the KKE, (Athens: Vol. I, No. 7), July 1921, pp. 232-233.

41. *Ibid.*, p. 239.

42. Lenin's *Works*, Vol. XIV, p. 186, as quoted in Vlahov, *Makedonija, op. cit.*, p. 221.

Balkan conferences. Only this time, the negotiators were communists who had to submit their individual interests to the general objectives of international communism. From the very beginning it was apparent that the Bulgarians were assuming a leading role in the Federation. The declaration quoted above had already endorsed a Bulgarian view of the national problem when it declared that "the Bulgarian people, although they have shed so much blood they have not gained their national unity; on the contrary, today, ethnically they are divided..."[43] There was no specific mention of Macedonia at this time. However, reference to the failure of the Bulgarian people to gain their national unity was a hint of the future course to be followed by the BCF on the national problems of the Balkans.

The position of the Comintern at this time was rather vague. Early in 1920, the President of the Executive Committee, Zinoviev, in a message of greetings to the communist parties of Bulgaria, Rumania, Serbia and Turkey, had condemned the policy of national oppression pursued by the Balkan governments, but mentioned only the Greek and Serbian governments by name when he wrote:

> Against the rule of the Serbian bureaucratic and landowning oligarchy, there are rising up the Macedonian Bulgarians, the Albanians, the Montenegrins, the Croats and the Bosnians. Against the rule of the Greek trading, speculating and profiteering bourgeoisie are fighting the Albanians of Epirus and the Turkish and Bulgarian peasants of Thrace.[44]

Early in 1922, there were strong indications that the Bulgarian communists were determined to bring the issue of Macedonia before the Conference of the BCF. Already, at the Third Balkan Conference held in Moscow on July 19-21, 1921, the Greek Party was ordered to fight openly and with determination against "the petit-bourgeois and chauvinistic superstitions" with which the consciousness of the Greek proletariat had been poisoned.[45] Anticipating — and fearing — an open pro-Bulgarian verdict by the Comintern, the KKE passed a resolution at the Party Conference of February 1922 which declared that the decisions of the Comintern were not compulsory but merely "documents of historical significance." The Comintern reacted promptly by attacking sharply the leaders of the Greek

---

43. Κομμουνιστικὴ 'Επιθεώρησις, op. cit., July 1921, p. 238.

44. Kommunismus, op. cit., March 5, 1920, as quoted in Barker, op. cit., pp. 48-49. It is worth noting that Comintern's initial document on the Macedonian Question referred to "Macedonian Bulgarians" and not to "Macedonians."

45. Κομμουνιστικὴ 'Επιθεώρησις, op. cit., November 1921, p. 409.

Party as ""opportunists" forcing them to capitulate and to promise that they would blindly follow the directives of the International.[46]

Unexpectedly, during the deliberations of the next Balkan Communist Conference held in Sofia in May-June 1922, the question of the ""autonomy of Macedonia and Thrace" was raised by Vasil Kolarov, the Bulgarian delegate, who presided over the meeting.[47] The Bulgarian communists, said Kolarov, needed the endorsement of all Balkan communists on this issue so that they might attract the thousands of destitute and longing refugees from Greek and Serbian Macedonia who had taken refuge in Bulgaria; otherwise, he argued, they would join the I.M.R.O. Yannis Petsopoulos, the Greek delegate, faced with a serious question and lacking instructions, asked for a postponement of the discussion. He was seconded by the Yugoslav delegate. Their request was supported by the Turks while the Rumanians chose to remain neutral.[48]

Petsopoulos' report to the Central Committee of the KKE upon his return to Greece, created much confusion since most of the Committee members had no idea of the prevailing situation in Greek Macedonia. An entire year was allowed to pass without the KKE making any decision on the issue.

In the meantime, the Comintern, primarily on account of the persistent and adroit pleading of Kolarov and Dimitrov, had gradually begun to orient itself toward the Bulgarian views. The addition of certain practical reasons finally convinced it to endorse fully the Bulgarian thesis.

On June 8, 1923, the Agrarian Covernment in Bulgaria was overthrown, and Premier Stambuliski murdered. The *coup* was executed by Chankov, the Officers League and the I.M.R.O. The communists, in what was probably the worst blunder in their history, maintained a benevolent neutrality toward the *coup*, which, in fact, was a revolt of the extreme right perpetrated against a leftist, socialist-agrarian regime. Their attitude drew an immediate and sharp rebuke by the Comintern, particularly since their numerous armed cadres could have played a decisive role in determining the outcome of the *coup*.[49]

Once in power, Chankov decided that he could crush the communists who had begun to show signs of restlessness. Anticipating the move, the

46. Ριζοσπάστης (newspaper of the KKE), Athens, February 20, 1922.
47. Barker, *op. cit.*, p. 50.
48. Kostas Bramos, Σλαβοκομμουνιστικαὶ 'Οργανώσεις ἐν Μακεδονίᾳ. Προπαγάνδα καὶ 'Επαναστατικὴ Δράσις [Communist-Slav Organizations in Macedonia; Propaganda and Revolutionary Activities], Second Edition (Thessaloniki: 1960), pp. 86-87.
49. For part of the text of Manifesto see Barker, *op. cit.*, pp. 50-51.

72

communists revolted in October 1923 but their attempt ended in disaster. The I.M.R.O., on whose support the communists should have relied, remained loyal to Chankov. By one account, the communists suffered 25,000 casualties and their leaders, Kolarov and Dimitrov were forced to run for their lives.[50]

His new success convinced Chankov that he had to make concessions to the I.M.R.O. to keep its loyalty. Realizing that the Bulgarian Macedonians constituted an explosive revolutionary element, he tolerated their irresponsible irredentism and even released from prison the I.M.R.O. leaders Protogerov and Alexandrov allowing them to reorganize their organization.

In the face of such tactics, the communists, having already suffered a significant setback, reached the conclusion that to maintain the leading position among the Balkan communist parties they had to show that they enjoyed significant power within their own country. To regain the strength they had lost, they had to attract the Macedonians, and to do that they had to offer them more than Chankov did, or could offer. They were confident that the slogan for a "united and independent Macedonia" would be extremely appealing, particularly if it were endorsed by all the communist parties including the Yugoslav and the Greek. Having reached this conclusion, they exerted all the pressure they could, through the Comintern and the BCF, to compel their neighboring comrades to endorse their Macedonian slogan.

Already in 1922, the Comintern had declared itself, at the suggestion of the Bulgarians, against the settlement of Greek refugees from Asia Minor in Greek Thrace and Macedonia. It even demanded that the Greek communists take a public stand against this settlement. The entire refugee program was attacked as merely a calculated scheme of the Greek Government to alter the ethnological composition of Macedonia and Thrace. The communists of Greece, as everyone else, were aware that the ethnological composition of the northern regions of the country, except for small pockets of Bulgarian Macedonians who lived in border districts, was definitely Greek especially after the departure of the Turks in 1923. Realizing, therefore, that only harm could result from the adoption of such a policy, they refrained as long as they could from condemning the Government's efforts to shelter the destitute refugees.

In December 1923, the BCF held its Fifth Conference in Moscow, just prior to the Comintern Congress scheduled to convene in the Soviet capital. The Bulgarian communists, having enlisted the backing of influen-

50. Bramos, *op. cit.*, pp. 88-89.

cial Soviet personalities — including Manuiliski and, naturally, Rakovski, both Comintern specialists on Balkan affairs — increased their pressure on the Greek and Yugoslav communists by demanding that the Conference adopt without delay their proposal for an independent Macedonia. Nikolas Sargologos,[51] the Greek delegate, initially objected to the Bulgarian proposal, but he was subsequently compelled to sign the resolution. He did so without the authorization of the Central Committee of his Party. The resolution, later ratified by the Comintern, referred to the Macedonian problem in these terms:

> The struggle of the peoples of Macedonia and Thrace for their national liberation and independence, emerges as one of the most essential factors for the success of the revolution in the Balkans. To reject the slogan for the autonomy of Macedonia and Thrace would mean to acknowledge an imperialist situation in the Balkans and the subjugation of the proletariat masses. For this reason, the Third Communist International has decisively raised the slogan for an ''autonomous and independend Macedonia and Thrace.''[52]

While the Bulgarians celebrated their triumph, the Greek and Yugoslav parties badly split over the resolution. Sargologos escaped the wrath of his comrades in the Central Committee by emigrating to the United States instead of returning to Athens. Stavrides, a Greek Macedonian, probably the best versed leading communist on the prevailing situation in Northern Greece where the Party had already succeeded in attracting a large number of workers, realized the inherent dangers of the resolution for the communist movement in Greece and proposed that the Central Committee ask for further clarifications from the Comintern. However, certain members of the Central Committee began to contemplate acceptance of the Comintern desision theorizing that since Bulgaria appeared to be on the verge of a Bolshevik-type revolution, the fraternal Balkan parties had an obligation to render to the CPB all the assistance they could.[53] Only Yannis Kordatos, edidor of the Party newspaper *Rizospastis,* remained adamant in rejecting outright the Comintern resolution. In an editorial he publicly declared that:

---

51. Sargologos had been Secretary-General of the KKE since October 1922. While he was on the way to Moscow, the KKE held a Congress (Nov. 1922) and voted him out of office although he was allowed to represent the Party at the Moscow conferences.

52. Christopher Naltsas, Τὸ Μακεδονικὸν Ζήτημα καὶ ἡ Σοβιετικὴ Πολιτικὴ [The Macedonian Question and the Soviet Policy], (Thessaloniki : Society for Macedonian Studies, Institute for Balkan Studies, 1954), p. 113.

53. Bramos, *op. cit.,* (1st Edition) p. 92.

The slogan for an autonomous Macedonia and Thrace is groundless, because Macedonia has been divided into three sections. The inhabitants of Greek Macedonia are all Greeks, as I personally know. If the Bulgarian communists want to attract the refugees of Macedonia and the *comitadjis*, that is a problem for the CPB [to solve], and neither the KKE nor any other Balkan communist party has any reason for getting involved. If such a slogan is useful for the CPB, it is disastrous for the KKE. We will not ruin the KKE to correct the mistakes of the CPB.[54]

The end result was that no decision was taken by the KKE on the resolution, although the pro-Comintern elements in the Central Committee appeared to be gaining ground as evidenced by the election of Pouliopoulos and Maximos to represent the Party at the Sixth Balkan Conference to be held in March 1924.

Similar, if not more adamant, was the reaction of the right wing of the Yugoslav Party, led by Sima Marković. Up to the Second Party Conference held in 1923 the rightists were able to bloc any action on the national issue. At the Third Party Conference in December 1923 a resolution was passed condemning Marcović and upholding the right of Yugoslav nationalities to self-determination and eventual secession. At the same time the Conference passed a resolution favoring Macedonian political autonomy. The right wing of the Party leadership did not accept the tenet of the resolution.[55] Factionalism, however, continued until 1925 — as will be seen in following pages — when Stalin personally intervened and the CPY finally capitulated accepting the Bulgarian-sponsored Comintern position on the Macedonian issue.

C. The Slogan for a "United and Independent Macedonia" and its Impact

1. Resolutions by the BCF and the Comintern

The year 1924 was probably the most decisive one for the position of the Balkan communist parties on the Macedonian Question. It started with the victory of the Bulgarians at the Sixth Balkan Communist Conference in March 1924 and ended with the unconditional acceptance of the Bulgarian view by the communist parties of Greece and Yugoslavia, which, as a consequence, were further weakened. Four years of preparation and

54. *Ibid.*, p. 92; also Naltsas, *op. cit.*, p. 113.
55. *Yugoslav Communism, op. cit.*, p. 40.

lobbying in Moscow by the Bulgarian communists had finally paid off in rich dividends.

The resolution of the Sixth Balkan Communist Conference completely ignored the fact that in Greek Macedonia — already settled with approximately 700,000 additional Greeks from Asia Minor — the Greek element formed a majority of more than 95 per cent of the total population. The view adopted was thoroughly arbitrary as it regarded Macedonia as a unique entity inhabited by many nationalities none of which had the majority. "Consequently," it stated, "the domination of any one of the Balkan states over Macedonia means national oppression of the majority of the Macedonian population." It is of particular interest to note that nowhere in the resolution is there any specific mention of a "Macedonian national group;" merely the inhabitants of the region are referred to as the "Macedonian population."

The largest part of the resolution, whose main thesis was the slogan for "a united and autonomous Macedonia," was aimed at convincing the I.M.R.O. followers and the masses of the *emigrés* in Bulgaria, that their position was clearly with the "progressive" communist movement which offered the best solution to their national aspirations. The resolution explicitly promised:

A united and autonomous Macedonia is now the slogan of the Macedonians in all corners of their Fatherland, which is covered with ruins. It is under this slogan that they are organizing and conducting the struggle...
In setting up the ideal of a workers' and peasants' government, the communist parties and the Communist Federation of the Balkans will assure peace, independence and liberty of development of all the peoples of the Peninsula, that it will be a voluntary union of independent Balkan Republics, *including the Republic of Macedonia and Thrace.*[56]

The Bulgarian drafters of the resolution were aware that their plan for a communist Balkan Federation could hardly be realized at that time, but they were counting the propaganda benefits they could reap in Bulgaria. They did not ask directly for a Bulgarian Macedonia. They preferred instead to remain firmly attached to doctrinal communist grounds which had the advantage of defeating the opposition of the Greek and Yugoslav communists while eliciting the support of the Soviets.

The endorsement of the BCF was the first significant success for the

56. Text in *International Press Correspondence*, May 1, 1924, quoted in part in Barker, *op. cit.*, pp. 50 - 51. (Italics added).

Bulgarian communists. The real triumph, however, came at the Fifth Comintern Congress which was held in May-June of 1924. Under pressure by the Bulgarian officials of the Comintern and with the support of Soviet delegates who apparently had become convinced that their political objectives in the Balkans could best be served by a policy pivoting around a strong communist Bulgaria, the Congress passed a resolution which, first, accepted as fact that the inhabitants of Macedonia — "the Macedonian people" — desired a united and independent state of their own; second, that their suppressed desire should be developed by the BCF into a proletarian revolutionary movement, and third, that the slogan of the BCF for a "united and independent Macedonia" was correct and truly revolutionary, whereas, the partition of Macedonia into three sections constituted an "opportunist stand." The Comintern issued explicit orders to the effect that "the communist parties of the Balkan Federation must support to the best of their ability the national-revolutionary movement of the oppressed nationalities of Macedonia and Thrace for the establishment of independent republics." To give more weight to the decisions of the BCF, the Comintern Congress entrusted the BCF with unifying the "leadership of the activities of the communist parties of the separate Balkan countries in regard to national questions, and particularly the Macedonian and Thracian questions."[57]

Much later (1950), the former Secretary-General of the KKE Stavrides, revealed that at the Congress the Bulgarians had convinced the other delegates by arguing that the slogan for a united and independent Macedonia would rally to the communist cause the following elements: The I.M.R.O., which had, more or less, formed a "united front" with the CPB; the Kutso-Vlachs, many of whom followed the Rumanian propaganda that they constituted a Rumanian minority; the Revolutionary Albanian Committee whose armed bands operated in the Kossovo region of Serbian Macedonia, and the Jews of Thessaloniki who, according to the Bulgarians, preferred an autonomous Macedonian state and were willing to support it financially. They argued that in the event of a plebiscite under the auspices of the League of Nations, all these elements would vote for autonomy and would, consequently, outnumber the Greeks and the few Serbs of Serbian Macedonia.[58]

The Greek representatives to the Comintern Congress, Pouliopoulos

57. Text in Κομμουνιστικὴ ᾿Επιθεώρησις, op. cit., October 1924, pp. 3483-49. For an English translation see Barker, op. cit., p. 58.
58. Stavrides, op. cit., pp. 259 - 260.

and Maximos, voted for the proposal. Neither had a good knowledge of the prevailing situation in Greek Macedonia. Pouliopoulos had never visited the region, while Maximos had spent only a few months in Kavala.[59] They endorsed the Comintern resolution preferring to prove themselves loyal communists than defend the national interests of their country and, as it turned out, the interests of their own Party as well.

The Yugoslav representatives followed the example of their Greek comrades and signed the resolution. However, the Party badly split over the issue. In the next, the Seventh Balkan Communist Conference held in Moscow in July, Sima Marković and I. Milioković were strongly condemned for pursuing a "rightist" and "opportunistic" policy with regard to various national questions which they viewed merely as ordinary political problems.[60]

The Seventh Balkan Conference used the strongest words yet in condemning the Greek and Yugoslav leaders who continued to raise objections to the Comintern's directives. In reference to the KKE, the new resolution declared that "the KKE would have committed a great mistake should it continue to take a contemptuous attitude toward the national revolutionary movement which has a tremendous significance for the revolution in the Balkans."[61] Then shifting its fire toward the dissenting Serbs, it stated:

> In Yugoslavia, the crisis is born especially on account of the increasing national struggle ... However, the Party is in danger of remaining a heresy, isolated from the great movements of the people if in fact it views with contempt the national struggle of the Croats, the Slovenes, the Macedonians, etc. It may also pass over to the camp of reaction if, at the time of the outbreak of the national struggle, it will continue to be preoccupied with the notion of supporting the idea of national unity as a segment of the Serb comrades does favor [today].[62]

Referring specifically to the Macedonian Question, the resolution attacked the Serbian Government for oppressing the movement of the "Macedonians" for national independence. It attacked also the Bulgarian Government for trying to infiltrate Macedonian organizations so that they might become loyal instruments of Bulgaria's own nationalistic objectives.[63] In this connection it is interesting to note the effort of the BCF, acting under the leadership of Bulgarian communists, to answer Greek

---

59. *Ibid.*, pp. 256-257.
60. Georgi Dimitrov, "The Seventh Balkan Conference," Κομμουνιστικὴ 'Επιθεώρησις, Vol. V, No. 9, September 1924, p. 297.
61. Κομμουνιστικὴ 'Επιθεώρησις, Vol. V, No. 10, October 1924, p. 338.
62. *Ibid.*, p. 339.
63. *Ibid.*, p. 341.

and Serbian contentions that only a small segment of the population in their respective parts of Macedonia was interested in an autonomous status. The resolution pointedly stated :

The Macedonian Question is a general Balkan problem and only as such it can be solved. The Macedonian land and the Macedonian people were divided between Serbia, Greece and Bulgaria. The great mass of the *emigré* Macedonian revolutionary element lives in Bulgaria and other countries, while revolutionary Macedonian organizations exist not only among the population of the Macedonian regions but also among the *emigrés* [in foreign lands]. *The Balkan communist parties will maintain a correct policy on the Macedonian Question only when they take into consideration the totality of the Macedonian revolutionary forces which are dispersed in various countries.*[64]

2. *The KKE in the Light of the 1924 Resolution*

The two resolutions of the BCF (Sixth and Seventh Conference) and the resolution of the Fifth Comintern Congress became the subject of wide controversy among the Greek communists. Not until October 1924 were they published in the Party theoretical review *Κομμουνιστικὴ 'Επιθεώρησις*. The controversy was finally solved at the Third Extraordinary Congress of the Party which was convened in Athens from November 26 to December 30, 1924. The issue on the agenda was the Macedonian Question. Stavrides, who had advocated the adoption of delaying tactics, was absent, deported to a Greek island. Thus, Pouliopoulos and Maximos were left to sway the Congress in favor of the Comintern resolution. They were undoubtedly assisted by the presence of Comintern observers attending the meetings. After long deliberations, and rejection of a memorandum sent by Stavrides arguing that Greek Macedonia was indisputably Greek and that, consequently, the Comintern resolution was inapplicable,[65] the Congress finally adopted the resolution of the Third International for a "united and independent Macedonia." By this decision, the KKE marked a turning point in its history, and almost definitely wrecked its chances for success in the country. It is not an exaggeration to suggest that the Party never really recuperated from the shock of this decision, at least not until 1935 when it was allowed to change to the slogan of "equal rights." It is, therefore, important to quote extensively from the Congress' "Report on the National Question :"

---

64. *Ibid.*, p. 340 (Italics added).
65. Stavrides, *op. cit.*, p. 250 and pp. 264-265.

The last imperialist wars in the Balkans and the treaties which followed them not only failed to solve the national question in Macedonia and Thrace but, on the contrary, they complicated it even more. The people of both countries [sic], having been subjected for long years to the imperialist raids of the bourgeoisie of the neighboring states and destituted by long wars, were faced with an economic crisis which finally led to their dismemberment between Serbia, Bulgaria, Turkey and Greece. This partition of the Macedonian and Thracian peoples was carried out in accordance with the political and military potential of each of the opponent, thieving states and in accordance with the conflicting interests of the Western European imperialist Powers... The partition, on the one hand, subjects the Macedonian people to the national rule of the bourgeoisie of the neighboring states and on the other, it renders the conflicts between these states more acute, thus constituting a threat for new wars.

Serbia, having failed to acquire a naval base at Fiume is seeking now to establish one by moving southwards to Thessaloniki with the support of Italy. On the other side, the designs of the Bulgarian bourgeoisie toward the Greek part of Macedonia and its desire to expand toward the Aegean Sea, constitute a new cause for an armed conflict... The peace of the people of the Balkans, on account of the conflicting imperialist designs over Macedonia and Thrace, is under the constant threat of war which may break out from one day to the next.

Despite the efforts of the Balkan bourgeoisies... these two peoples [Macedonians and Thracians] have always desired and struggled to be liberated from the foreign national yoke.

The partition of Macedonia between Yugoslavia, Greece and Bulgaria, accentuates even more the desire of the Macedonians to unite the three sections of their dismembered fatherland and to form a united and independent Macedonia...

The Bulgarian chauvinist bourgeoisie has always tried through its agents in the national Macedonian organizations to exploit the struggle for liberation of the Macedonian people and to place it in the service of its imperialist designs over the remaining portions of Macedonia. The Yugoslav and Greek bourgeoisies, on the other hand, through their policy of forced expatriation and denationalization, as well as through the settlement of the region with fellow national refugees, attempt to give the impression that the national issue in the Macedonian regions under their rule has been settled...

Then, the resolution went on to outline the policy which the KKE proposed to follow in Greek Macedonia :

The Congress accepts that the slogans of the Sixth and Seventh Balkan Communist conferences for a ''united and independent Macedonia" and for "a united and independent Thrace" are absolutely correct and truly revolutionary...

...Raising the elementary political slogan for the right of the peoples of Macedonia and Thrace to self-determination, including the right to secede from Greece, and the right to establish a united and independent state along with the other sections of their country (now oppressed by the other Balkan bourgeoisies), the KKE supports all the nationalpolitical claims of these oppressed peoples (national schools, national local self-government, religious freedom, respect for the popular national customs, etc.). In its struggle the KKE will support with all its strength the national revolutionary movement of the oppressed peoples of Macedonia and Thrace for the establishment of independent republics, and, along with all the revolutionary organizations of Macedonia and Thrace, it will form the united front of the Greek workers, peasants and the Macedonian and Thracian working masses against the national and social yoke of the Greek and Balkan bourgeoisies *for the union of the workers of the Balkans in a Balkan federation.*[66]

While the Congress was still deliberating, the Central Committee issued a manifesto to the Greek people to explain its policy on the Macedonian and Thracian issue. To allay the fears of the hundreds of thousands of refugees who had settled in the Northern Greek regions, the Manifesto pledged that in an independent Macedonian and Thracian state, national councils of refugees and farmers would be formed to divide justly the land.[67] It is, indeed, doubtful that the drafters of the resolution and of the Manifesto really believed that such arguments could convince the people, particularly of the northern regions who had a personal knowledge of the prevailing situation in their midst. It appears that the communist leaders tried hard to save face by utilizing, as best as they could, communist dialectics although they were personally aware that they could hardly convince their own followers.

The immediate reaction to the KKE's decision was that leading members of the Party resigned, while a storm was raised in both the Parliament and the Greek press against the Communist Party which was criticized for having adopted a clearly seditious policy. The Government, which until that moment had taken a rather naive view toward the com-

---

66. "Resolution of the Extraordinary Congress on the National Question" in *Tò KKE ἀπὸ τὸ 1918 ἕως τὸ 1931*, Vol. I, *op. cit.*, pp. 353-356, (translated from Greek by the author).

67. *Ριζοσπάστης*, December 14, 1924.

munists, reacted vigorously. Pouliopoulos was arrested and many Party officials were deported to the islands.

Stavrides, though opposing the resolution on the Macedonian issue,[68] in a critical moment for the Party was elected Secretary-General to replace Pouliopoulos. Immediately he dispatched reports to influential members of the Comintern to explain Greece's peculiar position and ask for their support in reversing the Comintern decision. Certain leading personalities of the communist movement, including Bukharin, Suvanin and Petrovski, replied that the "right to self-determination" is a basic principle of communism but that the KKE was not obliged to take any definite action towards effecting the autonomy of Macedonia. One thing, however, the Party could not or dared not do, was to change officially, without authorization, its line, a fact which seriously harmed its political prospects. Kordatos, writing in *Rizospastis* in 1927, accused the leadership of the Party in these revealing words:

> With their extremism [the new leaders of the Party] offered to the Government the excuse for general persecutions. But the most outrageous act was the slogan for the autonomy of Macedonia.
>
> Despite the fact that not even the slightest national movement existed in Greek Macedonia, since the Greek bourgeoisie had already deported the Slav population and had settled Greek refugees, the Communist Party raised, nevertheless, the issue. This policy was the *coup de grâce* [for the Party] which was dissolved not on account of the attacks of the Government but because it was DISAPPROVED BY THE WORKERS, since communism in Greece acted as the ally of BULGARIAN CHAUVINISM.[69]

Gradually, most of the leading Party members began to realize the harmful effects of the Macedonian policy on the Party. By 1927, even Pouliopoulos came out with the proposal that the slogan, "a united and independent Macedonia," should be substituted for the more ambiguous slogan, the right of the "Macedonian people" to self-determination, including the right of separation.[70]

Pouliopoulos' proposal remained unheeded as Party leadership had already been passed to Moscow-trained communists who piously followed the directives of the Comintern. Thus, the Third Regular Congress of the

---

68. Stavrides, *op. cit.*, pp. 267-272.

69. *Ριζοσπάστης*, February 25, 1927, (Emphasis by Kordatos).

70. "Statement by Pouliopoulos before the Third Regular Congress of the Party made on March 29, 1927," in *Τὸ ΚΚΕ ἀπὸ τὸ 1918 ἕως τὸ 1931, op. cit.*, Vol. II, pp. 133-134.

Party, held in March 1927, rejected Pouliopoulos' interpretation and considered as ''secondary'' the argument that there were no formulated ''Macedonian'' or ''Thracian'' people in the regions under consideration.[71] The new leaders realized that in 1923-1924, when the Party adopted the Comintern resolution, there was a strong revolutionary fervency, particularly among the dissatisfied national groups of the Balkans. The latter fact weighed heavily with the Comintern when it adopted its program on the national question. The revolutionary climate had greatly diminished by 1927; yet, the Greek communists felt that they were inescapably bound by the Comintern directives. Their only concession at the Third Regular Party Congress was to render a decision on the Macedonian Question which, though not abandoning the slogan for ''a united and independent Macedonia,'' cautioned against allowing the issue to become the primary slogan of the Party.[72]

Evidence to that effect was provided by the resolution of the next Second Plenum of the Central Committee (July 20 - 25, 1927), which merely mentioned the slogan at the bottom of the Party's 14-point program.[73] In the meantime, the communist members of the Parliament shied away from publicly supporting their Party's position on the Macedonian Question, a fact which raised the wrath of the Party leadership. At the Third Plenum of the Central Committee (February 15-18, 1928), the disobedient MP's were attacked for ''reformist eunuchism'' and were forbidden to represent the Party in Parliament.[74] The decision was confirmed by the Fourth Party Congress held in December 10-15, 1928. By this time, the KKE was careful to speak only of the ''oppressed nationalities'' which *were left* in Macedonia and Thrace.[75] Without saying so, the Greek communists were compelled to shift from a secessionist policy to that of the protection of minority rights.

All through 1929 and 1930 the slogan for ''a united and independent Macedonia'' was not raised in any of the major Party meetings or conferences.[76] Apparently the KKE's crushing defeat in the 1928 national elections forced the Party leadership to tone down its propaganda. The

71. Text of Resolution quoted in *ibid.*, pp. 40-41.
72. *Ibid.*, p. 41.
73. *Ibid.*, p. 116.
74. Text in *ibid.*, p. 242.
75. Text in Κομμουνιστικὴ Ἐπιθεώρησις, January 1929, pp. 9-14, (Italics added).
76. Ριζοσπάστης, February 21, 1930; also in Τὸ ΚΚΕ ἀπὸ τὸ 1918 ἕως τὸ 1931, Vol. II, *op. cit.*, pp. 355-356 and p. 423.

last effort to revive the discredited slogan was made at the Fourth Plenum of the Central Committee in December 1931 when the Party's decision to struggle for "an independent" — no more, "united" — Macedonia, was reaffirmed in the Party's Political Program. At the same time dissident elements of the Party were criticized for trying to minimize the importance of the national issue.[77] Finally in 1935, the KKE officially renounced its former policy and adopted the new slogan for "equal rights to all."

The failure of the KKE to attract the masses through its slogan for "a united and independent Macedonia and Thrace" should be mainly attributed to the fact that the people to whom this slogan was directed, simply did not exist. According to the statistics of the League of Nations, the ethnological composition of Greek Macedonia at this period [1926] was as follows:[78]

Greeks	1,341,000	88.8 %
Moslems	2,000	0.1 %
Bulgarians	77,000	5.1 %
Various	91,000	6.0 %
	1,511,000	100.0 %

The second reason should be found in the active opposition of many leading communists who chose to sever their ties with the Party rather than condone its tactics. Finally, a reason recently advanced by "Slav-Macedonians" living in Skopje, is that the failure of the slogan in Greek Macedonia during the inter-war period was due to a whole series of tactical errors by the Party. It was argued that the leaders of the KKE had been negligent in preparing the people psychologically to accept the radical slogan; that the slogan was applied in theory and abstract terms and no effort was made to make it an action slogan; that the KKE cadres were not properly briefed, and, finally, that the initiative of carrying out the policy for an independent Macedonia was not passed over to the Slavs of Macedonia who could "popularize" it more effectively as their own slogan.[79] It seems that there is sufficient truth in all these points — except the last one — because the KKE had neither the heart nor the popular sup-

77. Κομμουνιστικὸν Κόμμα τῆς ῾Ελλάδος [Communist Party of Greece], Πέντε Χρόνια ᾽Αγῶνες· 1931 - 1936 [New edition, corrected and completed], (Athens, Central Committee of the KKE, 1946), p. 43.

78. League of Nations, Greek Refugee Settlement (Geneva, 1926), chart at the end of the book.

79. Zografski, op. cit., p. 106.

port to agitate actively for such an unrealistic platform. Probably its main political blunder was that it talked too much for something it did so little about.[80]

3. The CPY following the 1924 Decision

The CPY followed exactly the unhappy experience of the KKE. How strongly Yugoslav communists objected to the BCF's 1924 decision is evidenced by Manuiliski's long speech before the Comintern Congress on June 30, 1924 when he accused leading Yugoslav communists of still being inbued with a social democratic ideology. Excerpts from his speech are quoted below:[81]

> These mistakes can be said to be of four fundamental types, all of which are survivals of the attitude of some Yugoslav comrades, especially of Comrades Marković and Miliokovič, who are now in prison... He [Comrade Miliokovič] asserts that in Yugoslavia there are no nations, but only linguistic differentiations. In his pamphlet, *The National Question in the Light of Marxism*, and in a number of articles published in the organ of the Yugoslav Communist Party *Radnik*, Comrade Marković brings forward, as a practical slogan for the Communist Party, the fight for the revision of the constitution, that is to say, he placed the whole question of national self-determination on a constitutional basis.

> Very characteristic is Comrade Marković's attitude towards the Macedonian question. You know that Macedonia plays at present, after its partition between Serbs, Greeks and Bulgarians, the very same role in the Balkans that the Balkans play in Europe. A fierce fight is being waged around Macedonia, and especially around the question of an outlet into the Aegean Sea and the fight for the port of Salonika between the small robbers in the Balkans.

> At the same time there is in Macedonia a strong national movement for the re-establishment of an independent State. What is Comrade Marković's attitude toward this national movement? In his articles he expressed the opinion that the Macedonian question is not by

---

80. The resolution of the Third Regular Congress on the National Question declared:

The mistake of the Party after the Extraordinary Congress of 1924 was that, in essence, it rendered the national question the center of all its activities. The mistake of the Party in 1925 should not be attributed to the incorrect basis of the slogan, but to its relative position toward the other slogans and activities of the Party.

Text in *Tò KKE ἀπὸ τὸ 1918 ἕως τὸ 1931,* Vol. II, *op. cit.,* pp. 40-41.

81. Published in *International Press Correspondence,* **August 4, 1924,** as quoted in Barker, *op. cit.,* p. 60.

any means a Balkan but a European problem, which cannot therefore be finally solved before a victory of the European proletariat over the bourgeoisie has been achieved. If the question is put in this way, what will be the result? only a passive attitude of the Communist Party to one of the most burning questions which is agitating the various Balkan nationalities at present. A careful study of the situation will show you that the origin of this kind of view is to be sought in the Second International. Marković holds the view that the proletariat must accept the bourgeois State such as it has been created by a series of wars and violations...

Comparing the relative positions of the CPY and the KKE, one is apt to observe that the former was much weaker than the latter. Whereas, in Greek Macedonia the irredentist elements did not even constitute a distinct group, in Yugoslav Macedonia the majority of the inhabitants, living under an oppressive regime which was trying hard to Serbianize them, felt closer to Bulgaria then to the Kingdom of the Serbs and Croats. Thus, a revolutionary movement could thrive on their resentment. Moreover, the Bulgarian communists exerted, through Comintern, more pressure on the CPY than on the KKE. A case in fact was an article by Stalin published in the June 30, 1925 issue of *Bolshevik* which accused the Yugoslav communists of taking an academic view of the right of nationalities to self-determination.[82] The Yugoslav communists could reply that Stalin himself had spelled out clearly that "the right of secession must not be understood as an obligation, as a duty to secede." "A nationality," he had written on another occasion, "may take advantage of this right and secede, but it may also forego the right, and if it does not wish to exercise this right, that is its business...We must not confuse a *right* with an *obligation.*[83] However, at that time, particularly after Stalin assumed the leadership of international communism, it was becoming increasingly dangerous to oppose Soviet demands. In a speech on March 30, 1925, reprinted in the April 15, 1925 issue of the *Bolshevik,* Stalin actually outlined the policy which the CPY ought to follow in the national question:

> The postulate of a revolution must be the starting point of the national programme. Further, it is imperative to include in the national programme a special point on the right of nations to self-determination, including the right of secession... Finally, the programme should include a special point providing for those nationalities in Yugoslavia which do not find it necessary to secede from

---

82. Barker, *op. cit.,* pp. 66-67; also, *Yugoslav Communism, op. cit.,* p. 40.
83. Joseph Stalin, *Marxism and the National and Colonial Question* (London: Lawrence and Wishart, 1936), p. 204, (Italics added).

that country... It is therefore... necessary to... have in the programme a point on autonomy, with a view to the transformation of the state of Yugoslavia into a federation of autonomous national states based on the Soviet System.[84]

The views of the Yugoslav communists who had opposed the Communist Bulgarian plan for Macedonia are best analyzed in Marković's book, *The National Question in the Light of Marxism*, published in Belgrade in 1923.[85] The author nowhere contended that there was a separate Macedonian people. He emphasized that the Macedonian Question could not be solved according to the interests of one or the other of the Balkan communist parties.

In 1923, at its Third National Conference held immediately after the BCF meeting which had first proclaimed the slogan for an independent Macedonia, the Party passed a resolution calling on the Macedonian peasants to struggle for an independent Macedonia which would *voluntarily* join a federation of independent Balkan republics.[86]

The resolutions of the Sixth and Seventh Balkan Communist Conferences, and particularly the resolution of the Fifth Comintern Congress forced the Yugoslavs to adopt without reservations the slogan for a united and independent Macedonia, despite the fact that influential members of the Party had raised serious objections. In the ''Platform of the Workers, and Peasants' Bloc,'' the Party demanded ''complete recognition of the right of all the oppressed peoples of Yugoslavia to political independence and freedom'' and openly named as its objective the formation of the ''independent republics of Croatia, Slovenia, Macedonia and Montenegro.''[87]

The Yugoslav Party, exactly as the Greek, found it necessary in its Third Congress held in Vienna in June 1926, to criticize its own work on the national problem. Specifically, the Congress demanded that the national-revolutionary organizations in Macedonia be revived and that a federation of communist republics be formed in the Balkans.[88] The official position of the Party was further clarified at the Fourth Party Congress

---

84. *Yugoslav Communism, op. cit.*, p. 41.

85. The official policy of the Yugoslav Communist Party, as recounted in the official documents of the Party, follows a similar pattern to that of the KKE. For a good account see Djoko Slijepcević, *The Macedonian Question; The Struggle for Southern Serbia* (Chicago: The American Institute for Balkan Affairs, 1958), pp. 198-206.

86. Italics added.

87. *Balkanska Federacija*, December 15, 1924, p. 134.

88. Slijepcević, *op. cit.*, pp. 202-203.

held at Dresden in October 1928 when a resolution was passed calling
upon the working class to lend its whole-hearted assistance to the struggle for an independent and united Macedonia."[89]

The situation remained unaltered until 1935, when the emergence of
National Socialism in Europe compelled Comintern to change its tactics.
Before discussing more thoroughly the events of 1935, it is necessary to
review a very important development in the Macedonian Question, namely,
the attempts of the communist parties and the I.M.R.O. to coordinate
their efforts in seizing control of Macedonia. This development presents
particular interest since, to some extent, communist tactics were influenced
by the desire to attract the followers of the I.M.R.O.

4. Communists and the I.M.R.O.

It has been previously mentioned[90] that the I.M.R.O. had actively
assisted Chankov in subduing the communists when they attempted their
coup in October 1923. Following the *coup,* however, the old quarrels
within the Organization between the followers of the irredentist, govern-
ment-sponsored, policy in Macedonia and the leftist "autonomists-fede-
ralists," came once again into the open.

The left wing began to discuss the possibility of collaborating with
the communists. It was this development which the Bulgarian communists
had long hoped for when they tried desperately to enlist the support of the
BCF and the Comintern for their slogan for "a united and independent
Macedonia." By 1924, this tendency had begun to mature with the left
wing of the I.M.R.O. which drew further away from pro-Government
elements in the Organization. The forthcoming split became even more
apparent when the elements defeated by Chankov, namely, the Agrarian
followers of the late Stambuliski and the communists, formed a common
front and approached the I.M.R.O. asking for its support. This development raised a storm among the rank and file of the Organization, though
there is evidence to suggest that the majority favored a kind of collaboration with the communists. Panitsa, left wing leader of the I.M.R.O.,
went secretly to Greece during the summer of 1924 and conferred with
Greek communist leaders on the possibility of receiving logistical support

89. Under severe criticism from many quarters, Marković finally capitulated
and recognized his "errors." *Yugoslav Communism, op. cit.,* p. 43.

90. *Infra,* p. 72. In the English language, both Barker, *op. cit.,* (pp. 36-77)
and Slijepcević, *op. cit.,* (pp. 188-198) have good sections on the subject. Consequently only a brief account will be given here.

and shelter behind the Greek frontier in the event a *coup* was undertaken jointly by the I.M.R.O. and the CPB against Chankov.[91]

Prior to these developments, the Bulgarian communists had made significant progress towards a rapprochement between the CPB and the I.M.R.O. In the March 1924 resolution of the BCF, a flattering paragraph had been inserted acknowledging the I.M.R.O. as ''the real organizer and leader of the revolutionary struggle of the Macedonian slaves, regardless of nationality...''[92] As Barker put it, this paragraph was designed to exploit the differences within the I.M.R.O., win over the anti-Supremist elements — including the federalists — and generate pressure from the ranks, so that the policy of the leaders might be compromised and exposed, forcing the Organization to join the communists.[93]

Finally, the communist efforts began to bear fruits. Negotiations during the month of March between I.M.R.O. leaders Alexandrov, Protogerov and Chaoulev, and Bulgarian communist representatives led to the conclusion of a Manifesto, signed by all three I.M.R.O. leaders, which bore close resemblance to the resolutions of the BCF. The main points, where the similarity was particularly striking, are quoted below.[94]

> Macedonia... has all the rights and conditions necessary for an independent political existence, forming an independent and self-governing State...

> As long as these States are administered by governments which support the conquering and imperialist policy of the treaties or in other words, so long as these States are not directed by governments who base their internal and foreign policy on the right of the self-determination of the peoples, the Macedonian people cannot expect from them any aid in its liberation.

> Deeply aware of this historic fact, I.M.R,O. arrives at the firm and decisive conclusion that in its revolutionary fight for the freedom of Macedonia, *it can only count on the extreme progressive and revolutionary movements of Europe*, fighting against the imperialist policy of their Governments, against the existing peace treaties, for the right of self-determination for their own people and for other peoples. That is why I.M.R.O. declares that, in the interests of Macedonian liberty, it will give all its support to all those in the Balkans who are fighting against the European policy of conquest and imperialism, realized either openly or through the intermediary of the Balkan Governments...

91. Stavrides, *op. cit.*, p. 236.
92. Barker, *op. cit.*, p. 52.
93. *Ibid.*, p. 54.
94. Text in *ibid.*, pp. 55-56.

I.M.R.O. declares that it is fighting and will fight with all the means permitted by the revolution :

1) For the liberation and the reunion of the separated parts of Macedonia in a fully autonomous and independent political unit, within its natural geographical and ethnic frontiers;

2) For the democratization of the States bordering on Macedonia and for their union in a Balkan Federation which alone can guarantee the political existence of an independent Macedonia and the independence of the other Balkan peoples...

Unfortunate for the Bulgarian communists, their carefully designed maneuver failed as soon as Chankov's Government became aware of the objectives of the Manifesto. Alexandrov and Protogerov repudiated their signatures. Soon, thereafter, Alexandrov fell victim of an assassination plot. A series of murders followed which claimed the lives of prominent communist Bulgarian Macedonians. The flirtation with the communists over, I.M.R.O. pledged its loyalty to the Government. Until the early thirties it remained a useful instrument in projecting vigorously the country's irredentist and revisionist claims.

At the same time, the leftist elements of the I.M.R.O. under Dimitar Vlahov, definitely broke away and formed the "United" I.M.R.O. The new group never attained a significant following, although for some time it was successful in attracting considerable attention through its journal, *Fédération Balkanique*.[95] The United I.M.R.O.'s aims, as outlined in the April 1, 1926 issue of its journal, resembled much the 1924 resolution of the BCF. The first article stated that the task of the Organization was to liberate the entire of Macedonia and form "an autonomous political unit belonging, as a member with equal rights, to the future Balkan Federation."[96]

The United I.M.R.O. failed to carry out its tasks, exactly as did all the various organizations which agitated on revisionist platforms during the inter-war period. Its lone contribution at the time, was to add to the confusion of Macedonian politics. Only years later during the occupation, the Organization, though non-existent in form — it appears to have been dissolved around 1936 — provided the Yugoslav communist movement in Macedonia with trustworthy and experienced cadres who espoused the Yugoslav Party's policy to built a "Macedonian" state.

---

95. *Ibid.*, p. 69. Barker comments that the United I.M.R.O. remained to the end little more than a small *emigré* group in Vienna.

96. *Ibid.*, p. 68.

THE EMERGENCE OF NATIONAL SOCIALISM: REVERSION
OF COMMUNIST TACTICS

A. The Seventh Comintern Congress

The communists of Greece and Yugoslavia who had been driven, *nolens volens*, into the vortex of Macedonian politics, found themselves in 1935 suddenly relieved of a slogan which had done much to discredit them in their respective countries. The reason was the emergence of the aggressively revisionist national socialists in Germany and the fascists in Italy. Communism, still taking its first steps, felt considerably weak to stem the threat posed by a well-organized, totalitarian movement of the extreme right. To achieve some substantial balance, it was necessary to abandon its ultra-revolutionary slogans and to attempt, in a more conciliatory manner, to form united fronts with the socialists, the agrarians and other left-of-center elements.

As early as 1932, the Comintern had shown signs of de-emphasizing its extreme revolutionary doctrines in order to strengthen the "antifascist camp." The Seventh Plenum of its Executive Committee passed a resolution which directed the communist parties to fight against capitalist attacks and armed intervention directed at the Soviet Union.[97]

The new defensive policy was endorsed at the Seventh World Congress of the Commintern held late in the summer of 1935. The question of "the oppressed nationalities" was, for the moment, forgotten. Grasping the opportunity, the Greek and Yugoslav communist parties abandoned, for the purpose of forming united fronts, the slogan for "a united and independent Macedonia." Instead, they proclaimed that they favored the granting of "equal rights to all nationalities."

B. The Greek Communists

The first evidence that the KKE was abandoning the old line on the Macedonian Question came in a decision of the Central Committee passed on June 11, 1935, just as the Venizelist Party of the Center was defeated by the royalist Popular Party. In its decision, the Central Committee explicitly referred to the difficulties of the Party in promoting its objectives under the handicap of its Macedonian policy. Declaring that the

---

97. Κομμουνιστικὸν Κόμμα τῆς Ἑλλάδος (Communist Party of Greece), Αἱ Ἀποφάσεις τῆς XII Ὁλομέλειας τῆς Ἐκτελεστικῆς Ἐπιτροπῆς τῆς Κομμουνιστικῆς Διεθνοῦς, Σεπτεμβρίου 1932 [The Decisions of XII Plenum of the Executive Committee of the Communist International, September 1932], (Athens, November 1932), p. 32.

Macedonian Question will find its final solution with the victory of the Soviets in the Balkans, the KKE decided that "from now on it will struggle for the complete equality of the minorities."[98]

Officially, the Party reversed its position at the Sixth Congress held in December 1935. Referring to the Macedonian Question, the resolution adopted by the Congress stated:

> Following the [unsuccessful Venizelist] *coup* of March [1935] our Party introduced the slogan of "complete equality for the minorities" in the place of the slogan for a "united and independent Macedonia and Thrace." This change of our slogan in regard to the national minorities of our country does not signify that we abandon the Marxist-Leninist principle of the self-determination of national minorities. The substitution of the old slogan for a "united and independent Macedonia and Thrace," is required by the very change of the national composition of the Greek part of Macedonia in close connection with the change of circumstances in which our revolutionary movement grows in the Balkans and more specifically in our country, having as its basic duty the anti-fascist, anti-war struggle.

> Marxism-Leninism requires that the communist parties base their policy and their slogans on firm and realistic grounds. In the part of Macedonia which Greece holds, Greek refugees have been settled. Today, in the Greek part of Macedonia, the population, in its majority, is Greek. And in the present circumstances, the Leninist-Stalinist principle of self-determination demands the substitution of the old slogan.

The resolution continued in the following terms to analyze the Party's future objectives for Macedonia:

> By no means does the change of our slogan portray a weakness of our work in Macedonia and among the national minorities. On the contrary, it is necessary to increase our efforts to secure for the minorities wide rights. Our Party does not cease to declare that *the Macedonian Question finally and definitely will be solved in a brotherly way after the victory of the Soviet power in the Balkans* which will tear to parts the dishonorable treaties of the exchange of populations and will take all practical steps to extinguish the imperialistic injustices. *Only then the Macedonian people will find their complete national restitution.*[99]

---

98. "Report of the Central Committee to the Sixth Congress" in *Κομμουνιστικὸν Κόμμα τῆς Ἑλλάδος* (Communist Party of Greece), *Δέκα Χρόνια Ἀγῶνες, 1935-1945* [Ten Years of Struggles, 1935-1945], (Athens: Central Committee of the KKE, 1945), p. 45.

99. *Δέκα Χρόνια Ἀγῶνες, 1935-1945, op. cit.*, pp. 66-67; (translated from Greek by the author) (Italics added); also, Barker, *op. cit.*, pp. 75-76.

The resolution clearly disavowed the former position of the Party which, in fact, had advocated the immediate detachment of Greek Macedonia and Thrace. However, it should be noted that a serious reservation was entered at the end indicating that the new line was purely a tactical maneuver which meant that the Macedonian Question was still considered open and that a definite solution would be found with the victory of communism in the Balkans. What that solution would have been was left obscure in the expertly-worded dialectical ambiguity which characterized the new document. Any twisted interpretation could easily be acceptable.

The resolution prompted the rank and file of the KKE to advocate the complete denunciation of all alien slogans for the future of Macedonia. Their immediate reaction was due to the realization that their failures in Northern Greece were the result of the Party's wrong policy on the Macedonian Question.[100] The Central Committee, however, desired no exaggerated interpretations of the new policy. It reacted strongly against the initiatives of minor Party officials and members and labeled their view that "Macedonia has become Greek" as a "rightist, opportunistic distortion of the Party line."[101] This interpretation remained the Party's policy until January 1949 when it reverted for a moment to the slogan of "a united and independent Macedonia" within the framework of a Cominform-sponsored Balkan federation.

C. The Yugoslav Communists

The Yugoslav communists likewise felt relieved to abandon the old line. In the summer of 1936 the Central Committee, meeting in Moscow, passed a resolution which resembled the resolution of the KKE. It specifically referred to the "fascist imperialist movements" which posed a threat to communism, as the reason which prompted the CPY to change its tactics "without abandoning the principle of the right of all peoples to self-determination." It went on:

> The Party opposes the breaking up of the territory at present occupied by the state of Yugoslavia, since it aims at achieving a reorganization of that state by peaceful means, on a basis of

---

100. Whereas the Party had elected 10 representatives to the Parliament in the 1926 elections, eight of which were from Northern Greek districts, in 1936, of the 10 representatives it elected, only three were from Northern Greece. Stavrides, *op. cit.*, p. 486.

101. *Κομμουνιστικὴ 'Επιθεώρησις,* No. 4, February 16, 1936.

national equality of rights. In the present circumstances, any movement aimed at the secession of the oppressed peoples would only assist the fascist imperialists and their warlike aims.[102]

In the remaining years before the outbreak of the Second World War, the communists in Yugoslav Macedonia appeared to gain in numbers despite — or probably due to — severe measures against the pro-Bulgarian inhabitants of the Vardar Banovina, as Yugoslav Macedonia had been renamed. This was contrary to developments in Greek Macedonia, where the dictatorial regime of General John Metaxas (1936-1941) had succeeded at least temporarily, in halting communist and Bulgarian agitation.[103]

Free from the bondage of the Comintern-imposed Macedonian policy, the Yugoslav communists attempted to form a ""Macedonian People's Movement"" which would agitate for a program of full autonomy for the Macedonian region within the framework of Yugoslavia. The Government's stern measures, however, caused its failure.[104]

In 1939 and 1940, opposition in Yugoslav Macedonia against the Central Government in Belgrade was rapidly reaching a climax. Most of the inhabitants of Yugoslav Macedonia were openly pro-Bulgarian, or at least, anti-Belgrade, and almost in their totality were favorably inclined toward an alignment with the Axis powers.[105] The communists, in the meanwhile, were particularly successful with the university and high school students of Skopje.[106] Constant demonstrations against central authority were the order of the day. On the whole, however, the demonstrators were Bulgarians protesting against Serbian rule, not communists rising against the oppression of the ""monarcho-fascist capitalists.""[107]

D. The Bulgarian Communists

In the two years prior to the war, the Bulgarian communists relinquished their leading role of the twenties. However, their interest in Macedonia was not diminished. There are indications that Bulgarian commu-

102. Slijepcević, op. cit., p. 205, quotes from the Historical Archives of the Communist Party of Yugoslavia, Vol. II, 1919-1937, p. 399. See also Yugoslav Communism, op. cit., p. 44.

103. Report dated December 17, 1949 in GFM, Archives A/59179/Γ5Ba/1949.

104. Kulishevski, 1948 Congress Speech, op. cit.

105. Secret Report dated May 10, 1940, in GFM Archives, A/13278/5/2/1940.

106. Skopje Consular Report dated December 24, 1939, in GFM, A/670/5/2/1940.

107. Skopje Consular Reports, GFM Nos. A/19064/5/2/1940, A/21292/5/2/1940, A/26758/5/2/1940.

94

nists mainly from the Pirin region had at times welcomed the cooperation of elements of the extreme rightist Macedonian group of Ivan Mihailov. They had also turned to the communists of Yugoslav Macedonia who had shown signs of being inclined toward a close relationship with the Bulgarian rather than the Yugoslav Communist Party. By one account, the initiatives of communist Bulgarian circles from Pirin Macedonia aimed at uniting the three parts of Macedonia into a future communist Macedonian state. There are no indications that the Central Committee of the CPB had any connection with these overtures.[108] It appears that the whole plan was one more manifestation of the acute regional sentiment which brought together the Slavs on both sides of the Yugoslav-Bulgarian border, irrespective of social or political inclinations.

As the storm of the Second World War was approaching the Balkans, the communist parties began to show signs of siding with the national policy of their respective countries. In the moment of national peril, and with the Soviet Union in an uneasy, unrealistic and clearly temporal alliance with Nazi Germany, the communists for a brief moment, indicated that they were willing to neglect the Party and fight for the cause of the Fatherland. At that short respite, before the tumbling of the *ancient régimes* the full initiative of the give-and-take of Macedonian politics passed to the governments in power in Sofia, Belgrade and Athens.

108. *The Voice of the Aegeans* [Organ of "Slav - Macedonian" *emigrés* in Skopje], Skopje, May 19, 1952.

CHAPTER V

WAR AND OCCUPATION IN MACEDONIA:
THE POLICIES OF THE NATIONAL GOVERNMENTS

THE EVE OF THE SECOND WORLD WAR

While the Balkan communists operating underground had already prepared detailed plans for the manipulation of national antagonisms over Macedonia, the Balkan governments, on the approach of a major armed confrontation in the area, began to show a renewed interest in the future of the coveted region.

In the late thirties, Greece, having relinquished her century-old policy of the "Great Idea," had focused her efforts on consolidating her internal peace and economic progress. Bulgaria had never abandoned her revisionist attitude over Macedonia and was viewed as the main trouble-maker of the Peninsula. Yugoslavia appeared at the time to follow a policy similar to that of Greece. Nevertheless, Macedonia, and particularly the fine port of Thessaloniki, remained a constant temptation to the policy-makers of Belgrade, a fact which was to become more evident with the approach of the war.

As far back as 1937, the then Yugoslav Prime Minister Milan Stojadinović had spoken to Count Ciano and Mussolini, of Yugoslavia's *Lebensraum* toward the Aegean Sea.[1] In June 1938, he informed Ciano that the question of an outlet to the Aegean, although not considered of immediate importance, was always open for the Yugoslav people.[2] When Greece was attacked by Italy in October 1940, the Yugoslav Government of Dragivsa Cvetković debated, and for a moment appeared to favor, entering Greece at the rear of her fighting Army in Albania, in order to take possession of Thessaloniki.[3] Only Greece's ability to drive back the Italians seems to have saved the city at that time.

---

1. Galeazzo Ciano, *Ciano's Diplomatic Papers, Being a Record of Nearly 200 Conversations Held During the Years 1936-1942* etc. (London : Odhams, 1948), pp. 103-152.
2. *Ibid.*, p. 214.
3. R. L. Knejević, "Prince Paul, Hitler and Salonica," *International Affairs,*

A. German-Yugoslav Negotiations for Macedonia

When the Germans began preparing their southward advance into the Balkans, they were fully aware of both Yugoslavia's and Bulgaria's desires to secure an exit to the Aegean by way of Greek Macedonia. The Foreign Office of the Third Reich, in accordance with its systematic policy of attracting the dissident elements of the coveted regions — particularly the ethnic minorities — paid special attention to Macedonia. Publication of an ethnographic map of all three parts of the region, numerous articles in the German press as well as scientific treatises by German scholars, all indicated a renewed German interest in Macedonia which favored mostly Bulgarian aspirations.[4]

The victories of the Greek Army in the Albanian front had convinced the Germans that before they were to venture an attack on the Soviet Union they had first to secure their flank in the Balkans. Their initial plan was to attempt winning the states of the Peninsula by political means. With the irredentist Bulgarians there could be no serious difficulty, especially since the Soviets were at that time allied to Nazi Germany. Greece was considered as too much involved in the war against Italy to follow a policy of favorable neutrality. Yugoslavia, thus, remained the main question mark.

The events of the last months prior to the German invasion of Greece in April 1941, are now well known. As early as the closing days of 1940, the Germans were actively engaged in trying to ascertain whether Yugoslavia might not abstain from objecting to a German intervention in Greece if, in exchange, she were offered the port of Thessaloniki.[5] When the German intentions were intimated to the Yugoslav Cabinet, they met

Vol. XXVII, No. 1 (January 1951), p. 42. The author stated that he had this information from certain documents which had fallen into the hands of the leaders of the March 27 *coup*. The documents were minutes of a cabinet meeting held in Belgrade the day of Italy's invasion of Greece (October 28, 1940), and showed that a lengthy discussion dealt with the question of entering Greece to take possession of Thessaloniki.

4. H. R. Wilkinson, "Yugoslav Macedonia in Transition," *The Geographical Journal*, Vol. CXVIII, Part 4, December 1952 (London : The Royal Geographical Society), p. 395.

5. Reporting to Mussolini on November 18, 1940, on his meeting at Salzburg with Hitler and Von Ribbentrop, Count Ciano said that he was asked by the Führer whether "Mussolini would be prepared to make a pact with Yugoslavia on these three points : Axis guarantee for the Yugoslav frontiers; cession of Salonica to Yugoslavia; demilitarization of the Adriatic by Yugoslavia." Ciano's Diplomatic Papers, *op. cit.*, p. 410.

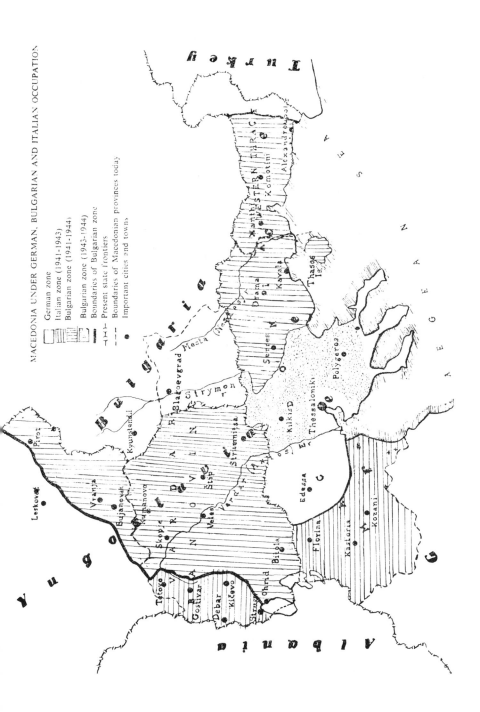

MACEDONIA UNDER GERMAN, BULGARIAN AND ITALIAN OCCUPATION.

German zone
Italian zone (1941-1943)
Bulgarian zone (1941-1944)
Bulgarian zone (1943-1944)
Boundaries of Bulgarian zone
Present state frontiers
Boundaries of Macedonian provinces today
Important cities and towns

Map 8

with considerable opposition particularly since it was felt that Yugoslavia was bound to Greece by an alliance. Gradually, however, the opposition weakened as it became evident that the Germans, in their negotiations with the Bulgarians were also offering as an inducement an exit to the Aegean by way of Greek Macedonia and Thrace.[6]

Finally, on March 25, 1941, the Cvetković Government signed the Axis Tripartite Pact. After the German invasion of the Balkans the Nazis issued the "Documents relating to the Conflict with Yugoslavia and Greece, 1939 - 1941" (No. 7, Foreign Office, Berlin, 1941), in which the surrender of Thessaloniki to Yugoslavia was twice mentioned. In the official Declaration by the Reich Government on April 6, 1941, it was stated that agreements reached with Cvetković in Vienna included the following clause:

Within the framework of the new European order, Yugoslavia would receive an outlet to the Aegean Sea, which at the particular wish of the Yugoslav Government was to comprise, territorially, Yugoslav sovereignty over the town and harbor of Thessaloniki.[7]

In the Memorandum accompanying the Declaration it was provided:

At the express wish of the Yugoslav Government, assurances were given that in the new state of affairs in Europe, Yugoslavia would receive an outlet to the Aegean Sea, thereby acquiring sovereignty over the city and part of Thessaloniki.[8]

A few days after the signing of the pact, the Cvetković Government was overthrown. In an attempt to pacify Hitler, the leader of the *coup*, General Dušan Simović, stated that there would be no change in Yugoslavia's international engagements. At the same time he attempted to renew close cooperation with the Greeks, but the course of history had caught up with him. On April 6, both Greece and Yugoslavia were invaded by the German divisions and, soon, were overrun.

---

6. In January 1941, the Japanese Ambassador in Ankara informed his Yugoslav colleague, Mr. Iliya Shumenković that a similar offer concerning Thessaloniki had already been made by Hitler to Bulgaria. Constantin Fotitch, *The War We Lost: Yugoslavia's Tragedy and the Failure of the West* (New York: The Viking Press, 1948) p. 44, footnote 1.

7. Germany, Auswartiges Amt., *Documents Relating to the Conflict with Yugoslavia and Greece* [Official Declaration by the Reich Government on April 6, 1941], 1931/41, No. 7, (Berlin: Deutscher Vertag, 1941), p. 21.

8. *Ibid.*, p. 30.

98

B. German-Bulgarian Negotiations for Macedonia

The Bulgarians appeared to be more successful than the Yugoslavs. Following the German invasion of Greek and Yugoslav Macedonia, Bulgarian troops and administrative officials were allowed to occupy large sections of Macedonia, ostensibly for "administration" purposes. Their apparent success was the result of long negotiations terminating with Bulgaria's siding with the Axis.

Immediately after Greece's engagement with Italy in a war in Albania, the Bulgarian Government began to orient itself toward joining the Tripartite Pact. Already, it had secured a Soviet guarantee that the territorial integrity of the country would be honored.[9] On November 21, 1940, a member of the Bulgarian Parliament, Peter Doumanov stood before the Chamber and declared it was time that Bulgaria free herself from the "timidity" which had marked her policy on the Macedonian Question. He went on to say:

> Two million [sic] Bulgarians are under foreign domination. Germany, with a population of 70 million shook entire Europe for two million fellow nationals living in Czechoslovakia. We, Bulgarians, with a population of six million and with two million co-nationals as minorities, i.e. one third of our population, we dare not openly fight for our minorities in Macedonia and Thrace. Some may say that Bulgaria is not Germany; Bulgaria should become for the Balkans what Germany is for Europe.[10]

The speech raised strong protest in Yugoslavia.[11] Until that time, the Bulgarian Government had discouraged open provocation while it secretly pressed the Reich for definite promises on the question of an outlet to the Aegean in exchange for Bulgaria's adherence to the Axis. From the diary of the then Bulgarian Prime Minister Filov—which was introduced at his trial in Sofia in November 1944—it is evident that the proposals for territorial concessions to Bulgaria in the direction of Greek Macedonia and Thrace were initiated not by the Germans but by the Bulgarians.[12]

Definite German acceptance of the Bulgarian terms reached the Bulgarian Government on January 18, 1941. A few weeks later, on February 8, the German General von Liszt and the Bulgarian General Boider signed

---

9. Achillevs A. Kyrou, *'H Συνωμοσία 'Εναντίον τῆς Μακεδονίας, 1940-1949* [The Conspiracy Against Macedonia, 1940-1949], (Athens: "Aetos," 1950), p. 30.
10. *GFM*, A/38408/6/4/1940.
11. *Politika* (Belgrade), December 6, 1940.
12. Filov's diary was published in installments in the Sofia newspaper *Ote-tsestven Front*, November 30, 1944 and ff., *GFM*, A/3367/1945.

a secret protocol allowing the Bulgarian Army to occupy Macedonia.[13] The Germans were offering the Bulgarians, Aegean Thrace from the Maritsa (Evros) river to the Mesta (Nestos) river. On March 1, Filov went to Berlin where he signed the Tripartite Pact. According to the March 1 entry in his diary, the Bulgarian and German leaders reached an agreement which Filov described as follows:

> Ribbentrop and Ciano handed me the letters by which, at the time of the settlement of the Balkan frontiers, we were to be given outlet to the Aegean Sea between the estuaries of the rivers Struma (Strymon) and Maritsa. This fact was to be kept a great secret to be made known only by the consent of both governments.[14]

It was understandable for the Germans—who at that time were tending similar offers to the Yugoslavs—to insist on secrecy. General Simović's *coup* freed their hands. According to Filov's diary, (entry of April 12), Hitler told the Bulgarian envoy Draganov that the Macedonian Question could now be settled in Bulgaria's favor. Already, on April 8, the Germans had requested that three Bulgarian divisions occupy Serbian Macedonia and take over the administration on the region,[15] thus freeing the German troops to pursue their operations in southern Greece and Crete. Similarly, on April 18, Bulgarian troops were allowed to occupy Greek Eastern Macedonia and Thrace, excepting the far eastern districts of Greek Thrace which bordered on Turkey. These the Germans did not want to trust to their Bulgarian allies.

Thus, at a time when Greece was entangled in a fierce war with Italy, her northern neighbors were conducting negotiations with the other partner of the Axis over the disposition of territorial spoils. Details of this diplomatic maneuvering were not known to the Greeks at the time.[16] The occupation, and the subsequent struggle against communism, preoccupied the Greek people to such an extent that they tended to forget the attitude of certain leaders in their neighboring countries. But it would seem unrealistic, indeed, to conclude that the behind-the-scenes bargaining of 1940-1941 did not leave a serious impact on Greek foreign policy, and

---

13. George Zotiades, *The Macedonian Controversy* [Second Edition], (Thessaloniki: Institute for Balkan Studies, 1961), p. 72 footnote 23.

14. "Filov's Diary," *Otetsestven Front, op. cit.*

15. *Ibid.*

16. Christopher Naltsas, *Τὸ Μακεδονικὸν Ζήτημα καὶ ἡ Σοβιετικὴ Πολιτικὴ* [The Macedonian Question and Soviet Policy], (Thessaloniki: Society for Macedonian Studies, Institute for Balkan Studies, 1954), p. 80.

a deep suspicion in the minds of the people as a whole, who tended to act negatively toward efforts to re-establish close relations with Yugoslavia and Bulgaria.

THE BULGARIAN OCCUPATION OF MACEDONIA

A. The Bulgarians in Greece

1. Occupation in Eastern Macedonia

In less than two weeks after the German invasion, and without technically declaring war on Greece,[17] Bulgaria proceeded to literally incorporate the Greek region of Eastern Macedonia within her realm. The Greek Government-in-exile was, thus, compelled to issue on June 11, 1941, a declaration stating that "a state of war should be considered as existing between the two countries."[18] The Bulgarians spoke and acted as if the regions they occupied had reverted to them permanently. In a speech before the Sobranje on September 28, 1941, King Boris declared:

> Thanks to this cooperation [with the Germans and the Italians] Macedonia and Thrace, these lands which have been so loyal to Bulgaria, which have been unjustly detached from her, and for which Bulgaria has been compelled to make innumerous sacrifices in the span of three generations, have now returned to the fold of the Bulgarian Motherland.[19]

Officially the Germans had not given their approval to Bulgaria's outright annexation of the territories, but the fact that no official protest was registered could be construed as a tacit consent.[20]

On June 10, 1942, a decree was published in the Bulgarian Government Gazette (No. 124) regarding the nationality of the inhabitants of the "liberated territories." By virtue of this decree, Bulgarian citizenship was automatically conferred upon all persons of "Bulgarian" descent residing in the "liberated regions" (Article 1). All other inhabitants were to become Bulgarian citizens by April 1, 1943, unless they declared their desire to retain their nationality or acquire another one. In either case, such persons were obliged to leave the "Bulgarian State" (Article IV). Presumably to make the opting for the Bulgarian nationality more attractive, Article

---

17. Kyrou, *op. cit.*, p. 43.
18. *GFM*, A/1272/11-6-1941.
19. *GFM*, A/4425/1/θ/1941.
20. Elizabeth Barker, *Macedonia; Its Place in Balkan Power Politics* (London: Royal Institute of International Affairs, 1950), p. 78.

VIII of the decree specified that all persons acquiring Bulgarian nationality were to be exempted from all taxes, levies and contributions.[21] The authorities were clearly aiming at the Bulgarization of the Greek regions through forced eviction of the Greek element and mass colonization of Bulgarians from Bulgaria.[22] This course of action was presumably chosen on the assumption that a future Peace Conference would be faced with a *fait accompli* with respect to the Bulgarian possession of these lands since the ethnological composition would, by that time, favor the Bulgarians. The procedure of evicting the Greek population was amply described in a study prepared by a team of Greek professors who conducted an on-the-spot investigation immediately after liberation. Excerpts are quoted below:

> At first individuals were expelled, later whole groups of inhabitants... Mass expulsions began in July (1941), when the Bulgarian Government had been persuaded by the results of the census of the population, that their strenuous efforts to alter the national conscience of the Greeks had failed... The order of priority was as follows: first were expelled those whose origin was from Old Greece, then refugees from Asia Minor of a generation ago, then families from the shores of the Black Sea, the Caucasus and Eastern Thrace —settled in Western Thrace and Eastern Macedonia according to the Treaty of Lausanne on the exchange of populations—lastly Greek families native of the place.[23]

The place of the evicted inhabitants would be taken by thousands of Bulgarian settlers. Premier Filov laid down the main terms of the colonization program in an interview published in the German newspaper *Borsen Zeitung* on November 11, 1941:

21. For the text of the Decree see *Bulgarian Atrocities in Macedonia and Thrace, 1941-1944: A Report of Professors of the Universities of Athens and Salonica* (Athens, 1945), p. 30, [hereafter referred to as *Bulgarian Atrocities*]. The nationality clauses of the Decree were not enforced on account of stern protests to the Reich authorities in Greece by the Nazi-imposed Athens government who succeeded in gaining successive postponements till the liberation of the country in October 1944.

22. On September 3, 1942, the Sofia newspaper *Zora* commented: "Now that the Greeks have been expelled for good from these Bulgarian regions, our Thracian brethren return in masses to their ancient homes. By means of the repopulation of these regions by Bulgarians, which is effected on a large scale, and by the "Bulgarization" of Western Thrace, these territories of Southern Bulgaria are colonized for a fourth time by those who have lived there for centuries." Text in: Greek, Under-Secretariat for Press and Information, *The Conspiracy Against Greece* (Athens: "Pyrsos", June 1947), pp. 30-31 [hereaftre referred to as *Conspiracy*].

23. *Bulgarian Atrocities, op. cit.*, p. 24.

In a few days we will begin with the colonization of the Aegean area... Thousands of Bulgarian families will be transported and settled in this area within the next weeks and months.

According to the Bulgarian Premier, the settlers were to pay the Bulgarian State for the dwellings and other buildings they would occupy which belonged to the Greek inhabitants who were forced to flee. On its part, the State undertook to provide them with transportation, and to those who were farmers, with agricultural loans on convenient terms.[24] Thus, many thousands of Bulgarians did settle in these regions.[25]

Parallel to the colonization, the Bulgarian Administration tried to alter the Greek character of the region by forbidding the use of the Greek language, closing the Greek schools, changing the Greek names of the streets to Bulgarian, and destroying many statues and memorials.[26] All these measures, plus murders and other deprivations forced at least 200,000 Greeks to find refuge in German or Italian-occupied Greece.[27] Such was the prevailing situation when Colonel Chrysochoou, under the cover-title of Supervisor of Nomarchies, was sent to the region by the Athens Government, with the knowledge and consent of the Greek Government-in-exile. In a moment of despair he proposed that the Government in Athens prepare plans to assist the mass evacuation of the population and its transfer to German-occupied Greece.[28]

At the end of the war the feelings of the Greeks, and especially those living in the Northern regions of the country, toward their Bulgarian neighbors, prompted a British observer to remark that "the only brotherly sentiment which Greek Macedonians felt towards the Bulgars was a disposition to raise Cain."[29]

2. Propaganda and Subversion in Western Macedonia

From the first days of the occupation, the Bulgarians indicated that they would not be satisfied with Eastern Macedonia only. Their objectives

24. For text of the Bulgarian Premier's interview see *Bulgarian Atrocities, op. cit.,* p. 31.
25. Naltsas, *op. cit.,* p. 211.
26. *Ibid.*
27. Constantine A. Doxiades, *Destruction of Towns and Villages in Greece,* Series No. 11, (Athens: Ministry of Reconstruction, 1947), p. 14.
28. Report dated July 30, 1942, in *GFM* E/474/I/1/1942.
29. Christopher M. Woodhouse, *Apple of Discord: A Survey of Recent Greek Politics in Their International Setting* (London: Hutchinson and Company, Ltd., 1948), p. 91.

included the acquisition of the Central and Western parts of Greek Macedonia with the port of Thessaloniki. Western and Central Macedonia constituted the lifeline not only of the German forces in Greece, but also of the German divisions fighting in Northern Africa. It was understandable, therefore, that the Germans would entrust neither to their Italian nor to their Bulgarian allies the administration of the vital port of Thessaloniki and the Vardar (Axios) Valley. Only some remote parts of Western Macedonia were included in the Italian zone of occupation.

The Bulgarians, on the other hand, were determined to extend their control to those regions by any means. The fact that in this area lived approximately 80,000 Slav-speaking inhabitants of whom a large segment had at the time of the German invasion, openly shown pro-Bulgarian sentiments, provided a further inducement and an excuse. On the whole, these Slav-speaking inhabitants had settled peacefully in the country and were it not for the Axis invasion and Bulgarian propaganda reviving in many old Bulgarian sympathies, they would have gradually been assimilated by the more populous Greek-speaking element.[30]

It was easy for the Bulgarians to persecute, evict or take as hostages thousands of Greeks from that part of Macedonia which was under their jurisdiction, but in German-occupied Western Macedonia, they needed to enlist the support of at least the Slavophones who were by no means entirely sympathetic to them. They had also to convince the Germans that Western Macedonia was heavily inhabited by Bulgarians; a very ambitious task, indeed.

The first objective, i.e. the proselytization of the Slavophones, had started even during the course of the Greco-Italian war when the Bulgarians succeeded in obtaining from Italy special treatment for Greek prisoners of war from Macedonia who were willing to declare themselves Bulgarians.[31]

The collapse of the Greek front in Macedonia before the onrushing German divisions created a psychological uneasiness among the inhabitants of the region. Militant Bulgarian-sympathisers waged a war of nerves against the native Greek population through the arrogant display of Bul-

---

30. Barker, *op. cit.*, p. 31.

31. Following the occupation of Greece, these prisoners of war were transported to Bulgaria and there is evidence to suggest that they were later sent back to Greece to form Bulgarian organizations. Kostas Bramos, Σλανοκομμουνιστικαὶ Ὀργανώσεις ἐν Μακεδονίᾳ: Προπαγάνδα καὶ Ἐπαναστατικὴ Δρᾶσις [Communist-Slav Organizations in Macedonia; Propaganda and Revolutionary Activities], First Edition (Thessaloniki: 1954), pp. 102-103.

garian flags, and rumors that momentarily the Bulgarian Army would occupy Western Macedonia.[32]

From May through July 1941, the situation worsened. The Greek Gendarmerie and officials of the local administration had followed the retreating army to the south. A number of Bulgarian sympathizers took advantage of the situation to form armed bands and terrorize the Greek population. The situation remained unchanged until July when the Greek authorities were allowed by the Germans to return to the region.[33]

The Bulgarians countered with a better organized, long-range plan to acquire control of the area. With the consent of the Germans, they established in Thessaloniki a Bulgarian Association which was founded ostensibly, ''for the cultural advancement and mutual assistance of its members.'' In fact, it became the center of Bulgarian efforts to seize Greek Western Macedonia through propaganda and, later, through coercion.

According to its Statute[34] (Article 4), only Bulgarians who were born in Macedonia, or Bulgarians of Macedonian origin could be admitted to the Association. Identity cards were issued for the members entitling them to special privileges and rich food rations,[35] a determining factor in swaying the loyalties of needy peasants in famine-stricken Macedonia. The Statute was confirmed on October 26, 1941, by General Von Krensky, German Commander of Thessaloniki and the Aegean, under condition that only Bulgarian citizens or Greeks of Bulgarian nationality could be admitted to membership. Furthermore, it was stipulated that the Association would be subjected to the laws of the German-installed Greek Government. It is interesting to note that it explicitly prohibited any financial advantages to the members,[36] a clause which was never observed.

The Greek Government in Athens strongly protested the establishment of this Bulgarian center in Thessaloniki. In a long memorandum to the Reich authorities in Greece, dated October 16, 1941, the Prime Minister complained that agents of the Bulgarian Association did not confine themselves to conducting propaganda but were engaged in acts of terrorism against the Greek population. In addition, the Prime Minister contended that leading Bulgarian agents were communists as were most of the recruited and secretly armed peasants. Indicative of the aims of the Bulga-

---

32. Naltsas, *op. cit.*, p. 217.

33. Demetrios G. Zapheiropoulos, *Tὸ KKE καὶ ἡ Μακεδονία* [The KKE and Macedonia], (Athens, 1948), p. 10.

34. Statute in *GFM*, E/1028/VI/1/1941 (File I/3a/1941-1942).

35. *Ibid.*

36. Order V5, Volk 4; in *GFM*, E/1029/VI/1/1941.

rians, said the Prime Minister, was the discovery by the German authorities in a village of Florina of concealed weapons which were enough to arm a whole battalion.[37]

The Germans failed to take any definite action on the basis of official Greek complaints, to curtail the discrepancies of the Bulgarians. This prompted the Bulgarians to adopt even more aggressive measures. Liaison officers were appointed to the German military headquarters in Thessaloniki and other cities. They soon became agents of an ambitious plan aimed at convincing the Germans that Western Macedonia was inhabited mostly by Bulgarians.[38] The Bulgarians tried also to expand their influence to the monastery community of Mount Athos. In February 1942, reports reached the Athens Government that the few Bulgarian monks of Mount Athos, apparently on instructions by the Bulgarian Government, were engaged in an effort to secure an order from the Germans for the eviction of the Greek authorities. Their plan aimed at internationalizing the monastery community—long the cradle of Orthodoxy in the Balkans—as a first step toward its subjection to Bulgarian control.[39]

The Germans, although they condoned the Bulgarian activities in German-occupied Macedonia, did not seem to consent to the Bulgarian demand to extend their authority into other regions as well. This German attitude convinced the Bulgarians that to succeed in their plans they had to rely on their own efforts. Thus, they were able to be entrusted with the distribution of foodstuffs donated by the International Red Cross. They declared that only those signing up as Bulgarians would receive food rations. However, even this method failed to produce impressive results as only 14,709 persons were given Bulgarian identity cards.[40]

The failure of the food distribution plan caused the Bulgarians to adopt more stringent methods. Through their liaison officers they succeeded in organizing and secretly arming their followers in the Western Macedonian districts. The German authorities were aware of the Bulgarian activities, but they were not inclined to take drastic measures against their allies.

37. No 51, dated October 16, 1941, in *GFM*, Nr. E/860/VI/3. The evidence was corroborated by a secret report of the Thessaloniki Police which informed the Government that anarchists and communists were admitted to the Bulgarian Association. *GFM*, File I/3a/1941-42.

38. Confidential report of the Edessa Gendramerie dated August 31, 1941. Text in *GFM* Archives. Also Naltsas, *op. cit.*, p. 263.

39. *GFM*, "Prime Minister's File," E/68, I/36/1942.

40. Bramos, *op. cit.*, [First Edition], p. 105.

As the situation deteriorated further, the Athens Government was compelled to protest, once again, to the Reich supreme authorities in Greece, in the strongest language permitted. The protest went as far as to accuse the local German authorities of tolerating and sheltering the activities of Bulgarian agents. It is worth quoting extensively from this document :

> The present Greek Government, having accepted to govern the country under extremely difficult conditions and circumstances, set out, as one of its primary objectives, the bridging of the chasm —which bad fortune had created between the Greek and the German peoples—, the re-establishment of the long-existing feelings of friendship and mutual esteem, and the *rapprochement* of the Greek people with the objectives and tendencies of New Germany. [The Government] finds itself in the difficult position of having to acknowledge that its efforts in these directions have not brought the desired results, principally on account of the utterly unpsychological attitude of certain military authorities toward the Bulgarian claims in districts inhabited by crushing majorities of pure Greek populations for which the Greek people have for decades, paid with heavy sacrifices.

> The Greek Government... would feel deep gratitude if it were assisted in its efforts by the German Government and by its local political and military representatives. [The Government's efforts] would be successfully carried out by the removal from German-occupied Greek Macedonia of every center of Bulgarian propaganda. Such are mainly today the Bulgarian Association of Thessaloniki and the Bulgarian liaison officers attached to the various German city headquarters...[41]

Greek protests, however, had little if any effect. The Bulgarian liaison officers—among whom a Lieutenant Kaltchev played a major role— continued to organize militarily their followers hoping that eventually they would be invited by the Germans to take over the administration of the region. Bulgarian hopes appeared to have a better chance when Greek partisans began to make their appearance on the mountains of Macedonia. In the Italian administered zone, the authorities permitted the pro-Bulgarian Slavophones to form armed security units,[42] which were entrusted with the maintenance of ''order and peace.''[43] It is interesting to note that, from the beginning, these newly-formed security units—popularly known as ''Ohrana battalions''[44]—did not receive their orders from the Italian

---

41. *GFM*, File No I/3b/1942, Nr. E/595/1/3a/v dated October 23, 1942. In the knowledge of the author, this is the first time that this document is published.

42. Naltsas, *op. cit.*, p. 217.

43. Zapheiropoulos, *op. cit.*, p. 19.

44. ''Comments and Oral Statement Made by the Liaison Representative of

authorities but from the Bulgarian liaison officers. In a short time they became notorious for their persecution of the Greek inhabitants. In the Kastoria region alone, they burned more than forty villages.[45]

The Italian Armistice in November 1943, removed a serious obstacle from Bulgaria's efforts to extend her control over most of Greek Macedonia. The Germans, engaged in critical combat in both the Eastern and Italian fronts, had neither the units to spare for occupation duty, nor the time to investigate the conduct of their Bulgarian allies in their zone of occupation. In the summer of 1943 they offered them an additional strip of land west of the Strymon river which included most of the Kilkis Prefecture and the northern part of the Thessaloniki Prefecture, including Chalkidiki.[46] After the war, at the Sofia trial of the leaders of the wartime Bulgarian government, the Crown Counselor, Jordan Sevov, revealed that the Bulgarian Government had debated at that time whether to extend the zone of occupation to include Thessaloniki. It had failed to reach an agreement primarily on account of the General Staff which raised objections for purely military considerations.[47] Finally, in the closing days of the occupation—late in 1944—the Bulgarians attempted clandestinely to extend their military authority into three more districts of Central and Western Macedonia, namely Edessa, Kastoria and Florina. This move, which was bound to be short-lived, had no other meaning than to register Bulgarian presence in a Greek region long claimed by the Bulgarians, apparently in the remote hope that the course of international developments might allow them to remain in possession of the regions they occupied.

On September 9, the Bulgarian Government was overthrown by the Fatherland Front. However, despite the Government change, the Bulgarians still hoped to remain in the occupied regions on the pretext of fighting the Germans. Stern Allied demarches forced them to leave all Greek lands by late November 1944.

Greece on Parts II and III of the Report, 'Memorandum on the Slavophones of Greece',' United Nations, Security Council, *Official Records*, 2nd year, Special Supplement, No. 2, Report by the Commission of Investigation concerning Greek Frontier Incidents to the Security Council, Vol. III (S/360 Rev. 1; July 28, 1950), (New York, 1950), pp. 323 - 327, [hereafter referred to as ''Memorandum on the Slavophones of Greece''].

45. *Ibid.*, p. 326.

46. Petros Monastiriotis, Οἱ Πρῶσσοι τῶν Βαλκανίων [The Prussians of the Balkans], (Cairo : 1944), p. 60.

47. Report by the Greek Ambassador to Ankara, dated January 10, 1945, *GFM*, A/7931/1945.

108

B. The Bulgarians in Yugoslav Macedonia

On April 17, 1941, Bulgarian troops were permitted to enter Southern Yugoslavia and take over large regions of Yugoslav Macedonia for "administrative purposes." As was the case with Greek Eastern Macedonia and Thrace, the Bulgarians acted on the assumption that the "New Lands" had been definitely annexed to the Bulgarian Fatherland. Their jurisdiction was extended to the whole of Yugoslav Macedonia except the Upper Vardar above Skopje and the north-western district around Tetovo, Gostivar and Kičevo which were allotted to the Italians.[48]

Contrary to Greek Macedonia, the Bulgarians were received here, on the whole, by a friendly population. Historical ties uniting the Slav populations on both sides of the frontier, and Bulgarian propaganda which had not ceased during the inter-war years, had kept alive the pro-Bulgarian feelings of the inhabitants.

From the first days of the occupation, the Bulgarian Government set out a carefully studied plan which, it was hoped, would induce the inhabitants of the region to demand the formal annexation of Yugoslav Macedonia to Bulgaria.[49] A major educational program was initiated whereby Bulgarian elementary and secondary schools staffed with teachers from Bulgaria were established in almost all towns and even villages. A Bulgarian university—The King Boris University—was opened in Skopje. Administratively, the Bulgarians attempted to consolidate their control by reallocating certain districts to form a new province including parts of Bulgarian Macedonia. The July 1942 Citizenship Law, which in Greek Macedonia became the pseudo-legal basis for the eviction of thousands of Greeks from their homes, was used here as a pretext to compel many Serbs to flee to Serbia.[50]

The Bulgarian authorities made no secret of their cooperation with the Bulgaro-Macedonian nationalists, especially the followers of the I.M.R.O., many of whom had joined special Bulgarian armed units to assist in the policing of the region.[51] The task of forming these units was assigned to General Ivan Marinov who accepted in his staff two I.M.R.O. liaison officers named Grupčev and Nastev.[52] At the same time, a Bulga-

48. Barker, *op. cit.*, p. 78.
49. "Filov's Diary," *Otetsestven Front, op. cit.*
50. Barker, *op. cit.*, p. 79.
51. "The trial of the I.M.R.O. followers in Sofia, August, 1946," *Glas* (Belgrade), August 19, 1946.
52. Secret Report, *GFM*, A/24317/2/1949.

rian nationalist organization named "Opstestvena-Cila," was entrusted with the task of preparing the ground for the eventual, gradual integration into Bulgaria of the districts not included in the Bulgarian zone of occupation. Political committees of this organization were set up in Tetovo, Gostivar, Kićevo, and Debar.[53]

However, despite the fact that all the prerequisites for the success of the Bulgarian objectives existed, it became increasingly evident that the native population was daily becoming disillusioned with the Bulgarians. A variety of reasons could be cited for this unexpected development. The most important was, apparently, the fact that the Slav peasants were surprised by the misconduct of the Bulgarian soldiers, who, far from acting as liberators, were frequently involved in situations very common in an army entering a foreign country. The Bulgarian authorities tried to correct the situation, but the first bad impressions remained. Then came stern reprisals by the Bulgarian occupation authorities, sometimes against innocent peasants, for murders of Bulgarian soldiers and officers committed by communist partisans. In April 1942, the communists attempted an uprising in the Monastir-Prilep district which was put down by the Bulgarian Army and Gendarmerie executing twelve local communists. The population reacted with mass demonstrations causing the death of the Bulgarian Gendarmerie commander and 15 gendarmes. In turn, the Bulgarians executed many villagers, men and women.[54]

Rather than project the elements held in common, these developments tended to stress those dividing the inhabitants of Yugoslav Macedonia from the Bulgarians. The strong regionalist spirit revolted against the lordly attitude of the Bulgarian authorities, a fact properly exploited by the communists, as will be seen in a subsequent chapter. The Bulgarians were, thus, engaged in a chain reaction, since reprisals against the partisans drove the native Slavs even farther away from Sofia and into the arms of the communists who were fighting under the slogan for a "Macedonian state" within Yugoslavia.

The last attempt by nationalist Bulgarians to win over Macedonia came when the Germans were preparing to withdraw from the Balkans. Ivan Mihailov, chief of the I.M.R.O. who had maintained friendly relations with the Nazis, attempted to establish an autonomous Macedonian state.[55]

---

53. *Ibid.*

54. "Monthly Confidential Report of the [Greek] Ministry of Interior," May 1942. In *GFM* Archives.

55. *Makedonska Tribuna*, (Indianapolis, U.S.A.), organ of Mihailov's (I.M.R.O.) followers in the United States, wrote in February 22, 1951 that in the closing months

But history had outrun him and rendered his plan outdated. Now the initiative had definitely passed to the communists who began to exhibit their lively interest in the potentialities of Macedonian politics.

THE GREEK AND YUGOSLAV GOVERNMENTS-IN-EXILE

At this point it becomes timely to review briefly the role played by the Greek and Yugoslav governments-in-exile with respect to the political future of the Balkans in general and Macedonia in particular. It is true that at the end, the real protagonists of the Macedonian Question during the years of the occupation remained Boris' Bulgaria and the Balkan communist parties. However, from 1941 to 1943, the Greek and Yugoslav governments, officially recognized by the Allies as the legitimate governments of their respective countries, were actively engaged in trying to shape in advance the post-war political destinies of their countries, a fact which cannot be allowed to pass unnoticed.

The Greek Government of Emmanuel Tsouderos had no sooner escaped from Crete following the capture of that island by the Germans in late May 1941, when it laid down the principles it thought should guide its policy after liberation. In a long memorandum prepared for King George II, Prime Minister Tsouderos emphasized that one of the deadliest threats to the security of the country was the establishment of an "autonomous Macedonia." Such a new "state," Tsouderos contended, would separate Greece from Yugoslavia, her traditional ally in the Balkans, and would result by necessity in a Yugoslav-Bulgarian *rapprochement* for the establishment of a South-Slav federation. Greece ought to prevent such a development at all costs.[56]

All through the summer and fall of 1941, the Greek and Yugoslav governments-in-exile were in close contact exchanging views as to postwar alignments in the Balkans. The Greeks had made clear to the Yugoslavs that they were willing to cooperate against the establishment of an autonomous Bulgarian-sponsored state in Macedonia, provided the Yugoslavs were ready to declare that they opposed the idea of a South-Slav federa-

---

of the German occupation, Mihailov had many talks with Bulgarian officials in Yugoslav Macedonia. In his talks he tried to convince them of the wrong policy they pursued trying to annex Yugoslav Macedonia to Bulgaria. Mihailov argued that the best course was first to adopt an autonomous status for Macedonia. Bramos, [First Edition], *op. cit.*, p. 136.

56. Secret Memorandum dated July 4, 1941, *GFM*, File A/16/1941.

tion which was viewed with apprehension by the Greek Government.[57] In August, the Yugoslavs informed the Greeks that they, indeed, opposed both the formation of a South-Slav union and any territorial changes against Bulgaria.[58]

Negotiations lasting until the end of 1941 finally led to the conclusion of an agreement, signed on January 15, 1942, by Prime Ministers Tsouderos and Slobodan Jovanović, concerning the establishment of a Balkan Union whose primary objective was "the Balkans for the Balkan peoples."[59] The accord was signed with Great Brirain's consent. The Soviet Union, although it could not be expected to view it as a happy development for her Balkan objectives, raised no opposition at the time of its signing.[60]

There could be no doubt that the agreement aimed principally at forming a *cordon sanitaire* against the expansionist policy of the Bulgarians, although Tsouderos had publicly stated on March 10, 1942, that the Greeks and the Yugoslavs looked with pleasure at the participation in the Union of the "lawfully constituted" governments of Rumania, Bulgaria and even Albania."[61] Secretly, the Greek Government agreed to Bulgaria's accession to the Union on condition that she would accept the strategic rectification of the Bulgarian-Greek frontier in favor of Greece and submit to certain restrictions which would render her incapable of committing a new aggression against her neighbors. To this Great Britain and the Soviet Union aggreed.[62]

In the meantime, the partisan movements in the occupied Balkan countries were growing in importance, and it soon became evident that the communists exerted a dominant influence in most of them. As the Allies were more and more interested in fomenting guerrilla warfare in the German occupied lands, they would not allow—at least at this state—the governments-in-exile to jeopardize their plans by untimely declarations of political solutions to be adopted after liberation. In September 24, 1942, Tsouderos and Jovanović met again in London and, under pressure, declared that for the duration of the war any pronouncement on the policy

57. *Ibid.*

58. Greek Ambassador to London Simopoulos, to Prime Minister Tsouderos, August 30, 1941; *GFM*, A/2961/1/θ/1941.

59. Text in *GFM*, File A/16/1942.

60. Greek Ambassador to Kuybyshev Pipinelis, to Prime Minister Tsouderos, January 25, 1942, *GFM*, A/7471/1942.

61. Prime Minister Tsouderos'speech at Oxford University. *GFM*. File A/16/1942.

62. Greek Ambassador to London Diamantopoulos, to the GFM June 10, 1942; *GFM*, A/10503/1942.

to be pursued toward their neighbors at the end of the war was premature. In a move undoubtedly aimed at courting the Bulgarians, the two Prime Ministers stated that they had no intentions against the independence of their neighbors.[63]

Thus ended the last attempt of the nationalist governments of Yugoslavia and Greece to solve definitely their mutual problems and to pave the way for sound, friendly relations between all Balkan states. Their effort failed primarily because of the emergence of Tito as the uncontestable political and military power in Yugoslavia. However, even had this not happened, it is doubtful whether their ambitious plan to solidify peace in the Balkans by compelling Bulgaria to renounce her traditional expansionist designs over Macedonia, could have any significant value. From the moment Tito was acknowledged as the main spokesman for Yugoslavia, the relations between Greece and Yugoslavia assumed the form of those between a communist, ambitious and expansionist-minded regime and a hard-pressed Greek government in a country seriously threatened by an armed communist insurrection whose main instigator was the new regime in Belgrade.

---

63. Text of the declaration in *GFM*, File A/16/1942.

CHAPTER VI

WAR AND OCCUPATION IN MACEDONIA:
THE ROLE OF THE COMMUNIST PARTIES

THE STRUGGLE FOR YUGOSLAV MACEDONIA [1]

A. The Conflict between the CPY and CPB

As soon as the Germans and their Bulgarian allies occupied Yugoslav Macedonia in April 1941, the communists, as if by signal, raised the banner of partisan warfare which in three and half years would bring them to absolute power.

The Regional Committee of the Yugoslav Communist Party in Macedonia immediately showed signs of insubordination toward the Central Committee of the Party. The first clash came over the issue of the deportation by the Bulgarian occupation authorities of the thousands of Serbs who had settled over the inter-war years in Yugoslav Macedonia.[2] The local communist leader, Metodije Sharlo-Shatorov, favored the deportation which would de-Serbianize the region. The worst came when he began exhibiting separatist tendencies by trying to place the local communist organization under the control of the Communist Party of Bulgaria.

In less than two months after the German invasion, his attitude toward the Central Committee of the CPY hardened. He dismissed from the local Central Committee the Serbs, replaced them with pro-Bulgarians, and declared that he would obey no more the orders of the Yugoslav Central Committee because his organization constituted part of the CPB.[3]

---

1. Certain sections of this Chapter have previously been published in the journal *Balkan Studies*, Vol. III, No. 2, (1962) pp. 375-396, under the title "The Making of Yugoslavia's People's Republic of Macedonia."

2. Kulishevski, "1948 Congress Speech," *op. cit.*

3. *Ibid.* Also, General Apostolski, "Reminiscences from August 2, 1944," in *Ten Years from the Establishment of the PFR of Macedonia*, Part II, (Skopje, 1954). Also Svetovar Vukmanović-Tempo's speech in Belgrade, July 24, 1948, *GFM* A/45511/Bal/1948.

114

It was clearly evident that pro-Bulgarian sentiment, then at a high peak among the largest segment of the population of Yugoslav Macedonia, had trespassed ideological barriers and had afflicted even the Yugoslav communists.

It is interesting to note that Sharlo's alliance with the Bulgarian Party remained firm even after Germany's invasion of the Soviet Union.[4] The Yugoslavs accused their Bulgarian comrades of disseminating propaganda which called on Yugoslav Macedonians not to take arms against the occupation authorities—who were mostly Bulgarians—because, allegedly, the Macedonian people had found the realization of their national expectations under the Bulgarian regime.[5]

The Yugoslav communists, organizing at that time their partisan movement, could ill-afford to lose control over their own party organization in Macedonia. Difficult as it was to convince the native inhabitants to take arms against the Bulgarian occupation authorities, it seemed almost impossible to fight jointly the nationalist and communist Bulgarians. In their frustration, they appealed to Moscow. Although during the inter-war period the Comintern had pursued a pro-Bulgarian policy over the Macedonian Question, the desperate need of the Russians to harass the Germans caused them to rule in favor of the CPY which, thus, was given control over Macedonia.[6]

For a time the situation remained unaltered. The Bulgarian communists and Sharlo's followers adhered to their policy of not attacking the occupation authorities.[7] On August 25, Tito set up a new Regional Committee under Kulishevski, but though he had Comintern's support, he could not make any progress among the communists of Macedonia, let alone the masses.[8] Tito tried in vain to get control of the situation. His appeals to the Central Committee of the CPB brought no change in the latter's Macedonian policy. Sharlo and his followers continued to defy him. In Sep-

---

4. It is interesting to note that the Bulgarian communists refrained from condemning initially the invasion and occupation of Greek and Yugoslav territories.

5. Achillevs A. Kyrou, Ἡ Συνωμοσία ἐναντίον τῆς Μακεδονίας, 1940-1949, [The Conspiracy Against Macedonia, 1940-1949], (Athens: "Aetos," 1950), p. 61, quoting Yugoslav and Bulgarian sources.

6. Lazar Mojsov, *The Bulgarian Worker's Party and the Macedonian National Question*, (Belgrade: Borba, 1948), p. 83.

7. Kulishevski's, "1948 Congress Speech", *op. cit.*

8. Elizabeth Barker, *Macedonia; Its Place in Balkan Power Politics* (London: Royal Institute of International Affairs, 1950), p. 89.

tember 1941, he was forced to denounce Sharlo openly.[9] Meanwhile, Kulishevski's efforts to organize partisan units were frustrated when in their initial baptism of fire his men were badly defeated. As misfortunes piled up for the Yugoslav communists, Kulishevski was arrested and the communist movement passed under firm Bulgarian control. The Central Committee of the Bulgarian Party dispatched from Sofia Petar Bogdanov and later Boyan Balgarianov who pursued a policy of no opposition to the Bulgarian occupation authorities. Yugoslav sources admit that the rule of the Bulgarian communists over the Macedonian Party organization remained dominant until 1943.[10]

However, relations between the CPY and the CPB had begun to show signs of improvement. Already by the end of 1942, the Bulgarian communists had initiated some form of cooperation with the Yugoslavs. They were even communicating with the Comintern through the channels of the CPY.[11] The recently formed Fatherland Front was moving away from the original position which called for no action. Now, Bulgarian communists began gradually to favor the tactics of the Yugoslav partisans though still they concentrated their efforts only in preparing their cadres for guerrilla warfare.[12] They did not engage in any activities which could be construed as aiming at the overthrow of the Sofia Government. Their primary preoccupation was to prevent the dispatch of Bulgarian soldiers to the Eastern front; to conduct passive resistance and to cultivate within the ranks of the Bulgarian Army the conviction that they should not fight against the Greek, Bulgarian, and Yugoslav partisans.[13]

---

9. Dedijer writes that Tito sent a letter to the Macedonian Central Committee in which he said : "The Macedonian Central Committee has failed to organize Partisan detachments, it has failed to organize any actions or sabotages, it has failed to act according to the request of the Comintern, but on the contrary, it has deliberately sabotaged these actions and run off to Sofia in order to escape our control." Vladimir Dedijer, *Tito* (New York : Simon and Schuster, 1953) p. 173.

10. Kulishevski, "1948 Congress Speech," *op. cit.*

11. Djoko Slijepcević, *The Macedonian Question; The Struggle for Southern Serbia.* (Chicago : The American Institute for Balkan Affairs, 1956), p. 213.

12. Slijepcević quotes a letter from the Secret Archives of the CPY written by Dr. Blagoje Nesković who was assigned by the Central Committee of the CPY as liaison to the Central Committee of the CPB. In the letter it appears that the Fatherland Front had, by this time, begun to press on with the formation of partisan units asking the Yugoslavs for advise. *Ibid.*, p. 215.

13. Blagoe Ivanov, "Answer to General Apostolski," *Rabotnitsesko Delo* (Sofia), May 23, 1949.

In Yugoslav Macedonia the situation did not change until the spring of 1943 when Tito's special emissary, Svetovar Vukmanović-Tempo, arrived in the region. Tempo, in addition to his personal skills and the full backing of his leader, was in possession of an ambitious plan by which the Yugoslav communists hoped to keep at least Yugoslav Macedonia under their control. This program was delineated by Tito in a letter to the Regional Macedonian Committee on January 16. At that time, Tito reproached the "outworn and liberal attitude towards autonomist tendencies of a national character," an obvious reference to the traditional pro-Bulgarian behavior of both the communists and the nationalists of the region. Instead, he promised that "the question of the existence, freedom, and independence of all peoples and, equally, of the Macedonian people" could be solved by means of the national liberation struggle. He went on to indicate that the principle of self-determination, to which the Communist Party ascribed, was conceivable only under conditions of "brotherhood and equality of peoples."[14] Thus, in rather ambiguous terms, Tito, as early as the beginning of 1943, gave evidence of his desire to give to Macedonia a form of self-government within the framework of Yugoslavia.

As soon as Tempo took over in Macedonia, partisan units began to make their appearance in the countryside and gradually to engage in counter-offence. Undoubtedly their position was enhanced by the fact that Moscow finally dispatched a direct order to the Bulgarian communists to initiate partisan warfare, particularly in Macedonia which was occupied by the Bulgarian Army.[15] Tempo did not restrict his activities to Yugoslav Macedonia but even came in touch with the Greek communist partisans and attempted to extend his influence over their organization as well.

B. The 1943 Jajce Resolution and its Impact

On August 2, 1943, the Central Committee of the Communist Party of Macedonia was elected in Prespa. In turn it initiated the formation of a "National Liberation Army." Early in October, its General Staff issued

---

14. Mojsov, *The Bulgarian Communist Party, op. cit.*, pp. 150, 168, 173, as quoted in Barker, *op. cit.*, p. 91.
15. Greek Ambassador to Kuybytshev, Politis, to the Greek Government-in-exile, (No. 139, dated April 4, 1943). *GFM* A 504/1943. Ambassador Politis wrote that he had learned from good authority that the Russians had given specific orders to the Bulgarian communists to start partisan activity, although such orders had not gone out to the communist parties of other occupied countries for fear of prematurily exposing their organizations.

a manifesto declaring that the Macedonian people met all the requirements necessary to win their freedom and independence, to gain on the
basis of self-determination true equality, and to build their own state in
brotherly unity with the Yugoslav peoples. Within the framework of this
unity, it added, the Macedonian people had all the conditions for realizing
their age-long dream unification.[16]

This was the most explicit definition up to that time of Tito's plans
for Macedonia. However, it seems that the dangerous implications for the
communist movements in Bulgaria and Greece of an open pursuance of
such a policy, compelled the Yugoslavs to proceed with caution.[17] Thus, on
November 29, 1943, the Jajce Conference of the Anti-Fascist Council of
National Liberation of Yugoslavia, which decided the organization of Yugoslavia on a federal basis, avoided any specific mention of the frontiers
of the proposed federative republic of Macedonia.

Even though no specific mention of boundaries was made, the Jajce
Resolution became an historic landmark in Yugoslav history and the beginning of more complications for the perennial Macedonian Question. The
Resolution put the Yugoslavs on record as, first, recognizing the existence
of a ‘‘Macedonian nation,’’ which had no historical foundation; second,
establishing a Macedonian state which, though dependent on the Central
Government at Belgrade, was accepted as equal to the other federative republics of Yugoslavia with substantial authority in self-government, and,
finally, disavowing completely Bulgarian pretentions over a land known
of old for the pro-Bulgarian sentiment of its inhabitants. The Resolution
stipulated that:

> On the basis of the right of all nations to self-determination inclu-
> ding the union with or secession from other nations...the Anti-
> Fascist Council of the National Liberation of Yugoslavia passes
> the following decisions :

> ... Yugoslavia is being built up on a federal principle which will
> ensure full equality for the nations of Serbia, Croatia, Slovenia,
> Macedonia, Montenegro, Bosnia and Hercegovina.[18]

Despite its initial hesitation, the Soviet Government and Party accepted the Jajce Program.[19] This did not apparently impede the Bulgarian

16. Barker, *op. cit.*, p. 93.
17. Lazar Mojsov, ‘‘About the South-Slav Federation,’’ *Kommunist* [Supple-
ment], (Belgrade, July-September, 1950).
18. Text in Barker, *op. cit*, pp. 94-95.
19. H. F. Armstrong, *Tito and Goliath* (New York : MacMillan and Co.,
1955), p. 187.

communists who, finding themselves in an inferior position similar to that of the Greek and Yugoslav communists in 1923-24, reacted strongly against the Yugoslav plans. The Fatherland Front issued a declaration in December 1943, less than a month after the Jajce Conference. It reiterated the well-known theory which Bulgarians, irrespective of their ideological inclinations, have advocated over the years, namely, that Macedonia is the cradle of the Bulgarian renaissance for which the Bulgarians have fought costly wars. It rejected outright the Yugoslav federative plan for Macedonia and declared itself in favor of the old slogan "Macedonia for the Macedonians," and the creation of "an integral, free and independent Macedonia which would be guaranteed by the Soviet Union and the democratic powers."[20]

For the Yugoslav communists, this was going too far. Having suffered frustrating humiliations all through the inter-war period on account of their Bulgarian comrades' expansionist policy over Macedonia, and having paid with prison terms and torture their stubborness to defend the unpopular Bulgarian-inspired directives of the Comintern, they could have no pity for the present position of the Bulgarians. This was especially so at a time when Bulgaria was condemned for having allied with the invaders of the Soviet Union, and when the latter had already sanctioned the Yugoslav plan. On January 24, 1944, Tito wrote to Georgi Dimitrov, then in Moscow, denouncing the Fatherland Front's position as being identical with the policy pursued at that time by the Germans, a policy clearly "hostile to the national-liberation struggle."[21]

In fact, the Yugoslav communists did not need to fear the Bulgarian objections. The tide of the war was reversing, and since they had already secured Soviet approval of their plan, they had at least secured control over their own part of Macedonia. In the meantime, as events were soon to prove, the Yugoslavs had prepared a grand design which, had it been realized, would have rendered them the undisputed masters of a sovietized Balkan Peninsula. Their plan aimed primarily at driving the Bulgarians into a South-Slav federation in which Yugoslavia would be represented by her six federative republics with Bulgaria forming the seventh. Also insured in the realization of this plan was the subordination of all three parts of Macedonia to Yugoslavia by way of the Federative Macedonian Republic whose nucleus would have been the Vardar region. To achieve the incorporation of Greek Macedonia — which would provide Yugoslavia with

20. Kulishevski, "1948 Congress Speech," *op. cit.*
21. Mojsov, "About the South-Slav Federation," *op. cit.*

her long-sought exit to the Aegean — the Yugoslav communists attempted to extend their influence among the small Slav minority living at that time in Greece, as well as among the leadership of the Greek Communist Party. For they clearly realized that were they to entertain any hopes for placing Greek Macedonia under their control, they would have to lure first the Greek communists.

THE STRUGGLE FOR GREEK MACEDONIA

Greek Macedonia—or more specifically the Western part of Greek Macedonia, since the Eastern part was under Bulgarian occupation—became the most contested region. Developments in this region during the last two years of the occupation, 1943-1944, have long confused those attempting to ascertain what really happened there. This is rather understandable since the various interests appear to have been thoroughly confused. The German and Italian occupation authorities, interested in maintaining security in the region, allowed their Bulgarian allies, who hoped to seize the region, to engage in propaganda and terror. The Greek communists organized strong units, and in their effort to assume control, were engaged in a struggle against the occupation authorities, the Bulgarian-organized "Ohrana battalions," the nationalist Greek partisans and later even the pro-Yugoslav Slavophones. The Greek puppet Government in Athens, through its officials and Gendarmerie in the region, tried in vain to contain Bulgarian and communist (Greek or Yugoslav) ambitions. Its efforts were discredited since it was considered to be an instrument of the Germans. The Greek Government-in-exile, through diplomatic representations to the Allies, tried equally to offset the gains of the Bulgarians and the communists of Yugoslavia.

That was the situation in Greek Macedonia; a confused situation, indeed, which will be examined in subsequent pages.

A. The KKE and the "Slav-Macedonians"

During the four years of the Metaxas' dictatorship, the outlawed KKE was reduced to insignificant numbers, abandoned even by some of its leaders; the German occupation, however, gave the Party the opportunity to organize itself again. In this it was assisted by the rather strange attitude of the Bulgarians who, through their Embassy in Athens, obtained from the Germans the release of a number of prominent communists interned in Greek prisons. Some of them were from Macedonia but, apparently, there could be no direct connection between them and the plans of Filov Government with respect to Macedonia.[22] How important some of them were for the KKE is evidenced by the release of Andreas Tzimas, a member of the Central Committee of the KKE, who was assigned by the Party the task of organizing partisan units in Macedonia. While Tzimas was recruiting members to form the first cells of the EAM (National Liberation Front) in Macedonia, he came in contact with some small armed groups composed mostly of pro-Bulgarian Slavophones who had gone underground probably at the suggestion of the Bulgarian communists.[23] The Slavophones in Western Macedonia, though barely forming five per cent of the entire population of Greek Macedonia, played such an important role in the power struggle between Greek, Yugoslav and Bulgarian communists, that their activities require careful investigation.

As in Yugoslav Macedonia, the first Slavophone communists were clearly pro-Bulgarian.[24] However, very few joined communist bands in 1941-1942, since most of them had been attracted by the Bulgarian propaganda directed either via the Monastir Bulgarian Army Headquarters, or via the Bulgarian Association of Thessaloniki. Some insignificant attempts to form separate ''Slav-Macedonian'' bands ended in failure.[25]

The Greek communists, through the EAM, began by early 1943, to have some success in organizing their movement. Still they were not certain whether to limit their activities against the Germans to strikes and sabotages in the cities, or to form partisan units and fight in the mountains.[26] Only later, when contact was established with the Yugoslav partisans, were the Greek communists assisted by their comrades across the border in or-

---

22. Two explanations may be offered: either that the staff of the Bulgarian Embassy in Athens was composed of communist sympathizers, a hypothesis which is substantiated by the fact that prior to the German invasion of the Soviet Union the Bulgarian communists were allowed considerable freedom of action; or, that the Bulgarian Government had hopes that it could utilize some Slav-speaking Greek communist cadres to carry out its own plans in Macedonia.

23. Kyrou, *op. cit.*, p. 51.

24. Naum Peyov, ''About the SNOB (Army) in the ranks of ELAS in Aegean Macedonia,'' *Voice of the Aegeans* (Skopje), December 1, 1950; Also Achillevs Kyrou, *op. cit.*, p. 51.

25. All these events, however, played no important role at the time. Even the EAM, as a mass movement had a very limited following. Nationalist Greek organizations like the ''Defenders of Northern Greece'' and PAO were more active, attracting a greater number of young patriots than any other organization at that early stage of the partisan movement.

26. *Radio Belgrade* (July 24, 1948) broadcasting a speech by Vukmanović - Tempo before the Congress of the CPY. *GFM* A/45511/Bal/1948.

ganizing their movement according to orthodox communist revolutionary doctrine.[27]

By the summer of 1943, two situations began to take shape. In Yugoslav Macedonia, Tito's partisans had consolidated their control of the regional communist organization and were engaged in full-scale partisan warfare. On the Greek side, the EAM had gradually grown in numbers, formed its armed organization, the ELAS (National People's Liberation Army), and begun timidly to be engaged in partisan activities. At the same time certain "Slav-Macedonian" elements began to make their presence felt. Such was the case of TITAN, an organization whose objectives coincided with those of the Yugoslav Macedonian partisans. Among its leading members were Naum Peyov, M. Keramidjiev, and M. Antonofski. These men occupied later important posts in the People's Republic of Macedonia at Skopje where they found refuge in 1949 following the failure of the guerrilla war.[28] At the same time Lazar Terpofski—a Moscow-educated "Slav-Macedonian" executed by the Germans late in 1943—was organizing small political groups of "Slav-Macedonians," within the ranks of the EAM-ELAS. The aim of these nuclei was to attract not only the Slavophones who had espoused the cause of the nationalist Bulgarians but, also, all the Slav-speaking inhabitants of the region who, in their majority, had remained loyal to Hellenism or neutral to the efforts of Bulgarian propaganda. Since an increasing number of these Slavophones was daily joining the ELAS—either out of patriotic motives or because they were drafted into it—a systematic work of proselytism was important to attract them to the cause of the Yugoslav Macedonians.

B. Yugoslav Interest in the Greek Partisan Movement

It was in the summer of 1943 that the first official Yugoslav communist intervention in the Greek communist movement took place. It assumed the form of a visit by Vukmanović-Tempo to the headquarters of the Greek partisans in Greek Macedonia. At a conference held between Yugoslav and Greek partisan leaders of all factions, including the Greek nationalist organizations EDES and EKKA,[29] Tempo discussed ways and means of improving military cooperation against the occupation forces.

---

27. *Ibid*. Also, Zahariades, former Secretary-General of the KKE, admitted that at that time the Greek communists depended mostly on the Yugoslavs; Nikos Zahariades, *Δέκα Χρόνια Πάλης* [Ten Years of Struggle], 1950, p. 41.

28. Zapheiropoulos, *op. cit.*, pp. 63-64.

29. *Ibid.*, p. 56.

Then he passed on to the subject of the Slavophones whom, for the first time, he claimed officially as Yugoslavs of ""Macedonian" nationality. His first point was to work out a plan, in cooperation with the Greek partisans, so that the thousands of Slavophones who had been attracted by Bulgarian propaganda and declared themselves Bulgarians, would desert the enemy ranks. Such an attitude exhibited by so many Slavophones was considered by the Yugoslavs as a deadly threat to their plans to make ""Macedonians" out of the Slav-speaking inhabitants of the region. His second point was to convince the Greek communists to let the Macedonian communists of Yugoslavia organize the Slavophones of Greece under an independent command. Although the Greek communists were indebted to their Yugoslav comrades for all sorts of assistance, they refused to accept the Yugoslav proposals.[30] Instead, they concurred to organize the Slavophones as an integral part of the ELAS and put into true application the principle of ""equal rights.""[31] As a result, in partisan occupied territories where the Slav idiom was known to a large segment of the population, schools began to function and papers published in that idiom.

The agreements with Tempo and the overt secessionist pronouncements of certain "Slav-Macedonian" leaders created a strong opposition within the ranks of the EAM. In its first Pan-Western Macedonian Congress held on August 10, 1943, certain EAM representatives strongly criticized the "Slav-Macedonian" leaders for engaging in seditious propaganda. They argued that the only concession able to be made was the granting of equal rights to the Slavophones in a future ""people's democracy.""[32]

---

30. William Hardy McNeil, *The Greek Dilemma; War and Aftermath* (Philadelphia : J. B. Lippincott Co., 1947), pp. 264-265.

31. Zahariades, writing after the Tito-Cominform split, said that the Greek communists had concluded during the occupation an agreement of cooperation with the Yugoslav communists but at the explicit terms that the Yugoslavs would cease their subversion of the Greek communist movement in Macedonia through propaganda among the "Slav-Macedonians." Zahariades, *op. cit.*, p. 41.

Similarly, the Bulgarian communists also accused Tempo's activities in Greek Macedonia. Bulgarian General Blagoe Ivanov writing in *Rabotnitsesko Delo*, May 23, 1949, said :

This character [Tempo], even then, [1943-1944] conducted an open struggle against the Greek comrades, against the KKE, and demanded, under the mask of communism, to go as far as Thessaloniki; to detach Greek Macedonia and to place it in the service of Serbian chauvinism. Naturally, the Greek communists had to react strongly against this line.

32. Zapheiropoulos, *op. cit.*, pp. 48-50.

C. The Slav-Macedonian National Liberation Front (S.N.O.F.)

Following Tempo's visit, the number of "Slav-Macedonians" joining the EAM-ELAS began to increase substantially, as did their pressure on the leadership of the KKE to grant them permission to form their own independent units. Their demand was halfway met when permission was given for the formation of the SNOF (Slav-Macedonian National Liberation Front). The SNOF made its appearance early in 1944, though there is evidence to suggest that clandestinely it had already existed for some months.[33]

The establishment of the SNOF was allowed only after it was made clear that it would remain under the command of the EAM and would fight, along with the ELAS, for the establishment of a communist regime in Greece in which the "Slav-Macedonians" would enjoy equality of rights. Apparently, "equality of rights" was not a suitable slogan for those extremist elements among the "Slav-Macedonians" who had fully espoused the Yugoslav views for the political future of Macedonia. Thus, the months which followed the formation of the SNOF appear to have been a period of constant clashes between the nationalist-minded Greeks of the EAM and the Yugoslav-oriented members of the SNOF.[34]

In February 1944, an Executive Committee of the SNOF was established with Pascal Mitrofski, Lazar Papalazarou, L. Lallas as members and Zisis Papatrayannis as secretary-general. Naum Peyov and M. Keramidjiev were appointed regional political advisers.[35] The SNOF pressed anew for formation of purely "Slav-Macedonian" partisan bands in Western Macedonia, which would operate independedly of the ELAS command. The ELAS, facing the rise of opposition within its ranks, rejected SNOF's demands. Peyov, one of the most extremist SNOF leaders, revolted

33. Christopher M. Woodhouse, *Apple of Discord: A Survey of Recent Greek Politics in their International Setting* (London: Hutchinson and Co., Ltd., 1948), p. 64.

34. Unfortunately, to trace the events of that period, one has to rely on accounts inaccurately reported because of partial knowledge of the facts or because of bias. Careful scrutiny of all available sources, examined in the light of research in official documents, may, probably, provide a better insight into the events of that crucial period. However, the author is not fully convinced that all the truth has been unveiled, and it may take decades before the existing gaps are covered. Unfortunately, these efforts might be further complicated by the fact that "Slav-Macedonian" *émigrés* in Skopje have been engaged in recent years — for obvious political reasons — in distorting the events, as the author has been convinced by some careful spot checking.

35. Zapheiropoulos, *op. cit.*, pp. 65-66.

in April 1944 against the ELAS and was forced to flee to Yugoslav Macedonia where he was offered refuge.[86] The leadership of the armed bands of the SNOF passed to Gotsev, an equally outspoken advocate for the incorporation of Greek Macedonia into Yugoslavia.

The conclusion from this confusing situation was that, at that time, the communist led EAM had no consistent policy with regard to Macedonia and more specifically toward the secessionist demands of the "Slav-Macedonians." Whereas the KKE officially was proclaiming that Greek Macedonia was an inseparable part of Greece,[87] locally, in Western Macedonia, the EAM adjusted its tactics according to the beliefs, sentiments and even opportunistic considerations of one or another of the local chieftains. One reason was probably the fact that by 1944 the EAM had been infiltrated by a large number of alien, non-Greek elements, who favored either Bulgarian autonomist plans or Yugoslav slogans for a united Macedonia within a federal Yugoslavia.[88]

Meanwhile, the Yugoslav communists faced with serious problems in their own part of Macedonia, could ill-afford, on account of the hasty action of a few "Slav-Macedonian" extremists in Greece, to provoke an open split with the Greek communists over the future of Greek Macedonia. Relations between the two parties were friendly. The boundary line had for all practical purposes been eliminated and Yugoslav Macedonian partisans frequently entered Greece in the course of fighting against the Germans. However, in many cases they crossed the Greek border solely to contact loyal elements among the "Slav-Macedonians" whom they ad-

---

36. *The Voice of the Aegeans*, December 1, 1950, (article by Peyov); Also, Zapheiropoulos, *op. cit.*, p. 71.

37. On July 10, 1943, the Polit Bureau of the Central Committee of the KKE, issued the following decision which was published in *Rizospastis*:

> The KKE, front-running fighter in the great struggle for the freedom, independence and [territorial] integrity of Greece, will develop further the national liberation struggle of the Greek people until the *independence* and *territorial integrity* of Greece are fully restituted. It calls on the entire Greek people, on all the organizations and on all the parties, to join their forces in an all-national liberation struggle to save Greek Macedonia and Western Thrace and to liberate enslaved Greece... Long live Greek Macedonia and Western Thrace.

Republished in *Πέντε Χρόνια Ἀγῶνες, 1931-1936* [Annex, New Edition], (Athens: Central Committee of the KKE, 1946), pp. 435-436 [Italics added].

38. Christopher Naltsas, *Τὸ Μακεδονικὸν Ζήτημα καὶ ἡ Σοβιετικὴ Πολιτικὴ* [The Macedonian Question and Soviet Policy], (Thessaloniki: Society for Macedonian Studies, Institute for Balkan Studies, 1954), p. 285.

vised and assisted in propagating the idea of a united Macedonian state among the Slavophones.[39]

In early summer 1944, the Yugoslavs finally convinced the EAM to allow Peyov and the "Slav-Macedonians" forced to flee to Yugoslav Macedonia, to return to Greece.[40] Their arrival in Greece gave more impetus to secessionist, pro-Yugoslav propaganda. In a meeting held at Halara on August 2, 1944, the Greek communists finally accepted one of the SNOF's major demands, namely, the drafting into the SNOF of unlimited numbers of Slavophones.[41] This concession led to the formation of the first SNOF battalion—the Gotsev battalion—with, allegedly, 700 men. Although nominally under ELAS command, the battalion soon began to pursue its own policies.

As the war in Macedonia neared its end, a new development became apparent. Unknown to the EAM, the communist, pro-Yugoslav "Slav-Macedonians" of the SNOF, entered into negotiations with the "reactionary," pro-Bulgarian "Slav-Macedonians" of the "Ohrana battalions" in order to induct the latter into the SNOF. Exposed as collaborating with the occupation authorities, they responded with eagerness, rightly considering it a unique opportunity to save their heads. By September, entire Ohrana units had joined the SNOF which, in turn, began to press the ELAS leadership to allow it to raise the SNOF battalion to division level.[42]

All through the month of September, relations between Gotsev and the ELAS command deteriorated rapidly especially since it became clear that Gotsev received his orders from the partisan headquarters of Yugoslav Macedonia. For a moment a crisis threatened to erupt within the ranks of the Greek partisans. General Sarafis, Supreme Commander of the ELAS, argued for the forceful disbandment of the Gotsev battalion while Siantos, Secretary General of the KKE, still favored the amelioration of the dispute through negotiation.[43] Indeed, an effort was made to ascertain fully Gotsev's true intentions. Early in October, "Captain" Slobotas (E. Kentros), member of the KKE and personal friend of Gotsev, visited him at his headquarters on orders from the Florina regional party organization. His report dated October 10, 1944, went as follows:

39. Zapheiropoulos, op. cit., p. 77.
40. The Voice of the Aegeans, December 1, 1950.
41. Zapheiropoulos, op. cit., p. 78.
42. Ibid., also, The Voice of the Aegeans, December 1, 1950.
43. Zapheiropoulos, op. cit., p. 88.

I called on Gotsev and I begged of him, in the name of our friendship, to tell me what was actually happening... He told me : "You
can do nothing because my battalion obeys neither the KKE nor the
ELAS. We are connected with Serbian Macedonia from where we
receive instructions and liaison men regularly, and in turn we send
them our own liaison men.

We received orders to draft as many men as possible, but they
should be pure Slav-Macedonians. The [Macedonian] Brigade of Serbia is giving us 5000 rifles and the appropriate number of sub-ma-
chine guns... Our conscription plan is on and we have accepted 300
new men. We will move on with the formation of a Slav-Macedonian Division...

... If you [the ELAS] want to attack me, I will not fight you, but
I will withdraw to Serbia. The Serbs have told us that "if they
chase you, you should come to us." [44]

Gotsev went on to tell Slobotas that neither the ELAS Command nor
he (Gotsev) could change the course of events. He contended that the
whole issue would be decided by the communist parties of Yugoslavia and
Greece. Slobotas concluded his report with the following revealing observations:

... All the reactionary elements which have played leading roles in
the Bulgarian propaganda [during the occupation] as well as leading
figures of the I.M.R.O. have assembled there [in the battalion]. They
have secretly assumed the command of the battalion, behind
Gotsev's back, without Gotsev realizing this because he is under their
influence. In fact, it is they who command the battalion, not
Gotsev. Unfortunately Gotsev cannot see this because he has been influenced by them. The situation in the battalion is chaotic. All the
fascist *comitadjis* find shelter there...

Two important facts became clear from this report. The first was
that the Yugoslav communists were rapidly arming the "Slav-Macedonians"
of the northwestern districts of Greek Macedonia, although they were careful not to provoke an open conflict with the ELAS, presumably in the
hope that the establishment of a communist regime in Greece would allow
the cession of Greek Macedonia to a "Macedonian" state of Yugoslav
making. The second fact was that by September 1944, I.M.R.O. elements
and well-known agents of the German and Bulgarian administration had
switched sides and had entered *en masse* the supposedly communist and
pro-Yugoslav SNOF. This probably explains why in the spring of 1945,

---

44. Original text in *GFM* Archives, A/30946/Γ5/1947, (translated by the author).

after the establishment of the legitimate Greek authorities in the region and the withdrawal of the followers of the SNOF to Yugoslav Macedonia, the Yugoslav authorities, fearing the Bulgarian propaganda, disbanded the organization and sent many of its members to distant northern regions.

Following Slobotas' report, the ELAS General Headquarters ordered the Ninth ELAS Division to attack the Gotsev battalion and compel it to submit to the orders of the ELAS. In the closing days of October, the battalion was, indeed, encircled and would have been annihilated were it not for the intervention of the regional KKE committee of Florina which vetoed the attack and helped Gotsev to cross the frontier into Yugoslavia.[45]

Liberation had by now come to Greece. On October 30, ELAS units and British liaison officers entered Thessaloniki following German evacuation of the city. A last effort, apparently at the suggestion of the Yugoslavs of Skopje, was made by the leadership of the "Slav-Macedonians" who had escaped to Yugoslavia. On October 23, SNOF leaders Gotsev, Keramidjiev and two others addressed to the KKE Regional Bureau for Macedonia a lengthy memorandum outlining a series of terms under which they would be willing to join the "liberation struggle" of the EAM.

Among the demands were, first, freedom to draft the Slavophones of the regions of Kastoria, Florina and Edessa into "pure" Macedonian units. (These were to have their own staff, although they would remain under the lines and political leadership of the EAM/ELAS); second, permission to establish in the above mentioned regions, a political organization — a "Macedonian National Liberation Front;" third, permission to establish a people's administration in Macedonian villages and towns. (The organization and government in these regions would be the responsibility of the "Macedonian National Liberation Front"); fourth, complete freedom to conduct open propaganda and indoctrination among the entire Macedonian people, and to teach them "the age-old, historical and national ideals of the Macedonian people, and also the fact that it is the inviolable right of the entire Macedonian people to live free and *united;*" fifth, end of the persecution of the "Macedonian" cadres, and sixth, end of the persecution, terror and falsification of the "true Macedonian conscience."[46]

It is evident that this document was dictated by the Yugoslav Mace-

---

45. Kostas Bramos, *Σλαυοκομμουνιστικαὶ Ὀργανώσεις ἐν Μακεδονίᾳ; Προπαγάνδα καὶ Ἐπαναστατικὴ Δρᾶσις* [Communist-Slav Organizations in Macedonia; Propaganda and Revolutionary Activities], Second Edition (Thessaloniki : 1960), p. 135; Curiously enough, the same Slobotas who had visited Gotsev in his headquarters, was the man behind the Florina KKE committee which saved Gotsev and his men.
46. Original text in *GFM* Archives.

donians, since less than a month before, Gotsev, in his talk with Slobotas, had displayed only a partial knowledge of the aims of the Yugoslav communists to establish a Yugoslav "Macedonian state" and cultivate a "Macedonian" nationality. The most important element revealed in this document was that the "Slav-Macedonians"—and through them the Yugoslav communists—felt free to demand openly from the Greek communists permission to prepare the ground for the eventual annexation of Greek Macedonia to Yugoslavia. As it was expected, the EAM turned down these demands which would have exposed the KKE as pursuing an anti-national, treacherous policy. However, the fact remains that the Yugoslav communists had given their Greek comrades notice of their ambitious plans for Macedonia. Once again Balkan nationalism was taking hold of the communists; only this time it was not the Bulgarian but the Yugoslav communists who were infected by an acute nationalist paroxism. The question unable to be answered at that time was whether, in the case of Greek Macedonia, Yugoslav nationalism or Greek nationalism would prevail.

D. The Wartime Position of the KKE on the National Issue

Throughout the occupation, the communist-led EAM appears to have avoided committing itself to either Yugoslavia's or Bulgaria's plans for Macedonia. There were instances, however, when certain local communists in Macedonia showed a tendency to identify themselves with alien aspirations. On the whole, these remained individual cases and there is no convincing evidence that their actions represented the Party views. Greek nationalists have tended to accuse the leadership of the KKE of unreservedly sanctioning the cession of Greek Macedonia to the Yugoslavs, the Bulgarians, or both. Most of this criticism was based on an alleged agreement said to have been signed at Karydies near Edessa, in January 1944, by Bulgarian Lieutenant Kaltsev and EAM representative Tzimas. Its main clauses were as follows:

1. The provinces Kilkis, Peonia, Almopia, Yannitsa, Edessa, Eordea, Florina, and Kastoria are ceded to the SNOF by the EAM-ELAS as zone of activities of the former.

2. The SNOF has the right to extend its zone of activities to other provinces more to the south after having assured the full control of the above provinces.

3. The Bulgarian Army occupying Macedonia undertakes the obligation to occupy the urban centers of Macedonia after the withdrawal of the Gernans and to hand them over to the EAM authorities.

4. The EAM and the SNOF decide in common to set up an autonomous Macedonian State of Soviet organization which shall request to be placed under the protection of Russia.

5. In order to assist the EAM and the SNOF the obligation is undertaken of officering the International Division with Bulgarian officers and ammunition. This Division will be formed at Kaimak Tsalan and be supplied with ammunition.

6. The Bulgarians are to undertake the discrediting by slander of all dynamic nationalist elements cooperating with the occupying authorities, in order that no nationalist movement be developed. Lastly, it has been decided that the flag of the Soviet Republic of Macedonia be the Bulgarian one, with inversed colours and a star in the centre.[47]

A careful analysis of the text reveals so many contradictions, that impartial writers have expressed serious doubts as to its authenticity.[48] In the first place, there is no certainty as to what organization or side each of the "delegates" represented. While it was generally believed that Tzimas signed on behalf of the EAM, some contend that Kaltchev signed on behalf of the SNOF, while others consider him as the representative of the I.M.R.O., the Bulgarian Government and even the CPB.[49] However, it is known, that by January 1944, Kaltchev was considered an arch enemy of Yugoslavia's ambitious plans for Macedonia and could hardly be expected to represent the pro-Yugoslav SNOF.[50] Moreover, some of the provisions of the alleged agreement indicate that only an official representative of the Bulgarian Army or the Bulgarian Administration could have signed it.

Even the substance of the agreement appears to lack a logical basis. Events have shown that the majority of the rank and file of the EAM-ELAS objected to the separatist tendencies of the SNOF. Consequently,

---

47. Text in *Conspiracy, op. cit.,* p. 14.

48. Barker, *op. cit.,* p. 82 and p. 115; Also, Woodhouse, *op. cit.,* p. 297.

49. *Conspiracy, op. cit.,* p. 14. Naltsas, *op. cit.,* p. 286 has confused the issue by contending that Kaltchev acted as a delegate of the Bulgarian authorities trying to get in touch with the SNOF, while, a few paragraphs later, he says that Kaltchev signed on behalf of the SNOF; Bramos [Second Edition] *op. cit.,* p. 124, is equally evasive as to whose behalf Kaltchev signed the document. Christides, *op. cit.,* p. 113, also fails to justify it.

50. Kulishevski, in his "1948 Congress Speech," said that Yugoslav Macedonian detachments were entering Greek Macedonia during the occupation to destroy "Kaltchev's anti-partisan units which were trying to stop the liberation movement in Aegean Macedonia." *GFM* A/19630/Γ2/1949.

an agreement, allegedly signed by an EAM representative, granting such wide jurisdiction to the pro-Yugoslav "Slav-Macedonian" organization can only be viewed with skepticism. What makes the agreement even less convincing is its fourth paragraph proclaiming the establishment of an autonomous "Macedonian State." Kaltchev has been accused by the Yugoslav "Macedonians" of being an agent of Greater Bulgarian aspirations over Macedonia. He would have affixed his signature to a document proclaiming the establishment of a Macedonian state, only if he were convinced that it meant the establishment of a Bulgaro-Macedonian state. Indeed, the Bulgarian colors of the flag show that the "Autonomous Macedonian State" would have been Bulgarian oriented. In that case, how could the SNOF—a pro-Yugoslav organization—extend its support to a clearly Bulgarian initiative?

Recent research has lifted some of the mystery covering this document. Evidence has been found which indicates that the document was not a fabrication of the Greek authorities, as the communists have contended. An unauthenticated copy was found in the seized archives of a communist band on July 7, 1945.[51] Before that, there were reports that on September 12, 1944, leaflets had been distributed in Thessaloniki which, allegedly, contained the provisions of the agreement.[52] A few years later no concrete evidence could be found that such leaflets had actually been circulated. On the contrary, in February 1947, a Greek Army unit operating against the guerrillas seized archives of the NOF (the successor of the SNOF) which included a document telling of a meeting held in January 25, 1944, between Kaltchev and top "Ohrana" leaders of the Florina district. At that meeting Kaltchev instructed his lieutenants to attempt to exterminate the Greek population and destroy the Greek partisan movement "which," he said, "is also purely Greek and is directed against the Bulgarian element."[53]

It is interesting to note that in his trial in Athens after the liberation (he was found guilty of crimes against Greeks and was executed), Kaltchev denied any knowledge of this agreement, and no witness could

---

51. *GFM* A/44666/1948.

52. Recently published archives of the German military authorities in Greece included a report on the alleged signing of the Karydies Agreement. However, it seems that the German authorities did not attach much credance to this document as evidenced by the lack of any pertinent comment. Pol. K, Enepekides: "The Wermacht Archives" *Tò Bῆμα* (Series), No 13, June 16, 1963.

53. *GFM* A/21205/Γ5Bb1/1947.

produce any convincing concrete evidence on the question of the Karydies document.[54]

Unless further evidence is produced, the logical conclusion is that such an agreement, at least in the form presented, could not have been signed. There is only the remote possibility that this was a private agreement, which, however, did not commit the organizations on whose behalf it was said to have been concluded. The criticism of the nationalist Greeks against the EAM-KKE could be justified only in the sense that the communists under their policy of "equal rights," allowed certain irredentist elements among the Slavophones to foment a separatist movement.

Yet, the seditious activities of a large segment of the Slavophones could not be blamed entirely on the attitude of the KKE. Years of illiberal treatment by incompetent local administrators, tolerated by dictatorial regimes, created a sense of persecution even among Slavophones who had been reared as Greeks and felt themselves to be Greeks. The communists did not create the irredentist minority; neither did the Yugoslavs. The extremist "Slav-Macedonians" who emerged as revolutionaries during the occupation were neither Bulgarians nor "Macedonians" of the Yugoslav type; they were merely a group of resentful Slav-speaking inhabitants from a remote part of Greece who, in their resentment against arbitrary measures by the authorities, turned first toward the Bulgarians and later toward the Yugoslavs.

This situation remained unaltered until the end of the communist guerrilla war in 1949 when all the irredentist "Slav-Macedonians" who were not killed in combat found shelter in the neighboring communist countries, mostly Yugoslavia where they were treated as Yugoslav nationals. Although it is not possible to ascertain exactly how many of the Slavophones of Greek Macedonia exhibited a Slav conscience during the occupation and the guerrilla war, it is safe to conclude that more than half can be classified in this category.[55]

---

54. *GFM* A/49923/1948.

55. Pallis places the figure at 65 % of all the Slavophones of Greek Macedonia. Alexander A. Pallis, *Macedonia and the Macedonians: A Historical Study*, (London: Greek Embassy Information Service, 1949) (mimeographed), p. 10. — H.R. Wilkinson, *Maps and Politics: A Review of the Ethnographic Cartography of Macedonia*, (Liverpool: University Press, 1951), p. 301, accepts Pallis' figure. — Yugoslav communist sources have revealed that during the occupation 5000 "Slav' Macedonians" belonged to active partisan units in Greek Macedonia while 12,000 others belonged to the ELAS reservists. Statement by Keramidjiev before the Second Congress of the People's Macedonian Front held in Skopje, May 1948 *Nova Mace-*

The KKE made no secret of its willingness to make certain concessions to the Slavophones in exchange for their support of the communist led partisan movement during the occupation. At the Eighth Plenum of its Central Committee, held in early January 1942, the KKE called on the "Slav-Macedonians" to join the national struggle for liberation of the Balkan peoples, "because only this guarantees their national and political liberation."[56]

Later, at the Panhellenic Conference of the KKE in December 1942, the Party declared that "the national minorities should be organized on the basis of the anti-Axis struggle, along with the Greek people, for the victory of Soviet Union and its Allies which constitutes the guarantee for the free and brotherly coexistence of all peoples."[57] And the Party's top theoretician, G. Zevgos, expressed openly the prevailing thinking in the KKE when he wrote in August 1943:

> If they]Bulgarians] took yesterday Eastern Macedonia and Western Thrace and today they advanced to Central Macedonia, there is no doubt that they will jump over to Western Macedonia also. However, in Greek Macedonia the racial mixture which existed prior to 1922 has ceased to exist. The Slavic and Turkish populations have emigrated on the basis of the Neuilly and Lausanne treaties and Greek populations—more than a milllon persons—have settled in Greek Macedonia and Thrace from the Balkans and Asia Minor... [the result was] that the ethnological composition of Greek Macedonia changed drastically and became as Greek as any other region of Old Greece... The Slav minority of Western Macedonia, numerically insignificant, is also struggling [against the occupying forces].[58]

Still suspected of trying to cede Greek Macedonia to Yugoslavia or Bulgaria, the Greek communists found it necessary to declare publicly not only that they considered Macedonia a Hellenic land, but that they also supported the national territorial claims of Greece. Thus, in his report to the 10th Plenary Session of the Central Committee Zevgos declared:

> Our people have struggled, and continue to struggle as few people have in this war. Therefore, they have the right to complete their

donija, May 24, 1948. — Dimitar Vlahov, *Makedonija, Momenti od Istorija na Makedonskiot Narod*, (Skopje : Drsavno Knigoisdatelatvo na Makedonija, 1950), p. 277, alleges that by 1943, 30,000 "Macedonians" were members of the ELAS, a figure which is grossly exaggerated and contradicted even by Yugoslav sources.

56. Naltsas, *op. cit.*, p. 268.

57. Text in Κομμουνιστικὴ Ἐπιθεώρησις, January 1943, p. 193.

58. G. Zevgos, "For Greek Macedonia and Thrace," Κομμουνιστικὴ Ἐπιθεώρησις, August 1943, p. 332.

national restitution with the unification, in a libezated Greece, of
all those territories which are inhabited by Greek populations [and]
to guard their security by local strategical rectification of the
frontier...[59]

Again in July 1944, Zevgos writing in the Party theoretical journal
Κομμουνιστική 'Επιθεώρησις, adroitly employed the arguments of the Leninist nationality doctrine to support views which today could be classified
as "nationalist-revisionist:"

According to the principle of self-determination, all peoples will
solve their national problems in a peaceful and final way. The minorities which live in other countries will acquire full national, economic, social and political equality of rights. Only in this way, the
minorities of Macedonia *and Epirus* and the hard pressed peoples of
the Balkans will solve once and for all their national problems.[60]

It is evident from this statement that Zevgos was advocating, on behalf of the KKE, equitable treatment of the national issue for Greece as
well as for the other Balkan countries. He would accept the principle of
equal rights for the "Slav-Macedonians" in a communist Greece. At the
same time he would expect a similar treatment for the Greek minority in
Albania. A few years later he and the then leadership of the Party were
severely reprimanded for having advanced "opportunist-chauvinist" views.

E. The KKE and the Bulgarians

From the first days of the occupation, the KKE denounced the take
over of Greek Eastern Macedonia and Thrace by the Bulgarians and publicly declared that "Boris, Filov and their comitadjis" would be punished.
In September 1943, Zevgos wrote that the Bulgarian leaders "will pay with
their heads for their crimes... We declare this in the most categorical way.
This is the only way to make the torturers pay for the crimes they commit
against the people."[61] And elsewhere he wrote: "The aggression of the
Bulgarians... is an imperialist, thieving operation. It means the dismemberment of Greece and the extermination of the Greek population."[62] More
important, yet, was the statement that:

59. Δέκα Χρόνια 'Αγῶνες, op. cit., p. 204.
60. G. Zevgos, "The National Minorities in the Common Struggle," Κομμουνιστική 'Επιθεώρησις, July 1944, p. 632.
61. G. Zevgos, "The National Problem and National Demagogy," Κομμουνιστική 'Επιθεώρησις, September 1943, p. 365.
62. G. Zevgos, "For Greek Macedonia and Thrace," op. cit., p. 332.

The KKE bases its policy on the principle of self-determination and for this reason it will not acknowledge any agreement or any occupation which will aim at annexing territories to fascist Bulgaria.[63]

Relations between the Greek and Bulgarian communists never reached the level of intimacy achieved between the Greek and Yugoslav communists.[64] There is not much information concerning their relations during the first two years of the occupation. Available data are of doubtful authenticity. Such is the case of an alleged agreement signed in Petrich, Bulgaria, on July 12, 1943, by Yannis Ioannides, a member of the Central Committee of the KKE and Dousan Daskalov, representing the CPB.[65] The agreement provided for the establishment of ''a Union of Soviet Republics in the Balkans including Greece, Macedonia and Serbia'' (Article 1) and for a territorial exit to Bulgaria and the Aegean (Article 4). Article 6 stated that Greek, Bulgarian and Serbian Macedonia would constitute ''an independent, autonomous Soviet Republic within the Balkan U.S.S.R.'' Greek and Bulgarian would be the official languages of the new state (Article 7).

To this day, the authenticity of this document has been accepted by Greek nationalists[66] while the communists have denied it.[67] Similarly, Bulgaria's Fatherland Front Government denied any knowledge of such an agreement when the issue was raised by the Greek Government before the United Nations in connection with her appeal concerning Bulgarian assistance to the communist guerrillas.[68] The Greek Government did, indeed, have substantial evidence about the signing of such an agreement, but it was far from conclusive.[69]

---

63. *Ibid.*, p. 333.

64. Barker, *op. cit.*, pp. 115-116.

65. Text in *Conspiracy*, *op. cit.*, pp. 11-12.

66. Bramos [Second edition], *op. cit.*, p. 125.

67. G. Zevgos, ''The National Minorities in the Common Struggle,'' *Κομμουνιστικὴ Ἐπιθεώρησις*, July 1944, p. 638, [Reprinted in October 1946].

68. *Radio Sofia*, Home Service, October 31, 1948, 12 : 01 p.m.

69. On August 1943, a merchant, later executed by the Germans, handed Naltsas — chief of the political section of the Thessaloniki national underground organization PAO — a copy of the agreement signed by Zografou, a leading EAM member. This was forwarded to the British service MO4 which was attached to the PAO headquarters and was transmitted to the Allied headquarters in the Middle East. Ten days later it was published in *Ἐθνικὴ Φωνή*, PAO's newspaper; *GFM* A/20323/Γ5Bb1/1948. Also Naltsas, *op. cit.*, p. 279, ft. 1. Later, in 1945, during anti-guerrilla operations in the Serres district, an unauthenticated copy of this agreement was found in communist archives seized near the Boula village. *GFM* A/20322/Γ5Bb1/1948.

Apart from communist denials, the conclusion of such an agreement raises certain questions: Why would the Greek communists make so many vital concessions to the Bulgarians for no apparent benefits in return? The KKE had struggled hard to avoid a similar Bulgarian plan during the inter-war period when the latter enjoyed Moscow's full backing; why should it now accept, when the Bulgarians were politically weak, what it had resisted—unsuccessfully—under Comintern pressure? Furthermore, the agreement provided for a "Macedonian" state, presumably under Bulgarian predominance, since the official languages would have been Bulgarian and Greek. How could Ioannides' actions be substantiated considering the fact that at that time the KKE was discussing with Tempo—and presumably accepting—the orientation of the "Slav-Macedonians" toward Yugoslavia? Finally, how could such a plan be envisioned with any chance of success, since the Bulgarians were aware that Stalin had given his support to the Yugoslav plan for Macedonia? That Yugoslav communists had no knowledge of the alleged Greek-Bulgarian agreement, either at the time or even later, is evidenced by the fact that they did not employ it in their attacks against Greek and Bulgarian communists following the Tito-Cominform split in 1948.

LIBERATION

The end of the war in the Balkans found the Yugoslavs with well advanced positions in the game of Macedonian politics which they had commenced without even being masters of their own part of Macedonia. During the inter-war period they had succumbed to the Comintern then under the influence of such prominent Bulgarian personalities as Vasili Kolarov and Georgi Dimitrov and had favored the policy of ceding their part of Macedonia to a unified Macedonian state which—they maintained no illusions—would have developed into a second Bulgarian state. Liberation found them in power in Yugoslav Macedonia, though not without local opposition; in strenuous diplomatic negotiations with the Bulgarians for control of Bulgarian Macedonia; and in overt agit-prop activities in Greek Macedonia where they tried to win over to their cause the Slavophones and pressure the Greek communists to adopt their plan for a unified Macedonia.

A. The Establishment of the People's Republic of Macedonia

Yugoslav Macedonia became officially a federative state of the People's Republic of Yugoslavia on August 2, 1944, when the Anti-Fascist

136

Assembly of the National Liberation of Macedonia [Antifasiskoto sobranie na naradnoto osloboduvanie na Makedonija] met for the first time and proclaimed the formation of the People's Federative Republic of Macedonia. The new state was immediately accepted by the Central Committee of the Communist Party of Yugoslavia. Publicly, it was recognized that the People's Republic of Macedonia, as all other republics of Yugoslavia, had the right to secede, but this was to remain purely theoretical.[70]

From the very beginning it became evident that the new state aspired not only at consolidating Yugoslav control in a traditionally irredentist minded region, but also at providing a pivotal structure around which Bulgarian and Greek Macedonia could eventually be united. Thus, immediately after the establishment of the People's Republic of Macedonia, the Central Committee of the Communist Party of Macedonia issued the following declaration :

> Macedonian people : In your three-year popular liberation struggle you achieved your unity and you established your own army and set the foundations of the federative Macedonian state. With the participation of the entire Macedonian people against the fascist occupiers in Yugoslavia, Bulgaria and Greece *you will achieve the union of all parts of Macedonia which the Balkan imperialists seized in 1913 and 1918.*
>
> As for the demand for the complete unification of the Macedonian people, there are today on your side all the other peoples of Yugoslavia, the Anti-fascist People's Liberation Council of Yugoslavia and the heroic People's Liberation Army of Yugoslavia.[71]

A little later, Milovan Djilas, in a speech at Kolarać, on November 7, 1944, declared that "the question of the unification is today before the Macedonian people who have the right to unite themselves wherever they may live." He further explained that the unification of Macedonia was not merely a theoretical question but one of *vital interest to the security of Yugoslavia.* [72]

The new state immediately drew to itself the most diversified figures who had played an active role in old Macedonian politics, irrespective of

---

70. *Yugoslav Communism, op. cit.,* p. 97. Dimitar Vlahov wrote that it was true that Macedonia had the right to secede, if it so desired, but went on to say that "there is not even one conscientious citizen who would like to secede from his common homeland, the P.R. of Yugoslavia, because, thus, our democracy would fall into the hands of the imperialists." Vlahov, *Makedonija, op. cit.,* pp. 275-276.
71. Text was reprinted in a brochure published at Skopje in 1954 under the title, *Ten Years from the Establishment of the P.R. of Macedonia.* [Italics added].
72. *Politika,* November 8, 1944. [Italics added].

the sides they had espoused at the time. The most illustrious of them all was Dimitar Vlahov, first Premier of the federative republic. Vlahov had been an outspoken Bulgarian during the Macedonian Struggle (1903-1908) and was later elected Bulgarian delegate to the Turkish Parliament. He espoused the cause of the "federalist" Macedonians, and in 1925 appeared as leader of the "United" I.M.R.O. It was during the closing years of the war that he emerged as an "authentic Macedonian."

The leaders of the People's Republic of Macedonia, were trusted by the Central Committee of the CPY to place their communist loyalties over and above their regional chauvinism. Thus, they were granted wide jurisdiction by the central government to cultivate among the traditionally Bulgarian inclined inhabitants of the region, a Macedonian national consciousness and to combat any anti-Yugoslav tendencies that might occur. This sudden wide authority invested in the newly appointed leaders a messianic zeal not only to turn Bulgarians into "Macedonians" but also openly to claim Bulgarian and Greek Macedonia as parts of one country. At the same time, they shifted their attention to the removal of the remnants of pre-war Serbian rule. But, in their desire to cut off Serbian heritage, they went a little too far, a situation which the Yugoslav communist centralists in Belgrade were not willing to leave uncontrolled. Thus, when the Executive Committee of the Macedonian Religious and National Assembly appealed to the Serbian Patriarch to allow them to form their own independent Macedonian Orthodox Church, their petition was denied.[73]

Not for a moment did the new Yugoslav leaders hesitate to use the ace they held in their hands, i.e. "Macedonian statehood," to put pressure on their neighbors, the Bulgarians and Greeks. If in following years they pressed hard to win over Bulgarian and Greek Macedonia, they did it not merely to expand territorially or, even less, to satisfy the regionalists of the Skopje region; their ultimate objective—as events were to testify later—was the hegemony of the Balkans, and to that end they were not willing to retreat, even before the Soviets. The Macedonian Question was simply a very useful pawn in their dangerous game of power politics.

B. Yugoslav-Bulgarian Negotiations for Federation (1944-1945)

On September 9, 1944, Bulgaria changed sides. The communist dominated Fatherland Front took over the reigns of the Government and ten

---

73. What they failed to win at that time was granted to them in 1958 when the Macedonian Orthodox Church was established. However, the Serbian Patriarch continued to maintain nominal control over the entire Church.

days later the entire Bulgarian Army of approximately 500,000 was placed under Soviet Marshal Tolbukin who ordered it to cut off the retreating Germans from Greece and Yugoslavia. The Bulgarians responded eagerly hoping that even at that late moment they might avoid the consequences of their wartime conduct. Since the Germans were retreating through Yugoslavia, the Bulgarians had to pursue them in their neighbor's territory. The Yugoslav communists, however, were not inclined to accept their former enemy as a liberator, even under the cover of communism, and, consequently, they imposed many obstacles and restrictions on the movements of the Bulgarian Army. Later, the Bulgarians accused the Yugoslavs of allowing 14 German divisions to withdraw unharmed from the Balkans because of these restrictions.[74]

There was no doubt that the Yugoslavs were determined not to accept the Fatherland Front Bulgarians as equals. Instead, they tried to take advantage of the situation and dictate their own terms for cooperation.

The first hint of Yugoslav intentions came in a statement made by the Yugoslav Minister of Foreign Affairs who expressed the hope, in July 1944, that Bulgaria would join the new Yugoslav Federation and that efforts could be made toward the formation of an all-Balkan federation.[75]

In September, immediately after the successful Bulgarian *coup*, General Vukmanović-Tempo and Lazar Kulishevski met with the Central Committee of the CPB in Sofia to discuss the future of Macedonia. Yugoslavia's quick action aimed at capitalizing on Bulgaria's weak diplomatic position and the internal weakness of the Bulgarian Party. According to Yugoslav sources,[76] the Bulgarians accepted at that meeting the principle that wide autonomy be granted to the inhabitants of Pirin, i.e. Bulgarian Macedonia, "to prepare them for the unification with the Federative Republic of Macedonia in Tito's new Yugoslavia." It was made clear that the slogan, "united Macedonia," did not signify the immediate unification of the region, but that both parties accepted it in principle and that the necessary propaganda among the population would be conducted to prepare it for unification.[77] Apparently the Yugoslav leaders felt that it was not

74. Col. Al. Getman, "How Tito helped Hitler and Assisted Churchill," in *Rabotnitsesko Delo*, October 16, 1950.

75. *Osservatore Romano* (Rome), July 12, 1944.

76. Letter by Kulishevski to the Central Committee of the CPB dated September 1944. Reprinted in *Ten Years Since the Establishment of the P.R. of Macedonia*, *op. cit.*

77. Lazar Mojsov wrote: "Although from the Yugoslav side the question of the incorporation of Pirin into the People's Republic of Macedonia was not raised

only the Bulgarian Macedonians who were not ready for unification, but that their own ''Macedonians'' were fairly much Bulgarians in feeling. There were, undoubtedly, serious doubts as to whether so many Bulgarians in a newly created ''Macedonian'' state could be absorbed. However, the Yugoslav leaders knew that time could easily turn against their plans and, consequently, they definitely turned down the Bulgarian proposal that unification be linked to the question of the signing of a close alliance between the two countries.

The content of this initial agreement between Yugoslav and Bulgarian communists resembled the wartime negotiations between the Yugoslav and Greek partisans. First, the Bulgarians recognized as a fact that the inhabitants of their part of Macedonia ceased to be Bulgarians and became ''Macedonians,'' in the ethnic connotation of the word. The rest came naturally. It was agreed that Macedonian national units would be formed in Pirin Macedonia under the Bulgarian General Staff (the war was still going on in the Balkans) and that national liberation committees would be established in all Bulgarian Macedonian towns. On the political side, a Regional National Liberation Committee was to be formed under the supervision and control of the Fatherland Front to carry out in the Pirin district the tasks of the Bulgarian Government as well as to prepare the people for unification. The entire plan was a well calculated move on the part of the Yugoslav communists to draw within their fold Bulgarian Macedonia—and later Greek Macedonia— when conditions in Yugoslav Macedonia became ripe enough to ensure a fairly smooth merger.

The Bulgarian communists had no reasons to rejoice over the terms imposed on them. Following a meeting of the Central Committee of the CPB, Vlado Poptomov explained the position of the Bulgarian communists in a regional conference in Gorna Djumaja. He accepted the fact that in Yugoslav and Bulgarian Macedonia conditions were mature for unification,[78] but maintained that difficulties still existed. The Macedonians of Pirin, he said, felt themselves free under the Fatherland Front, and no question of unification was raised by them. Instead, there were many who

---

as an action slogan, this question required its fundamental solution, i.e., proof was sought that the leadership of the CPB had truly gotten rid of its Great Bulgarian chauvinism;'' Mojov, ''About the South - Slav Federation,'' *Kommunist* [Supplement] (Belgrade : July-September, 1950).

78. He said that the EAM should be assisted in Greece so that the situation there might develop favorably for the unification of Macedonia.

wondered why Pirin Macedonia should be united to Vardar (Yugoslav) Macedonia and not vice versa.[79] The Yugoslavs lost no time over such weak Bulgarian protests and double talk. They set themselves to the task of realizing an even more grandiose plan than mere annexation of Bulgarian and, at the most, Greek Macedonia. Their scheme was to establish a South-Slav federation in which they would become the undisputed masters. They knew that now was the time to do it.[80]

All through the months of November and December 1944, negotiations were conducted on the basis of a Yugoslav proposal for the establishment of a federation whereby Yugoslavia would be represented by six units—six republics—while Bulgaria by only one. The fact that Bulgaria was placed first on the list of the seven republics of the planned federation was simply adding insult to injury.

Fighting for time, the Bulgarians submitted in turn a proposal which in fact provided for a Yugoslav-Bulgarian federation on equal terms. The Yugoslavs realized that no progress could be made by merely exchanging notes and sent Kardelj to Sofia. Kardelj stayed in the Bulgarian capital for three days—December 22 to 24—and met with Traiko Kostov, Vasili Chervenkov and Kimon Georgiev.[81]

The Bulgarian leaders proposed in place of a South-Slav federation a defense treaty or a pact of mutual assistance. This Kardelj rejected contending that something more ambitious should be concluded to attract the imagination of the masses to the idea of an eventual union. The Bulgarians retreated and accepted, initially, the idea of a South-Slav federation. However, their views on the question of representation differed substantially from those of the Yugoslavs.[82] The difference is evident in the two draft proposals. The Yugoslav draft was as follows:

1. Democratic federal Yugoslavia and Bulgaria are being united in one federal state *which will consist of 7 federative units*—Bulgaria, Serbia, Croatia, Slovenia, Macedonia, and Bosnia and Hercegovina—which will have a joint Parliament and a single customs territory.

79. From a secret report by Liupso Arsov and Vera Acheva to the Central Committee of the CPY, dated November 9, 1944.

80. Kardelj wrote to Tito from Sofia on December 23 that ''now is the time and I doubt that it will ever repeat itself;'' *Borba*, December 29, 1949.

81. Blagoe Popofsky, *Judicial Provocation in Sofia* [A study published in Skopje] 1950.

82. Moje Pijade, *On the Question of the Balkan Federation* [Study written in 1949 and published again in brochure form in 1951], Skopje, 1951.

2. The joint activities of the federal state include military affairs, foreign policy and customs, and also all other activities which will be included in the Constitution of the federation as joint affairs and, therefore, under the competence of the federal organs.

3. A joint Bulgarian-Yugoslav commission will be established in Belgrade, to be called the "Commission of South-Slav Unity" with the task of preparing a draft constitution on the joint federal state. This Commission will consist of representatives of Bulgaria and of the six federative units of the Democratic Federal Yugoslavia which will be appointed by the corresponding governments.[83]

The Bulgarian draft, clearly aiming at an equal status and representation, stated:

The governments of Bulgaria and Yugoslavia declare that they are acceding to the union of South-Slavs, by means of creating a joint state, organized on a federal basis, which will be called the "South-Slav Federation" —Federacija Juznih Slovena (FJ-US)—, with joint Parliament, with joint ministries of foreign affairs and armed services, and with all other joint institutions and Ministries which will be finally determined in the joint Constitution of the South-Slav Federation to be drafted in consequence of the final realization of this agreement.

The beginning of the realization of this Federation will take place with the effective functioning of the specially created organ of the federation, namely the temporary Council of the South-Slav Unity (PSJSJ), with its seat in the city of Belgrade. *This Council will be formed on the parity principle of representatives from both governments.*[84]

Since no progress could be made in Sofia, Yugoslav and Bulgarian leaders were invited in January 1945 to Moscow for an arbitration of their differences. Yugoslavia was represented by Moje Pijade while Kimon Georgiev and Anton Yugov represented Fatherland Front Bulgaria.[85] Georgi Dimitrov who was in Moscow at the time, kept a close watch on the negotiations, and though remaining behind the scenes apparently played an important role in advising the Bulgarian delegation. According to Yugoslav accounts Stalin favored, initially, the Bulgarian view but changed sides when the Yugoslavs explained to him that the various individual regions of Yugoslavia, i.e. Serbia, Montenegro, etc., had their own historical evo-

83. Text in *Borba*, December 29, 1949. [Italics added].
84. *Ibid.*, [Italics added].
85. Mojsov, "About a South-Slav Federation," *op. cit.*

lution.[86] In the light of more recent disclosures,[87] it seems doubtful that Stalin would have allowed Yugoslavia to assume an omnipotent position in the Balkans through her plan for a South-Slav federation. Even if it is assumed that he accepted the validity of the Yugoslav argument, there is evidence to suggest that he did not force the Bulgarians to submit to it. Instead, the two delegations were advised by the Soviet Government to delay, for the moment, any decision on the question of the federation and, instead, to proceed with the conclusion of a treaty of political, military and economic cooperation and alliance. The treaty could be supplemented by an exchange of letters between the two Prime Ministers who would express their desire to prepare the way for a South-Slav federation to be realized within the shortest possible time. The Soviets contended that they were prompted to suggest a temporary postponement on account of the weak position of the CPB within Bulgaria where the federation plan was attacked by the non-communist opposition parties.[88] The Bulgarian and Yugoslav communists tried, indeed, to follow Soviet advise to draft the treaty. However, British representations to Moscow, supported by the Americans, canceled their plans.[89]

The question of Macedonia played a significant role in federation negotiations. The initial Yugoslav draft, discussed by Kardelj in his visit to Sofia in late December 1944, called for a unified Macedonian state to be represented as an equal in a South-Slav federation. The Bulgarians knew that if they rejected without justification this proposal they would be accused openly of chauvinism. Instead, they tried to gain time and moved to a second line of defense. They would accept a unified Macedonian state in a South-Slav federation but on the condition that it would be formed simultaneously with the coming to force of the federation. Kardelj, as well as the other Yugoslav leaders, knew well that the federation plan, especially as outlined by Belgrade, could hardly be achieved overnight. They put all kinds of pressure on the Bulgarians, even going as far as to accuse them of an anti-Leninist attitude for trying to lower a clear question of a people's self-determination to the level of political bargaining. In the end, Bulgarian intransigence forced the Yugoslavs to retreat.[90] Their only gain

---

86. *Borba,* January 20, 1945, as quoted by Mojsov; *Ibid.*

87. Milovan Djilas, *Conversations with Stalin* [Greek Edition], (Athens: K. H. Kamarinopoulos, 1962).

88. Mojsov, "About the South - Slav Federation," *op. cit.*

89. *Ibid.* Also Pijade, *op. cit.*

90. The Greek Government was first informed of Bulgaria's diplomatic acti-. vity at the end of 1944 by a lengthy report of its chargés d'affaires in Iran, Mr.

was that Bulgarian communists had officially accepted the thesis that
the people of the Pirin district, as well as those of Vardar Macedonia
were not Bulgarians but ''Macedonians,'' a people of a new ethnic stock.
In the draft treaty, agreed upon by the two delegations, the Bulgarians assumed the obligation toward Yugoslavia ''to regulate all questions concerning that part of Macedonia which reverted to Bulgaria under the terms of
the Peace Treaty of 1913.'' The Yugoslavs undertook similar obligations
toward the Bulgarians for the regions they had annexed from them at the
end of the First World War. However, even this agreement failed to be
ratified on account of British and American protests.

The Yugoslavs, thus, failed to win Bulgarian Macedonia at a moment when Bulgaria was at the nadir of her political power. They had,
nevertheless, made sufficient strides in that direction which, it was hoped,
would bear fruits in the years to come. Only Stalin's unexpected feud
with the Yugoslav Central Committee in 1948 caused the cancellation of
the ambitious plans.

C. The Bulgarian Communists and Macedonia (1945)

In Bulgaria, Yugoslav attempts to build a Greater Macedonian state
and annex Pirin Macedonia in the process were, on the whole, received negatively, causing serious embarrassment to the communists. The response
was understandable for a nation which—rightly or wrongly—had considered
Macedonia, especially Yugoslav Macedonia, as part of the Bulgarian Fatherland. It should be remembered that when Germany offered the Bulgarian Army occupation of Greek and Yugoslav Macedonia, the Bulgarians,
irrespective of political affiliations, had supported the move as a justification of their national rights. Even the communists in the beginning failed
to register any opposition. It was only toward the end of the war, when
Moscow and the CPB were anxious to see the pro-Axis government fall,
that Bulgarian communists began to denounce publicly the seizure of Greek
and Yugoslav Macedonia.[91]

G. Koustas who on January 20, 1945, advised Athens of Bulgaria's willingness to
support the formation of a ''Macedonian state'' in Yugoslavia and even to cede
its part of Macedonia receiving in exchange Greek Thrace. *GFM* A 1113, Bulg. 1945
 91. Vulko Chervenkov, wrote in June 1944:
 The occupation of Thrace and Macedonia by the Bulgarian Army and their
 forceful annexation has nothing in common with the unity of the Bulgarians,
 exactly as 29 years ago the occupation of these regions, with the assistance
 of the Germans, led Bulgaria not toward unity but toward destruction. The
 present occupation of Thrace and Macedonia by the Bulgarians serves simply

However, after the overthrow of the pro-Nazi regime, the Fatherland Front flirted for a moment with the idea of remaining in the occupied Greek and Yugoslav regions. The seriousness of the threat, particularly for Greek Macedonia to which the legitimate Athens Government did not have the means to send military forces, was demonstrated by the fact that Stalin instructed in September the Soviet representative to the European Advisory Commission to inquire whether the Bulgarians might not be left in possession of parts of Western Thrace assigned to them by Hitler. America's uncompromising refusal to leave an ex-enemy in possession of an ally's territory, forced the Soviets to withdraw their proposal.[92] Nevertheless, the Bulgarian communists have contended, as in the case of Yugoslavia, that the Bulgarian Army was instrumental in achieving the liberation [sic] of Greece.[93] Before their departure the Bulgarians carried off cart loads of war "booty" from Greek Macedonia and Thrace and turned over the political and military administration of the area to the EAM.[94] Elizabeth Barker probably described best the situation in Greek Macedonia after the departure of the Bulgarians, when she wrote:

Hitler's imperialist designs and leads Bulgaria to a destruction which will be even more terrible than that of 1918.

Vulko Chervenkov, "The Myth of the National Unity of the Bulgarians with the Assistance of the German Thieves," *The Slavs* (Moscow), June 1944. Chervenkov's article coincided with a campaign by the Soviet press (May-July 1944), aimed at forcing the nationalist Bulgarians to abandon the Government and join the communist led Fatherland Front. For Soviet articles: *GFM* A/15250 - 19252/1944, A/17429 - 17366/1944, A/17348 - 15254 1944. Georgi Dimitrov, in a letter sent from Moscow on September 18, 1944, to the Central Committee of the CPB, emphasized the great importance for the Party to assist in eradicating the remnants of Bulgarian chauvinism. He wrote:

"Without the merciless destruction of Great Bulgarian chauvinism, that deep-seated wound in the living organism of our country, it is not possible to create the renaissance of a new Bulgaria. It is necessary, along with the prevention of the harmful work by the bearers of this deadly contagious [policy] to carry out a tremendous ideological campaign, which would explain things to the people and its intelligentsia, so that every trace of the Great Bulgarian ideology and adventurous policy should vanish.

Quoted in Mojsov, "About the South-Slav Federation," *op. cit.*

At their trial held in Sofia, December 20, 1944, the leaders of the wartime Bulgarian Government were accused of having "sanctioned the occupation of Yugoslav and Greek lands by the Bulgarian Army and condoned the cruel oppression of the Yugoslav and Greek nations which brought dishonor to the Bulgarian name." Text in *GFM* A/7931/Bulg./1945.

92. Armstrong, *op. cit.*, p. 189, footnote 2.
93. *Rabotnitsesko Delo*, May 23, 1949.
94. Naltsas, *op. cit.*, p. 344.

Although the Greeks were relieved by the belated Bulgarian withdrawal, they were left with an overpowering hatred of all Bulgars, whether pro-German or Communist. In fact the average Greek probably detested and feared the Bulgarian Communists, who represented the great Slav menace to Greece from the north, even more than he had hated their predecessors.[95]

Inside Bulgarian Macedonia the communists tried to consolidate their control by persecuting the remnants of Ivan Mihailov's I.M.R.O. which had cooperated with the Germans in the occupation of Yugoslav Macedonia and, to a lesser extent, Greek Macedonia. Many were imprisoned or deported as "reactionaries." In the trial of the I.M.R.O. members held in Sofia in 'August 1946, it was revealed that following the evacuation of the Balkans by the Germans, Mihailov had succeeded in escaping abroad. I.M.R.O. leadership then passed to Vlanda Kurtev and Georgi Nastev who went into hiding. In December 1945, the Organization tried to regroup armed I.M.R.O. units and even attempted to come into contact with Bulgarian opposition leaders. In January 22 members of the I.M.R.O. were arrested trying, allegedly, to proselytize new members.[96] Not all Bulgarian Macedonians favored the lost cause of the I.M.R.O. extremists. A number of them had espoused communism and had, indeed, occupied important posts in the Party.

In the meantime, various opposition elements, and particularly the Bulgarian Social Democrats, conducted all through 1945 and 1946 a forceful parliamentary and press campaign against making any concessions to the Yugoslavs.[97] Despite official communist condemnation of such pronouncements, there is no doubt that the communists welcomed this criticism as strengthening their position vis-à-vis Yugoslav demands.

Tito appears to have found this situation intolerable. In a strongly worded speech delivered at Skopje on October 12, 1945, he said:

We have received reports from brotherly Bulgaria, telling of certain elements who claim that the Macedonians are not free... There are some people in Bulgaria who are composing memoranda and sending them to the Great Powers, demanding the union of Macedonia —i.e. of Pirin, Aegean and Vardar Macedonia—under the protection of foreign powers. As if we needed protectors; as if we were not of age! As a mature nation we will win Macedonia's right to be

---

95. Barker, *op. cit.*, p. 83.

96. *Glas* (Belgrade), August 19, 1946.

97. *Narodno Zemedelsko Zname* (Sofia), December 12, 1946; *Otetsestven Front* (Sofia), December 19, 1946.

united. All these memoranda are nothing but a screen; they are the machinations of those who always strove to create discord among the Balkan peoples... Suddenly, they began to say that the Macedonians were not free, that Macedonians should be united and given better living conditions. Yet, these very people have been here for three and a half years and what have they done? You have a good notion of what they have done.[98]

Thus, for the Bulgarian communists who had consolidated their control over the Pirin region, the most serious threat was not posed by the "reactionary" I.M.R.O., but by the "brotherly" Communist Party of Yugoslavia.

D. Greek Macedonia in 1945

The departure of the Germans from Greece in late October 1944 left the entire country in the hands of the EAM/ELAS. Only Athens and the islands were under the control of the Greek Government-in-exile which had returned under strong British military escort. In Macedonia, official representatives of the Athens Government were installed in Thessaloniki, but their authority was subject to the dictates of the local EAM Committee. Remnants of the nationalist partisan units operating in Eastern Macedonia were annihilated by the ELAS with the help of the Bulgarian Army which, as has been revealed, was delaying its departure from Greece.

Thus, from November 1944 to February 1945—when the Varkiza Agreement terminated the abortive first communist *coup*—most of the Greek countryside and the entirety of Macedonia was in the hands of the communists. Rumors circulated that during the critical months of December and January, the Yugoslavs were advising their Greek comrades to withstand British pressure, promising them military support. Confidential reports had reached the Greek authorities early in January providing evidence that the Yugoslavs had offered to assist the Greek communists with troops.[99] Outrageous as this information might have seemed at the time, there is now corroborative evidence pointing to its accuracy. Following the Tito-Cominform break, the Bulgarian communists undoubtedly aiming at reaping propaganda benefits, revealed that just after the withdrawal of the Germans, the Yugoslavs were laying plans for armed intervention on the side of the Greek communists, thus, preparing the ground for the annex-

---

98. Monitored by the British Broadcasting Corporation, October 22, 1945, *GFM* A/24581/Γ2/1945.

99. *Report*, dated January 9, 1945, *GFM* A/913/Mac./1945.

ation of Greek Macedonia.[100] In addition, there is indisputable evidence that during those critical months, pro-Yugoslav "Slav-Macedonians" in Greek border regions were encouraged by the Yugoslavs to increase their secessionist propaganda.[101]

The inability of the communists to achieve a quick *coup* ended the revolt. On February 12, 1945, an agreement was signed at Varkiza between the Government and the EAM, by which the latter undertook to disband its armed forces in exchange for the promise of an early plebiscite to decide on the constitutional regime of the country.[102] All over Greece, ELAS units began to disarm. Soon, however, there were charges of communist hypocrisy; that guns and ammunition were hidden; that whole units were crossing the frontier to Yugoslavia and Bulgaria to prepare themselves for a "third round."[103] There were also counter charges of Government excesses, terrorism by extreme nationalist bands, and persecution of minorities. It seems that there was some truth in all of these charges and counter charges.

When the first Government armed forces, the National Guard and the Gendarmerie entered Western Macedonia in April and May 1945, the ill-feeling which had accumulated during the occupation boiled to the surface. The National Guard, for its part, was evidently prone to accept almost all complaints against "Slav-Macedonians" who had committed crimes during the occupation either as collaborators of the Germans and the Bulgarians, or as members of the communist bands of the ELAS and the SNOF. Undoubtedly, innocent suffered along with the criminals, although very few were killed.[104] In fact, the treatment of the Slav minority in Greece never reached the extent of cruel persecution which was reserved, immediately after the war, for national minorities in the communist Balkan countries.[105]

---

100. *Otetsestven Front*, January 15, 1952.

101. *GFM* A/913/Mac./1945.

102. Text of the Varkiza Agreement in *Conspiracy, op. cit.*, pp. 33 - 37.

103. It has been commonly accepted that the "first round" was the communist takeover of the Resistance movement; the "second round" was the unsuccessful communist *coup* in December 1944; as it developed later, the "third round" was the large scale guerrilla war (1946 - 1949).

104. McNeil, *op. cit.*, p. 266.

105. In Rumania and Yugoslavia the German and Hungarian minorities suffered many deprivations, deportations, internships in labor camps and mass trial executions, all of them justified by the Rumanian and Yugoslav regimes as due punishment for the atrocities committed by these minorities in collaboration with the occupying forces against the local Rumanian and Yugoslav populations. For details : Evangelos

By no means were acts of revenge directed solely against the ''Slav-Macedonians'' as members of an alien minority. On the contrary, the vendetta which revived with the disarming of the ELAS groups seems to have been aimed at those who had collaborated with the occupation forces and with the communists. If violence seemed directed more toward the ''Slav-Macedonians,'' it was due to the fact that, a large part of the minority under the protection of either the German-Bulgarian occupation authorities, or under cover of the communist-led partisan bands, had gone out of its way to terrorize the native Greek population. A foreign observer wrote with regard to this situation :

> In Macedonia, where the Greek loyalists suffered atrociously from the Bulgarians and from Slavophones with Bulgarian sympathies, as well as from the Communists, there appears to have been some administrative terrorism, although without the direct connivance of the central authorities. In 1945 and 1946, when the power of the Communists was at its lowest (although it was still considerable) and loyalist bands were active all over Greece, murders by loyalists became almost as frequent as murders by Communists.[106]

Already peace appeared to be returning to the region. Approximately 25,000 ''Slav-Macedonians'' crossed the border to Bulgaria and Yugoslavia.[107] Those remaining could be generally grouped into three categories : those fanatically attached to Hellenism who over the years fought against the Bulgarian and communist interests; those who did not have the moral strength or a sufficiently developed national consciousness to resist the tempting offers and terror of Bulgarians and communists and who, thus, shifted their allegiance away from the Greek State; and, those who permitted themselves to be made the agents of Bulgarian and Yugoslav

Kofos, ''Balkan Minorities under Communist Regimes,'' *Balkan Studies*, Vol. II, No. 1, 1961, pp. 22 - 46.

106. Fritz August Voigt, *The Greek Sedition* (London : Hollis and Carter, 1948), pp. 45 - 46.

107. Yugoslav Macedonians have accepted the figure 25,000; *Nova Makedonija*, May 24, 1948. A Soviet spokesman in the United Nations placed it as high as 30,000; Barker *op. cit.*, p. 116. Originally 10,000 went to Bulgaria (Statement by Bulgarian Premier Kimon Georgiev, *Agence Anatolia*, August 4, 1945), and 15,000 crossed the border to Yugoslavia; Dimitar Vlahov, *Govori i Statii, 1945 - 1947* [Speeches and Articles, 1945 - 1947], (Skopje, 1947, p. 100), [Greek trans.] Greek official sources listed the ''Slav - Macedonians'' who fled to Bulgaria and Yugoslavia after the Varkiza Agreement and the departure of the Germans, at 15,000 but apparently their information was not accurate; *Memorandum* of the Greek Delegate to the United Nations Balkan Investigation Commission, dated April 25, 1950, *GFM* A/30362 Γ5/ Ba/1950.

communist designs on Macedonia. The largest number of the Slavophones who remained in Greece after the liberation appeared to belong to the second category.[108]

The "Slav-Macedonians" who went to Bulgaria did not stay there long. The Bulgarian communists, having relinquished the initiative to the Yugoslavs, urged the "Slav-Macedonians" from Greece to go to Yugoslav Macedonia [109] where those able to carry arms were inducted into camps and trained in guerrilla tactics in order to participate in the communist uprising being prepared against Greece.

As later disclosed, the Yugoslavs undertook to assist the preparation of a communist revolt in Greece because they hoped that a communist regime in their southern neighbor would regard their plan for the annexation of Greek Macedonia with, at least, less hostility. It is probably for this reason that they paid particular attention to training the "Slav-Macedonian" emigrés, because from their ranks they could expect to draw the most loyal elements to support their annexationist plan.

In addition to providing the means of preparation for the rebellion, the Yugoslavs embarked during 1945 on a major campaign to discredit Greece internationally and, thus, provide a more fertile ground for the advancement of their objectives in Macedonia.

Even as early as November 1944—less than a month after the arrival in Athens of the Papandreou Government—the Yugoslavs began to accuse the Greek authorities of maltreating the "Macedonians." In his Kolarać speech, delivered on November 7, 1944, Milovan Djilas declared:

... the armed forces under the command of the Papandreou Government exercise a violent terror against our Macedonian populations without any serious reason. The Macedonians in Greece, who did not have other course but to demand the organization of themselves to fight against the German aggressor, want to speak their own language and exercise their national rights.[110]

---

108. Philippos Dragoumis, *Προσοχὴ στὴ Βόρειο Ἑλλάδα: 1945 - 1948* [Watch Northern Greece: 1945 - 1948], (Thessaloniki: Society for Macedonian Studies, 1949), pp. 67 - 69.

109. The Plovid (Bulgaria) newspaper *Otetsestven Glas* (April 26, 1945), published an announcement of the Bulgarian Ministry of Social Welfare which read as follows:

The Macedonian state of Federal Yugoslavia has begun the concentration of all Macedonians who arrived in Bulgaria as refugees. All Macedonians who are interested in returning to federal Yugoslavia should report to [the listed] office.

110. *Politika*, November 8, 1944.

Yugoslav statements for a united and independent Macedonian state within federal Yugoslavia had seriously disturbed the Greek Government which had just crushed—December 1944—a serious internal uprising in Athens. Repeatedly the Greek Foreign Ministry asked its Ambassador in London to secure British support against Yugoslav pretentions in Macedonia. On January 15, 1945, Ambassador Athanasios Aghnides telegraphed his Minister in Athens that the Foreign Office had informed him of the British Government's assurances from Marshal Tito to the effect that he planned indeed, to establish a Macedonian state within the framework of the Yugoslav Federation, but without incorporating any part of Greek Macedonia.[111] A little later, Foreign Secretary Anthony Eden brought the issue before a Big Three meeting at the Yalta Conference in an effort to secure guarantees for Greece.[112]

However, the Greeks did not feel secure by these assurances, particularly since official Yugoslav pronouncements appeared menacing. On April 4, 1945, Greek Ambassador to Moscow Jean Politis, in a talk with Yugoslav Foreign Minister Ivan Subasić, on the eve of the signing of the Soviet-Yugoslav Pact, brought the discussion around to the Macedonian question and asked the Yugoslav Minister for clarifications of Yugoslav policy with regard to Macedonia. Cabled Politis to his Government:

> Subacić answered guardedly that the official Yugoslav view remained the same [that Greek Macedonia will not be incorporated], but added that no one could predict how the situation would develop in Yugoslavia's southern frontiers; he went on to say that even if such a case were to arise, his personal view was that it would be solved in an official way between old allies and friends such as the Greeks and the Yugoslavs.[113]

As was to be expected, Subasić' vague statement created more apprehension in the Greek capital. It was already becoming clear that Subasić had no real authority, inasmuch as in the new Yugoslav Government formed on March 7, 1945, only five of the 28 ministers were not communists.[114] Thus, the Minister's expression of "personal views" that the situation, "if raised," would be solved amicably, increased instead of calming

---

111. Ambassador to London Aghnides to the Ministry of Foreign Affairs; January 15, 1945, *GFM* A/388/22894/Γ1/1945.

112. Ambassador Aghnides to Ministry of Foreign Affairs; February 14, 1945; *GFM* A/1593/Mac./1945.

113. Ambassador to Moscow Politis to Ministry of Foreign Affairs; April 11, 1945; *GFM* A/4331/1945.

114. *Yugoslav Communism, op. cit.,* p. 117.

the fears of the Greeks. Weak as they were internally and having trusted their foreign affairs to a socialist who believed that Greece should try to pursue a middle course between Great Britain and the Soviet Union,[115] they tried to adhere to a policy of moderation and non-provocation,[116] hoping vainly that still there could be some kind of an accord with Yugoslavia.[117]

In the meantime, the Yugoslavs were increasing their propaganda against Greece for alleged maltreatment of "Yugoslav populations" residing in Greek Macedonia. In addition to press reports, Belgrade officials were expressing thinly concealed claims over Greek Macedonia.[118] On July 22, serious evidence was produced indicating that no Greek policy of moderation could restrain Yugoslav plans for Macedonia. In a note addressed to the Greek Foreign Ministry, Yugoslavia protested, in language once the accepted harbinger of war, against the alleged "persecution committed against the Macedonians—our co-nationals."[119] The Greek Govern-

---

115. Greek Foreign Minister at the time was George Sofianopoulos. In a secret report from the United Nations Conference in San Franscisco, dated May 7, 1945, addressed to the Regent, he advised that Greece should change its policy "in order to secure the sympathy and the favor of the Soviet Union" (Report No. 125). In another report (No. 71), addressed again to the Regent, referring to talks he had with Mr. Anthony Eden, he stated that he had advised the British Foreign Secretary that :

> ... the dangers to Greece from her northern neighbors, Hoxda's Albanians, Tito's Yugoslavs, and Fatherland Front Bulgarians were so great that Greece, in addition to Britain's help, was compelled to ask for the good will and support of the Russians.

GFM, File "The Minister's Most Important Talks," 1945.

116. Greece repeatedly and categorically turned down specific requests by anti-Titoists to be allowed to organize on Greek soil special forces of Yugoslav *emigrés* whose number could reach 7,000. This request was made in August 1945, at the time when, ironically enough, Yugoslavia had launched its major indoctrination and training program of Greek communist *emigrés* in Yugoslavia preparing to invade Greece.

117. Sofianopoulos talking to U. S. Assistant Secretary James C. Dunn, explained that Greece was willing to do her best not to provoke Yugoslavia, to which the American diplomat agreed. Sofianopoulos to Regent, No. 26, April 19, 1945; GFM "The Minister's Most Important Talks" op. cit.

118. In a London press conference on June 13, 1945, Yugoslav Ambassador Dr. Ljudo Leontić said that "the settlement of the Bulgarian and Greek portions of Macedonia will be the subject of mutual arrangements." GFM A/21448/1945.

119. GFM A/18583-18481/Γ1/1945; Text of the Yugoslav Note in : Yugoslavia, Office of Information, *Book on Greece* (Belgrade : Office of Information, 1948), p. 106.

ment rejected the note and, in turn, sent a note of protest to the Allies. The U.S. Ambassador in Athens, Mr. Lincoln MacVeagh, informed on July 31, the Greek Prime Minister Voulgaris, that the Yugoslav Government had sent a similar note to the U.S. Government. He went on to propose to the Greek Prime Minister that a commission of investigation composed of representatives of the U.S., British and Soviet missions in Belgrade and Athens be appointed to inquire into the issue.[120] Greece accepted the proposal on condition that the commission extend its investigations to Yugoslavia as well.[121] In the end, the American proposal did not materialize because the Yugoslavs refused to accept the commission inside their borders, where plans were already underway for the launching of the guerrilla war which would shake Greece for the next three years.

After that, the Yugoslavs rarely missed the opportunity of stating publicly their desire to incorporate Greek Macedonia into the People's Republic of Macedonia. On August 2, 1945, General Vukmanović declared his Government's policy on the unification issue before a large crowd at Skopje. The speech, promptly reported in that city's press, contained the following paragraph:

> Comrades, you know very well that there is a part of the Macedonian people which is still enslaved. We must openly state this case. We are not the only ones to do this; there are tens of thousands of Macedonian men and women who suffer and mourn today under the yoke of the Greek monarcho-fascist bands.[122]

The most categorical statement on this point was made on October 11, by President Tito himself, again in a speech at Skopje. His remarks, recorded in the Skopje newspapers, were particularly enlightening:

> We will never renounce the right of the Macedonian people to be united. This is our principle and we do not abandon our principles for any temporary sympathies. We are not indifferent to the fate of our brothers in Aegean Macedonia and our thoughts are with them. We will steadfastly defend the principle that all Macedonians must be united in their own country.[123]

The *causus* for Yugoslavia's interference in the Greek communist rebellion had thus been established. In less than six months a major guer-

---

120. *GFM* A/19746/1945.
121. *Ibid.* The Greek answer was given to Ambassador MacVeagh by Jean Politis who had replaced Mr. Sofianopoulos in the Foreign Ministry.
122. *Bulletin* (Skopje), August 10, 1945.
123. Text in *GFM* A/24581/Γ2/1945.

rilla war was on throughout Greece; a guerrilla war prepared and fully assisted by Yugoslavia in collaboration with Bulgaria and Albania.

At this point, before we proceed with an examination of the consequences of the ''Guerrilla War''—as it has passed into Greek history—it is necessary to review two major developments supporting the thesis that nationalism had remained one of the major motivating elements in the foreign policy of the newly established communist regimes in Sofia and Belgrade. The first was the peace negotiations (1946-1947) which led to the signing of the Paris Treaty, and the other, the strenuous Yugoslav-Bulgarian negotiations which led to the conclusion of the Bled Agreement of 1947, probably the most ambitious step ever taken in the direction of closely linking the two Balkan Slav states.

CHAPTER VII

FROM LIBERATION THROUGH THE TITO-COMINFORM SPLIT

The years 1946-1949 mark probably the most crucial period for Macedonia and, in fact, for the future historical process of the entire Balkan Peninsula.

The major events which shaped the course of future relationships in this part of the world were: The Peace Treaty with Bulgaria which actually reinstated that country in good international standing despite its war behavior; the Yugoslav-Bulgarian negotiations which brought the two countries to the verge of forming a South-Slav federation; the three-year-old guerrilla war in Greece which seriously threatened to convert her into a communist satellite; and, finally, the most significant development of all, Yugoslavia's expulsion from the Cominform.

THE PARIS PEACE CONFERENCE

The Greeks had looked forward to the Peace Conference as the moment of retribution for their wartime sufferings and the day of reward for having sided with the victorious Allies at the most critical moment of the war. They hoped that their reward would take the concrete form of territorial concessions, as was the case at the end of the First World War. They failed to grasp the significance of the major international developments occurring in the course of the Second World War. As a consequence, an entire nation felt deeply injured and disillusioned at the outcome of the Peace Treaty.

There was scarcely a Greek politician, journalist or intellectual who would not let himself be carried by the vision of a powerful and enlarged Greece "respected by her allies and feared by her enemies."[1] The national claims were warmly applauded by all parties of the Right, Center and Left. Even the communists joined in by demanding the application of the right

---

1. Michael Dendias, *La Thrace grecque et la débouche bulgare sur la mer Egée* (Paris: B. de Boccard, 1946), p. 15.

of self-determination to such Greek lands as the Dodecanese islands, Cyprus and Northern Epirus in Albania.[2]

From July 29 to October 11, 1946, the Paris Peace Conference convened to advise the Foreign Ministers of the Great Powers on the question of terminating the state of war with the Axis countries. Actually, it was the Fourth Conference of the Foreign Ministers, held between November 4 aud December 11, 1946, which actually terminated the state of war. The peace treaties, however, were not signed until February 10, 1947.[3]

At the Peace Conference, Greece presented claims totaling $700,000,000 for damages suffered by the Bulgarians during the occupation. At the end she was awarded only $45,000,000.[4] In addition to reparations, the Greek delegation requested, for security reasons, a readjustment of her frontier by allocating to her an area of approximately 2,000 square kilometers, thus reducing the length of the Greek-Bulgarian frontier from 480 to 350 kilometers.[5] The request was denied.

If rejection of the Greek claims met with disappointment, presentation at the Conference of Bulgarian counter claims over Western Thrace was received by the Greek people with shock and indignation. The Soviet Union and its satellite countries strongly supported the Bulgarian position.[6] Manuiliski, the Ukrainian delegate, insisted that Bulgaria should have a "peace with justice," with no economic strings attached. He openly favored the cession of Western Thrace to Bulgaria so that she might have access

---

2. "Final speech by N. Zahariades before the Twelfth Plenum of the Central Committee of the KKE", (June 25 - 27, 1945) in : Kommunistikon Komma tis Ellados, Δέκα Χρόνια 'Αγῶνες, 1935 - 1945, (Athens: Central Committee of the KKE, 1945), p. 294. On June 1, 1945, the Politburo of the Central Committee of the KKE passed a decision on the question of national claims referring to the North Epirote Question in the following words :

The KKE has always declared that the question of Northern Epirus is still unsolved. This question should be solved freely by the entire North Epirote people. It is the people who will decide what to do. . .

However, if the majority [of the democratic people in the EAM] decides that Northern Epirus should be occupied by direct military action of the Greek Army, the KKE will express its opposing views but will accept the decision.

Text in Δέκα Χρόνια 'Αγῶνες ; 1935 - 1945, op. cit., p. 253.

3. Dimitri S. Constantopoulos, The Paris Peace Conference of 1946 and the Greek - Bulgarian Relations, (Thessaloniki: Institute for Balkan Studies, 1956), p. 5.

4. William Hardy McNeil, The Greek Dilemma; War and Aftermath (Philadelphia : J. B. Lippincott and Co., 1947), pp. 252 - 253. Incidentally, Greece has not yet (December 1963) received any payment from Bulgaria.

5. Constantopoulos, op. cit., pp. 17 - 18.

6. Ibid., p. 18.

to the Aegean.[7] The Yugoslav representative also backed the Bulgarian request finding it "perfectly justified."[8]

In a memorandum submitted to the Foreign Ministers' Council, in June 1946, Bulgaria based her claims on the following grounds: first, that Western Thrace had always been geographically, ethnically and historically an integral part of Bulgarian lands; second, that Bulgarian loss of Western Thrace had resulted in the economic decline and destitution of entire provinces; third, that the Aegean coast was necessary to the hinterland which —it was contended—extended beyond the Danube as far as Rumania and Poland; fourth, that Bulgaria's foreign trade ought to be conducted inexpensively through ports on the Aegean, and, fifth, that a free port could not satisfy Bulgaria because the heavy investment required for construction of port facilities could not be undertaken unless full sovereignty were accorded Bulgaria. Futhermore, the Bulgarians argued that Western Thrace was a superfluous and unnatural appendage to Greece which she could afford to cede to Bulgaria since she was expected to receive the Dodecanese islands. A final point raised was that the Bulgarians who left the region after its restoration to Greece at the end of the First World War, were "eager to return to their homeland."[9] The fact that large scale shifts of populations during the interwar period had completely hellenized the region (the only alien element that had remained was the Turkish minority approximating 80,000) was completely ignored by the Bulgarians.[10]

Another interesting point revealed during the deliberations was that the Bulgarian communists who, barely two years before, had harshly condemned the "bourgeois-chauvinist circles of Sofia" for having unjustifiably occupied Greek Macedonia and Thrace, were now resorting to the same arguments they themselves had discredited. They even attempted to justify the policy of the wartime Bulgarian Government.[11]

7. Volms H. Cassidy (ed), *Paris Peace Conference, 1946: Selected Documents* ("Conference Series" No. 103). (Washington: U. S. Government Printing Office, [1947)], Department of State Publication No. 2868, p. 899.

8. The official Yugoslav statement was made before the Political and Territorial Commission for Bulgaria, (15th Meeting). Quoted in *Conspiracy, op. cit.*, p. 64.

9. Bulgaria, *Memorandum : Bulgaria and her Peace Problems*, (Supplementary Statement submitted to the Council of the Four Foreign Ministers at Paris, June 1946), pp. 5 - 6.

10. Statement by Bulgarian Foreign Minister Georgi Kulitchev, *Otetsestven Front*, April 27, 1946.

11. In Annex 3 of the Bulgarian *Memorandum* quoted above, the following paragraph was added (pp. 6 -7):

In 1941, the picture is rather different. With the victorious advance of the

Aside from the unexpected Bulgarian counter claims, the most significant development at the Conference was that the Bulgarian position met with the full support of the Soviet Union and Yugoslavia. The Bulgarians acknowledged publicly the importance of Yugoslavia's backing in rejecting the Greek claims.[12]

Yugoslavia's attitude at the Peace Conference appears to have been conditioned by the fact that by the end of 1946, Bulgaria had begun to contemplate seriously the acceptance of Yugoslav requests concerning Pirin Macedonia.[13] If, in exchange for the cession of the Pirin district to a Macedonian state of Yugoslav affiliation, Bulgaria were offered Western Thrace, than the deal would not appear to be so painful and might even be welcomed. Of course, barring a new war, only a communist regime in Greece could be expected to consent, under pressure, to the cession of Western Thrace.

The Bulgarian delegates left the Peace Conference having entered a reservation that they did not abandon their claim over Greek Thrace. Greece did likewise with regard to the question of the strategic rectification of the Greek-Bulgarian border.[14] Similar official statements from the Bulgarian side were made in 1946 and 1947. In December 1946, the Bulgarian Prime Minister Georgi Dimitrov stated that the question of Western Thrace was of ''vital importance to Bulgaria and will not be withdrawn from the

---

Nazi armies, who after heavy fighting burst through the Rupel gorge, the Aegean region remained, so to speak, a no man's land. Basing its rights on former possession, the Government of King Boris decided to send a Bulgarian army into this district in order to restore as it considered the situation of before 1920. There can be no question of an attack. The entry of the Bulgarian forces took place without any resistance and without any fighting, since the territories had already been evacuated by all armed forces and civil authorities and the Bulgarian authorities immediately set about restoring the damages caused by the passage through of the German units, and feeding the Greek population which was in a miserable plight. Even those who condemn for political or moral reasons the occupation of the Aegean district by the Bulgarians cannot deny that without them anarchy and famine would have resulted there [sic].

12. Statement by Bulgarian Ambassador to Belgrade, Sava Ganovski, March 1947; *GFM* A/22807/Bulg./1/1947.

13. On November 16, 1946, *Rabotnitsesko Delo* wrote that ''present-day Bulgaria favors the autonomy of Macedonia in the framework of federal Yugoslavia so that an end be placed on the hardships of the oppressed Macedonian people.''

14. United Nations, General Assembly, *Official Records*, Third Session, Suppl. No. 8, ''Report of the U. N. Special Committee on the Balkans'' (A/574), (Lake Success, 1948), p. 11, footnote 88). (Hereafter referred to as *UNSCB 1948 Report* A/574).

political stage until it finds its final solution." [15] Again in February 1947, a few months before the signing of the Bled Agreement, Dimitrov, asked by Western reporters if Bulgaria considered the Peace Conference as solving the question of Western Thrace, answered: "Of course not. The question remains open and waiting for its favorable solution." [16]

Even after the Tito-Cominform split, in 1949, the United Nations Special Committee on the Balkans had noted in its Report to the General Assembly that "Bulgaria has continued to support that country's old claim to Western Thrace with its outlet to the Aegean Sea." [17] As late as 1950, the Bulgarian Thracian organizations continued their irredentist propaganda. [18]

TOWARD A YUGOSLAV-BULGARIAN AGREEMENT; 1946-1948

A. Internal Problems in the People's Republic of Macedonia

It has already been noted [19] that Yugoslavia was increasingly critical during 1945 of pronouncements about Macedonia by certain Bulgarian elements, most of whom belonged to the Opposition parties still tolerated. Not only did these outspoken Bulgarians object to Yugoslav plans for Pirin Macedonia, but they did not hesitate to claim that the Skopje region was, in fact, a Bulgarian land. Yugoslav sensitivity was apparently due to the fact that such statements could obstruct the de-Bulgarization process, then in its most critical state. There is sufficient evidence available at this time to indicate that the Yugoslavs came across serious difficulties, in those days, in their internal Macedonian policy.

Early in January 1945, General Vukmanović, addressing a meeting of the Macedonian Anti-Fascist Organization in Skopje, revealed that opposition to the new regime in Macedonia was active and he singled out the dangers of "internal antagonism" and of "regionalist" tendencies. [20]

More details became known later in a report published by Mito Mitsaikov, State Secretary of Internal Affairs (Security) of the People's Republic of Macedonia. Referring to the period of 1945-1947, Mitsaikov

---

15. *Rabotnitsesko Delo*, December 13, 1946.

16. *Borba*, February 13, 1947.

17. United Nations, General Assembly, *Official Records*, Fourth Session, Suppl. No. 8, "Report of the U.N. Special Committee on the Balkans" (A/935), (Lake Success, 1949), p. 6. (Hereafter referred to as *UNSCB 1949 Report*, A/935).

18. *Trakiiska Duma* (Sofia) March 25, 1950 and August 15, 1950.

19. *Supra*, p. 145.

20. Report on Yugoslav press articles, February 2, 1945, *GFM* A/1869/Mac./1945.

stated that O.Z.N.A. (Security) had to combat in Macedonia the organs of many foreign interests which were preparing a counter-revolutionary *coup*. During 1945-1947 alone, 600 members of armed bands were arrested and hundreds made to return to their homes. During the same period, 1000 "spies" of the Bulgarian, German and Italian occupation authorities were arrested. Even more revealing of the prevailing situation in Yugoslav Macedonia and the opposition of the inhabitants to the regime, is Mitsaikov's statement that up to 1948 "134 fascist, terrorist organizations and groups had been discovered in the P.R. of Macedonia." [21] There could be no doubt that the majority of these organizations were composed of Bulgarian sympathizers drafted from among the local inhabitants.

B. Bulgarian Concessions

By the end of 1946, the Bulgarians had made serious concessions to the Yugoslav demands. More and more Bulgarian officials were speaking in less guarded terms about Macedonia's eventual autonomous status. Already, on May 13, 1945, Bulgarian Foreign Minister Petko Stainov, speaking to Zveno members in the Plovid Officers' Club, was quoted as saying that "Macedonia should become an independent, free state within the borders of Yugoslavia because only in this way will there be peace among the Slavs of the Balkans." [22] A year later, on June 24, 1946, Georgi Dimitrov speaking to Yugoslav students visiting Sofia appeared to endorse tacitly even the six-to-one Yugoslav federation plan, which would include a united Macedonia. He said:

> ... these two Slavic countries [Bulgaria and Yugoslavia] have now an open road for a closer unity... till the moment when they will get the common state roof without frontier when they will create a South-Slav federation of Serbs, Bulgars, Macedonians, Croats, Montenegrins,, Slovenes, when Belgrade, Sofia, Zagreb, Skopje, Cetinje and Ljubljana shall be cities and capitals of the peoples within the great federation of South-Slavs. [23]

Dimitar Ganev, then a member of the Central Committee of the CPB and presently [1963] President of the People's Assembly, spoke in the same spirit in September 1946, when he indicated that Macedonia would be united,

---

21. *Nova Makedonija*, Skopje, May 14, 1949.

22. Text in *GFM* A/21620/Bulg. 2/1945.

23. Georgi Dimitrov, *Reci, Doklad; Statii*, Vol. III, 1942-1947, (Sofia : Bulgarian Workers' Party — Communist, 1948), p. 295, as quoted in Lazar Mojsov, "About the South-Slav Federation," *Kommunist* [Supplement], (Belgrade : July-September, 1950).

with the People's Republic of Macedonia as its basis.[24] It cannot be considered merely a coincidence that all these statements occurred at the time of the peace negotiations where Yugoslavia was exhibiting a very benevolent attitude toward her ex-enemy's demands over Greek Thrace.

At its 10th Plenum, in August 1946, the Central Committee of the CPB decided "to work systematically for the cultural rapprochement of the Macedonian population of Pirin Macedonia with the People's Republic of Macedonia to propagate the People's Republic of Macedonia and its achievements... to advance the study of the Macedonian language and history among the inhabitants of Pirin, and to attach a Macedonian character to the newspaper *Pirinsko Delo*." The Resolution further suggested that "special attention must be given to a series of measures concerning the cultural autonomy and development of national consciousness of the Macedonian population... in order to facilitate its union with the main portion of the Macedonian people in the People's Republic of Macedonia."[25] The Resolution was not communicated to the rank and file of the Party at that time. Apparently the leaders were still afraid of the nationalism of their followers and hoped for a more opportune moment to make it public. Acts, however, revealed more than words could tell.

In October of that year, Gotse Deltchev's relics were removed from Sofia and presented in an official ceremony to the People's Republic of Macedonia. Thus, the most representative and illustrious figure of the Slav struggle to win Macedonia at the turn of the century, lost its Bulgarian character, by official decree, and was invested posthumously with a Macedonian ethnic identity. A little later, along the same road from Sofia to Skopje followed the 3500 volumes of the ethnological collection of the former Scientific Macedonian Institute of Sofia.[26] Early in February 1947, a census was taken in Pirin Macedonia. The inhabitants could choose between the "Macedonian" and the Bulgarian nationality. Most chose the former.[27] Many factors were instrumental in influencing the Bulgarians of Pirin to declare themselves "Macedonians." New bookstores had been opened and books in the "Macedonian" dialect propagated "Macedonian" nationalism freely. Cultural groups and teachers from the People's Republic of Macedonia cultivated the spirit of independence, which was mis-

---

24. *Glas* (Belgrade), September 24, 1946.

25. Dimitar Vlahov, *Makedonija : Momenti od Istorijata na Makedonskiot Narod* [Macedonia : Moments in the History of the Macedonian People], (Skopje : Drsavno Knigoisdatelatvo na Makedonija, 1950), p. 319.

26. *Politika*, August 15, 1947.

27. *GFM* A/20495/Γ1/1947.

taken for complete independence from *any* central authority. This, the local inhabitants mistrusted and hated when they were not openly opposing it. In addition, the communist regime in Sofia was increasingly assisting this proselytism. Despite severe opposition from many quarters, the Bulgarian Government assured the Pirin inhabitants that they would have nothing to lose from a closer association with the People's Republic of Macedonia.

C. The Bled Agreement

On August 2, 1947, Dimitrov and Tito met at Bled and signed a series of protocols, known as the Bled Protocols, which included an agreement on common policy with regard to the "Greek Question," and an agreement on cultural autonomy for Pirin Macedonia. They announced also that a pact of alliance was in the making.[28] By the agreement on Pirin, the Bulgarian Government recognized the separate ethnic rights of the inhabitants of Pirin. To the Yugoslavs the agreement meant that the region would develop nationally, politically and economically in a way that would facilitate its incorporation into the People's Republic of Macedonia.[29]

In anticipation of the conclusion of a South Slav federation the Yugoslavs were careful to limit their immediate aims to the level of "cultural autonomy."[30] This was confirmed a little later when Tito returned Dimitrov's visit and signed with him at Evksinograd, near Varna on November 27, an agreement of friendship, co-operation and mutual assistance. Following this agreement, Tito declared before a large crowd in Sofia that the treaty the two leaders had just signed brought the two countries so closely together that a federation would only be a formality.[31]

In return for their concessions in Macedonia, the Bulgarian leaders could point to a similar Yugoslav concession on the question of the "Western regions," allocated to Yugoslavia at the end of the First World War though they constituted portions of Bulgaria proper.[32] Naturally, the

28. *Yugoslav Communism, op. cit.*, p. 153.

29. *Proceedings of the First Congress of the Communist Party of the P.R. of Macedonia held 19-24 December 1948, GFM* A/19630/Γ2/1949.

30. Edvard Kardelj, *Yugoslavia's Foreign Policy*, Address delivered in the Federal Assembly on December 29, 1948 (Belgrade, 1949), p. 55.

31. *Borba*, November 26, 1947.

32. Georgi Dimitrov, *Political Report to the Fifth Congress of the Bulgarian Communist Party* (Sofia: Ministry of Foreign Affairs, Press Department, 1948), p. 64. The Yugoslavs also renounced the $25 million of Bulgarian war reparations allocated to them at the Peace Conference. Mojsov, "About the South-Slav Federation," *op. cit.*

price could scarcely compensate the Bulgarians. The loss of the Pirin district was not merely the loss of a few thousand square miles of territory, but the abandonment of a century-old national dream, shared by all Bulgarians irrespective of political or social orientation, to incorporate the entire region of Macedonia from Lake Ohrid to the Nestos (Mesta) River, from the Shar Mountains to Mount Olympus.

Although by this time open opposition had been sufficiently curtailed, there was widespread discontent in Bulgaria over the agreements, a fact manifested in the obstructionist attitude of officials of the administration and even of the Party. Particularly revealing was the following article published in the Party's newspaper *Rabotnitsesko Delo*, dated October 9, 1947:

> Through great sacrifices, the Macedonian people have acquired their just right to be considered a free people with equal rights. They have proven to their enemies—the Greater Bulgarians, the Greater Serbs and the Greek chauvinists—who refused to acknowledge to them the right of their own identity, that they are a living people, capable of managing their own affairs according to their own interests. They have established their free Macedonian state within the framework of federal Yugoslavia. Through a superb, heroic effort, they are creating their material and cultural civilization... [Their successes] fill with joy not only the Macedonian people of Vardar Macedonia, but also the Macedonian population of Pirin... as well as all Macedonians wherever they might be...

> ... These people have the right to live and develop as a Macedonian people, to raise their national consciousness and to develop their Macedonian civilization.

> Our people have nothing to lose from the practical realization of these just rights of the Macedonians; on the contrary, they will gain even more, in the brotherly hearts [of the Macedonians]. Only misguided and irreconcilable Greater Bulgarian chauvinists and foreign agents in our country can deny them these rights. The imperialist, assimilative policy of the Bulgarian bourgeoisie is foreign to the Fatherland Front...

The article went on to reveal that there was strong opposition to the principles proclaimed by the Party organ. The following passages are particularly enlightening:

> Unfortunately, the remnants of this chauvinistic policy have not been fully discredited and their influence still poisons the actions of certain elements in our country. There are still certain persons in our country, even within the ranks of the Fatherland Front, who are of the opinion that within the borders of the country there are

no Macedonians, there is no Macedonian population. The geography textbooks of the 4th grade and the 3rd and 7th grades of the high school, published by the Ministry of Education in 1945, 1946 and 1947, contain not a few individual examples of Greater Bulgarianism and chauvinism. The books mention that within the frontiers of Fatherland Front Bulgaria, live only Bulgarians, Turks, Armenians, Jews, Gypsies, etc., but no mention is made of the Macedonians... Sometime ago, officials of the Ministry of Information objected to granting financial aid to the new theater in Gorna Djumaja because it bore the name, "The Macedonian National Theater"...

These gross and dark expressions of Bulgarian super-chauvinism cannot and should not be tolerated in Fatherland Front Bulgaria. The Bulgarian people should overcome these destructive influences which are the remnants of the bourgeois-fascist past; they should grow in the spirit of the correct policy of the Fatherland Front. This policy grants to the Macedonians of Pirin all the rights to be educated as part of the Macedonian people—who already possess their own state—to be tought their own history, to speak their mother tongue, to have their own books and develop their own civilization.

Dimitrov appeared to be succeeding in transforming, in the name of communist internationalism, Bulgaria's traditionally agressive nationalism. Even the most skeptical observers began to accept that a genuine transformation was taking place in Bulgaria. It was customary, at the time, to attribute these developments to Moscow's Balkan policy. Recent available information, however, corroborated by Milovan Djilas' book, *Conversations with Stalin,* has revealed that Stalin had nothing to do with this Bulgarian-Yugoslav rapprochement. On the contrary, when a year later all the elaborately prepared plans for a united Macedonian state and a South-Slav federation broke down, the reason was not to be found in the contradictions of Balkan nationalism but, rather, in the centralist manifestations of Soviet policy.

D. Soviet Reactions

Georgi Dimitrov, caught by the vision of a powerful South-Slav Communist federation, allowed himself to be carried away to a point which Stalin could not tolerate. In a press conference in January 31, 1948, Dimitrov stated that the question of a people's federation or confederation, encompassing Bulgaria, Yugoslavia, Albania, Rumania, Czechoslovakia, Poland, Hungary and even Greece, was bound to come into existence. *Pravda* initially published his remarks without any comment; sharply condemned them a few days later. "What these countries require," wrote

Pravda, ''was no questionable and fabricated federation or confederation or customs union; what they require is the consolidation and defense of their independence and sovereignty by mobilizing and organizing internally their people's democratic forces.''[33] On February 10, the Bulgarian and Yugoslav leaders were summoned to Moscow where they were subjected to a tormenting criticism by Stalin himself for undertaking an ambitious political program without first securing his permission. The Bulgarians were represented by G. Dimitrov, V. Kolarov and T. Kostov while the Yugoslavs sent Bakarić, Kardelj and Djilas. Tito remained in Belgrade pretending to be sick.[34] Most of the criticism was reserved for the Bulgarians, apparently because Stalin wanted to subdue, once and for all, any desire for independent action on the part of the most trusted Eastern European Party. Dimitrov was forced to apologize. The Yugoslavs, however, remained non-committal. Apparently, it was this meeting that convinced Stalin that he had to adopt more drastic measures toward the intransigent and ambitious Yugoslavs in order to force the overthrow of the leadership of the Yugoslav Party.

THE GUERRILLA WAR IN GREEK MACEDONIA

Though by the end of 1947, the incorporation of Bulgarian Macedonia into the People's Republic of Macedonia appeared to be closer than ever, in Greece the communists, assisted by Yugoslavia, Bulgaria and Albania, had unleashed a large-scale guerrilla war aimed at the overthrow of the existing regime. The most critical military operations took place in Macedonia, and, indeed, the fate of that region depended much on the outcome of the rebellion.

A. The KKE on the Macedonian Question at the Outbreak of the Rebellion

It is interesting to note that on the eve of the outbreak of hostilities, the Greek communists publicly disclaimed persistent rumors that they favored the cession of Macedonia to Yugoslavia or even to Bulgaria. In Party conferences and official publications they upheld the principles of the 1935 Party Congress which had abandoned the slogan of ''a united

33. Vladimir Dedijer, *Tito* (New York : Simon and Schuster, 1953), pp. 313-114.
34. Milovan Djilas, *Conversations with Stalin,* [Greek edition], (Athens : K. H. Kamarinopoulos, 1962), p. 143.

and independent Macedonia" for the principle of "equality of rights for the Slav-Macedonians."

In 1945, Yannis Zevgos, the top theoretician of the KKE, declared publicly that Macedonia was a Hellenic land.[35] For this attitude he was severely reprimanded by Secretary-General Zahariades in 1949, when the Party returned to the slogan of "a united and independent Macedonia."[36]

The decision to launch an open rebellion was taken at the 12th Plenum of the Central Committee of the KKE held in Athens on June 25-27, 1945.[37] In setting out the policy of the Party on the national issue, Zahariades declared:

> We are against any forced change of the boundaries of 1939 from any side. The only democratic solution we recognize is the principle of the self-determination of peoples. This principle applies also to the Dodecanese islands, Cyprus and Northern Epirus.[38]

At the same time he said that equal rights should be granted to all national minorities including "the Macedonian minority." Zahariades further explained his Party's position on this issue at the Seventh Party Congress held in Athens in late 1945, when he said:

> ... We declare that a fundamental prerequisite for the peaceful co-existence with the Yugoslav Republic is the absolute respect of the rights of the Slav-Macedonian minority and the securing for this minority of a regime of full equality of racial, religious and linguistic rights. This is the only way to avoid conflicts, misunderstandings and discussions over Greek Macedonia, which is inhabited by 90 per cent Greeks, a fact which renders it an inseparable part of the Hellenic land.[39]

Partsalides, a member of the Central Committee, was even more categorical in his final speech to the Congress. While, he declared that

35. Δέκα Χρόνια 'Αγῶνες, 1935 - 1945, op. cit. pp. 8 and 29.

36. Vasilis Bardjiotas, "Πάνω στὴ Μελέτη τῆς 'Ιστορίας τοῦ ΚΚΕ" [On the the Study of the History of the KKE], Νέος Κόσμος (Monthly theoretical organ of the KKE), March 1951, p. 13.

37. 'Απόφαση τοῦ Πολιτικοῦ Γραφείου τῆς Κ.Ε. τοῦ ΚΚΕ γιὰ τὴν 'Υπόθεση Μπούλκες [Decision of the Politburo of the Central Committee of the KKE on the Bulkes case], Νέος Κόσμος, June 1951, p. 6.

38. 'Απόφαση τῆς 12ης 'Ολομέλειας τῆς Κ.Ε. τοῦ ΚΚΕ [Decision of the 12th Plenum of the Central Committee of the KKE], (Athens: Central Committee of the KKE, 1945), p. 48.

39. "Zahariades' Introductory Speech before the Seventh Party Congress," Τὸ 7ο Συνέδριο [The Seventh Congress], Issue C, (Athens: Central Committee of the KKE, 1945), p. 30.

166

Greece had the right, on the basis of the principle of self-determination, to project her national claims over the Dodecanese islands and Cyprus, the same principle could not apply to Greek Macedonia, even in the border regions where the "Slav-Macedonians" lived in more compact groups.[40]

On the basis of these and other public statements by leading members of the KKE, as well as by details revealed during the heated exchanges between Greek and Yugoslav communists in 1949-1952, it appears that the KKE was willing to make certain concessions to the Yugoslavs, such as recognizing the Slavophones as a Yugoslav minority and even extending to them national rights. However, it does not seem probable that the KKE made at that time any promises to the Yugoslavs for territorial concessions in Macedonia.

All through 1945 and 1946, Zahariades continued to uphold in public the position of the Party on the national question as outlined at the Seventh Congress.[41] Naturally, the Yugoslavs could not be expected to be fully satisfied with these half-concessions but, hoping for the best, they extended their full support to the guerrilla war which the KKE had begun in the summer of 1946.[42]

B. Yugoslavia and the Guerrilla War in Greece

By early 1946, approximately 25,000 communists from Greece were assembled in Yugoslavia. The Yugoslav Government, as has been ascertained by the United Nations Security Council's Investigation Commission dispatched to the Balkans, had established a camp in Bulkes where refugees from Greece received military training and political indoctrination.[43] At the same time they attempted to elicit loyal friends, particularly among the Slav-speaking refugees, who would be willing to carry out the Yugoslav objectives in Greek Macedonia.[44] Their efforts apparently

40. *Ibid.*, p. 27.

41. Kostas Bramos, Σλανοκομμουνιστικαὶ 'Οργανώσεις ἐν Μακεδονίᾳ. Προπαγάνδα καὶ 'Επαναστατικὴ Δρᾶσις [Slav-Communist Organizations in Macedonia. Propaganda and Revolutionary Activity], (Thessaloniki: 1953), p. 145.

42. Following the Tito-Cominform rupture in 1948, Svetovar Vukmanović sharply criticised the KKE for its policy in 1945-1946 which, he alleged, did not provide for the right of self-determination to the "Slav-Macedonians." He accused the Greek communist leaders of having followed a clearly opportunistic attitude on the issue. Svetovar Vukmanović, *How and Why the People's Liberation Struggle in Greece Met with Defeat*, (London: 1950), p. 50.

43. Report of the U.N. Investigation Commission quoted in *Conspiracy*, *op. cit.*, p. 161.

44. In 1951, in its official publication, Νέος Κόσμος, the KKE revealed that

met with sufficient success, especially among those Slavophones who had been members of the SNOF during the closing days of the war and had, subsequently, sought refuge in Yugoslavia. It is interesting to note that upon their entrance to Yugoslavia, the SNOF bands had been dissolved, their leader Gotsev named colonel of the Yugoslav Army and a significant number of his followers allowed to join the Yugoslav Army. By December 1946, fully trained and indoctrinated, they were discharged from the Army and were dispatched to join the ranks of the Greek guerrillas.[45]

The conduct of the guerrilla war falls outside the scope of this book. Only developments which had a direct impact on the fate of Macedonia will be examined. The protagonists in the struggle for Greek Macedonia were: First, the Yugoslavs who encouraged and assisted the Greek guerrillas [46] (even when Stalin was convinced that there was no hope of success).[47] They hoped apparently that eventually a communist government in Greece would be willing to cede Greek Macedonia to a Skopje-centered Macedonian state. Second, was the NOF [National Liberation Front], the new "Slav-Macedonian" organization which was formed by the Yugoslav-trained "Slav-Macedonians" and acted as the instrument of Yugoslav plans in Greek Macedonia. Third, were the Greek communists who were badly divided over the issue of the irredentist "Slav-Macedonians."

Except for direct material assistance to the guerrillas and the NOF, Yugoslavia carried, all through the war, an open campaign to discredit and intimidate Greece. At the same time, through the press, radio, numerous books and pamphlets, as well as by speeches of Government officials in Yugoslavia and the United Nations, she tried to show that Greece had no

---

in 1945, the communist refugees were assembled in Bulkes where they lived as an organized group. Many cadres of the "Democratic Army of Greece" (the communist guerrilla force) received their specialized training at Bulkes. *Νέος Κόσμος,* June 1951, *op. cit.,* p. 6.

45. *GFM* A/21270/Bal/1948. After the Tito-Cominform break, the leadership of the KKE accused the Yugoslavs of trying to manipulate indoctrination at the Bulkes camp for the purpose of proselytizing agents for their "Greater Serbian" chauvinistic claims over Greek Macedonia. *Νέος Κόσμος,* June 1951, *op. cit.,* p. 7.

46. After the communist defeat in August 1949, Zahariades revealed that the KKE had decided to launch an open armed rebellion only because they were promised in 1946 the unswerving support of the Yugoslavs. "If we knew of this treachery (Tito's closing of the frontier in July 1949) we would not have started in 1946." D. Zapheiropoulos, *'Ο 'Αντισυμμοριτικὸς 'Αγὼν* [The Anti-guerrilla Struggle], (Athens, 1956), p. 660.

47. Djilas, *op. cit.,* p. 152. Dedijer, *op. cit.,* pp. 321-322.

168

rights over Macedonia.[48] An effort was made by the theoreticians of the new "Macedonian" state to prove that Greece did not have even ethnological grounds to posses the region.[49] Most of the Yugoslav propaganda was discharged *via* the Skopje Government. This prompted an on-the-scene observer to remark that Skopje's attitude toward Greece resembled that of Sofia's in its most nationalistic mood, or of the I.M.R.O. in its moments of greatest revolutionary fervor. "The [Yugoslav] Macedonian Government," he wrote, "cries to the world of Greek terror, just as Sofia long shrieked of Turkish terror... From Skopje run underground lines of conspiracy to Greece, just as they used to run from Sofia into Turkey."[50]

---

48. On August 26, 1946, *Borba* published an article under the title "Aegean Macedonia" which read as follows:

> Greek imperialists have no right to keep the Macedonians any longer under their yoke; they can no longer allege that Belgrade and Sofia also oppress some portions of Macedonia and that a free Macedonian people with state organization does not exist.
>
> . . . .
> This question is part of the struggle for peace and democracy and for the self-determination of the peoples. That is why our country cannot remain indifferent to the extermination of our populations in Greece and to their right and request to opt and unite themselves with their brethren in Yugoslavia.

A month later, on September 22, the Premier of the People's Republic of Macedonia, Dimitar Vlahov, delivered a speech in Monastir, published in *Nova Makedonija*, on September 26, 1946, which referred to Greek Macedonia as follows:

> We openly declare that Greece has no right whatsoever over Aegean Macedonia...The Macedonian people are struggling for their union within the Macedonian People's Republic which is an integral part of the Federal People's Republic of Yugoslavia.

49. Hristo Antonofsky, an extremist irredentist from Greek Macedonia living in Skopje, declared that the ethnological composition of Greek Macedonia was as follows:

"Macedonians"	258,000
Greeks	250,000
"Caramanlides"	210,000
Armenians	80,000
Lazi and other Caucasians	74,000
Others	37,000

In addition to discovering new "nationalities," Antonofski conveniently excluded the population of Thessaloniki, the Chalkidiki Peninsula and even the Kozani district, all parts of Macedonia known for their indisputable Greek ethnological composition even prior to the First World War. All estimates refer to the period following 1941.— Hristo Antonofski, *Egejska Makedonija* [Aegean Macedonia] (Skopje: G.O. na Zdruzhanieto na be Galcite od Eg. Makedonija, 1951), p. 50.

50. R. H. Markham, *Tito's Imperial Communism* (Chapel Hill, N. C.: The University of North Carolina Press, 1947), p. 228.

Never had Greco-Yugoslav relations deteriorated to such a low point. In 1947, the United Nations General Assembly found that Albania, Bulgaria and Yugoslavia had given assistance and support to the guerrillas fighting against the Greek Government, and called on these states to cease offering assistance.[51]

The United Nations Special Committee on the Balkans attributed the deterioration of Greco-Yugoslav relations definitely to the latter's support of the guerrilla war.[52]

C. Bulgaria and the Guerrilla War

While Yugoslavia was fully involved in the Greek guerrilla war, Bulgaria maintained a reserved attitude toward Yugoslav interference in Greek Macedonia. For the detached observer, it was a most curious attitude, inasmuch as this was the only period in Bulgaria's history since the establishment of the Exarchate in 1870, that Sofia was disinclined to actively participate in developments concerning a region long attracting the nation's interest. Instead, she limited herself to occasional statements about her historical rights over Greek Western Thrace and, more important, she offered harbor and material assistance to the Greek guerrillas,[53] pleading that a friendly regime at her vital southern frontiers was to her national interest.[54] A "National Committee for Assistance to the Greek Democratic People" was organized including members of the Sobranje and Madame Rosa Dimitrova, wife of the Bulgarian Premier. In its appeal to the Bulgarian people for contributions on January 2, 1948, the Committee stated that "a victory of the Greek people is definitely in Bulgaria's interest." [55]

In fact, Bulgaria's outward indifference toward Macedonian affairs remained unaltered until Yugoslavia's expulsion from the Cominform. Later, however, it was revealed that in 1947-1948 the Bulgarians had tried secretly to reduce Yugoslav dominance over the NOF by infiltrating it with their own agents among the Slavophones.

---

51. United Nations, General Assembly, *Official Records*, Second Session, First Committee, 72nd Meeting, p. 115.

52. *U.N.S.C.B. 1948 Report*, (A/574), *op. cit.*, p. 12.

53. *Ibid* , p. 16.

54. Georgi Dimitrov, *La Front de la patrie*, p. 12.

55. *U.N.S.C.B. 1948 Report*, (A/574), *op. cit.*, p. 16.

170

D. The Role of the "Slav-Macedonians" in the Rebellion

The exact date of the establishment of the NOF is not known. It appears, however, that its political and organizational bases were set in the spring of 1945, following the withdrawal from Greece of the SNOF followers.[56] There is no evidence that the Greek communists were directly involved in the NOF's formation, an essentially Yugoslav inspired organization.[57] Only after the Seventh Congress of the KKE and Zahariades' visit to Yugoslavia in 1946, to discuss details of the planned rebellion, did the KKE accept the NOF. In the spring of 1945, Zahariades recognized it officially — though not publicly — and allowed it to be admitted to the EAM where, in addition to the communists, other leftist groups had also been assembled.[58] By 1947, it was definitely ascertained that the NOF had formed armed units which operated under the command of the guerrillas' supreme commander, Markos Vafiades.[59]

According to its Statute, the NOF's primary purpose was to win for the "Macedonian people" their national rights "within the framework of democratic Greece" [Article 1].[60] There is no evidence that at this time the NOF agitated for a separate national status. Aware, apparently, of the small percentage of "Slav-Macedonians" amidst the Greeks of Macedonia, it attempted to attract members from "other national minorities" [Article 2] and other "mass people's organizations" [Article 3]. This maneuver resembled the I.M.R.O.'s first Constitution of 1893 which had initially declared it would welcome to its ranks all those sharing its program.[61]

The NOF followed the organizational pattern of all similar communist

---

56. Bramos (First Edition), *op. cit.*, pp. 143-144.

57. In the post-Cominform era, the "Slav-Macedonian" *emigrés* in Yugoslavia accused the Greek communists of having opposed NOF's establishment following the Varkiza Agreement. "The Aegeans in the Cominform countries," *Voice of the Aegeans* (Skopje), August 6, 1952.

58. *Ibid.*

59. Elizabeth Barker, *Macedonia; Its Place in Balkan Power Politics* (London: The Royal Institute of International Affairs, 1950) p. 118.

60. Document in *GFM* A/27302/Ba./1948.

61. The NOF's aims were further amplified in an accompanying document which outlined its platform as follows:

...NOF...is determined, along with all the national democratic powers which recognize this right, to struggle for winning equality of national rights and, thus, secure for our People an equal national life, equal political, civic and cultural rights and its full democratic guarantee within the ranks of an independent and democratic Greece.

Document in *GFM* A/27302/Aut. Mac./Ba./1948.

groups. The Congress, meeting once a year, was the sovereign body. Executive authority was vested in the Central Council which appointed a nine member Executive Committee to carry out decisions [Articles 6, 7]. To reach the masses, the NOF was organized on a regional basis with regional, sectional, city and even unit (village, factory, etc.) councils [Articles 8-10]. Women also could join their own NOF organization, the Women's Antifascist Front (A.F.Z.) [Article 13].

While the NOF's objectives did not appear, in writing, to go further than a demand for equality of rights, official Yugoslav statements for the unification of Macedonia and direct Yugoslav support of the NOF — in the form of Yugoslav instructors under the cover of "Macedonian volunteers" — raised serious doubts as to the true objectives of the group. Similarly, the activities of certain NOF leaders who continually pressed the guerrilla headquarters for more authority in the conduct of the operations and more jurisdiction in the administration of guerrilla controlled countryside, tended to support the thesis that "equality of rights" was not the maximum of the NOF's objectives.

By the end of 1947, the NOF had succeeded in spreading its network among the Slavophones of the border regions of Edessa, Florina and Kastoria. However, when in November, it appealed, in a conference of guerrilla cadres held at Ano Vrontou, for permission to extend its organization to Eastern Macedonia, its petition was turned down by Headquarters.[62]

In the meantime, in guerrilla controlled mountain regions, the KKE had granted the NOF the right to establish schools, newspapers and even churches in the Slav-Macedonian dialect.[63] According to NOF estimates, by May 1948, 7000 children had learned the "Macedonian" language, while 4000 adults had been taught writing and reading in evening schools.[64]

Despite Yugoslav and Greek communist support, the NOF was able to organize only the Slavophones who were completely under guerrilla control. In fact, there were two categories of Slavophones who had joined the guerrilla movement; those who willingly did so, and those who were drafted into it. Zahariades claimed, after the rebellion, that the communists had won to their cause "undoubtedly the majority of the Slav-Macedonians."[65]

62. *GFM* A/15470/Γ5/Bb1/1949.

63. Vlahov, *Makedonija, op. cit.*, p. 298; Also, *Oletsestven Front*, January 15, 1962.

64. Report by the NOF delegate Michael Keramitjiev to the Second Congress of the Macedonian People's Front held at Skopje, May 1948, *Nova Makedonija*, May 24, 1948.

65. Nikos Zahariades, Δέκα Χρόνια Πάλης [Ten Years of Struggle], (November 1950), p. 48.

172

However, a significant number of Slavophones opposed the NOF and the communists in general. There are many examples of entire villages of Slav-speaking inhabitants which formed home-guard units against the NOF incursions.[66] In March 1948, the NOF issued a declaration urging the Slavophones not to join the Greek Army because "the Macedonian people were already building a new life in equality with the Greek people in the free regions."[67]

In January 1948, the number of "Slav-Macedonian" guerrillas was estimated at 11,000.[68] Although some leaders of the guerrillas were suspicious of the motives and objectives of the NOF, the "Democratic Army," concentrating its activity in the northern departments of the country, was forced to depend increasingly on the "Slav-Macedonians."

On January 13, 1948, the first NOF Congress was held in guerrilla controlled territory to vote for the NOF Statute. It was attended by 500 representatives[69] and the "ministers" of the "Provisional Government," Yannis Ioannides (Interior) and Leon Stringos (National Economy).[70] A little later, on April 21, the first Congress of the A.F.Z. was held, attended by "Minister of Justice" Porfyrogenis. Despite the fact that major Greek communist figures attended the NOF conferences, the mutual mistrust between the rank and file of Greek guerrilas and the NOF followers grew daily.[71]

The NOF did not have to fight only for recognition by the Greek communists; it had also to contend with the old, pro-Bulgarian nationalist propaganda conducted by a revived I.M.R.O. As was the case with Yu-

66. Doros G. Pefanis, Οἱ ῞Ελληνες Σλανόφωνοι τῆς Μακεδονίας καὶ οἱ ῞Ελληνο - Βλάχοι: Μελέτη Πολιτική, ῾Ιστορική, Κοινωνικὴ [The Greek Slavophones of Macedonia and the Greco-Vlachs] Second Edition, (Athens, 1949), pp. 18-19. The author quotes official reports indicating that Slavophones had joined the National Army to fight against the NOF and the guerrillas.
67. Text in *GFM* A/26516/Ba/1948.
68. Pantelis Vagenas, "The Democratic Army and the Slav-Macedonians," Δημοκρατικὸς Στρατὸς (Vol. I, October 1948) pp. 408-412. The Greek Army General Staff estimated that 20 per cent of the guerrillas were "Slav-Macedonians." *GFM* A/74677/Bal/1948.
69. ᾿Εξόρμησις, February 1948 (publication of the Guerrilla Headquarters).
70. *GFM* A/36877/Bal/1948.
71. Report of the Greek Army General Staff, dated January 28, 1948, *GFM* A/19319/Bal/1948. Two years later, information reached French intelligence circles that in the early part of 1948, Vafiades had discussed with Tito the cession of certain Greek Macedonian border regions for the latter's support of Greek claims over Northern Epirus. To the knowledge of the author, these reports have not been corroborated by other sources.

goslav, and to a lesser extend Bulgarian Macedonia — where it had created difficulties in the "Macedonization" process — the I.M.R.O., in war ridden Greek Macedonia, was also engaged in attracting the Slavophones to its own slogans. Supported by non-communist Bulgarian-Macedonian organizations in the United States and Canada, as well as by circles of the Bulgarian Opposition parties, the I.M.R.O. declared that it struggled for an independent Macedonian state outside the framework of Yugoslavia.

In all its pronouncements, the I.M.R.O. was anti-Soviet and anti-communist. Whether the communist Bulgarians had any connection with these activities — as some suspected — is doubtful, although many communist Bulgarian personalities bitterly objected to their Government's retreat before Yugoslavia on the Macedonian problem. Such elements might have tolerated, or even abated the I.M.R.O.'s activities, but concrete evidence, in this respect, is lacking.[72]

The NOF tried to contain the I.M.R.O.'s influence — which actually never reached any significant dimensions — by publicly denouncing it. In a leaflet circulated among the "Slav-Macedonians" it was stated that the "NOF struggles uncompromisingly against the autonomist movement...and the terrorist bandit organization I.M.R.O. led by Ivan Mihailov."[73]

The I.M.R.O. was more successful after the confusion created among the "Slav-Macedonians" by the Tito-Cominform dispute. By January 1949, it became known that the I.M.R.O. agitated in favor of a plan for an independent and united Macedonian state to be placed under the protection of the United States, Great Britain and the Soviet Union. A significant number of hesitant "Slav-Macedonians" were attracted by the propaganda of the Western oriented I.M.R.O. probably in the hope they might be able to save their lives in the event of the rebellion's defeat.[74]

E. The United Nations on the Macedonian Question

The seditious activities of the "Slav-Macedonians," most of whom had organized themselves in the NOF, brought many delegates in the United Nations to the conclusion that the conflict's only solution was the

---

72. Report dated February 16, 1948. *GFM* A/22166/Ba/1948; Also, *Pirinsko Delo* November 17, 1947, wrote that Mihailov's propaganda was actively aiming at "subverting the national consciousness of the Macedonian people."

73. *GFM* A/27302/Ba/1948.

74. Statement by captured "Major" Constantine Giogas ("Fanis"), chief of the Intelligence Office of the General Headquarters of the guerrillas. February 1949. Statement in *GFM* A/23696/Γ5/1949.

exchange of minorities between Greece and her Slav neighbors. Yugoslavia reacted strongly against these proposals. Dimitar Vlahov, writing in June 1947, appealed to the Slav organizations of North and South America, Canada and Australia to raise a campaign in their respective countries against "these diabolic designs aimed at the Macedonian people."[75] Nevertheless, the General Assembly, in its 1947 Resolution, recommended that Albania, Bulgaria, Yugoslavia and Greece "study the practicability of concluding agreements for the voluntary transfer of minorities."[76] However, the continuation of hostilities in that region precluded any action on the subject. An offer by the Australian Foreign Minister Evatt to mediate the question of alien minorities on both sides of the border, was turned down by Greece on the grounds that she could not enter into negotiations with Yugoslavia on this subject because she would be thus recognizing the latter's right to express an interest in the Slavophones. This, Greece was unwilling to accept.[77]

It may be noted here that what was not achieved through the good offices of the International Organization during the heat of the guerrilla war was realized, for all practical purposes, at the end of the rebellion when thousands of "Slav-Macedonians" crossed the border and took refuge in Yugoslavia. Albania, Bulgaria, as well as other Eastern European countries.

Such was the situation in Greek Macedonia up to the summer of 1948 when, suddenly, Cominform's announcement of the expulsion of Yugoslavia took the world by surprise and affected the course of the guerrilla war and the fate of Greek Macedonia.

THE IMPACT OF THE COMINFORM'S DECISION
ON THE MACEDONIAN QUESTION

Stalin's decision to denounce Tito, since he could not subdue him, had a direct impact on the fate of the guerrilla war in Greece, and more generally, on Yugoslavia's Macedonian plans. Following a full year's indecisiveness, the Yugoslavs ended their support of the Cominform oriented Greek guerrillas and, thus, helped significantly in the crushing of the

---

75. Dimitar Vlahov, "The Problems of the Aegean Macedonia," *Slobensko Bratstvo*, (Belgrade), June 1947.
76. United Nations, General Assembly, *Official Records*, Second Session, First Committee, 72nd Meeting, (Lake Success, 1947), p. 115.
77. Permanent Deputy Minister of Foreign Affairs Pipinelis' cable from Paris to Greek Foreign Ministry dated November 17, 1948. *GFM* A/57503 Γ5/1948.

rebellion.[78] The new turn of events, the mass exodus of the "Slav-Macedonians," and the defeat of communism in Greece, apparently solved the Macedonian question for Greece. As far as Bulgaria was concerned, she was now in a position to keep the Pirin district for herself.

The end result was that Yugoslavia's chances for the acquisition of Macedonia — and for the hegemony of the Balkans — which appeared promising at the time of the Bled Agreement, suffered a definite setback. Barring unanticipated developments, Yugoslavia had to abandon her expansionist Macedonian policy, at least for the foreseeable future, and seek new orientations in her foreign policy. On the other hand, Bulgaria considered that the temporary weakness of her Slav neighbor offered her the opportunity to bring forth anew the issue of the formation of a Bulgarian sponsored autonomous Macedonian state.

A. The Last Year of the Guerrilla War: July 1948 — August 1949

1. From July to December 1948

Cominform's decision took the leadership of the Greek communists by surprise and created deep confusion among the rank and file of the "Democratic Army" and the NOF. The dilemma was, indeed, critical; to choose Tito over Stalin would have been an unpardonable treachery to the principles of international communism; to side with the other Cominform countries and attack Tito, would have jeopardized the rebellion — then at its most critical stage — since the bulk of the support came by way of Yugoslavia. Both the KKE and the NOF were badly split over the decision.

During the first weeks, and even months, there was no public change in the attitude of the KKE toward Tito. Secretly, however, at the Fourth Plenum of the Central Committee, convened on July 28, 1948, the KKE adhered to the Cominform's Resolution on Yugoslavia but refrained from making public its decision at that time. Similar was its attitude at the Fifth Plenum, on January 30, 1949.[79]

---

78. Zahariades probably made a correct estimate of the harm done to the rebellion by Yugoslavia's closing of the frontier, when he wrote : "Even though the Monarchofascists [i.e. the Greek Army] could manage to push us off, temporarily from Vitsi and Grammos, they could have never achieved the eviction from Greece of the main forces of the Democratic Army of Greece, were it not for Tito's treachery. It is from this angle that Tito's treachery played a decisive role in the outcome of the operations at Vitsi and Grammos in 1949." Zahariades, Δέκα Χρόνια Πάλης, op. cit., p. 63.

79. "The Rebellion," Sovietology (Athens), January 1962, pp. 25-26.

Throughout the summer and fall of 1948, the leadership of the KKE began discreetly to remove from NOF positions of leadership the most outspoken advocates of Yugoslav aims. On August 8, 1948, just a month and a half after the Cominform's announcement, the Plenun of the Executive Council of the NOF removed from the Secretariat Michael Keramidjiev, ostensibly for failing to mobilize the masses of the "Slav-Macedonians" and for engaging in fractional activities in order to assume the leadership of the Organization. The fact is that his removal was ordered because he had remained loyal to Tito.[80] Vangel Kotsev, trusted by the KKE to follow the Cominform's new policy toward Yugoslavia, was chosen as the new head of the NOF. The decision was ratified by a Conference of NOF military cadres held on September 24. Zahariades and Vlandas were present at the meeting,[81] a fact which indicated thad the NOF was rapidly passing under the pro-Cominform leadership of the KKE.

From that moment on, an open struggle became apparent between the pro-Yugoslav and pro-Cominform factions. By December, the Cominformists appeared to have won, as evidenced by the fact that pro-Yugoslav elements had fled *en masse* to Yugoslavia. Safely at Skopje, they accused the leadership of the KKE of lacking "love" and "trust" for the "Slav-Macedonians." In addition, they complained that the KKE had failed to promote the "Slav-Macedonians" to senior ranks in the guerrilla army, had intentionally discriminated against them and assigned them to front line duty.[82]

The KKE could ill afford to lose the support of the "Slav-Macedonians." The intelligence officer of the General Headquarters of the guerrillas, "Major" Fanis, captured by the Greek Army, revealed that in January 1949, 30 per cent of the "Democratic Army" was composed of "Slav-Macedonians." Of these, the majority favored secessionist or autonomist solutions for Macedonia.[83] Daily, the number of "Slav-Macedonians" inclining toward the Bulgarian sponsored plan for an autonomous Macedonian state, which had the Cominform's support, increased. This was partly due to the fact that Bulgaria began to reinforce the guerrilas with the dispatch of trusted residents of Greek extraction in Bulgaria, including a few who were already reserve officers in the Bulgarian Army. By May 1949,

---

80. Secret Report dated November 3, 1948, in *GFM* A/59224/Bb1 1948.
81. *Bulletin* (issued in "Slav-Macedonian" by the Central Council of the NOF), No 8, September 29, 1948.
82. Captured guerrilla documents in *GFM* A/17516 Γ5 Bb1 1949.
83. *Ibid.*

the NOF reported that approximately 1200 "brother Bulgarians" had arrived in Greece.[84]

During the closing weeks of 1948, friction between the lesser cadres of Greek and "Slav-Macedonian" guerrillas became more acute. The NOF leadership, however, realizing the importance of the "Slav-Macedonians" for the rebellion, pressed the KKE to adopt its secessionist demands. In the December issue of *Democratikos Stratos* (No. 12, pp. 528-529), organ of the Guerrilla Headquarters, a letter was published signed by K..., apparently a member of the NOF hierarchy. It spoke of the common struggle of the "Slav-Macedonians" and the Greek people and demanded that the *national claims* of the "Slav-Macedonians" for an independent, national and separate state identity should not be refused.

2. The KKE's New Macedonian Policy: The January 1949 Resolution

Acceptance of the demands of the "Slav-Macedonians" by the KKE came late in January 1949. At the Fifth Plenum of the Central Committee held on January 30-31, the KKE passed a Resolution which opened the way for Greek Macedonia to be ceded to a future "Macedonian state." The text referring to the Macedonian question was as follows:[85]

> In Northern Greece, the Macedonian (Slavo-Macedonian) people have offered everything to the struggle, and [now] fight with such overwhelming heroism and self-sacrifice that it commends admiration. There should be no doubt that with the victory of the Democratic Army of Greece [and] of the people's revolution, the Macedonian people *will realize their full national restitution, as they themselves want it,* offering today their blood to win it.

To make certain that no one misinterpreted the statement concerning the "national restitution" as an endorsement of Yugoslavia's position, the Resolution went on:

> At the same time, the Macedonian communists should guard against the fractionist and disrupting activities of alien-motivated, chauvinistic and reactionary elements aimed at breaking the unity of the Macedonian (Slavo-Macedonian) and Greek people, a fact which would benefit only our common enemy, monarcho-fascism and Anglo-American imperialism.

---

84. Bramos (First Edition), *op. cit.*, p. 172.

85. Text in *GFM* File A/Γ5/Bb1/1949. Italics added. The Resulotion was broadcast by Radio "Free Greece" on February 6. It is also quoted in part in Barker *op. cit.*, p. 119.

Taking notice of the great dissatisfaction among a significant segment of the Greek communists with the concessions made to the "Slav-Macedonians," the Resolution contained a clear directive:

> ...at the same time, the KKE should radically remove all obstacles, attack all Greater Greek chauvinistic expressions and activities which create disappointment and displeasure among the Macedonian people and, thus, assist the fractionists in their traitorous activities and support the work of the reactionaries...

That Yugoslavia was not yet mentioned by name as the worst enemy of the Macedonian people, must be attributed to the fact that the Greek guerrillas were still receiving support from and refuge in Yugoslavia.

Steadily, however, the situation worsened. It was in January that Tito's most trusted man among the Greek communists, "Prime Minister" and "Commander-in-Chief of the Democratic Army" Markos Vafiades was relieved of his duties and expelled from the Party. At that time it was publicly alleged that his removal was due to ill-health.[86] His fate was shared by other lesser officials of the Greek guerrilla movement as well as of the NOF. Actually, Vafiades had been replaced in the position of Commander-in-Chief by Zahariades himself in November 1948.[87] The reason for his expulsion was not exclusively the result of his pro-Yugoslav attitude. As revealed at the Third Party Conference held in 1950, Vafiades had, by the fall of 1948, reached the conclusion that "monarcho-fascism" had more or less stabilized its position in Greece, and that without the open intervention of the Soviet Union, the guerrilla movement had no chance of winning. Zahariades, on the contrary, supported the view that the rebellion should, nevertheless, go on. The issue was said to have been brought before Stalin himself who, although expressing serious doubt as to its fate in conversations with Yugoslav and Bulgarian leaders in Moscow early in 1948, he ruled in favor of Zahariades' view. Apparently, Stalin had decided that a pro-Cominform guerrilla army on the southern Yugoslav border could seal off Yugoslavia on all sides and, thus, force Tito to capitulate. Consequently, Vafiades was accused of "defeatism" and "lack of internationalism."[88]

Vafiades also had different views on the Macedonian issue. According to what Tito confided to a high-ranking Western diplomat in Belgrade a year later, Vafiades had objected to raising late in 1948, the Macedo-

---

86. *Ibid.*
87. *Sovietology,* January 1962, p. 35.
88. *Ibid.,* p. 36.

nian problem because he believed that such a course would rally even the most fanatic communists around the Athens Government. In this respect, he had cautioned the extremist elements of the NOF not to agitate for the establishment of an independent Macedonian state but to limit themselves to their demands for equal rights. Zahariades paid no attention to Vafiades' sober observations and proceeded with the Resolution of the Fifth Plenum which constituted a significant landmark in the KKE's Macedonian policy. It should be added that the Resolution did not make any specific mention of the KKE's intention to adopt a policy favoring the eventual establishment of an independent Macedonian state within a Balkan federation. Very soon, however, statements by top KKE leaders outlined the real intentions of the framers of the Resolution.

A few days after the convocation of the Plenum, on February 3 and 4, the Executive Council of the NOF held its own Second Plenum. Announcing that the NOF Second Congress would be held in March, the Resolution of the Plenum referred to the Macedonian issue in the following specific terms:

> ...the Second Congress will also declare the NOF's new policy lines. It will announce the Union of Macedonia into a complete, independent and equal Macedonian nation within the People's Democratic Federation of the Balkan peoples...[89]

Zahariades, present at the meeting, endorsed the Executive Council's decision when he declared before the NOF leaders:

> The [NOF] Congress should make clear what constitutes the national mission of the Macedonian people who, with their participation in the struggle, are moving toward achieving the independent [Macedonian] state within the framework of the Balkan Federation.[90]

3. Reaction against KKE's New Policy

The announcement of the intention to form an "independent Macedonian state within a Balkan federation," generated a profound reaction in many quarters. The Greek Government, particularly disturbed, instructed its diplomatic representatives to inform the friendly governments on the seriousness of the situation. In Washington, the State Department assured the Greek Ambassador that the establishment of a "Macedonian" state which would include Greek Macedonia would be viewed as an act against the ter-

---

89. Text broadcast by Radio "Free Greece" on February 27, 1949, 08:30, GFM A/22864 Γ5/Bb1 1949; also Barker, op. cit.. p. 120.
90. Bulletin, February 5, 1949, GFM A/27238/Bb1/1949.

ritorial integrity of Greece and, consequently, would be contrary to the Truman Doctrine.[91] The United States Government asked its embassies in the communist capitals to follow closely developments in connection with the Macedonian problem.[92] Similarly, the British Foreign Office kept a vigilant eye on the situation, although it expressed the opinion that the Soviet Union would not create a crisis by granting its permission for the formation of Macedonian state.[93] Both Great Britain and the United States considered the necessary diplomatic measures to be taken in the event the situation were to deteriorate.[94]

By April, however, the Western allies of Greece were confident that Moscow was not willing to press for the establishment of an autonomous Macedonian state because such an action could easily "touch a spark to the Balkan powder keg."[95]

The Bulgarian Government, similarly exhibited a cautious attitude, although it approved of the position adopted by the KKE and the "Slav-Macedonians."[96]

On their part, the Yugoslavs, faced with mounting Cominform pressure on all their extended frontiers, interpreted the KKE's decision as part of a general Cominform plan aimed at utilizing the slogan for an independent Macedonia in the campaign to disrupt the People's Federal Republic of Yugoslavia and overthrow the leadership of the CPY.[97] Initially, the Yugoslavs tended to be mild in their criticism of the Greek communists, apparently maintaining hopes that they could retain their friendly relations with the Greek Party. Moje Pijade, in an article "On the Question

---

91. Ambassador Dendramis (Washington) to Greek Foreign Ministry, March 11, *GFM* A/23706/Γ5/Bb1/1949.

92. Dendramis to Greek Foreign Ministry, March 18, *GFM* A/24622/Γ5/Bb1/1949.

93. Ambassador Melas (London) to Greek Foreign Ministry, March 12, *GFM* A/23610,Γ5Ba/1949.

94. Dendramis to Greek Foreign Ministry, April 4, reporting on talks with British Foreign Minister Bevin and State Department officials, *GFM* A/27704/Γ5Ba/ 1949; Also Dendramis to Greek Foreign Ministry, March 23, *GFM* A/25308/Γ5/Bb1/1949.

95. Dendramis to Greek Foreign Ministry, April 4, *GFM* A/21288/Γ5Ba/1949.

96. The Bulgarian Communist Party paper *Rabotnitsesko Delo* (May 19), referred to the struggle of the Macedonian people as a struggle "for national liberation, a people's republic and communism;" quoted in Barker *op. cit.*, p. 123. The Sofia paper *Trud*, in its editorial of February 14, 1949, praised the new stand of the Greek Communist Party for an independent Macedonia and for a Balkan Federation as the only correct way of solving the Macedonian question, emphasizing that it corresponded with the standpoint of the CPB as well. Quoted in Mojsov, "About the South-Slav Federation" *op. cit.*

97. Mojsov, *Ibid.*

of a Balkan Federation," clearly stated his country's position on the new "Macedonian state":

> During the war and now during this difficult postwar period of Greek history, the Macedonian people of Aegean Macedonia were conscious of the fact that fighting alongside with the Greek people to establish a people's democracy in Greece, they were fighting at the same time, for the right of their national self-determination and their national liberation.[98]

He went on to state that the KKE's recognition on this right was correct but the timing of its projection was wrong because the primary objective ought to remain the struggle for the victory of the people's democracy in Greece. "There is no need," he wrote, "for these people [the "Macedonians"] to be urged to make a clear declaration which not only is incapable of rallying the forces of the Macedonian people but, on the contrary, it can create unnecessary discussions and confusion in the united ranks of the Greek and Macedonian fighters." At that moment the Yugoslavs were desperately fighting for time hoping, apparently, that a reversion in Stalin's attitude could once again allow them to take the initiative in Macedonian politics. Events were to prove them wrong.

Only a year later, when all hope for a Yugoslav-Soviet rapprochement had been lost and the communist uprising in Greece had finally been defeated, did the Yugoslavs allow themselves to express their true feelings concerning the KKE's Fifth Plenum decision on the Macedonian issue. Svetovar Vukmanović, in a book published in 1950, said of the KKE's attitude:

> ...Here, in fact, one had an attempt on the part of the Government of the Soviet Union and the other Cominform elements to detach the People's Republic of Macedonia from the People's Federal Republic of Yugoslavia and render it subordinate to the Soviet Union.[99]

This was, indeed, a dramatized though correct appraisal of the dynamics of Macedonian politics which even in our days far exceed the limits of a normal territorial dispute between neighboring states and project themselves on the sphere of Great Power politics.

Back in Greece, the uproar against the communists mounted. Although it was commonly believed that since the war the communists had pledged

---

98. Moje Pijade, *On the Question of a Balkan Federation* [Study written in 1949 and published again in brochure form in 1951], Skopje, 1951.

99. Vukmanović, *op. cit.*, p. 54.

Macedonia to the Bulgarians first and then to the Yugoslavs, this was the first time that the KKE had dared to advocate in public the detachment of the region from Greece. At the same time, opposition within the ranks of the guerrillas was growing. Objections were raised both by those who favored an alliance with Yugoslavia and by those who, although they had remained loyal to the Party hierarchy, were worried that a return to the 1924 slogan would alienate the masses from the Party.[100]

The reaction throughout the country, the opposition of the Titoist elements, the hesitancy of many leading members of the Party, and probably words of caution from Zahariades' supporters in the Cominform countries, compelled the KKE to tone down its public pronouncements. On March 8, Radio "Free Greece" broadcast a statement contending that despite the propaganda of the Greek Government, the KKE had not agreed to the setting up of a Macedonian state within a Balkan Federation. It merely proclaimed itself in favor of the "self-determination of the Macedonians" who, having fought side by side with the Greek people, would decide for themselves, after the victory, the manner in which they wish to live and be governed.[101] Similar disclaimers were also made by the the NOF. Radio "Free Greece" broadcast on March 9, a statement by the NOF's Executive Council declaring:

> ...the enemies of the Macedonian people...are spreading rumors that the 2nd NOF Congress will announce the setting up of a united Macedonian state, that this state would be joined to Yugoslavia, Greece, Bulgaria or to a Balkan Federation...The truth, however, is different... Tens of thousands [of Slav-Macedonians]...fight, arm in hand, or behind lines, for freedom, for a people's democracy, for the complete national restitution of the Macedonian people...Our people gave everything to this struggle. As a result of their great sacrifices and common victory, *they will win their freedom and will arrange by themselves their life, their government and their social structure.*[102]

Indeed, the Second NOF Congress meeting in late March, failed to announce — in so many words — the formation of a united Macedonian state, as it had been indicated at the February meeting of the Plenum of

---

100. Captured document of the Sixth Guerrilla "Division" dated May 23, 1949, answering a request for clarifications by the 132nd "Brigade" on the new slogan for the Macedonian Question, Text in *GFM*.

101. Barker, *op. cit.*, p. 122.

102. Radio "Free Greece," March 9, 1949, 15 : 00, *GFM* A/23590/Γ5/Bb1/1949, [Italics added].

its Executive Council. Instead, it reiterated the old position that the "Macedonian" people will be able to decide freely their own status after the victory of communism in Greece.

Another important decision taken by the Congress in the presence of top officials of the KKE was the formation of a separate, independent Macedonian communist organization called the "Communist Organization of Aegean Macedonia," (KOAM).[103] This new organization, more than any statement, indicated that the KKE was preparing the ground to relinquish its authority in Greek Macedonia to the "Slav-Macedonians," since no two communist parties can function over the same territory.

The conclusion to be drawn from the decisions of the Congress was that the NOF, with the approval of the KKE, officially sanctioned the pro-Cominform, pro-Bulgarian orientation of the "Slav-Macedonians" in Greece. It was in this spirit that Keramidjiev and Gotsev, both leading advocates of Yugoslavia's Macedonian policy, were formally condemned.[104] "General" Karageorgis expressed, on behalf of the Central Committee of the KKE, his approval of the decisions of the Congress and pledged that the "Slav-Macedonians" would receive wider recognition, including the appointment of NOF officers to Supreme Headquarters.[105]

Within a week, the "Provisional Democratic Government" was reshuffled to include two high-ranking NOF members. Pascal Mitrovski was appointed Minister of Food and Stavro Kotsev Director for National Minorities in the Ministry of Interior.[106]

During the ensuing months, until the final defeat of the communists in August, NOF leaders continued to conduct their secessionist propaganda.[107] Suspicion on the part of the guerrilla rank and file that the NOF continued to promote alien objectives mounted but could not be openly

---

103. Intelligence Report, June-September 1949, pp. 3-4 *GFM* A/56176/Γ2/1949.

104. Both of them had already crossed the border to Yugoslavia. From Skopje they conducted a persistent campaign urging the "Slav-Macedonians" to desert to Yugoslavia. In August, Gotsev had been reported occupying an important post in the Ministry of Welfare of the Reople's Republic of Macedonia. *GFM* A/45283/Γ5/Bb1/1949. The KKE accused Marshal Tito of establishing in Skopje a rival organization of "Slav-Macedonians" and sending agents to Greece to urge "NOFites" to desert the "Democratic Army." "Decision of the Sixth Plenum of the Central Committee of the KKE" broadcast by Radio Bucharest on November 5, 1949, 14 : 30 (in Greek), *GFM* A/54830 Γ5/Ba/1949.

105. Speech delivered before the Congress on March 26 and broadcast two days later by Radio "Free Greece" *GFM* A/26759 Γ5/Bb1/1949.

106. Radio "Free Greece" April 5, 1949, as quoted by Barker, *op. cit.* p. 123.

107. *GFM* A/32362 Γ5Bb1/1949.

184

expressed at that critical moment when the National Army had begun its final and determined offensive to wipe out the rebellion. Only in September, when the rebellion had finally been crushed, were the submerged feelings allowed to be voiced openly.

4. End of Yugoslav Support to the Guerrillas

Despite rising provocations by the KKE on the Macedonian issue, the Yugoslavs contained themselves to voicing only mild criticisms. On April 10, Lazar Kulishevski declared before the Third Congress of the Yugoslav Popular Front that the attitude of Yugoslavia toward ''our people in Aegean Macedonia and the struggle of the Greek people in general, has not changed on account of the Cominform decision.''[108] Late in May, the Yugoslav delegate to the United Nations intimated that Yugoslavia would continue assisting the Greek guerrillas even though the Soviet Union might decide to abandon them.[109] Indeed, despite their year-old quarrel with the Soviets, Yugoslavia maintained in the United Nations her polemical attitude toward the "monarcho-fascist" Greeks.

However, faced with enemies on all sides of his extended borders, Marshal Tito was in need of a friendly or even a neutral neighbor in the south. When he became fully convinced that this could not be achieved through the KKE, he did not hesitate to come into a *modus vivendi* with Athens and, on July 23, he formally closed the frontier to the Greek guerrillas.[110]

This decision constituted the near fatal blow to the rebellion, then nearing its end as the National Army methodically was closing in on the guerrillas. Vile denunciations by the Greek communists were directed against Tito who was accused of being, allegedly, an undercover agent for British and of having sabotaged the rebellion from its very beginning.[111]

Tito's reply was given at a meeting attended by pro-Yugoslav NOFites

---

108. *U.N.S.C.B. 1949 Report*, (A/935), *op. cit.*, p. 13.

109. Ambassador Alexis Kyrou (U. N. Headquarters) to Greek Foreign Ministry, May 23, 1949, GFM A/32730 Γ5Α2 1949. The Report (1949) of the U.N. Special Committee on the Balkans established that all through the first part of 1949, Yugoslavia had continued to give moral and material aid to the guerrillas. "This country" continued the Report, "allowed the use of its territory for the passage of guerrillas to and from Greece, facilitated the return to Greece of guerrillas after hospitalization, and furnished some supplies of war materials." *U.N.S.C.B. 1949 Report*, *op. cit.*, p. 18.

110. H. F. Armstrong, *Tito and Goliath* (New York: MacMillan and Co., 1955), p. 228, footnote 4.

111. Zahariades, Δέκα Χρόνια Πάλης, *op. cit.*, p. 55.

in Skopje on July 28. In his speech, the Marshal attacked the leadership of the KKE for never having seriously considered the national rights of the "Slav-Macedonians." He appealed to all Slavophones — as well as to the rank and file of the KKE — to join him in his anti-Cominform struggle promising in return his full support.[112] A few days later, on August 2, speaking again in Skopje, he reiterated his country's position on the Macedonian issue declaring that all parts of Macedonia should be united in one state, apparently under Yugoslav sponsorship.

In the meantime, the Bulgarians used the closing of the frontier to accuse the Yugoslavs of stabbing the Greek guerrilla movement in the back "an act of treachery toward our brothers of Aegean Macedonia."[113] At the same time, Bulgaria increased her agitation for the establishment of an independent Macedonian state. The confusion which prevailed in the closing days of the rebellion is clearly portrayed in the 1949 Report of the United Nations Special Committee on the Balkans:

> Radio broadcasts, newspapers and statements of public officials in Bulgaria and Yugoslavia have continued to support conflicting claims for the *detachment* of Greek or "Aegean" Macedonia from Greece and for the establishment of a unified Macedonia in some form or another.[114]

5. The Departure of the "Slav-Macedonians" from Greece

In August, the National Greek Army led by Field Marshal Alexander Papagos, launched a decisive attack on the Vitsi-Grammos massive which resulted in the death, capture or departure of tens of thousands of guerrillas and the end of the communist rebellion in Greece.

In terms of human losses, the three-year old guerrilla war had cost Greece much more than what the Greco-Italian and Greco-German wars had cost together. The following table, which does not list the guerrilla losses, is sufficiently revealing (figures are given in round numbers):[115]

---

112. Report, *GFM*, A/56176/Γ2/1949, *op. cit.*

113. "Manifesto of the Third Plenum of the Union of the People's Youth of Petrich [Bulgarian Macedonia] to the Youth of Vardar," *Rabotnitsesko Delo*, July 31, 1949.

114. *U.N.S.C.B. 1949 Report*, (A/935), *op. cit.*, p. 5.

115. G. A. Leventis, Ἡ Κατὰ τῆς Μακεδονίας Ἐπιβουλὴ [The Conspiracy Against Macedonia], (Athens: Military Publications, 1962), p. 285. The figure of those who fled to the communist countries is quoted from *Sovietology*, January 1962, p. 52.

Killed	70,000
Abducted children	28,000
Evicted from their homes (inside Greece)	1,000,000
Emigrated (voluntarily or forced)	40,000

As with the mass eviction of Greeks from Asia Minor in 1922-1923, a great national calamity had its beneficial side-effects. Along with the thousands of guerrillas, abducted children and adults, the "Slav-Macedonians" who, for well over eight years, had collaborated either with the Bulgarian and German occupation authorities or with the KKE, left the country in large numbers. Thus, Greece was delivered of an alien-conscious minority which had actively threatened her security and internal peace. Although figures for the "Slav-Macedonians" who escaped to satellite countries and Yugoslavia vary on account of lack of thorough statistics, the Greek authorities estimated that they amounted to approximately 35,000.[116] Undoubtedly, among them were Slav-speaking Greeks — as distinguished from the "Slav-Macedonians" with an alien conscience — who had been taken as hostages or forcefully inducted into the guerrilla bands and then compelled to follow the retreating guerrillas into exile.

The entire guerrilla force, including the leadership of the KKE and the members of the "Provisional Greek Government" escaped to Albania during the last week of August. Most of them were temporarily sheltered in camps in southern Albanian towns. In the aftermath of the defeat, the leadership of the KKE which had fought under the battle-slogans, "the enemy shall not pass from Vitsi," and "Grammos shall become the graveyard of monarcho-fascism," blamed the defeat for the most part on the "Slav-Macedonian" units which had fought with no heart and deserted the ranks at the approach of the attacking National Army. These open accusations brought to the surface the mutual suspicions and animosity suppresesd during the critical moments of the military operations.[117]

On October 4 and 5, many "NOFites" were arrested in the refugee

---

116. Bramos, (Second Edition), *op. cit.*, p. 237, estimates them at 18,000-20,000. The Skopje newspaper *Pirinsko Glas* (November 6, 1950) reported that by the end of 1950 over 30,000 "Macedonian" refugees from Greece were living in Yugoslavia. This figure is corroborated by Greek official sources. *GFM* A/59179/Γ5Ba/1949.

117. A leading member of the NOF Youth Organization who escaped from Vitsi to Albania and thence to Yugoslavia, reported that during the closing days of the guerrilla war, particularly after the closure of the Yugoslav frontier, the NOF had come under serious suspicion from the leadership of the KKE, as pursuing a Titoist Macedonian policy; this was despite the large-scale liquidations which had supposedly cleared the "Slav-Macedonian" organization of Titoist elements.

camps in Albania on the grounds that they had been Yugoslav agents who actually brought about the defeat of the rebellion. Among the arrested were Pascal Mitrofski, member of the "Provisional Government," Pavle Rakovski, Lazo Pop Lazarov, Mina Fotev, Ourania Pirovska, member of the Central Council of the NOF, and others.[118] Additional pro-Yugoslav "Slav-Macedonians" managed to escape to Yugoslavia, while a significant number followed the mass of guerrillas on the road to exile, first to Bulgaria and then to the various Eastern European countries including the Soviet Union.

The departure of the "Slav-Macedonians" from Greek Macedonia doubtless prevented the adoption of certain stern security measures, i.e. mass deportation or transfer, which the Greek Government under pressure of public opinion, might have considered in order to safeguard the northern departments of the country from a recurrence of Yugoslav or Bulgarian subversion. As it turned out, the only concrete measure taken by the Greek Government was the refusal to allow the return of those who had fled. This measure, still in existence, applied to a mass return of the *emigrés*, irrespective of their self-classification as "Slav-Macedonians" or Greeks. Only individual petitions are examined at present.

The 1951 official census of Greece reported that war, occupation, guerrilla casualties and the mass exodus of 1949, had reduced the number of Slav-speaking inhabitants of Greek Macedonia to 42,000. Greek authorities were confident that these Slavophones possessed a Greek conscience and only their language tended to differentiate them from the rest of the inhabitants of Macedonia.[119]

The end result from the tragedy of the three-year guerrilla war was that, for Greece, the Macedonian Question — even in the form of a "minority question" — had been solved as an internal problem. Occassional propaganda attacks from the "Slav-Macedonians" in exile, from the Skopje irredentists, and from the aged emigrants of Northern America who

---

118. *Borba*, November 27, 1949. Years later, some of them found their way to Skopje where a few of them were offered leading positions in the Administration of the People's Republic of Macedonia.

119. Very revealing in this respect—because of its secret nature at the time—is an intelligence report dated December 17, 1949, prepared for Commander-in-Chief A. Papagos. It stated that a substantial number of Slav-speaking inhabitants in Greek Macedonia, not only resisted the communist, Yugoslav and Bulgarian propaganda but had formed home-guard units to fight the guerrillas. These units proved particularly damaging to the efforts of the guerrillas and the "NOFites," both on the battleground and in the propaganda warfare. *GFM* A/59179/Γ5Ba/1949.

188

tended to regard nostalgically developments in the Balkans in the light of their experience of 30 to 50 years ago, could have no damaging effect on the security of the country since no alien element existed any more to carry out foreign objectives.

B. *Bulgaria's New Dominant Role in Macedonian Politics*

The Bulgarian-Yugoslav dispute was now steadily replacing the Greco-Yugoslav conflict over Macedonia. Only this time, it was Yugoslavia which was placed on the defensive. Propaganda attacks and counter-attacks, guerrilla raids and subversion between the two countries in the familiar grounds of Northern Macedonia had a striking resemblance to the acute inter-war controversy. The only difference in the familiar nationalist feud was that every action was allegedly justified in the name of Marxism-Leninism. Undoubtedly, the Bulgarians had once again secured Moscow's favor, since Stalin made no secret of his desire to overthrow Tito by any means, including subversion in Macedonia.

The Yugoslav-Bulgarian dispute over Macedonia was not caused by the Cominform decision; rather its existence came to the surface on account of that decision. Although the Tito-Dimitrov negotiations had brought the two countries substantially near to solving their differences over the region by means of South-Slav federation, Stalin's uncompromising attitude of opposition definitely jeopardized its chances.

It is interesting to note that after their return to Belgrade from the Soviet Union, the Yugoslavs attempted to implement the Bled and Evxino-grad agreements by contacting the Bulgarians on the issue of putting them into effect.[120] This was a major affront directed at Stalin personally. It is surprising that the Yugoslav leaders could so misjudge his determination to crush any nationalist deviation on the part of parties which he considered as mere appendices to the Communist Party of the Soviet Union; unless the Yugoslavs believed that the Bulgarians were equally willing to follow them in their independent course, in which case Stalin, presented with a *fait accompli*, could be expected to retreat. The Bulgarians, however, were not eager to espouse Yugoslavia's ambitious plans. To most of them the Bled agreements appeared as a capitulation to the Yugoslavs. To go even further and antagonize the Soviets must have seemed a political afront and a national catastrophe. In short, they had little to gain and much — very much, indeed — to lose.

---

120. Kardelj, *Yugoslavia's Foreign Policy, op. cit.,* pp. 54-55.

There is no evidence to assume that the leadership of the BCP had begun, as early as March, to adopt a new course away from the Yugoslavs. Judging from their initially cautious reaction to the June Cominform decision, they were not aware of the mounting tension between the Central Committees of the CPY and the CPSU.[121] When the Cominform decision was announced on June 28, 1948, the Bulgarian Government still hoped that it could maintain the close ties which so laboriously had been woven between the two neighboring countries. On June 29, it informed the Yugoslavs that the Cominform Resolution in no way alters the existing friendly relations between the two countries.[122] Soon, however, Bulgaria was compelled to fall in line with the other communist countries. Once that course was chosen, Bulgaria became the most active agent of the Cominform's policy, especially concerning Macedonian developments.

On July 12-13, less than three weeks after the Cominform decision, the Central Committee of the CPB held its 16th Plenary session, in Sofia. Among other things the Plenum discussed the question of halting all Yugoslav propaganda in Pirin Macedonia. Further it gave evidence that from that moment, Bulgaria was determined to oppose Yugoslavia's general Macedonian policy.[123] Bulgarian Foreign Minister Vladimir Poptomov—a native of Macedonia—set clearly the new orientations of Bulgaria's policy toward the Macedonian Question, when he spoke of Pirin Macedonia "as part of Macedonia which belongs to Bulgaria."[124]

The first concern of the Bulgarians was to consolidate once again, their control over their own people in the Pirin district. "Macedonian" language and history, taught by teachers from Skopje, were banned from the schools of the region. The "Macedonian" page of the newspaper *Pirinsko Delo* was taken out; the "Macedonian" national theater was converted into a purely Bulgarian one, and no more students were allowed to go to schools in Skopje.[125] To offset any Yugoslav gains among the Pirin inhabitants, the Bulgarian Government formed "literary circles" to propagate the new line. The Yugoslavs retorted that the Bulgarians were

121. Royal Institute of International Affairs, *The Soviet-Yugoslav Dispute; Text of the Published Correspondence.* (London: R.I.I.A., 1948).
122. "Bulgarian Government's Note No. 6266-I, dated June 29, 1948," in Yugoslavia, Ministarstvo inostranih poslova, *White Book on Agressive Activities by the Governments of the USSR, Poland, Czechoslovakia, Hungary, Rumania, Bulgaria and Albania towards Yugoslavia* (Beograd, 1951), p. 78.
123. *Ibid.*, p. 91. Also Vlahov, *Makedonija, op. cit.*, p. 320.
124. *White Book, ibid.*, p. 91.
125. Vlahov, *Makedonija, op. cit.*, p. 321.

pursuing "a policy of denationalization and exploitation which is so characteristic of stale capitalism and Greater Bulgarian chauvinism."[126]

Nevertheless, the Bulgarians appeared determined to eradicate all
remnants of Yugoslav influence and guide the inhabitants of Pirin firmly
back to Bulgarian nationalism. Indicative of the prevailing atmosphere was
the fact that not only Yugoslav Macedonian books were burned but, also,
certain Bulgarian books written immediately after the war at the suggestion
of Georgi Dimitrov for the purpose of critisizing strongly the Bulgarian
chauvinistic pretensions over Macedonia.[127] Anti-Yugoslav propaganda paid
particular attention to the "Macedonian" language, labeling it an artificial
language that no one spoke in Pirin Macedonia. It was contended that its
purpose "was not to unite the Macedonian people or advance their culture,
but to suppress and supplant the Bulgarian language spoken and read by
all Slav Macedonians."[128] To cement their control over the Pirin Macedonian organizations, they expelled the Titoist elements from the Central
Macedonian Committee at Sofia and formed in its place a Provisional
Macedonian Committee under loyal Bulgarian Macedonians. To add to the
confusion, the leadership of the Bulgarian Macedonians declared that their
aim was to revive the faith in the "Macedonian" cause, develop a "Macedonian" consciousness, and unify the Macedonians under the flag of the
Fatherland Front and the slogan, "Macedonia for the Macedonians" [sic].
Once again, the same old slogans were employed to advance entirely different
aims. In this connection, the name "Macedonian" was employed as a
geographical term to distinguish a segment of the Bulgarian people.

The Yugoslavs maintained some hope for salvaging their friendship
with Bulgaria in Georgi Dimitrov. The patriarch of Bulgarian communism
had, indeed, shown a sincere desire to meet the Yugoslavs more than half
way in order to prepare the ground for the formation of a strong South-

---

126. "Denationalization is a steady task of the Bulgarian policy in Pirin Macedonia," *Pirinski Glas* (Skopje), June 1954.

127. *Oslobodjenje* (Serajevo), August 27, 1950.

128. The Bulgarian P. Gevgeliev wrote :

It is true that we have given up the teaching of "Macedonian history,"
a high-falutin term for the ravings of a handful of maniacs in Skopje who
are so far gone in their nationalistic dementia and mental aberration as to
claim that the present Macedonian people are descendants of Alexander
the Great. These 'historians' seem to overlook the fact that the Slav tribes
came to this territory fully a thousand years after the death of Alexander
the Macedon.

P. Gevgeliev, "Skopje Revives Macedonian Spectre," *Free Bulgaria* (Vol. III,
October 15, 1948), pp. 299-230.

Slav bloc. However, Stalin's merciless attacks on him at the Moscow meeting had apparently reduced him to an obedient instrument of Soviet policy. Standing before his Party's Fifth Congress in December 1948, he accused Tito of having "betrayed the great doctrine of Marxism-Lenin-ism."[129] Referring to Macedonia, he complained that the Yugoslavs took advantage of Bulgarian concessions to conduct a Greater Yugoslav chauvinist propaganda in Bulgarian Macedonia.[130] "The people of the Pirin district" he declared, "for centuries feel themselves tied economically, politically and culturally to the Bulgarian people and do not desire their separation before the realization of a federation between Yugoslavia and Bulgaria."[131] He went on to outline his country's official position on the Macedonian Question in the following terms:

> Our Party has always advocated and continues to advocate that Macedonia belongs to the Macedonians. True to the traditions of the Macedonian revolutionaries, together with the honest Mace-donian patriots, we are deeply convinced that the Macedonian people will translate into reality their national unity and will ensure their future as a free nation with equal rights only within the framework of a federation of Southern Slavs.[132]

Since no such federation was in sight, especially as envisioned by the Bulgarians, there was not even the slightest chance for separation of the inhabitants of Pirin from the Bulgarian Fatherland.

Thus, by the end of 1948, Bulgarian policy over the Macedonian Question aimed at eradicating all remnants of Yugoslav propaganda among the Bulgarian Macedonians and championing the cause of Macedonian unity, exactly as the Bulgarian communists had done in the twenties. No attempt was made, as yet, to denounce the existence of "Macedonians." It was merely declared repeatedly that the Macedonians of Pirin were closely connected with the rest of the Bulgarians. Only in 1949, in the course of the further deterioration of Bulgarian-Yugoslav relations did the Bulgarian position on the Macedonian Question harden.

In the best tradition of Macedonian politics, the initiative changed hands and passed from Yugoslavia to Bulgaria, historically the most outspoken contender for Macedonia. Throughout 1949, Bulgarian agents secretly crossed the frontier to revive the morale of the pro-Bulgarian

---

129. Georgi Dimitrov, *Political Report to the Fifth Congress, op. cit.*, p. 62.
130. *Ibid.*, p. 69.
131. *Ibid.*, pp. 69-70.
132. *Ibid.*, p. 70.

elements among the population of the People's Republic of Macedonia.[133] At the same time Bulgarian propaganda — supported by the Soviet Union and all the Cominform countries — accused Yugoslavia of maltreating the people of Vardar Macedonia.[134]

All through 1949 and 1950, the campaign of slander and subversion gained such momentum that both Tito and the Western Powers began to fear seriously that the Cominform countries — particularly Bulgaria and Albania — were preparing a major guerrilla war in Southern Yugoslavia.[135] For its part, Yugoslavia was forced to remove troops from the Greek frontier to reinforce her borders toward Bulgaria.

There was sufficient foundation for Bulgarian contentions that the people of the People's Republic of Macedonia — called interchangeably "Bulgarians" and "Macedonians" — were not so happy with the Yugoslav administration, particularly following the stern measures applied by the regime as a consequence of the Cominform's subversion. Reliable sources revealed that Tito, realizing that his Macedonian policy of the early 1940's could strike back at the foundations of his federal state, had informed Dimitar Vlahov in Skopje that any attempt in the People's Republic of Macedonia to create internal disturbances would be mercilessly crushed.[136]

By Belgrade's orders (decision of Fifth Congress of the CPY), the First Congress of the Communist Party of Macedonia was convened in Skopje, in 19-24 December 1948, to prepare the defense against Bulgarian propaganda. The Congress decided to initiate a major indoctrination-education program to establish that from its first steps the Macedonian communist movement was the work of the "Macedonians," not of the Bulgarians; that the attitude of the Bulgarian communists *vis-à-vis* Macedonia had been chauvinistic; and that Macedonia was not liberated by the Bulgarian Army but by the Communist Party of Macedonia.[137] More important yet, the Congress issued detailed instructions for the "Macedonization"

133. Bidoe Smilevski, member of the Politburo of the Central Committee of the Communist party organization in the P.R. of Macedonia, publicly admitted this situation. *Nova Makedonija*, June 7, 1949; Also *Politika*, July 1, 1949.

134. Dedijer, *Tito, op. cit.*, p. 388.

135. Royal Embassy in Washington to Greek Foreign Ministry, March 29, 1949; GFM A 25962/Γ1/1949 Report, GFM A/39675/Γ2 1949, dated July 9, 1949. Royal Embassy in Moscow to Greek Foreign Ministry, February 25, 1950, GFM A 23791/Γ1 1950.

136. Royal Embassy in Paris to Greek Foreign Ministry, March 21, 1949, GFM A/24927/Γ2/1949.

137. Congress documents published in *Nova Makedonija*, December 19-25, 1948.

of Yugoslav Macedonia through mass education, economic development and large scale propaganda. *Borba* reported that an Institute for the National History of the Macedonian People was founded in Skopje in December 1948.[138] Particular care was paid to the "Macedonian" language. A major effort was undertaken by linguists to remove from the local dialect most of the Bulgarian elements and substitute with borrowings from Serbo-Croatian. So successful was this painstaking work that ten years later, the Bulgarian Macedonians of Pirin had difficulty in understanding the Skopje radio broadcasts. On the other hand, the new language could easily be read and even translated by Serbo-Croatian speaking persons.

What, however, remained of immediate concern to Yugoslav authorities was the serious internal situation in the federative republic. All through 1949, a stream of confidential reports was reaching the Greek capital on numerous arrests in the People's Republic of Macedonia aimed at squashing at birth any pretension of an open uprising.[139] Even military units in which soldiers from the Skopje and Monastir districts were serving, were transferred from the People's Republic of Macedonia and their place was taken by units composed of Bosnians, Serbs, Croats, etc.[140] Much later it was acknowledged that a very serious situation had developed at that time in the People's Republic of Macedonia. In a speech at Titov Veles, V. Georgov, member of the Executive Council of the People's Republic of Macedonia, revealed that "the campaign conducted at that time [1948 - 1953] on the part of the [Cominform] states, stimulated a number of known racists, opportunists, national-chauvinists, defeatists and criminals to commit traitorous acts."[141]

Among the "national-chauvinists" were important leaders of the Macedonian Communist Party. The Chairman of the Presidium of the Assembly, Fotov, was found shot in his home on New Year's Eve (1951) and among the arrested were former ministers of the local government as well as leading members of the National Assembly and the Party. On January 4, 1951, the new Government under Lazar Kulishevski, trusted by Belgrade, attacked both Bulgaria and the Soviet Union for fomenting subversion in the People's Republic of Macedonia.

It appears that the situation could have developed into a fairly grave one were Bulgaria determined — with the support of the Soviet

138. *Borba*, January 23, 1949.
139. *GFM* A/21819/Γ2/1949; *GFM* A/28468/Γ2/1949; *GFM* A/36582/Γ2/1949.
140. *GFM* A/25616/Γ2/1949.
141. *Nova Makedonija*, November 2, 1958.

194

Union — to instigate an open guerrilla uprising of the kind Yugoslavia was supporting in Greece at that time.

Tito's reaction to Bulgarian measures, took initially the form of a series of trials in Skopje and Nish of Bulgarians who had served with the Bulgarian occupation authorities. The belated trials — four years after liberation — were actually aimed at convincing the inhabitants of the People's Republic of Macedonia that the Bulgarians who had behaved intolerably during the occupation did not differ much from those of the new regime at Sofia, since many officials of the latter had occupied importantposts during the wartime Bulgarian Administration.[142]

Similarly, the Bulgarians had problems in their own part of Macedonia where pro-Yugoslav elements were still evident. Deportations to the interior of the country, and mass arrests of Pirin residents were chosen as the most suitable method to purify the region from the Titoist Macedonians. In vain did the Yugoslav press loudly denounce the measures.[143] The Bulgarians responded that the measures were directed against the extremist followers of Mihailov's I.M.R.O.; but they were hardly convincing.[144]

To silence criticism for the 1944-1947 policy, Trajko Kostov, Secretary of the Party and Vice President of the Bulgarian Government, was chosen as scapegoat. In November 1949 he was indicted, accused of having connived with Tito and Western "imperialists" to cede Pirin Macedonia to Yugoslavia and drive Bulgaria into a South-Slav federation under Yugoslav domination. The Yugoslavs reported that Kostov, far from being a Yugoslav agent, hat always been hostile to Yugoslav plans for Macedonia. According to the Yugoslavs, Kostov had played an important role in liquidating the armed uprising in Yugoslav Macedonia during the first years of the Bulgarian occupation (1941-1942). He had opposed Dimitrov, in his efforts for a Bulgarian-Yugoslav rapprochement and a South-Slav federation. Moreover, he was the Bulgarian delegate who had signed the

---

142. Commenting on the trial of the Asen Bogdanov group held in Skopje on November 21-25, 1948 *Nova Macedonia* wrote on November 26:

Our people cannot forget the crimes committed against it by the fascist occupation...How strange it is that the organizers and executioners of those crimes in Macedonia are actually today absolutely free [in Bulgaria] and some of them even hold major posts in the political and military administration of the Bulgarian Fatherland Front.

Similar trials were held in April (*Borba*, March 19-22, 1949) and June 1949 (*Politika*, July 1, 1949).

143. *Borba*, October 29, 30, November 30, 1949; Also *New York Herald Tribune*, October 22, 1949.

144. *Rabotnitsesko Delo*, September 2, 1950.

Comintern Resolution on behalf of the CPB.[145] Nevertheless, Kostov was executed as a traitor and Dimitrov, the true founder of the policy of Bulgarian-Yugoslav close alliance, emerged, apparently, unharmed.[146]

Amidst the truly grave developments in the relations between Yugoslavia and Bulgaria were certain incidents with light undertones. Such were the Bulgarians' efforts to rally history to prove their views. While just three to four years previously, Gotse Deltchev's relics were donated by Sofia to Skopje — in recognition of his "Macedonian" identity — in 1951, the Bulgarians, quoting his turn-of-the-century speeches, tried to show his Bulgarian orientation to the "pure Macedonian cause."[147]

145. "The Aims and Nature of the Sofia Trial," *Borba*, December 4, 1949.

146. Following the Eighth Party Congress in November 1962, Kostov was posthumously reinstated and declared a hero of the Bulgarian Fatherland. It is not merely a coincidence that his reinstatement followed the most recent Yugoslav-Bulgarian rapprochement.

147. Dino Kiosev, "The Macedonian people follow the teachings of Gotse Deltchev and Yanne Sandaski," *Rabotnitsesko Delo*, May 6, 1951.

CHAPTER VIII

THE DECLINE OF THE CONTROVERSY

THE LAST YEARS OF THE STALINIST ERA: 1949 - 1954

Tito's expulsion from the Cominform and the measures adopted by the Soviet bloc to bring about his downfall, seriously affected the Macedonian Question. Though replete with dangers, the fifties marked a gradual decline in the controversy over Macedonia. Stalin's death in 1953, only confirmed this fact.

The turn of events proved that in the age-old contest over the region, nationalist considerations were still dominant among the peoples of the southern Balkans and their leaders; in fact, they were more dominant than the newly introduced Leninist principles of national self-government and cultural autonomy.

As the tensions of the forties gradually gave away to more subtle forms of power contest, the Macedonian issue began to take new shapes, although basically its inherent inflamable potentialities remained unaltered.

The most significant developments in the closing years of the Stalinist era were mainly three: first, the acute Bulgarian-Yugoslav feud — which has already been examined; second, the inter-KKE conflicts over the policy to be pursued toward the "Slav-Macedonians" and, third, the normalization of Greek-Yugoslav differences which, for all practical purposes, closed the question as far as Greek Macedonia was concerned.

A. The KKE and the "Slav-Macedonian" Issue in Exile

The seal of the guerrilla war was affixed by the Sixth Plenary Session of the Central Committee of the KKE held in October 1949. In its Resolution the Party attributed defeat to Tito's treachery and the superiority of the national armed forces. It was unknown at the time that long before Tito's decision to stop rendering his assistance, the rebellion had been doomed by Stalin himself. The epitaph of the rebellion, as inscribed in the Resolution, read as follows:

To continue a thoughtless armed conflict would have been the expression of a petit-bourgeois despair and would have allowed the enemy to thrust a final *coup* on the people's movement. The Central Committee of the KKE took a wise decision in adapting tactical retreat.[1]

Among the new tasks of the Party was "the conservation and consolidation of the ties between the Greek and Macedonian people." The slogan for a "united and independent Macedonia within the framework of a Balkan federation" did not appear in the Resolution, though it was not renounced either. The KKE preferred to limit itself, at the time, to a rather vague statement referring to the broad Leninist principle of equality of national rights. Zahariades explained, a year later in 1950, that the term "equality" meant the political autonomy and the self-government of the "Slav-Macedonians."[2]

1. Inter-Party Recriminations

Once the Greek communists found themselves assembled in the Cominform countries, the old quarrels on handling the issue of the "Slav-Macedonians" were revived. M. Partsalides, a member of the Central Committee, in a detailed report dated February 14, 1950, contended that the substitution of the slogan of "equal rights" in 1949 for a policy aimed at the "complete national restitution of the Slav-Macedonians of Greek Macedonia," was a mistake. He criticized the NOF's statement for "a national restitution within the framework of a Balkan federation" as well as the decision to establish the KOAM which, in fact, meant the establishment of a separate party organization for the "Slav-Macedonias."[3]

Partsalides reiterated his criticisms before the Seventh Plenum of the Central Committee held May 14-18, 1950.[4] He revealed, moreover, that the decision of the Fifth Plenum of January 1949, was prompted by the desire to offset the fractionist subversion of the Titoist elements.[5] Never-

---

1. Text of the Resolution, broadcast over Radio "Free Greece" and reprinted in the Czechoslovak newspaper, *Rude Pravo*, November 6, 1949.

2. Nikos Zahariades, Δέκα Χρόνια Πάλης [Ten Years of Struggle], November 1951, p. 126.

3. Report published in Νέος Κόσμος, August 1950, p. 482.

4. "Speech by Partsalides before the Seventh Plenum of the Central Committee of the KKE," Νέος Κόσμος, August 1950, p. 489.

5. Zahariades also admitted, just after the end of the rebellion, that the Fifth Plenum Resolution for the "self-determination of the Slav-Macedonians" was prompted by the need to counteract the subversive and fractionist activities of the

theless, the leadership of the Party failed to take stern measures against Tito's agents who agitated in favor of a Macedonian state with Thessaloniki as its capital.

Partsalides did not even hesitate to criticize Secretary-General Zahariades for still defending the decision of the Fifth Plenum.[6] Zahariades on his part, maintained that the slogan for the "self-determination of the Slav-Macedonians" did not correspond to the general interests of the movement but, nevertheless, he did not think that it was the wrong slogan.[7] He then turned to the offensive and blamed his opponents for voicing "nationalist" opinions.[8]

His views prevailed both at the Seventh Plenum of the Central Committee and at the Third Party Conference held in October 1950. In his book, Δέκα Χρόνια Πάλης, written in November 1950, in no uncertain terms, he delineated the KKE's position on the issue as follows:

> The KKE recognized to the Slav-Macedonian people of Aegean Macedonia *the right of self-determination including separation*. The Fifth Plenum took a correct decision when it raised this question... When we talk of equality of rights we do not mean anything else but autonomous status, the true autonomy in its Leninist-Stalinist meaning, i.e. political self-government.[9]

It was, indeed, strange, if not utterly short-sighted, for Zahariades to support in 1950 the discredited policy of detaching Macedonia from Greece, which was exactly what the KKE's policy amounted to despite the peculiar communist dialectics. The explanation should be sought in less apparent reasons.

The year 1950 was an uncertain, critical year, with the anti-Tito campaign reaching its climax. It has already been seen that Tito's most exposed positions were the People's Republic of Macedonia and the Albanian populated region of Kossovo-Metohia. Consequently, were the Cominform willing to undermine his position in the country, the most suitable regions to start with would have been Macedonia and Kossovo. Already, Bulgaria was conducting large scale propaganda alleging maltreatment of the "unredeemed Macedonian brethren of Vardar Macedonia." Daily, the press gave evidence of Bulgaria's expansionist intentions toward

---

Titoists. Nikos Zahariades, Καινούργια Κατάσταση - Καινούργια Καθήκοντα [New Situation-New Duties], November 1949, p. 42; Also, Νέος Κόσμος, August 1950, p. 489.

6. Νέος Κόσμος, Ibid., pp. 489 and 499.

7. Zahariades, Καινούργια Κατάσταση..., op. cit., p. 42.

8. Νέος Κόσμος, August 1950, p. 489.

9. Zahariades, Δέκα Χρόνια Πάλης, op. cit., p. 126. (Italics added).

Yugoslav Macedonia. "The Macedonians in Bulgaria," wrote the official newspaper of the CPB,[10] "are inseparately united to their brethren on the other side of the border and it is only natural that they cannot follow the latter's fate passively... The Macedonian people will be liberated, will be united and will enter with equal rights the family of the people's democracies with the Soviet Union at the top." And on another date: "The Macedonians in those two parts of Macedonia [Greece and Yugoslavia] will be liberated according to the teachings of Iliden and the example of the Macedonians in Bulgaria, i.e. in alliance with the workers in Greece, with the KKE at the head, and with internationalist communists in Yugoslavia."[11]

Such Bulgarian statements, echoed throughout the Soviet bloc, must have impressed Zahariades that their origin was not simply Sofia but Moscow. At a time when the symbols of Titoism in the satellite countries had begun to fall, no nationalist deviations could be tolerated; particularly in the vital question of Macedonia. Zahariades was thoroughly familiar with Soviet sensitiveness, having graduated in the twenties from a Soviet Institute for cadres. He was also a master of opportunism. While his opponents, motivated by nationalist considerations, pursued a course which could be best described as *narrow* opportunism, Zahariades maneuvered his Party — and doubtless strengthened his own position — through the channels of *broad* opportunism. In January 1949, with the Resolution of the Fifth Plenum, he had hoped to win the wholehearted support of the Cominform while, at the same time, rallying around the Party the "Slav-Macedonians" who were particularly valuable to the guerrilla operations. In late 1950, having lost a war, he still hoped to remain in firm control of the Party while maintaining Moscow's favor. To him there was no other course for the Party to follow.

2. Rivalry between Skopje and the KKE

By the end of 1950, all but a few followers of the KKE remained in Albania where they had originally sought refuge.[12] In Yugoslavia, those

---

10. *Rabotnitsesko Delo*, August 1, 1950.
11. *Rabotnitsesko Delo*, August 2, 1950. There are numerous Bulgarian statements made in the same spirit. See for example a statement by Hristo Kalaidziev, President of the Union of the Macedonian Cultural Associations in Bulgaria, published in *Rabotnitsesko Delo*, September 13, 1950.
12. Greek delegate to the United Nations, Politis, announced to the United Nations General Assembly that only 1500 combattants remained in Albania by late 1950. United Nations General Assembly, *Official Records*, Fifth Session, First Committee, 392nd Meeting (November 10, 1950), New York, 1950, p. 298.

who chose to remain loyal to the Cominform and the leadership of the KKE were allowed to go to the Soviet Union or to satellite countries; the rest were concentrated in the People's Republic of Macedonia where most of them were summarily invested with a "Macedonian" nationality. In Skopje they were assisted in forming their own organization and conducting a vigorous irredentist campaign which was to strain repeatedly Greek-Yugoslav relations.

By 1950, according to the Skopje paper *Pirinski Glas,* the "Slav-Macedonians" from Greek Macedonia had formed their own association to improve their cultural level and to maintain contact with "Macedonian" emigrants in America, Australia and elsewhere. The Association even possessed a newspaper, *Egejskiglas* ("The Voice of the Aegeans") and issued a number of propaganda brochures.[13]

The Yugoslav Macedonians tried to attract as many as possible of the "Slav-Macedonians" who had followed the KKE to the satellite countries. As was to be expected, the KKE reacted with fury to the Yugoslav attempts, and a feud, lasting to this day, broke out between Greek and Yugoslav communists over the allegiance of the "Slav-Macedonians."

The leadership of the KKE, thus, found itself fighting on two fronts to defend its Macedonian policy. Many of its followers were unwilling to execute the directives of the Third Party Conference of November 1950. Indicative of the prevailing situation is the following article written in the February 1951 issue of *Νέος Κόσμος* by Vasilis Bartziotas, member of the Central Committee of the KKE (excerpts follow):

...The Party organizations have neglected their political work among the Slav-Macedonians. This attitude means that our comrades have not realized the political significance of the work among the Slav-Macedonians, and they intentionally or unintentionally express Greater Greek ideas. The party organizations show no interest in educating the Slav-Macedonians in their own language or in solving the problems they have. They let the Titoist agents rove around and cultivate among the Slav-Macedonians the chauvinistic worm.

On the other hand, the Greater Greek ideas give ammunition to the Titoist agents and assist them in their fractionist activities. Occasionally, in production, they make distinctions between Greeks and Slav-Macedonians in the various sections of the plant. Elsewhere, they allow the Slav-Macedonians to use their own language, but they raise obstacles to their celebrations. This way they render assistance and comfort to the work of the Titoist agents...

13. *Piriniski Glas,* November 6, 1950.

The slogans of the Titoists toward the Slav-Macedonians are: "no Slav-Macedonians are appointed to the Party organizations" (which, of course, is a lie); "we were nice while they needed us to shed our blood on Vitsi-Grammos; now they have abandoned us;" "the Macedonian cadres are pushed aside;" moreover, [the Titoist agents] accuse our Slav-Macedonian cadres who fought courageously in the ranks of the Democratic Army and refused to become Tito's agents of being "stooges of the Greeks." They claim, moreover, that we assign the "heaviest jobs" to the Slav-Macedonians...[14]

It is evident that opposition to the Party's decisions was as wide-spread and active as was Yugoslav Macedonian propaganda among the "Slav-Macedonians."

3. The Formation of "Iliden"

In the summer of 1951, a conference of leading "Slav-Macedonians" in exile proposed the disbanding of all existing "Slav-Macedonian" organizations and the formation of a centralized organ under the KKE. The Central Committee of the KKE, accepted the proposal in its September 12 meeting and in October brought it before the Second Plenum of the Central Commitee.[15] The Plenum, in turn, decided that a Congress of "Slav-Macedonian" representatives be held to form the new organization which would be named the *Narodno-Osvobotitelen Revolutsionarna Organizatsia "Iliden."*

The decision was followed by a wide-range effort of the KKE leadership to explain to the confused "Slav-Macedonians" that the NOF had to be discredited publicly because, after all, it was not a "national-liberation" organization, as it had been claimed over the years, but an alien, "counter-revolutionary, imperialist" organization conceived and established by the Yugoslavs and their agents among the "Slav-Macedonians" in Greek Macedonia.[16] It was at this time that it was revealed that the KKE had been convinced of the NOF's Titoist ties as early as the spring and summer of 1949, but had refrained from dissolving it for fear that it might jeopardize the rebellion at its most critical moment.[17]

---

14. Vasilis Bartziotas, "Some Conclusions on the Condition and Work of our Party Organizations in Foreign Countries, following the Third Party Conference," *Νέος Κόσμος,* February 1951, pp. 19-20, [translated by the author].

15. Stavros Kostopoulos and Tasos Yousopoulos, "Toward the Congress of the Slav-Macedonians," *Νέος Κόσμος,* January 1952, p. 26.

16. *Ibid.,* p. 26. Mitrofski, Keramidjiev, Gotsev, Rakovski and others were singled out as "leading traitors."

17. *Ibid.,* p. 27.

The reasons prompting the KKE to establish in 1952 a new "Slav-Macedonian" organization, should be sought first, in the Party's desire to contribute to the anti-Yugoslav campaign, and second, in the need for an instrument to exert its authority over the thousands of the "Slav-Macedonians" scattered throughout the Eastern European countries; thence, the repeated references to the "Unity of the Slav-Macedonian and Greek peoples." [18] To attract the masses of the "Slav-Macedonians," the KKE promised to provide for their cultural, educational and national advancement. It solemny pledged, moreover, to uphold their *national claims*.

In the January 1952 issue of *Νέος Κόσμος*, the right of the "Slav-Macedonians" to remain *masters in their homeland* was guaranteed. The pledge went as follows :

> This clear position of our Party, guarantees to the Slav-Macedonians their territorial, economic, social, cultural, educational and religious self-government within the framework of the Greek state. This will be the prize for the common struggles of the Slav-Macedonians with the Greek people... No honest Greek patriot can deny that the Slav-Macedonians should be masters [*nikokyrides*] and lords [*kyriarchoi*] in their homeland. [19]

The "separate, united Macedonian state within the framework of a Balkan federation" appeared to have been abandoned by the KKE for a policy of a separate political entity for the "Slav-Macedonians" within the framework of Greece. Soon, however, the convocation of the "Iliden" Congress made it clear that no real change of policy had been introduced.

The Congress was held on April 1-3, 1952. [20] In its Declaration it endorsed the KKE's basic position that the Greeks and "Slav-Macedonians" were inseparably united. It vowed to guide its followers toward the realization of equal national rights "political autonomy, meaning territorial, administrative, economic, social, educational, cultural and [even] religious self-government." However, the Declaration went a step further than the KKE's publicly declared policy, when it stated :

> The Slav-Macedonian people maintain their inalienable right to their complete national restitution, their unity with their brethren — at the moment of the victory of the peoples' democracies in Greece

18. *Ibid.*, p. 30.
19. *Ibid.*, p. 28.
20. "Declaration of the *Iliden* Congress to the Slav-Macedonian People of Aegean Macedonia," *Νέος Κόσμος,* May 1952, pp. 21-23.

and Yugoslavia — *in a united, independent Macedonia of the free peoples of the Balkans and of the Slav peoples.*[21]

That a future Macedonian independent state would, in fact, be simply a Bulgarian offspring was becoming evident from the passage of the Declaration stressing that while the Macedonians in Vardar and Aegean Macedonia were enslaved, only in Pirin Macedonia "have our brethren won their freedom."[22] Bulgaria endorsed "Iliden's" proclamation through a Radio Sofia announcement in August, which pointed out that the KKE had recognized the right of self-determination of the "Slav-Macedonians" to build their own united state.[23]

From that time on, during its short existence,[24] "Iliden," through its Presidium, its Central Council and its territorial councils in Sofia, Bucharest, Prague, Budapest and Warsaw, tried to instill in the Slav-speaking *emigrés* a separate national consciousness. Newspapers and pamphlets were published in their dialect, special programs were broadcast over Radio "Free Greece," as well as over the radio stations of the host countries. Schools were established to teach in the "Slav-Macedonian" dialect illiterate adults as well as thousands of children abducted during the guerrilla war.[25] The educational program was definitely anti-Yugoslav and pro-Bulgarian in its orientation. The dialect used in the textbooks and radio commentaries was the spoken dialect which resembled Bulgarian. The literary Slav-Macedonian language, being formulated in the People's Republic of Macedonia, was rejected as a Serbo-Croatian invention.

While attention was focused on the indoctrination of the "Slav-Macedonians" in exile, an effort was made to create "Iliden" underground cells in Greek Macedonia through the dispatch of *agents provocateurs* and the emission of radio propaganda.[26] It was a futile attempt which was bound to fail, as Greek Macedonia had been divested of its alien-conscious "Slav-Macedonians."

"Iliden" passed unnoticed by the public in Greece. Only Greek and

---

21. *Ibid.*, p. 22. (Italics added).

22. *Ibid.*, p. 21.

23. *Radio Sofia*, August 2, 1952, 22 : 00.

24. The "Iliden" Organization was dissolved in 1957, but it had ceased to play any significant role much earlier.

25. In its July 25, 1952 broadcast, Radio "Free Greece" announced that the Party's publishing enterprise, "Nea Hellas," had put out a series of books for children in the "Slav-Macedonian" dialect. The first broadcast in "Slav-Macedonian" over Radio "Free Greece" took place on June 18, 1952.

26. Radio "Free Greece," October 2, 1954.

204

Western diplomatic and intelligence services could follow its existence and activities. Indeed, the organization began to stumble even a year after its founding. The Second Plenum of its Central Council, meeting in November 1953, pointed out a series of problems[27]: that the "Slav-Macedonians" were no more attracted by the Organization; that they did not pay their dues; that there were many alien agents in their ranks who advocated return to Greece or the People's Republic of Macedonia; that the schools did not function well, etc. Fighting for a lost cause, the Plenum made only a routine reference in its resolutions to "freedom, independence, food, democracy, peace, full national and equal rights."[28]

By 1954, its members began to desert it, either taking the road to Skopje or integrating themselves into the life of the host country. This tendency grew as the KKE began to orient itself toward a major change in its Macedonian policy to be introduced in 1956.

B. Greek-Yugoslav Relations and Macedonia

While the Greek communists had been caught in a "Macedonian Question" of their own making, and the Yugoslav-Bulgarian feud over Macedonia was at its worst, timid attempts were made to improve the poor state of Greek-Yugoslav relations. The political climate appeared to favor the rapprochement of the two countries. By closing her frontier to the guerrillas, Yugoslavia could offer invaluable assistance to the Greek Government's effort to crush the rebellion which was still on in the summer of 1949. Greece could offer to the hard-pressed Yugoslavs the only friendly outlet from the dangerous encirclement of hostile Cominform countries. Indeed, Marshal Tito for reasons of his own, closed the border in July and ordered Radio "Free Greece" out of Yugoslavia to Rumania.[29] The end of the rebellion created the proper atmosphere for the resumption of a Greek-Yugoslav dialogue. Still, however, there were major problems ahead. Not willing to expose himself to more criticism from the Cominform, Tito moved with caution. Throughout 1949, he repeatedly confided to Western diplomats in Belgrade that the restitution of working relations between his country and Greece would depend on his neighbor's willingness to desist from oppressing her "democratic citizens" and accord the

27. P. Vagenas, "The Second Plenum of the Central Council of the "Iliden" Organization," *Νέος Κόσμος,* January 1954, pp. 31-40.
28. *Ibid*, p. 40.
29. *U.N.S.C.B. 1949 Report* (A/935), *op. cit.,* p. 7.

"Macedonian minority" full social, cultural rights and complete political autonomy within Greece, under the guarantee of the United Nations and of the four Great Powers.[30] Meanwhile, Yugoslav propaganda from Belgrade and Skopje, as well as from the assembly halls of the United Nations, continued its anti-Greek tirades.[31]

1. Diplomatic negotiations

Finally, under mounting provocations and threats from Cominform countries, the Yugoslav leaders decided to come to terms with Greece — and the West — in order to offset pressure from the East. The opportunity was offered by the April 1950 elections in Greece which brought to power a new Government under General Nikolaos Plastiras, a moderate liberal of the Center. On April 27, Marshal Tito declared that political developments in Greece provided a possibility for improving the relations between the two countries. He then made public his intention to send an Ambassador to Athens. Two days later, General Plastiras welcomed Tito's announcement and promised that Greece would reciprocate by appointing her own Ambassador to Belgrade. On May 9, the two countries announced that they had reached an agreement to exchange ambassadors simultaneously.[32]

Suddenly, the Macedonian Question threatened to wreck negotiations. On May 16, Edward Kardelj, explaining his Government's decision before the Foreign Relations Committee of the People's Assembly, referred to the treatment accorded the "Macedonian" minority in Greece and said it was such that it upset Yugoslav public opinion.[33] Yugoslav personalities publicly claimed that the granting of cultural rights to the "Macedonian" minority in Greece be considered a basic prerequisite for the true normalization of relations between the two countries.[34] The Skopje radio and press referred in harsh terms to alleged tortures committed in Greek Macedonia.[35]

---

30. Report dated May 29, 1949, *GFM* A/34065 Γ2/1949.

31. During the discussions of the "Greek problem" in the United Nations General Assembly, Greek chief delegate Pipinelis spoke in conciliatory terms about Yugoslavia, but both Djilas and Bebler, the Yugoslav representatives, ignored the offer and sided with the Soviet bloc countries to accuse Greece of terrorism of her "democratic citizens." U. N. General Assembly, *Official Records, Political Committee,* Fourth Session, 1949, 27th Meeting (September 28) and 276th Meeting (September 29), pp. 6 and 14.

32. *New York Times,* May 10, 1950.

33. *Politika,* May 17, 1950.

34. *New York Herald-Tribune,* May 25, 1950.

35. *Radio Skopje,* May 18, 1951, 20 : 00 [in Serbo-Croatian], quoted in Kostas

While publicly high Yugoslav officials were making such statements, the Yugoslav chargé d'affaires in Athens, Mr. S. Shehović, presented to the Greek Government an official note warning that "non-democratic" treatment of the "Macedonian" minority would obstruct the normalization of relations between the two countries.[36] Trying to justify his Government's attitude, Marshal Tito explained to the American Ambassador in Belgrade, that Yugoslav insistence on the issue of the "Macedonian" minority in Greece was prompted out of concern for Cominform and in particular Bulgarian accusations which alleged that he tried to "sell the Macedonians of Greece"[37]

It is true that the Bulgarians were already placing Tito in the same category as the Greek "monarcho-fascists" on the question of the treatment of the "Macedonians."[38] "The Titoists," wrote the Bulgarian newspaper *Izgrev*, "have conspired with the Athens leaders against the Macedonian fighters and against the entire Macedonian movement of the Greek people."[39] Yugoslavia's interposition of the Macedonian issue in the negotiations with the Greek Government was interpreted by the Bulgarian paper as a move aimed at a "new chauvinistic exploitation" of the issue.[40]

The Greek press responded with harshness. It was evident that the Greeks were determined to sacrifice their rapprochement with Yugoslavia rather, than mortgage their national security by recognition of a non-existent "Macedonian" minority. The Yugoslav Ambassador, already in Athens, was compelled, under the circumstances, to return to Belgrade without presenting his credentials.[41]

The British and the Americans tried, behind the scenes, to mediate the differences between the two countries. The British Ambassador in Athens told Prime Minister Plastiras that while he viewed favorably the Greek cause, he thought that the two governments should proceed with the exchange of ambassadors despite Yugoslav statements.[42] Similar was the

---

Bramos, Σλαβοκομμουνιστικαὶ 'Οργανώσεις ἐν Μακεδονίᾳ· Προπαγάνδα καὶ 'Επαναστατικὴ Δρᾶσις [Slav-Communist Organizations in Macedonia; Propaganda and Revolutionary Activity], First Edition (Thessaloniki, 1953), p. 245.

36. Talk between Prime Minister Plastiras and British Ambassador Clifford Norton, June 21, 1950. *GFM*, File A/Γ4 1950.

37. Report dated June 24, 1950. *GFM* File A/Γ4 1950.

38. *Rabotnitsesko Delo*, August 1 and 2, 1950.

39. *Izgrev*, June 9, 1950.

40. *Ibid.*

41. *New York Herald-Tribune*, June 25, 1950.

42. Plastiras-Norton Talk, *op. cit.*

position of the U.S. Embassy in Athens,[43] and the American Ambassador in Belgrade hinted broadly to Marshal Tito that it would be beneficial to all if the interested countries would desist from interfering with the treatment and status of their minorities in neighboring countries.[44] Greece made it clear to her allies that she was determined to cease all negotiations with Yugoslavia until the question of the ''Macedonian'' minority was fully clarified.[45]

Convinced of Greece's determination, the British assumed the task of finding a way to bring the two Balkan countries once again close together.[46] Their efforts apparently met with some success, since the Yugoslavs informed them that they did not really espouse the view attributed to them, namely, that the development of Greek-Yugoslav relations should depend on the treatment of the ''Macedonian'' minority.[47] Thus, quietly, the Yugoslavs were abandoning one condition which was definitely unacceptable to Greece. However, on the important point of the existence of a ''Macedonian'' minority in Greece, they remained firm in their views. The Greek Government chose to interprete the Yugoslav explanations as a declaration of intention not to claim the right of interference with the status of Greek citizens. The road for the establishment of normal diplomatic relations between the two countries was once again open.

The interpretation given by the Greek Government was, naturally, arbitrary since there was no serious indication that the Yugoslavs were genuinely inclined to give up their intention to demand, at the proper time, special treatment for the few Slavophones who had remained in Greece. Actually, the Yugoslavs supported the Soviet proposal to the United Nations that the question of ''increasing terrorism in Greece'' be included on the agenda of the General Assembly.[48] Similarly the Yugoslav press and radio continued to raise the question of minority rights for the ''Macedonians'' of Greece.[49]

43. *GFM* A/39721/Γ4,1950.
44. Greek Embassy in Belgrade to Greek Foreign Ministry (No 2085), dated June 24, 1950. *GFM* File No. A/Γ4/1950.
45. Greek Foreign Ministry to Greek Embassy in Washington, July 17, 1950, *GFM* A/39721/Γ4/1950.
46. *New York Herald-Tribune,* September 4, 1950.
47. British Embassy in Athens to Greek Foreign Ministry, August 14, 1950, *GFM* File A/Γ4/1950.
48. *New York Herald-Tribune,* September 4, 1950.
49. *Politika,* October 12, 1950; *Nova Makedonija,* June 6, and 16, 1950. On June 20, *Nova Makedonija* wrote that ''our public opinion demands concrete guar-

Even more objectionable to the Greeks was the fact that Skopje continued to talk about the "unification" of Aegean Macedonia — as well as Pirin — with Vardar Macedonia.[50] In an interview with C. L. Sulzberger of the *New York Times*, President Tito made his Government's position clear when he said that "Yugoslavia has no territorial claims upon Greek Macedonia, nor does she desire frontier alterations, but she would wish to see certain minority rights granted to the Slavonic elements in that territory." He was categorical on the question of the existence of a "Macedonian" minority in Greece. "[The Macedonian minority] does exist," he said, "and we cannot allow that subject to be forgotten, first, for reasons of principle, and second, because the Cominform, especially Bulgaria, continually attack us on this issue. But we have in mind no territorial claims."[51]

Despite the fact that Yugoslavia did not renounce her claim over the minority issue, Greece realized that since no condition for special minority rights was projected, she could proceed with the normalization of diplomatic relations. On December 27, 1950, the two countries exchanged ambassadors and a new era began.

2. From Normalization to Alliance

The impact of this new development on the Macedonian Question was not yet fully realized. Despite the continuation of anti-Greek propaganda emanating principally from Skopje, the two countries were able to move ahead in a satisfactory way.[52] Of course, adverse occurrences were

---

antees so that no policy of natural extermination and loss of national identity be enforced on our brethren in Aegean Macedonia."

50. Dimtse Belofski, member of the Central Committee of the Communist Party of Macedonia, speaking at the Skopje National Theater during the celebrations for the Iliden uprising, ended his speech as follows:

...the People's Republic of Macedonia, within the framework of federal Yugoslavia, under the leadership of the CPY and comrade Tito, constitutes the foundation of a happy, united living for all Macedonians of tomorrow. Text in A/92765/Γ4/1950.

51. *New York Times*, November 7, 1950. *Radio Belgrade*, December 14, 1950, made the unrealistic claim that there were 250,000 "Macedonians" in Greek Macedonia—five times the official Greek figures for the Slavophone Greeks. On August 28, 1953, *Yugopress* advanced a more sober estimate—120,000—although that also was exaggerated.

52. The U. N. Special Committee on the Balkans reported in 1951 : "With regard to Yugoslavia, however, the Special Committee has noted with satisfaction the improvement in relations between that country and Greece through direct negoti-

frequent, particularly on account of the inflamatory propaganda from nationalists in Skopje. Yugoslav officials repeatedly tried to convince the Greeks that Skopje acted independently of the central Government, mainly because it was assigned the task of countering Bulgarian propaganda and subversion in Macedonia. The unfriendly attitude of the Skopje nationalists continued all through 1951, and for a moment, in the summer months, it again reached a critical level.[53]

By 1952, the relations between the two countries began to develop in a friendly way. Parliamentary delegations were exchanged, various agreements were signed and the ground was sufficiently prepared for the conclusion of a Pact between the two countries. The Macedonian Question had been pushed to the background. Greece wished, of course, that Yugoslavia would officially disclaim any pretensions over Greek Macedonia, either in the form of outright annexation or in the indirect way of an expressed interest over the protection of a minority which, in fact, had ceased to exist. Yugoslavia did not seem eager to make such a formal statement. However, under tactful pressure from many sides, she finally ordered an end to the inflamatory propaganda of the Skopje irredentists, a fact Greece welcomed as a genuine contribution toward instituting cordial relations with Belgrade, its natural ally in the Balkans.[54]

On February 28, 1953, following long negotiations, a treaty of friendship and cooperation was signed in Ankara between Yugoslavia, Greece and Turkey. The following year, on August 9, the treaty was implemented by a military alliance signed at Bled. By late 1954, despite occasional outbursts from Skopje, all indications pointed to the complete elimination of the Macedonian dispute.

However, a wind of change was coming from Moscow, as Stalin's

---

ations as revealed by the exchange of Ministers, the signature of a postal agreement on 2 February 1951, a rail traffic agreement on 12 February 1951, an air transport agreement on 16 March 1951, and finally a trade agreement on 10 April 1951. The Special Committee has likewise noted with satisfaction the continuing repatriation with the cooperation of the International Red Cross, of a certain number of Greek children and adults..." *U.N.S.C.B. 1951 Report* (A/1857), *op. cit.*, p. 5.

53. Similar complaints were made by the Yugoslavs when the Greek Government passed a law in 1953 confiscating the land of those who had left the country illegally and did not return to claim their property within the specific time provided in the law.

54. As a friendly gesture, Yugoslavia ordered the disbanding of the Aegean Macedonian Association—composed of ex-guerrillas—and closed their paper, *The Voice of the Aegeans*, whose inflamatory articles had been an endless source of friction between the two countries.

14*

heirs were orienting Soviet policy toward a rapprochement with the Yugoslav outcast. The Macedonian Question was destined to affect anew Balkan politics, though this time in a much milder form.

THE ERA OF UNEASY CO-EXISTENCE

Stalin died on March 5, 1953. A few months later, significant changes began to shape the conduct of Soviet and satellite international policies. Their implications were soon felt on the Balkans in the form of a Soviet-Yugoslav and Bulgarian-Yugoslav reconciliation.

In June 1953, Belgrade and Moscow exchanged ambassadors and Marshal Tito found it opportune to remark, on June 14, that the new Soviet Government had a "real desire" to rehabilitate and improve its foreign policy methods. During the remaining part of 1953, and all through 1954, Soviet and Yugoslav statements indicated a steady improvement in the relations between the two countries which prepared the ground for Nikita Khrushchev's visit to Belgrade on May 26, 1955. In his airport speech, the Soviet Party leader acknowleged Yugoslavia's right to build socialism in her own way. He pledged that his country had no intention of interfering in internal Yugoslav affairs or objecting to Belgrade's desire to maintain good relations with both East and West. Tito accepted the Soviet apologies and pledges but moved cautiously without compromising his independent status.

As was expected, the Soviet-Yugoslav reconciliation also affected the relations between Belgrade and Sofia, a fact which reflected on the amelioration of their quarrels over Macedonia.

A. Yugoslav-Bulgarian Reconciliation; 1955-1957

First came a ban on mutual recriminations and seditious propaganda. In the closing months of 1954, Yugoslavia dissolved the "Cultural Association of the Pirin Macedonians" which had its headquarters in Skopje. In November it stopped Radio Skopje's fifteen-minute program to Pirin Macedonia, and in December, it closed down *Pirinski Glas*, the newspaper of the refugees from Bulgarian Macedonia. Finally, in January 1955, it lifted the restrictions on the departure of those who desired to return to Bulgaria and other Eastern European countries.

Although rumors circulated freely, there is no definite evidence to suggest that the two countries had reached the point of conducting negotiations for a territorial transfer which would involve Bulgarian Macedonia and the "Western Bulgarian regions" held by Yugoslavia since the end of the First World War. There were, however, certain circumstances which indicate that Bulgaria was again ready to make significant concessions to Yugoslavia. Very revealing of Bulgarian intentions was the fact that the inhabitants of Pirin were renamed "Macedonians," a classification setting them aside as a national group from the rest of the Bulgarians.[55] During the period 1949-1953, the name "Macedonian" used to distinguish the inhabitants of a certain region, not a separate national group.

In public, the Bulgarian leaders were particularly cautious not to give the impression that they were making concessions to the Yugoslavs.[56] In private conversations, however, high officials of the Bulgarian Government, including Foreign Minister Neichev, expressed freely the view that Pirin Macedonia was inhabited by a population not Bulgarian, but rather related to the people of the People's Republic of Macedonia. They made no secret of the fact that, eventually, the Pirin Macedonians would join the People's Republic of Macedonia, although the time was not yet ripe for that.

Why the Bulgarians made such statements is, indeed, uncertain. A probable explanation is that the Soviets, in their determination to draw the Yugoslavs away from their close relationship with Western countries — the tripartite Balkan Pact had been signed only in 1954 — realized that Yugoslav sensitiveness and ambitions over Macedonia ought to be handled with understanding. In all probability. the Bulgarians were made to understand that they ought to cooperate and even make certain concessions to the Yugoslavs, such as recognizing a "Macedonian" national identity for the inhabitants of Pirin and stopping all anti-Yugoslav propaganda. No doubt, the Yugoslavs were attracted by the vision of returning to the group of states to whom they belonged ideologically. If that could be done more or less on their own terms, on other issues, as well as on the vital Macedonian problem, they would have no reason but to welcome the offer.

---

55. The 1956 Bulgarian statistics distinguishing again the "Macedonians" as a separate ethnic group, listed 6,506 Bulgarians and 188,000 "Macedonians." *Statistical Bulletin of the People's Republic of Bulgaria* (Sofia: Central Statistical Service of the Council of Ministers, May 1959), p. 19.

56. In September 1956, returning a visit by a Yugoslav Parliamentary group, a Bulgarian delegation under Todor Zhivkov visited Belgrade and Skopje. In a banquet at Skopje, Premier Kulishevski, toasting the Bulgarians, expressed the conviction that "not a single problem" existed between the two countries which could not be solved since there was a mutual desire to discuss in a comradely and friendly way all the problems. Zhivkov's noncommittal answer was that the firm friendship and cooperation between the two countries would be a contribution not only to peace in the Balkans but to the entire world. *Otetsestven Front*, September 28, 1956.

In February 1956, the Twentieth Congress of the CPSU was convened in Moscow. In the presence of a Yugoslav delegation, Khrushchev denounced publicly Stalin and his methods, although he did not go so far as to condemn the 1948 Cominform decision which led to the expulsion of Yugoslavia. Yet, a great step had been taken for a more genuine rapprochement between Belgrade and Moscow.[57] A few months later, in June, Tito paid an official visit to Moscow. Upon his return to Belgrade he belittled the military aspects of the Balkan Pact and stressed its secondary features of economic, cultural and political cooperation between the signatories.[58]

On the Greek side, the Bulgarian-Yugoslav reconciliation and apparent rapprochement were viewed with careful attention but not serious apprehension. With the departure of the "Slav-Macedonians" in 1949, there was no real issue as far as Greece was concerned. Occasional comments from Skopje on the alleged existence of a "Macedonian minority" in Greece passed unnoticed in the climate of cordial relations existing between the two countries. It is a fact that Yugoslavia never made in public a declaration to the effect that no "Macedonian" minority existed in Greece. However, assurances had been given by Yugoslav officials that Yugoslavia had no intention of demanding that Greece recognize the few Slav-speaking inhabitants as constituting a Slav minority. For well understood domestic reasons, the Yugoslav leaders refrained from publicly making similar statements.

B. New Yugoslav-Bulgarian Feud over Macedonia: 1958-1960

The improvement of Soviet-Yugoslav relations begun in 1953, suddenly came to a halt in 1957 and by 1958 had reversed its course, dangerously approaching the state of relations of the post-Cominform Resolution years. Thus, Yugoslav-Bulgarian differences over Macedonia were brought again to the surface.

Soviet-Yugoslav relations suffered their first setback during the Soviet suppression of the Hungarian revolt when the Yugoslavs failed to endorse Soviet measures. In November 1957, a more serious problem emerged when, at the Moscow Conference, of all communist parties, the Yugo-

57. In Bulgaria, Khrushchev's denunciation of Stalin resulted in the fall of Premier Vulko Chervenkov, an outspoken enemy of Tito. Mid-European Studies Center, Free Europe Committee, Inc. *Yugoslavia* (New York: F. A. Praeger, 1957), p. 35.
58. *New York Times*, June 28, 1956.

slav delegation opposed Soviet and Chinese demands for the re-establishment of a Cominform-type organization.[59] The depth of the ideological conflict between Yugoslavia and the Soviet bloc was revealed in the spring of 1958.

In March, Yugoslavia communicated to the various communist parties a draft program for the Seventh Congress of the League of Yugoslav Communists to be held between April 22 and 26. The Yugoslav draft was bitterly denounced by the Soviet Union on the grounds that it equated the Soviet Union with Western "imperialists" in two respects, namely, that both constituted military-political blocs — not world social systems as the Soviets maintain — and that both pursued their policies from a position of strength.[60] The latter point was in direct contradiction to the Soviet peace campaign and could not very well be tolerated. Despite Soviet objections, the Yugoslav communists refused to alter their draft points, with the result that their Congress was boycotted by the Soviet bloc delegates. On May 5, the Peking newspaper *People's Daily* launched a major attack on the Yugoslav leaders, stigmatizing their policy as "anti-Marxist-Leninist" and "out-and-out revisionist."[61] The Chinese about-face had a familiar ring to the ears of the Yugoslav leaders. Ten years earlier it had been the Cominform which had used similar language. In both instances the initial attack was followed up by a barrage of criticism from all the communist satellites. Moscow delayed its own formal criticism by approximately a month, although *Pravda* reprinted the *People's Daily* article. On June 3, Premier Nikita Khrushchev choce the capital of Bulgaria to express his full agreement with the Chinese criticisms of the Yugoslavs. There, at the Bulgarian Communist Party Congress, and "amidst cheers and chants which lasted for four minutes,"[62] Khrushchev publicly stated that Tito's denunciation by the Cominform in 1948, was basically correct and answered the interests of the revolutionary movement. He then went on to label Yugoslav "revisionists" the "Trojan Horse" of the enemies of Communism.[63]

Once again, Tito appeared as an outcast of the Soviet dominated communist family. The consequences of his ejection from the Soviet world were soon to follow. On May 28, economic credits promised to the Yugo-

59. *New York Times,* May 8, 1958.
60. *Radio Moscow* (Soviet European Service in Swedish), Commentary by Ivan Stepanov, June 15, 1958, 17 : 00.
61. *Christian Science Monitor,* May 13, 1958.
62. *Christian Science Monitor,* June 4, 1958.
63. *New York Times,* June 4, 1958.

slavs by the Soviet Union in 1957 were postponed for five years.[64] Reports from Bulgaria and Albania indicated the beginning of attempts to foment trouble for Yugoslavia among the latter's ethnic groups.[65] The Macedonian Question, real or fabricated, was re-emerging.

The Bulgarians wasted no sympathy on their Yugoslav comrades who had fallen into the Kremlin's disfavor for the second time in a decade. Their press and leaders began to discuss the history of Macedonia, emphasizing the benefits enjoyed by the inhabitants of Bulgarian Macedonia and the disadvantages under which the people of Yugoslav Macedonia lived. Boris Vaptsarov, First Secretary of the CPB for the district of Blagoevgrad [Bulgarian Macedonia] in an address before the Seventh Congress of the Party, accused the Yugoslav communists of following incorrect "bourgeois" and nationalistic policies with regard to the Macedonian problem.[66] Other speakers from the Pirin district assured the Congress that their people did not feel themselves different in any sense from the rest of the Bulgarian people with whom they shared a common heritage.[67]

A few days later, on June 8, the Belgrade newspaper *Politika,* cautioned the Bulgarian leaders that "the inflaming of Greater Bulgarian chauvinism from the tribune of the Party Congress will not have the least positive effect on the relations between Bulgaria and Yugoslavia."[68]

During the summer of 1958, the Yugoslav-Bulgarian dispute over Macedonia became exceedingly acute. Yugoslav newspapers charged the Bulgarians with reviving old claims over Yugoslav Macedonia as a contribution to the Soviet bloc's renewed campaign against Yugoslavia. Articles appeared almost daily in Bulgarian papers recounting alleged wrongs suffered by the population of Yugoslav Macedonia.[69]

The most caustic attack against the Yugoslavs was delivered by Dimitar Ganev, Secretary of the Central Committee of the CPB, a Bulgarian-Macedonian himself. Speaking at Razlog, in Pirin Macedonia, on September 21, he said:

It is known to all what kind of relationship the Greater Serbian communists and their agents at Skopje have with the Macedonian

64. *Christian Science Monitor,* May 28, 1958.
65. *Newsweek,* June 9, 1958, p. 12.
66. *Radio Sofia* (Bulgarian Home Service), June 4, 1958; 07:00.
67. Speech by delegate Jovan Angelov before the Congress.
68. *Politika,* June 8, 1958.
69. Paul Underwood, "Ancient Specter Rises in Balkans: Macedonian Question Revived by Bulgarians who Oppose Oppression by Yugoslavs," *New York Times,* September 28, 1958.

population... They demand that the Macedonian people sever their ties with everything that is Bulgarian, denounce their past and their history, which generally is the same as the history of the Bulgarian people... The Macedonian people are forced to denounce their mother language, which was spoken by their fathers and grandfathers, and they are compelled to adopt a fully Serbianized, artificial language which they do not know...

Today no one in Vardar (Yugoslav) Macedonia has the right, or dares to declare himself Bulgarian, although many have a Bulgarian national consciousness. Such is the true image of the nationalist policy pursued by the Yugoslav leaders who are deep in the mud of Greater Serbian chauvinism.[70]

This was apparently too much for the Yugoslavs who, in the course of just a few months, saw the old specter of Bulgarian nationalism over Yugoslav Macedonia revive in its old familiar, disturbing proportions. On October 4, 1958, the Yugoslav Government addressed a note to the Bulgarian Government complaining that Bulgarian officials, as well as the press, were carrying on a campaign whose purpose was to "inflame chauvinist passions in the Bulgarian people and to stir ambitions for territorial claims toward the People's Republic of Yugoslavia." Bulgaria was placed on warning that her actions were viewed as an interference in the internal affairs of the country and as an attack on the unity of the peoples of Yugoslavia and its territorial integrity.[71] From that day the Yugoslavs passed to the counteroffensive with articles in the domestic press and brochures destined for foreign distribution.[72]

On May 21-23, 1959, the Third Congress of the Macedonian League of Communists was held, apparently to provide the opportunity for publicizing the loyalty of the Yugoslav Macedonians to Belgrade. Premier Kulishevski, in his speech before the Congress, declared that the solution to the Macedonian Question *"depends on the democratic movement of all the other peoples of the Balkans,"* and that recognition of the basic national rights to the Macedonians living outside the borders of Yugoslavia depends "on the degree of democracy in the internal politics of the coun-

---

70. Published in *Rabotnitsesko Delo*, September 22, 1958. (The translation is from a reprint of the speech in Skopje's *Nova Makedonija*, November 23, 1958.)

71. The text of the Yugoslav note was distributed by TANYUG and broadcast over Radio Belgrade (In English to Europe), October 4, 1958, 12:45; *New York Times*, October 5, 1958.

72. "La nation macédonienne et la campagne anti-yougoslave—documents," *Revue de la politique internationale* (Belgrade, June 1959), pp. 18-21.

tries concerned."⁷³ According to Kulishevski, the proper and definite solution to the Macedonian Question would depend on the establishment of
a "democratic" regime in Greece and a "truly democratic" government in
Bulgaria. In no uncertain terms, he outlined his country's position as follows:

> The Macedonian Question was and continues to be the question
> of the recognition of the Macedonian nationality and its democra-
> tic rights for a national, free development, i.e. those rights which
> are irresistibly affirmed in the contemporary world and which ought
> to be sacred in a socialist country.
>
> In the framework of the Balkans as a whole, the Macedonian
> Question is objectively the result of the partition of the Macedonian
> people, of their feeling of being divided and of the fact that the
> Macedonian population living outside the People's Federal Repub-
> lic of Yugoslavia — under the pressure of the negation of their ele-
> mentary rights and their national existence — is deprived of the pos-
> sibility of benefiting from a more liberal development within the
> confines of a minority status.⁷⁴

Turning to the policy pursued by the Bulgarians in their own part
of Macedonia, Kulishevski said:

> The Bulgarian leaders do not need the teachings of history. They
> have completely denounced Dimitrov, the decisions of the Tenth
> Plenary Session of the Central Committee of the Bulgarian Work-
> ers' Party (Communist) [1946], which were adopted at the insistence
> of Dimitrov himself, and all his warnings regarding Greater Bulga-
> rian chauvinism.⁷⁵

Relations between Yugoslavia and the Soviet bloc remained unfriendly. In November 1960, at the Moscow Conference of the Communist
and Workers' parties, Yugoslav revisionism in foreign and domestic affairs
came under sharp criticism. In February 1961, the Central Committee of
the CPY issued a Resolution which objected to the anti-Yugoslav tone of
the Moscow Declaration.⁷⁶ Approximately at this time the Soviet Institute
of International Relations published a book entitled "International Relations and the Foreign Policy of the Soviet Union; 1950-1959." It blamed
Yugoslavia for continuing to accept U.S. assistance and for failing to denounce the Balkan Pact.⁷⁷

73. Text in *Nova Makedonija*, May 22, 1959 (Italics added).
74. *Ibid.*
75. *Ibid.*
76. *Borba*, February 28, 1961.
77. *Borba*, March 6, 1961. By 1961, the Balkan Pact was considered a dead

It is interesting to note that while Yugoslav-Bulgarian differences over the Macedonian Question during 1958-1959 were sharply accentuated, Yugoslav-Greek relations remained fairly unmarred by this issue. The two governments signed on June 18, 1959, a long-postponed agreement on free border traffic allowing the inhabitants of the respective regions, up to a defined line, to move freely on both sides of the frontier. The agreement was sharply criticized by a large segment of the Greek public which expressed apprehension fearing that the Yugoslavs might avail themselves of the opportunity to conduct their "Macedonian" propaganda among the Greek border populations.

Gradually, certain minor incidents cast shadows on the otherwise cordial Greek-Yugoslav relations.[78] Various Greek papers, either for reasons of sensationalism or because they opposed the Government, carried some articles not necessarily in the spirit of good Greek-Yugoslav relations. The attitude of the Skopje publications was similar. However, the responsible authorities on both sides tried to ignore the incidents. Yugoslav officials reassured their southern neighbors that Yugoslavia had no territorial claims over Greece.[79] Privately, they urged that the two countries should not allow their differences to come into the open because only the Bulgarians could profit from such a situation. They did not hide their concern over Bulgarian expansionist tendencies.

Such was the situation until the summer of 1961 when Soviet-Yugoslav relations showed signs of improving. On July 8, Yugoslav Foreign Minister Koća Popović paid a visit to Moscow. The trip was reported "as useful for developing the relations between the two countries."[80] Apparently by that time, Khrushchev, preparing his history making 22nd Party Congress scheduled for November 1961, had finally decided to push forward his moderate foreign and domestic policies; the policies which would bring him into open conflict with the dogmatists, both in the Soviet Union and in China. Consequently, a rapprochement with Tito appeared easier and rather natural, if not necessary.

Although the Yugoslavs spoke in guarded terms about the improvement of their relations with the Soviet Uuion, there could be no doubt that

letter by all three signatories. However, none would like to assume the responsibility of denouncing it formally.

78. Such was the case of a speech made by Tito on October 2, 1960, before representatives of Yugoslav immigrants in Canada, in which the Yugoslav leader was quoted as having said that "unfortunately not all Macedonians are free today."

79. *Politika*, November 18, 1960.

80. *Borba*, July 8, 1961.

they rejoiced at the new turn of events. Their guarded optimism appeared to be justified after the 22nd Congress of the CPSU, as Soviet-Yugoslav relations in 1962 experienced a rapid improvement. Visiting Bulgaria in May, Khrushchev referred to Yugoslavia as one of the great Balkan countries which was "also building socialism." No doubt, the Bulgarians felt Soviet pressure to re-establish friendly relations with the twice condemned outcast of the Soviet bloc. On September 25, Soviet President Brezniev visited Yugoslavia and opened the way for Tito's visit to the Soviet Union in December.

Although no major official declarations were made at the time, it appears that Khushchev and Tito laid down in Moscow the foundations for a close cooperation on almost all issues, particularly the international ones. Despite tirades from Peking and Tirana, Yugoslavia was accepted as a full-fledged socialist state. The impact on the Macedonian Question of Yugoslavia's new position in the socialist camp remained, by the spring of 1963, a matter of speculation. However, the Soviet-Yugoslav rapprochement in 1962 did affect Bulgaria's attitude substantially.

After Khrushchev's May visit to Sofia, Bulgaria's new attitude toward Yugoslavia began to acquire a striking resemblance to that of 1955. Prior to this, the Bulgarians tried to stand firm on their position regarding Macedonia. On April 3, 1962, the Bulgarian chargé d'affaires in Athens, Lambriev, paid a private visit to former Greek Foreign Minister Stefanopoulos. As reported in the Greek press, Lambriev stated to Stefanopoulos that his Government did not accept the Yugoslav theory that there is a "Macedonian" nation, but only Bulgarian speaking inhabitants. As for Yugoslav agitation for "Aegean Macedonia," Lambriev said that his Government considered such a question non-existent.[81] Similar views were expressed by high-ranking Bulgarian officials in Sofia to a correspondent of an Athens daily. The Bulgarians made it clear to the Greek journalist that they did not recognize the Macedonian state of Skopje and its "Macedonians" whom they considered Bulgarians.[82]

As expected, the Yugoslav press reacted strongly, accusing the Bulgarians of openly pursuing a chauvinistic policy.[83] The Lambriev interview was considered serious enough for Belgrade to send a note of protest to Sofia. On April 13, Yugoslav Foreign Office spokesman Kunć said that

81. *Καθημερινή*, (Athens), April 3, 1962.
82. *Tὸ Βῆμα*, (Athens), April 10, 1962.
83. *Nova Makedonija*, April 8, 1962.

the purpose of Lambriev's remarks portrayed unfounded chauvinistic views aimed at again undermining Yugoslav-Bulgarian relations.

Soon, however, the Bulgarian leaders found themselves confronted with an international situation which compelled them to improve their relations with Yugoslavia.[84] How much ground the Bulgarians had lost in less than a year was revealed in October when the three Balkan neighbors celebrated the 50th anniversary of the Balkan Wars of 1912-1913. In Greece, the theme of the celebrations was that the two Balkan Wars had brought freedom to the Hellenic parts of Macedonia. In Bulgaria, all chauvinistic references to national claims — frequent in previous years — were completely ignored.[85] For her part, Yugoslavia grasped the opportunity to project further her position in Macedonia. Not only the Skopje press, but all major Yugoslav newspapers proclaimed that, despite the struggles of the "Macedonians," the Balkan wars divided them and placed them under the suppressive and assimilative policy of the neighboring countries. Only in Vardar Macedonia, under the leadership of the CPY, did the "Macedonians" find their just national restitution.[86] Once again, by the end of 1962, the odds in the Yugoslav-Bulgarian dispute over Macedonia appeared to favor the Yugoslav side.

The reconciliation with the Soviet Union appeared to have minimized for Yugoslavia Greece's role as a direct access route to the West. The Skopje nationalists availed themselves of the opportunity to reiterate their views that not only a "Macedonian" minority existed in Greece, but that this minority was ill-treated by the Greek authorities.[87] The Greek press, as usual, reacted with indignation, and Greek Foreign Minister Evangelos Averoff declared in Parliament that his Government's position was that no "Macedonian" minority existed in Greece. In answer to this statement, an official spokesman of the Yugoslav Foreign Ministry publicly stated that for Yugoslavia a "Macedonian" minority did exist in Greece.[88]

This statement created an uproar in Greece, not because it actually

84. Following Khrushchev's visit, Bulgarian Party Secretary Todor Zhivkov, in a speech on May 23, declared that "we will preserve and improve our relations with Yugoslavia and the peoples of Yugoslavia... [because] Yugoslavia follows the socialist road." *Rabotnitsesko Delo,* May 30, 1962.

85. *Rabotnitsesko Delo,* October 18, 1962; *Narodna Armiya,* October 18, 1962; *Otetsestven Front,* October 18, 1962; *Radio Sofia,* October 19, 1962.

86. *Borba,* October 21, 1962; *Politika,* October 21, 1962.

87. Press conference by Premier of the People's Republic of Macedonia. Alexander Grlsko, at Skopje; *Καθημερινή,* November 15, 1961.

88. *Borba,* December 16, 1961.

contained any new element in Yugoslav policy, but because it was felt that it was the first time in many years that an official spokesman of the central government in Belgrade had publicly taken such a categorical stand.[89] The Greeks had been led to believe that what was said in Yugoslavia about Greek Macedonia was merely the result of the agitation of a few irredentists at Skopje whose views were somehow tolerated for domestic reasons, but not fully espoused officially by the central Government.

Late in January 1962, the Greek Government closed the frontier to its citizens in the border regions who had free passes to travel to Yugoslavia. Heated exchanges between the press of the two countries continued[90] and by the middle of the summer, relations between the two friendly countries had reached the lowest point in a decade.[91] Only by December was it possible for the two countries to reach a *modus vivendi* on the issue of "Macedonian" minority, without backing from their basic positions.

A new era appeared to be developing in Greek-Yugoslav relations, without recriminations and extremist nationalist manifestations.

C. The KKE and the Yugoslavs 1955-1962.

To complete the picture, it is necessary to review briefly the position of the KKE which, though powerless in exile, still played an important role in the Macedonian issue.

Events since 1955 have had a profound impact on the Greek communists in the *diaspora*. The most important was the expulsion of Zahariades from the post of the Secretary-General of the Party, at the Sixth Plenum of the Central Committee in 1956. Zahariades had built over the years an image of himself which closely resembled that of Stalin. Even his most unpopular decisions — as the 1949 Resolution on the Macedonian Question — were accepted by the rank and file of the Party with surprisingly little effective opposition. His fall, which was brought about

---

89. In an interview with V. Vasiliou, correspondent of the Athens daily Ἀκρόπολις, Foreign Minister Popović said that a similar declaration was made on May 28, 1960, by the spokesman of the Yugoslav Foreign Ministry. Text of the interview in *Revue de la politique internationale*, Belgrade, February 5, 1962, p. 23.

90. Indicative of the deterioration of relations was an article published in *Nova Makedonija* which went as far as to accuse Greece of pursuing a policy of "genocide" against its "Macedonian" minority. *Nova Makedonija*, September 6, 1962.

91. The Greek Government issued the following terse press release in November: "There is no issue of a Macedonian minority in Greece and we will never discuss a non-existent issue. Persistence on this subject can shake the Greek-Yugoslav relations..." Καθημερινή, November 11, 1962.

by the open intervention of the Soviet authorities, was followed by the official condemnation of Zahariades' Macedonian policy.

In a strongly worded statement, the new leadership of the Party under Koliyannis, condemned the 1949 Resolution as one "of the most serious leftist, sectarian mistakes."[92] Zahariades was personally criticized for having dissolved the NOF and initiating the formation of "Iliden." In fact, "Iliden" was dissolved as being too anti-Titoist and "harmful to the spirit of unity among the Slav-Macedonians, as well as to the strengthening of brotherly relations between the Greek and Slav-Macedonian people and the peoples of the People's Republic of Yugoslavia."[93]

The new policy of the KKE, was that of "equal rights for the Slav-Macedonians." These rights were outlined as follows:

> The Slav-Macedonian minority should have all the rights of the Greek citizen; the right to use freely its language, to be educated in the mother tongue, in its own schools — exactly as the Turkish minority — and generally to enjoy the right to cultivate and to develop its national culture not only without any obstacles on the part of the Greek state but with its material and moral aid.[94]

The new leadership of the KKE, without abandoning its close relationship with the CPB, adopted a more conciliatory attitude toward Yugoslav claims over the Macedonian Question. Still, however, it did not stop to be alert against the infiltrations of Skopje's propaganda among the "Slav-Macedonians," whom the KKE had every reason to want to keep under its control. From 1957 to the end of 1962, the Yugoslavs were successful in attracting many "Slav-Macedonians" who left the Eastern European countries in order to settle in the People's Republic of Macedonia. All these "Slav-Macedonians" were supposed to have cut their ties with the KKE and, in their majority, to have been invested with a Yugoslav citizenship. By the end of 1962 it was estimated that *emigrés* from Greek Macedonia in Southern Yugoslavia numbered approximately 40,000.

In the last five years, relations between the Greek and Yugoslav communists have followed the pattern of Yugoslav-Soviet relations. As late as the Eighth Congress of the KKE — held in late August 1961 — the Yugoslav communists were under severe fire by their Greek comrades for their alleged chauvinistic attitude on the Macedonian Question. Presenting its Report to the Eighth Congress, the Central Committee wrote:

---

92. "The Macedonian National Question in the Light of the Decisions of the Sixth Plenum," *Νέος Κόσμος,* February 1957, p. 8.

93. *Νέος Κόσμος,* February 1957, p. 11.

94. *Ibid.,* p. 8.

In these common struggles [Occupation, Guerrilla War] unbreak-able ties were established between the Greek and Slav-Macedonian peoples. This unity constituted, even from years past, the target of our common enemies and particularly the *Yugoslav revisionists,* who undermined it systematically with fractionist and chauvinistic slogans. *This unfriendly, fractionist work has recently increased.*[95]

The new Moscow-Belgrade rappochement in 1962 forced the Greek communists to halt their attacks on the Yugoslavs. Whenever they refer to the "Slav-Macedonian" issue — and they do so rarely now — [96] they refrain from any anti-Yugoslav remarks. Whether in late 1963, the close cooper-ation envisioned between the Soviet bloc and Yugoslavia would compel the Greek communists — and for that matter, the Bulgarian communists — to accept the Yugoslav demands appears uncertain, although not necessarily improbable.

95. "Report of the Central Committee," *Νέος Κόσμος,* September 1961, p. 125 (Italics added).

96. The Radio of the KKE ("The Voice of Truth") in its January 19, 1962, broadcast reported the Party's new position which was devoid of any anti-Yugoslav hints. Similar was an article published in *Ἀγωνιστὴς* (July 30, 1962), organ of the KKE in Czechoslovakia.

CONCLUSIONS

The course of the events recorded and analyzed in the preceeding pages, establishes in a sufficiently clear way the fact that the Macedonian Question has been a combination of age-old national antagonisms, messianic ambitions, Great Power politics, racial suspicions, economic considerations and, more recently, conflicting socio-political ideologies. The emergence of communism in the Balkans has brought basically little, if any, change to the ingredients of the problem. The introduction of Leninist principles, while it altered the appearance of the issue, has left the substance intact.

A careful study of Part II reveals a series of flagrant violations of basic tenets of Marxism-Leninism which were frequently superceded by "old-fashioned" nationalist aspirations. None of the three Balkan communist parties is free from blame.

The *Bulgarian communists*, from the infancy of their Party, espoused the extremist nationalist claims of the bourgeois régimes of their country. Naturally, Leninist phraseology and technics were employed to cover the fact that the communists aspired equally at the age-old vision of San Stefano Bulgaria. That this policy, which lasted all through the inter-war period, tended to place in an awkward position the communists of Yugoslavia and Greece, did not appear to hinder their moves. Communist Bulgarian inconsistency with Leninist principles continued also after the end of World War II. In less than twenty years since liberation, the Bulgarian communists five times adopted totally contradictory views on the Macedonian issue. Thus, in 1944-1948 not only did they relinquish in favor of the Yugoslavs their territorial claims over Macedonia, but even accepted the Yugoslav theory that the Slav inhabitants of Macedonia as a whole were "Macedonian," i.e. a new ethnic group. Following the Tito-Cominform split — from 1948 to 1954 — the Bulgarians passed to the offensive by advocating the establishment of a Bulgarian-sponsored Macedonian state within a Balkan communist federation. By official act, the "Macedonians" became Bulgarians again. Only when the new Soviet leadership thought it expedient to try to bring Tito back to the communist fold in 1955, did Bulgaria drop her pretentions over Macedonia and acquiesced to recognition of the existence of ethnic "Macedonians" even inside Bulgaria. But, this was only a short-lived retreat which lasted only for the duration of the new

Soviet-Yugoslav rapprochement. In 1958, amidst sharp criticism of the Yugoslav "revisionists" by the entire Soviet bloc, the Bulgarians lost no time to declare their independence on the Macedonian issue, welcome back the "Macedonians" as "Bulgarians" and do away with the theory of the "Macedonian nationality." But Moscow's new international orientations brought about a new reconciliation with Belgrade. As a result Sofia found itself abandoning the polemics on the Macedonian issue. There were indications that following the Tito - Zhivkov meeting in Belgrade in January 1963, the Bulgarians might harden their position to Yugoslav demands. However, Soviet-Yugoslav relations have not apparently reached perfection to compel the Bulgarians to decide definitely whether "Macedonians" do exist outside the People's Republic of Macedonia.

The *Yugoslav communists,* contrary to the Bulgarians, appear to be thankful to Marxist-Leninist theories for strengthening their position in Macedonia. While the inter-war Yugoslav governments were forced into an unenviable defensive position for their handling of the Macedonian issue, the Yugoslav communists, by employing adroitly the national doctrine and creating a new nationality, passed to the offensive. Thus, even during the occupation, they felt themselves strong enough to demand recognition of their policy by the communist parties of Bulgaria and Greece. Later, in the mid-forties, their claims assumed the form of demands for a unified Macedonian state which would have included Greek and Bulgarian Macedonia ostensibly under Yugoslav control. That no ethnological foundations existed for the advancement of such claims, did not seem important to the Yugoslav communists at the time. However, since 1950, expansionism has been abandoned. Yugoslavia continues, of course, to adhere to the theory that "Macedonians" exist in Bulgaria and Greece, but she raises no territorial claims; she merely presses for recognition by the neighboring states of "Macedonian" minorities which should be granted national minority rights.

The *Greek communists* found themselves in the least enviable position of all Balkan communists whenever the Macedonian issue was raised. In the forty years of its existence, the KKE was, in fact, the victim of Bulgarian-Yugoslav conflicting claims over Macedonia. Its position was a sorry one, indeed. On the one hand, it was blamed inside Greece of high treason for trying to cede Greek territories to foreign states and, on the other, it was faced with the opposition of its rank and file who argued that since Greek Macedonia was inhabited, in fact, by Greeks alone, the policy of secession was contrary to Leninist national doctrine. In the inter-war period—at least up to 1935—the KKE was under strict orders by the Comintern to accept the Bulgarian view; and it capitulated. In the forties, in urgent need for support from Yugoslavia and Bulgaria, it acquiesced to their demands to pledge Greek Macedonia to alien political objectives. To maintain a facade of principled and consistent policy, it accepted the tenet that the Slavophones of Greek Macedonia are "Slav - Macedonians" entitled to national rights; these rights were interpreted to mean sometimes complete "liberation" and "secession" from Greece, sometimes acceptance of a separate ethnic minority status.

It becomes clear that for the communists the Leninist nationality doctrine was a convenient means of projecting conflicting individual interests. National security, national cohesion, conversion to communism, defense of the Party's rule against "counter-revolutionaries," were some of these interests. But, far and above, the conflicting objectives were "old-fashioned" nationalist manifestations, not different from those of the *anciens régimes.*

At present, despite past behavior, all three interested countries disclaim any and all pretensions over neighboring territories. Greece has done this since the end of the First World War. Yugoslavia, following the experiences of the feud with the Cominform, when she saw herself falling victim to her own pretensions in Macedonia, has officially abandoned territorial claims and has reorientated her foreign policy toward peaceful coexistence. As it happened, this policy paid richer dividents for the country's international standing and economic and national stability. Bulgaria, since Stalin's death, has similarly, officially disclaimed any pretensions over neighboring territories.

Then, the question may be asked: Is there really a "Macedonian Question?" If the term "Macedonian Question" refers to outstanding territorial issues the answer is negative. However, a whole series of lesser "problems" is still connected with Macedonia.

Yugoslavia has not, as yet, fully converted to "Macedonianism" the traditionally Bulgarian-inclined population of the People's Republic of Macedonia. Yet, twenty years since its establishment, a distinct national consciousness—named "Macedonian" after the land—is slowly emerging among the Slavs, particularly the youth of the region. There is also another problem which appears to disturb the central government in Belgrade. That is the "regionalist, chauvinist" manifestations of the new "Macedonians" of Skopje which tend to disrupt the ultimate aim of the government toward "Yugoslavism," i.e. integration of all nationalities of the country. If the Yugoslav leaders do succeed in this task and turn new Yugoslavia into a "melting pot," then it will not be a surprise if they pass in the history of that troubled country as national benefactors. Solving a difficult internal problem will simultaneously remove a bothersome obstacle in the relations with the two neighboring countries. Greek-Yugoslav relations, in particular, will benefit the most and the familiar and traditional road of friendship and mutual respect will be once again open.

Bulgaria's problem today arising from Macedonia, is how to cope with Yugoslavia's declared policy that there is a distinct national group, which by implication, if not by direct declaration, renders the inhabitants of Bulgarian Macedonia ethnic ''Macedonians,'' as those of the People's Republic of Macedonia. While Bulgaria may sincerely agree that now, or in the near future, the inhabitants of Yugoslav Macedonia have become ''Macedonians,'' it is doubtful that she will accept this thesis for the Bulgarians of the Pirin district, especially since Skopje's ''Macedonization'' process has not seriously affected them.

For Greece, there is no problem, since the alien-conscious elements left the country, initially during the Greco-Bulgarian exchange of the twenties, and later, after the crushing of the communist rebellion in 1949. Some 40,000 inhabitants which were listed in the 1951 census as Slav speaking, had proven themselves to have a Greek national consciousness. At present they may be termed as bilingual Greeks since they speak both Greek and and a peculiar Slavonic idiom. Greece's ''Macedonian problem'' emerges only when either of the two neighboring countries advance demands for recognition of an ethnic minority which interchangeably is termed Bulgarian or ''Macedonian.'' Since, in fact, no such ethnic group exists within the country, the suspicion arises among the Greeks, that the request for minority rights is a pretext for ulterior aims. It is an encouraging sign that neither Bulgaria nor Yugoslavia put forward such requests at the present time.

Today the policy of peaceful coexistence, on the one hand, and the Sino-Soviet dispute on the other, which has prompted the Soviets to welcome the cooperation of even the ''revisionist'' Yugoslavs, have pushed the Macedonian issue to the background. Now all three Balkan states appear to advance the positive elements in their relations which, doubtlessly will bear all-round beneficial results. Under such circumstances, the ''Macedonian Question'' can and should be considered a subject for the student of history rather than an issue for the policymaker.

BIBLIOGRAPHY

I. UNPUBLISHED DOCUMENTARY SOURCES

Archives of the Royal Ministry of Foreign Affairs, (include documents of the Nazi imposed Athens Government 1941-1944 and the Greek Government-in exile 1941-1944).

II. DOCUMENTS

A. BULGARIA

Ministry of Foreign Affairs. *Memorandum: Bulgaria and her Peace Problems* (Supplementary Statement submitted to the Council of the Four Foreign Ministers at Paris). Paris:1946.
Ministry of Foreign Affairs, Press Department. *Political Report to the Fifth Congress of the Bulgarian Communist Party* (presented by Georgi Dimitrov). Sofia: 1949.
Council of Ministers, Central Statistical Service. *Statistical Bulletin of the P. R. of Bulgaria.* Sofia:1959.
Statute of the Bulgarian Association of Thessaloniki. Thessaloniki: 1941 (unpublished).

B. GERMANY

Auswartiges Amt. *Documents Relating to the Conflict with Yugoslavia and Greece* [Official Declaration by the Reich Government on April 6, 1941], 1931/41, No. 7. Berlin: Deutscher Vertag 1941.
The Vermacht Archives; 1941-1944 [in Greek]. Athens: *To Vima:* June 1963.

C. GREAT BRITAIN

Foreign Office. *Treaty of Peace with Turkey and Other Instruments Signed at Lausanne on July 24, 1923, Together with Agreements between Greece and Turkey Signed on January 30, 1923, and Subsidiary Documents Forming Part of the Turkish Peace Settlement.* "Treaty Series," No. 16. London: H. M. Stationery Office, 1923.

D. GREECE

Ministry of Foreign Affairs. *Treaty of Peace between the Allied and Associated Powers and Bulgaria with an addended Protocol Signed at Neilly,* 14-27/11/1919 [in Greek]. Athens: National Printing Office, 1919.

Ministry of Foreign Affairs. *Traité de paix entre les puissances alliées et associées et la Turquie*. Signé le 10 août 1920 à Sevres (text in French, English and Italian).

Ministry of Foreign Affairs. *Traité entre les puissances alliées et la Grèce relatif à la Thrace*. Signé le 10 août, 1920, à Sevres [text in French, English and Italian].

Ministry of Foreign Affairs. *Acts Signed at Lausanne on 30/1/1923 and 24/7/1923* [in Greek]. Athens: National Printing Office, 1923.

Ministry of Foreign Affairs. *Treaty of Peace between the Allied and Associated Powers and Bulgaria* [in Greek]. Collection of Treaties, Conventions and Agreements. No. 18. Athens:National Printing Office, 1947.

Ministry of Interior. *Monthly Confidential Report, May 1942* (unpublished).

National Statistical Service. *Annuaire Statistique de la Grèce, 1928,* Athens: National Printing Office, 1928.

— *Statistical Yearbook of Greece,* Athens : National Printing Office 1946.

Under-Secretariat for Press and Information. *The Conspiracy Against Greece.* Athens: "Pyrsos," June 1947.

E. UNITED STATES OF AMERICA

Congress (Senate), Committee on the Judiciary. *Yugoslav Communism: A Critical Study,* [author: Charles Zalar]. Washington: U. S. Government Printing Office, 1961.

Department of State. *Paris Peace Conference, 1946: Selected Documents*, [Editor: Volms H. Cassidy]. "Conference Series" No. 103. Publication No. 2868. Washington: U. S. Government Printing Office.

F. YUGOSLAVIA

Federal Institute of Statistics. *Petit Manuel de la Yougoslavie, 1962.* Belgrade, 1962.

Kardelj, Edvard. *Yugoslavia's Foreign Policy; Address Delivered in the Federal Assembly on December 29, 1948.* Belgrade, 1949.

Ministrarstvo inostranih poslova. *White Book on Aggressive Activities by the Governments of the USSR, Poland, Czechoslovakia, Hungary, Rumania, Bulgaria and Albania towards Yugoslavia.* Belgrade, 1951.

Office of Information. *Book on Greece.* Belgrade, 1948.

Proceedings of the First Congress of the Communist Party of the P. R. of Macedonia, December 19-24, 1948. Skopje: *Nova Makedonija,* December 1948.

G. LEAGUE OF NATIONS

Greek Refugee Settlement. Publication of the League of Nations No. 11, "Economic and Financial". Geneva, 1926.

H. UNITED NATIONS

General Assembly *Official Records.* Second Session, First Committee. Summary Record of Meetings, 16 September to 19 November 1947. Lake Success, 1947.

General Assembly. *Official Records.* Fifth Session, First Committee, Summary Records of Meetings, New York, 1950.

General Assembly. *Official Records.* Fourth Session, First Committee, Summary Records of Meetings, 20 September to 6 December 1949. Lake Success, 1949.

General Assembly. *Official Records.* Third Session Supplement No. 8. "Report of the United Nations Special Committee on the Balkans" (A/574). Lake Success, 1948.

General Assembly. *Oficial Records.* Fourth Session Supplement No 8 "Report of the U. N. Subcommittee on the Balkans" (A/935). Lake Success, 1949.

General Assembly. *Official Records.* Sixth Session Supplement No. 11. "Report of the U. N. Special Committee on the Balkans" (A/1857). New York, 1951.

Security Council. *Official Records.* Second Year Special Supplement No. 2. "Report by the Commission of Investigation Concerning Greek Frontier Incidents to the Security Council," Vol. III (S/360/Rev. 1; July 28, 1950), "Memorandum on the Slavophones of Greece." New York, 1950.

I. GREEK COMMUNIST PARTY (KKE)

Αἱ ἀποφάσεις τῆς ΧΙΙ ῾Ολομελείας τῆς ᾽Εκτελεστικῆς ᾽Επιτροπῆς τῆς Κομμουνιστικῆς Διεθνοῦς [The Decisions of the XII Plenum of the Executive Committee of the Communist International], Athens: November 1932.

Central Committee. *Τὸ ΚΚΕ ἀπὸ τὸ 1918 ἕως τὸ 1931* [The KKE from 1918 to 1931], two vols. Athens, 1947.

Central Committee. *Πέντε Χρόνια ᾽Αγῶνες, 1931-1936* [Five Years of Struggle], New Edition, corrected and completed. Athens, 1946.

Central Committee. *Δέκα Χρόνια ᾽Αγῶνες, 1935-1945* [Ten Years of Struggle; 1935-1945]. Athens, 1945.

Central Committee. *Τὸ ῞Εβδομο Συνέδριο τοῦ ΚΚΕ* [The Seventh Congress of the KKE], five pamphlets. Athens, 1945.

Central Committee. *᾽Απόφαση τῆς 12ης ῾Ολομέλειας τῆς Κ.Ε. τοῦ ΚΚΕ* [Decision of the 12th Plenum of the Central Committee of the KKE]. Athens, 1945.

J. ROYAL INSTITUTE OF INTERNATIONAL AFFAIRS

DEGRÁS IANE. *The Communist International 1919-1943: Documents.* Vol. I, 1919-1922. London: The Institute, 1956.

The Soviet-Yugoslav Dispute: Text of the Published Correspondence. London: The Institute, 1948.

III. BOOKS

ANASTASOFF, CHRIST. *The Tragic Peninsula: A History of the Macedonian Movement for Independence Since 1878.* St. Louis, Mo.: Blackwell Weilandy Co., 1938.

ANDONOFSKI, HRISTO. *Egejska Makedonija* [Aegean Macedonia]. Skopje: G. O. na Zdruzhanieto na be Galcite od Eg. Makedonija, 1951.

ARMSTRONG, H. F. *Tito and Goliath.* New York: MacMillan and Co., 1955.

AVGERINOU, MELPOMENI. *Μακεδονικὰ 'Απομνημονεύματα καὶ Διπλωματικὰ Παρασκήνια* [Macedonian Memoirs and Diplomatic Backstage]. Athens: "To Kratos," 1914.

BALLAS, NIKOLAOS. *'Ιστορία τοῦ Κρουσόβου* [History of Krussovo]. Thessaloniki: Institute for Balkan Studies, 1962.

BARKER, ELIZABETH. *Macedonia; Its Place in Balkan Power Politics.* London: The Royal Institute of International Affairs, 1950.

BRAMOS, KOSTÁ. *Σλαβοκομμουνιστικαὶ 'Οργανώσεις ἐν Μακεδονίᾳ: Προπαγάνδα καὶ 'Επαναστατικὴ Δρᾶσις* [Slav-Communist Organizations in Macedonia; Propaganda and Revolutionary Activities]. First Edition, Thessaloniki, 1953. Second Edition, Thessaloniki, 1960.

Bulgarian Atrocities in Macedonia and Thrace, 1941-1944: A Report of Professors of the Universities of Athens and Salonika. Athens, 1945.

CHRISTIDES, CRISTOPHER J. *The Macedonian Camouflage in the Light of Facts and Figures.* Athens: The Hellenic Publishing Company, 1949.

CHRYSOCHOOU, ATHANASIOS I. *'Η Κατοχὴ ἐν Μακεδονίᾳ* [Occupation in Macedonia]. Six Volumes. Thessaloniki: Society for Macedonian Studies, 1949-1952.

CIANO, CALLEAZZO. *Ciano's Diplomatic Papers, Being a Record of Nearly 200 Conversations Held During the Years 1936-1942, e.t.c.* London: Odhams, 1948.

COLOCOTRONIS, V. *La Macédoine et l'Hellénisme; Etude historique et ethnologique,* Paris: Berger-Levrault, 1919.

CONSTANTOPOULOS, DIMITRIS. *The Paris Peace Conference of 1946 and the Greek-Bulgarian Relations.* Thessaloniki: Institute for Balkan Studies, 1956.

CVIJIC', JOVAN. *Remarques sur l'ethnographie de la Macédoine.* Second Edition, augmented. Paris: G. Roustan, 1907

DEDIJER, VLADIMIR. *Tito.* New York: Simon and Schuster, 1953.

DENDIAS, MICHAEL. *La Thrace grecque et la débouche bulgare sur la mer Egée.* Paris: B. de Boccard, 1946.

DJILAS, MILOVAN. *Conversations with Stalin* [Greek Edition]. Athens: K. H. Kamarinopoulos, 1962.

DIMITROV, GEORGI. *Selected Speeches and Articles.* London: Lawrence and Wishart, 1951.

DOXIADES, CONSTANTINE A. *Destruction of Towns and Villages in Greece.* (Series No.11). Athens: Ministry of Reconstruction, 1947.

Dotation Carnegie pour la Paix Internationale. *Enquête dans les Balkans: rapport présenté aux directeurs de la Dotation par les membres de la Commission d'Enquête.* Paris, 1914.

DRAGOUMIS, PHILIPPOS. *Προσοχὴ στὴ Βόρειο 'Ελλάδα, 1945-1948* [Watch Northern Greece; 1945-1948). Thessaloniki: Society for Macedonian Studies, 1949.

E VELPIDI, C. *Les états balkaniques,* Paris, 1930.

FOTICH, CONSTANTIN. *The War We Lost; Yugoslavia's Tragedy and the Failure of the West.* New York: Viking Press, 1948.

Free Europe Committee, Inc., Mid-European Studies Center. *Yugoslavia.* New York: Frederick A. Praeger, 1957.

GREGORIOU, EMMANUEL TH. *"Ελληνες καὶ Βούλγαροι* [Greeks and Bulgars]. Thessaloniki: Society for Macedonian Studies, 1954.

GUECHOFF, IV. E, *L'Alliance balkanique.* Paris: Librairie Hachette et Cie, 1915.

GUECHOFF, IV. E. *La folie criminelle et l'enquête parlementaire,* Sofia, 1914.

HRISTOV, ALEXANDAR. T. *The Communist Party of Yugoslavia in the Solution of the Macedonian Question; 1937-1944* [mimeographed Greek translation]. Skopje: "Kultura", 1962.

IDAS (ION DRAGOUMIS). *'Ηρώων καὶ Μαρτύρων Αἷμα* [Blood of Heroes and Martyrs]. Second Edition. Athens, 1914.

JELAVICH, CHARLES. *Tsarist Russia and Balkan Nationalism: Russian Influence in the Internal Affairs of Bulgaria and Serbia; 1879-1886.* Berkeley: University of California Press, 1958.

KARAVANGELIS, GERMANOS. *'Ο Μακεδονικὸς 'Αγών. 'Απομνημονεύματα* [The Macedonian Struggle; Memoirs]. Second edition, edited by Vasilios Laourdas. Thessaloniki: Institute for Balkan Studies, 1959

KERNER, R.J. and HOWARD, H. N. *The Balkan Conferences and the Balkan Entente, 1930-1936; A Study in the Recent History of the Balkans and Near Eastern Peoples.* Berkeley: University of California Press, 1936

KRAINIKOWSKY, ASSEN IV. *La question de la Macédoine et la diplomatie européenne.* Paris: Librairie Rivière & Cie, 1938.

KYROU, ACHILLEFS A. *'Η Συνωμοσία ἐναντίον τῆς Μακεδονίας: 1940-1949* [The Conspiracy Against Macedonia; 1940-1949]. Athens: "Aetos" 1950.

KYROU, ALEXIS A. *'Ελληνικὴ 'Εξωτερικὴ Πολιτικὴ* [Greek Foreign Policy]. Athens, 1955.

KYROU, ALEXIS A. *Οἱ Βαλκανικοὶ Γείτονές μας* [Our Balkan Neighbors]. Athens, 1962.

LADAS, STEPHEN P. *The Exchange of Minorities: Bulgaria, Greece and Turkey.* New York: Macmillan and Company, 1932.

LAOURDAS, VASILIOS. *Τὸ 'Ελληνικὸν Γενικὸν Προξενεῖον Θεσσαλονίκης, 1903-1908* [The Greek General Consulate of Thessaloniki; 1903-1908]. Thessaloniki: Institute for Balkan Studies, 1961.

LAOURDAS, VASILIOS. *'Η Μητρόπολις Νευροκοπίου: 1900-1907. 'Εκθέσεις τῶν Μητροπολιτῶν Νικοδήμου καὶ Θεοδωρήτου* [The Metropolis of Nevrokop; 1900-1907. Reports of the Metropolitans Nikodemos and Theodoritos]. Thessaloniki: Institute for Balkan Studies, 1961.

LAOURDAS, VASILIOS. *'Η Πηνελόπη Δέλτα καὶ ἡ Μακεδονία* [Penelope Delta and Macedonia]. Thessaloniki: Institute for Balkan Studies, 1958.

232

LENIN, VLADIMIR ILICH. *The Right of Nations to Self-determination; Selected Writings.* New York: International Publishers, 1951,

LEVENTIS, G.A. Ἡ κατὰ τῆς Μακεδονίας Ἐπιβουλὴ [The Conspiracy Against Macedonia]. Athens: Military Publications, 1962.

MACARTNEY, C.A. *National States and National Minorities.* London: Oxford University Press, 1934.

MCNEILL, WILLIAM HARDY. *The Greek Dilemma: War and Aftermath.* Philadelphia and New York: J. B. Lippincott Company, 1947.

MARKHAM, R.H. *Tito's Imperial Communism.* Chapel Hill N.C.; The University of North Carolina Press, 1947.

MAVROCORDATO, JOHN. *Modern Greece.* London: Macmillan Company, 1931.

MIHAILOFF, IVAN. *Macedonia; A Switzerland of the Balkans.* St. Louis, Mo.: Pearlston Publishing Company, 1950.

MILIOFSKI, KYRIL. *The Macedonian Question in the National Program of the Communist Party of Yugoslavia: 1919-1937*, (mimeographed Greek tranlation from "Macedonian"). Skopje: "Kultura", 1962.

MITREV, DIMITAR. *The Communist Party of Bulgaria and Pirin Macedonia,* (mimeographed Greek translation from "Macedonian"). Skopje: "Kultura" 1960.

MOJSOV, LAZAR. *Bulgarskata Rabotnitka Partije (Kommunisti) i Makedonskoto Nacionalno Prášnje* [The Bulgarian Workers (Communist) Party and the Macedonian Question]. Belgrade: Borba, 1948.

MOJSOV, LAZAR. *Okolu praesanjeto na Makedonskoto nacionalno malcinstvo vo Grcija.* Skopje, 1954.

MONASTIRIOTIS, PETROS. Οἱ Πρῶσσοι τῶν Βαλκανίων [The Prussians of the Balkans]. Cairo, 1944.

NALTSAS, CHRISTOPHER. Τὸ Μακεδονικὸν Ζήτημα καὶ ἡ Σοβιετικὴ Πολιτικὴ [The Macedonian Question and Soviet Policy]. Thessaloniki: Institute for Balkan Studies, 1954.

PAPAEVGENIOU, ATHANASIOS. Βόρειος Ἑλλάς: Μειονότητες [Northen Greece: Minorities]. Thessaloniki: Society for the Advancement of Greek Letters, 1946.

PEFANIS, DOROS G. Οἱ Ἕλληνες Σλαβόφωνοι τῆς Μακεδονίας καὶ οἱ Ἑλληνόβλαχοι: Μελέτη Πολιτική, Ἱστορική, Κοινωνικὴ [The Greek Slavophones of Macedonia and the Greco-Vlachs: A Historical, Political and Social Study], Second edition. Athens, 1949.

PETSOPOULOS, YANNIS. Τὰ Πραγματικὰ Αἴτια τῆς Διαγραφῆς μου ἀπὸ τὸ ΚΚΕ [The Real Reasons of my Expulsion from the KKE]. Athens, 1946.

PIPINELIS, PANAYOTIS. *Caitiff Bulgaria.* (Published by authority of the Greek Ministry of Information). London: Hutchinson and Company, 1944.

PIPINELIS, PANAYOTIS. Ἱστορία τῆς Ἑλληνικῆς Ἐξωτερικῆς Πολιτικῆς, 1923-1941 [History of Greek Foreign Policy; 1923-1941]. Athens: Saliveros Company, 1948.

RADOSLAVOFF, VASIL. *Bulgarien und die Weltkrise.* Berlin, 1923.

ROTHSCHILD, JOSEPH. *The Communist Party of Bulgaria: Origins and Development, 1883-1936.* New York: Columbia University Press, 1959.

ROUCEK, JOSEPH S. *Balkan Politics: International Relations in No Man's-Land.* Stanford, California: Stanford University Press, 1948.

SETON-WATSON, HUGH. *The Pattern of Communist Revolution: A Historical Analysis.* London: Methuen and Company, Ltd., 1953.

SETON-WATSON, HUGH. *Eastern Europe between the Wars; 1918-1941.* Cambridge: University Press, 1945.

SETON-WATSON, R. W. *The Rise of Nationality in the Balkans.* London: Constable and Company, Ltd., 1917.

SLIJEPCEVIC, DJOKO. *The Macedonian Question; The Struggle for Southern Serbia.* Chicago: The American Institute for Balkan Affairs, 1956.

SOULIOTIS-NIKOLAIDES, ATHANASIOS. Ἡμερολόγιον τοῦ Πρώτου Βαλκανικοῦ Πολέμου [Diary of the First Balkan War]. Thessaloniki: Institute for Balkan Studies, 1962.

SOTEROPOULOS, H. K. Αἱ Σλαβικαὶ ᾿Οργανώσεις καὶ ἡ ᾿Ανθελληνικὴ των Προπαγάνδα [The Slav Organizations and their anti-Hellenic Propaganda]. Athens, August 1960.

SPENCER, FLOYD ALBERT. *War and Postwar Greece; An Analysis Based on Greek Writings.* Washington, D.C.: Library of Congress, European Affairs Division, 1952.

STALIN, JOSEPH. *Marxism and the National and Colonial Question: A Collection of Articles and Speeches.* New York: International Publishers, (no date).

STALIN, JOSEPH. Ὁ Μαρξισμὸς καὶ τὸ ᾿Εθνικὸ καὶ ᾿Αποικιακὸ Πρόβλημα [Marxism and the National and Colonial Question]. Athens: Marxist Library, 1933.

STAVRIANOS, L. S. *Balkan Federation: A History of the Movement toward Balkan Unity in Modern Times.* Northampton, Mass.: The Department of History of Smith College, 1944.

STAVRIDES, ELEFTHERIOS, A. Τὰ Παρασκήνια τοῦ ΚΚΕ, ἀπὸ τῆς ῾Ιδρύσεώς του μέχρι τοῦ Συμμοριτοπολέμου [Backstage of the KKE; from its Founding to the Guerrilla War]. Athens, 1953.

STOJANOVIC, MIHAILO D. *The Great Powers and the Balkans, 1875-1878.* Cambridge: University Press, 1939.

SWIRE, JOSEPH. *Bulgarian Conspiracy.* London: R. Hale, Ltd., 1939.

ULAM, ADAM B. *Titoism and the Cominform.* Cambridge, Mass.: Harvard University Press, 1951.

VASDRAVELLIS, I. K. Οἱ Μακεδόνες εἰς τοὺς ὑπὲρ τῆς ᾿Ανεξαρτησίας ᾿Αγῶνας, 1796-1832 [The Macedonians in the Struggles for Independence, 1796-1832]. Second edition. Thessaloniki: Society for Macedonian Studies, 1950.

234

VILLARI, LUIGI (editor). *The Balkan Question; The Present Condition of the Balkans and of European Responsibilities*. London: John Murray, 1905.

VLAHOS, NIKOLAOS. V. *Τὸ Μακεδονικὸν ὡς Φάσις τοῦ 'Ανατολικοῦ Ζητήματος 1878-1908* [The Macedonian Question as a Phase of the Eastern Question, 1878-1908]. Athens: Petroudis and Christou, 1935.

VLAHOV, DIMITAR I. *Govori i Statii, 1945-1947* [Speeches and Articles]. Skopje: Drsavno Knigoisdatelatvo na Makedonija, 1947.

VLAHOV, DIMITAR I. *Iz Istorije Makedonskog Naroda* [From the History of the Macedonian People]. Belgrade, 1950.

VLAHOV, DIMITAR I. *Makedonija; Momenti od Istorijata na Makedonskiot Narod* [Makedonia: Moments in the History of the Macedonian People] Skopje: Drsavno Knigoisdatelatvo na Makedonija, 1950

VOGAZLIS, D. K. *'Η Μακεδονία : 'Ιστορική, 'Εθνολογικὴ καὶ Νομικὴ Συγκριτικὴ Μελέτη* [Macedonia: A Historical, Ethnological and Legal Study] (unpublished). Athens, 1962.

VOGAZLIS, D. K. *Φυλετικὲς καὶ 'Εθνικὲς Μειονότητες στὴν 'Ελλάδα καὶ τὴ Βουλγαρία* [Racial and National Minorities in Greece and Bulgaria]. Athens: Society for Thracian Studies, 1954.

VOIGT, FRIT AUGUST. *The Greek Sedition*. London: Hollis and Carter, 1949.

VUCINICH, WAYNE S. *Serbia Between East and West : the Events of 1903-1908*. Stanford, California: Stanford University Press, 1954.

VUKMANOVIC, SVETOVAR. *How and Why the People's Liberation Movement in Greece Met with Defeat*. London, 1950.

WILKINSON, H. R. *Maps and Politics: Review of the Ethnographic Cartography of Macedonia*. Liverpool: University Press, 1951.

WOLFF, ROBERT LEE. *The Balkans in Our Time*. Cambridge, Mass.: Harvard University Press, 1956.

WOODHOUSE, CHRISTOPHER M. *The Apple of Discord: A Survey of Recent Greek Politics in their International Setting*. London: Hutchinson and Company, Ltd., 1948.

XYDIS, STEPHEN G. *Greece and the Great Powers, 1944-1947; Prelude to the Truman Doctrine*. Thessaloniki: Institute for Balkan Studies, 1963.

ZAHARIADES, NIKOS. *Δέκα Χρόνια Πάλης* [Ten Years of Struggle]. November 1950.

ZAHARIADES NIKOS. *Καινούργια Κατάσταση, Καινούργια Καθήκοντα* [New Situation, New Duties]. November 1949.

ZAPHEIROPOULOS, DEMETRIOS. *Τὸ ΚΚΕ καὶ ἡ Μακεδονία* [The KKE and Macedonia]. Athens, 1948.

ZAPHEIROPOULOS, DEMETRIOS. *'Ο 'Αντισυμμοριακὸς 'Αγών: 1945-1949* [The Anti-Guerrilla Struggle]. Athens, 1956.

235

ZOGRAFSKI, DANCE. *Egejska Makedonija* [Aegean Macedonia]. Skopje: "Iliden," 1951.

ZOTIADES, GEORGE. *The Macedonian Controversy*. Second edition. Thessaloniki: Institute for Balkan Studies, 1960.

IV. ARTICLES, PAMPHLETS, BROCHURES

BARDJIOTAS, VÁSILIS. «Πάνω στὴ μελέτη τῆς ἱστορίας τοῦ ΚΚΕ» [On the Study of the History of the KKE]. *Neos Kosmos*, March 1951.

BARDJIOTAS, VASILIS. «Μερικὰ συμπεράσματα γιὰ τὴν κατάσταση καὶ δουλειὰ τῶν κομματικῶν ὀργανώσεών μας στὶς ξένες χῶρες μετὰ τὴν III συνδιάσκεψη τοῦ Κόμματος» [Some Conclusions on the Condition and Work of our Party Organizations in Foreign Countries following the III Party Conference], *Neos Kosmos*, February 1951.

CHERVENKOV, VULKO. "The Myth of the National Unity of the Bulgarians with the Assistance of the German Thieves," *The Slavs*. Moscow, June 1944.

DAKIN, DOUGLAS. "The Greek Proposals for an Alliance with France and Great Britain: June-July 1907," *Balkan Studies*, Vol. III, No. 1. Thessaloniki: Institute for Balkan Studies, June 1962.

DAKIN, DOUGLAS. "British Sources Concerning the Greek Struggle in Macedonia; 1901-1909," *Balkan Studies*, Vol. II, No. 1. Thessaloniki: Institute for Balkan Studies, June 1961.

DIMITROV, GEORGI. «Ἡ Ἑβδόμη Βαλκανικὴ Συνδιάσκεψις» [The Seventh Balkan Conference], *Kommunistiki Epitheorisis*, Vol. V, No. 9. Athens, September 1924.

DIMITROV, GEORGI. *Le Front de la patrie* (No date, no publisher).

JELAVICH, BARBARA. "Russia, Bavaria and the Greek Revolution of 1821/1863," *Balkan Studies*. Vol. II, No. 1. Thessaloniki: Institute for Balkan Studies, June 1961.

KNEJEVIC, R. L. "Prince Paul, Hitler and Salonica," *International Affairs*, Vol. XXVII, No 1. London, January 1951.

KOFOS, EVANGELOS. "Balkan Minorities under Communist Regimes," *Balkan Studies*, Vol. II, No. 1. Thessaloniki: Institute for Balkan Studies, June 1961.

KOFOS, EVANGELOS. "The Making of Yugoslavia's People's Republic of Macedonia," *Balkan Studies*, Vol. III, No. 2. Thessaloniki: Institute for Balkan Studies, December 1962.

KOSEV, DIMITAR. "Revisionističeski Falsifikacii na Bulgarska Istorija y Skopskite Istorici" [The Revisionist Falsifications of Bulgarian History and the Historians of Skopje], *Istoriceski Pregled*, Vol. I. Sofia, 1959.

KOSTOPOULOS, STAVROS and YOUSOPOULOS, TÁSOS. «Πρὸς τὸ Συνέδριο τῶν Σλαβομακεδόνων» [Toward the Congress of the Slav-Macedonians], *Neos Kosmos*, January 1952.

MOJSOV, LAZAR. "About the South-Slav Federation" (from an English translation), *Kommunist* (Supplement). Belgrade, July-September 1949.

MOJSOV, LAZAR. "The National Resurgence of the Macedonian People," *Macedonia*. Belgrade: "Jugoslavia," 1957.

PALLIS, ALEXANDER. A. *Macedonia and the Macedonians: A Historical Study*. London: Greek Information Service, 1949.

PALLIS, ALEXANDER A. "Racial Antagonisms in the Balkans," (Lecture delivered at Birmingham University). January 27, 1945.

PIJADE, MOJE. *On the Question of the Balkan Federation* (English translation of a brochure). Skopje, 1951.

POPOFSKI, BLAGOE. *Judicial Provocation in Sofia* (English translation of a brochure). Skopje, 1950.

TOZIS, JOHN A. «'Αμερικανικαὶ καὶ 'Αγγλικαὶ πληροφορίαι περὶ τῆς ἐπαναστάσεως τοῦ 1854 ἐν Μακεδονίᾳ» [American and British Sources for the Revolt of 1854 in Macedonia], *Makedonika*, Vol. III, 1953-1955. Thessaloniki: Society for Macedonian Studies, 1956.

VAGENAS, P. «Ἡ Δεύτερη Ὁλομέλεια τοῦ Κεντρικοῦ Συμβουλίου τῆς 'Οργάνωσης "Ἰλιντεν"» [The Second Plenum of the Central Council of the "Iliden" Organization], *Neos Kosmos*, January 1954.

WILKINSON, H. R. "Yugoslav Macedonia in Transition," *The Geographical Journal*, Vol. CXIII, Part 4. London: The Royal Geographical Society, December 1952.

ZEVGOS, G. «Οἱ 'Εθνικὲς μειονότητες στὸν Κοινὸ 'Αγῶνα» [The National Minorities in the Common Struggle], *Kommunistiki Epitheorisi*. Athens, July 1944.

ZEVGOS, G. «Τὸ 'Εθνικὸ πρόβλημα καὶ ἐθνικὴ καπηλεία» [The National Problem and National Demagogy]. *Kommunistiki Epitheorisi*. Athens, September 1943.

ZEVGOS, G. «Γιὰ τὴν 'Ελληνικὴ Μακεδονία καὶ Θράκη» [For Greek Macedonia and Thrace], *Kommunistiki Epitheorisi*. Athens, 1943.

V. NEWSPAPERS, PERIODICALS, RADIO STATIONS

A. NEWSPAPERS

Agonistis. Prague
Akropolis. Athens

Borba. Belgrade
Bulletin. Publication of the Greek Communist Guerrillas
Bulletin. Skopje

Christian Science Monitor. Boston, Mass.

Egejska Makedonija [Aegean Macedonia]. Skopje

Glas. Belgrade

Izgrev. Sofia

Kathimerini. Athens

Makedonska Tribuna. Indianapolis, Indiana

Nova Makedonija. Skopje
Narodno Zemedelsko Zname. Sofia
New York Times
New York Herald - Tribune
Narodna Armiya. Sofia

Otetsestven Front. Sofia
Observatore Romano. Rome
Otetsestven Front. Plovid
Oslobodjenje. Serajevo

Politika. Belgrade
Pirinsko Delo. Blagoevgrad
Pirinsko Glas. Skopje

Rizospastis. Athens
Rude Pravo. Prague

Trakiiska Duma. Sofia
Trud. Sofia

To Vima. Athens

Zora. Sofia

B. PERIODICALS

Balkan Studies. Institute for Balkan Studies. Thessaloniki
Demokratikos Stratos. Publication of the Greek Communist Guerrillas (irregular)
Exormisis. Publication of the Greek Communist Guerrillas (irregular)
Free Bulgaria. Sofia
The Geographical Journal. The Royal Geographical Society. London
Glasnik. Skopje
International Affairs. Royal Institute of International Affairs. London
Istoricecki Pregled. Sofia
Makedonika. Society for Macedonian Studies. Thessaloniki
Kommunistiki Epitheorisis. Inter-war and war-time official theoretical journal of
    the KKE
Kommunist. Official theoretical journal of the CPY. Belgrade
Neos Kosmos. Official theoretical of the KKE since 1950

Newsweek. U. S. A.

Revue de la politique internationale. Publication of the Union of Journalists of Yugoslavia. Belgrade

The Slavs. Moscow

Slobensko Bratstvo. Belgrade

Sovietology. Athens

C. RADIO STATIONS

Radio Belgrade

Radio "Free Greece" (Greek Communist Guerrillas)

Radio Moscow

Radio Skopje

Radio Sofia

Radio "Voice of Truth" (Exiled leadership of the KKE). Bucharest

INDEX

A

Belofski, Dimtse 208 ft. 50
Berat 21
Bevin, Ernest 180 ft. 94
Bismark 17
Bitola (see Monastir)
Blagoev 64
Blagoevgrad (see also Gorna Djumaja) 4, 214.
Bled Agreement (1947) 153, 175, 188
Bled Pact 1954 (see Balkan Pact)
Bogdanov, Asen 194 ft. 142
Bogdanov, Petar 115
Boider, General 98
Bolsheviks 57, 58
Boris, King 100, 133, 157 ft. 11
Boris University (Skopje) 108
Bosnia-Hercegovina 17, 18, 64, 117, 140
Bosnians 70, 193
Brezniev 218
Britain (see Great Britain)
British Service MO4 134 fl. 69
Broad Socialists 64
Bukharin 81
Bulgaria (see under Balkan Communist Federation, Communist Party of Bulgaria, Fatherland Front, Greece, IMRO, Western Thrace, Yugoslavia) 16-17, 18-20
Foreign relations 40, 42, 45-46, 79, 95, 97-99, 107, 111, 225
Germany 97-99
Greece 38, 42, 45, 48, 100, 111, 151 ft. 115, 153, 155-158, 164, 169, 174, 185, 217, 226
Macedonia (see also Bulgarian Macedonia, Greek Macedonia, P.R. of Macedonia) 20, 21, 26, 27, 36-37, 38, 41, 77, 85, 96, 98, 100-110, 139, 157, 162-163, 169, 173, 175, 176-177, 180, 185, 188-192, 203, 211, 214-215, 218-219, 223-224, 226
Russia 14, 15, 16, 19
Serbia 19, 37-38, 40-41
Soviet Union 96, 116, 155-157, 163-164
Yugoslavia 51, 98, 111, 138-143, 157, 159-162, 188-192, 194-195, 199, 208, 210-220, 224, 226
Bulgarian Association of Thessaloniki 104, 105, 106, 120
Bulgarian Church (see Bulgarian Exarchate)
Bulgarian Exarchate 12, 14, 15, 20, 21, 23, 24, 25, 31, 32, 169
Bulgarian Macedonia 3, 4, 5
internal situation 43, 50, 93-94, 138, 143, 145-146, 159-163, 173, 189-191, 194, 203, 211.
and the Yugoslavs 135, 138, 139, 143, 157, 161, 189-191, 194, 210-211, 216, 224

Bulgarian-Macedonians (see Macedonian Bulgarians)
Bulgarian nationalism 12, 13-14, 17, 21, 51, 98, 163, 215, 223
Bulgarian-Serbian Treaty (1912) 37, 39, 41
Bulgarian Social Democrats 145
Bulgarian Socialist Party (see Socialist Party of Bulgaria)
Bulgarians (see also under Macedonian Bulgarians) 12, 13, 70, 98
"Bulgarophiles" 50
Bulkes 166, 167 ft. 45
Buxton, Victoria 28

C

"Caramanlides" 168 ft. 119
"Caucasians" 168 ft. 119
Central Macedonia (see Greek Macedonia)
Central Macedonian Committee (Bulgarian) 190
Central Powers 41
"Centralists" 27, 52, 58
Chalkidiki 10, 107
Chankov, Alexander 40 ft. 25, 51, 71, 72, 87, 88-89
Chaoulev 88
Chervenkov, Vulko 143 ft. 91, 212 ft. 57
Chinese communists 213, 217, 218
Chrysochoou, Athanasios 102
Ciano, Count 95, 96 ft. 5, 99
Circassians 24
Cominform
    and Bulgarian communists 189
    and Yugoslav communists 169, 174, 175, 176, 180, 181, 184, 188, 189, 192, 204, 205, 206, 208, 212, 213
    and Greek communists 199, 200
Comintern (see also Communist Party of Yugoslavia, KKE) 64, 65
    congresses of, 64, 66, 73, 76, 84, 86, 90
    and Macedonia 70-73, 76, 82, 114, 115, 118, 135, 225
    and the National issue 66-67, 70
    and National Socialism 87, 90
Comitadjis, 23, 28, 30, 31, 33, 74
Commission of South-Slav Unity 141
Communism and Nationalism (see under Nationalism, Marxism-Leninism, Self-determination)
Communist Organization of Aegean Macedonia (see K.O.A.M.)
Communist Party of Albania 69
Communist Party of Bulgaria (see also

Greek national claims 132-133, 154-157
"Greek Problem" 205 ft. 31
Greek puppet Government 101 ft. 21, 102,
104, 105, 106, 119
Greek Revolution (1821) 9-10
Greek revolutions in Macedonia 10, 11,
17
Greeks in Albania 133, 174
Greeks in Macedonia 9-11, 12 23-24, 25,
31, 62, 74, 83, 101, 168
Grlsko, Alexander 219 ft. 87
Grujev, Damjan 25
Grupćev 108
Guechoff, Ivan 40 ft. 25
Guerrilla War (1946-1949) (see also under
KKE) 165, 172, 174-176, 184, 185,
196-197, 201, 222
Albania 153, 164, 169
Bulgaria 153, 164, 169, 176-177
Departure of "Slav-Macedonians"
174, 186-187
Soviet Union 178
Yugoslavia 149, 153, 164, 166-167,
169, 174, 175 ft. 78, 178, 185,
196-197
Gypsies 68, 163

H

Hadji-Dimov, Dimo 52, 53, 61
Hercegovina (see Bosnia-Hercegovina)
Historical Macedonia 4
Hitler, Adolf 96, 97, 99, 144
Hungarian Revolt (1956) 212
Hungary (see also Austria-Hungary)
163

I

Ignatiev, Count 14, 17
"Iliden" Organization 201-203, 203 ft.
24, 221
Iliden uprising (1903) 33, 60, 65 ft. 23,
199
I.M.R.O. (see also under Comitadjis,
"Federalists," Supreme Committee,
"United" IMRO) 25, 26, 28, 29, 30,
32-33, 41, 43, 46, 48, 50-54, 61, 66,
71, 88-89, 108-109, 126, 145-146, 170,
172-173
Bulgarian Government and, 26-
27, 51, 52, 89, 194
Communists and, 53, 58, 71, 76,
87-89
Socialists and, 59, 60, 62
Institute for the National History of the
Macedonian People (Skopje) 193

Inter-Allied Commission (1919) 41
International Socialist Federation 62
Istria 65
Italian Armistice (1943) 107
Italy, 39, 46, 79, 90, 95, 103, 106-107,
108
Ioannides, Yannis 134, 172
Ivanov, Blagoe 122 ft. 31

J

Jajce Resolution (1943) 117-118
Jews
in Bulgaria 163
in Thessaloniki 10, 24, 62, 68, 76
Jovanović, Slobodan 111

K

Kaimak-Tsalan Mountain 129
Kalaidziev, Hristo 199 ft. 11
Kalapothakis, Demetrios 35
Kalfov-Politis Protocol 48, 49
Kaltchev, Lieutenant 106, 128, 129, 130
Karageorge 9
Karageorgis 183
Karavangelis, Bishop Germanos 34
Kardelj, Edvard 140, 142, 164, 205
Karev, Nikola 59, 60
Karydies Agreement 128, 131
Kastoria 4, 16, 21, 34, 37, 107, 127, 128,
171
Kavala 2, 4, 40, 68
Kentros, E. (see Slobotas)
Keramidjiev, M. 121, 123, 127, 171 ft.
64, 176, 183, 201 ft. 16
Khrushchev, Nikita 210, 212, 213, 217,
218, 219 ft. 84
Kićevo 108, 109
Kilkis Prefecture 107, 128
King Boris (see Boris, King)
Kiunstendil 4
KKE (see also under Balkan Commu-
nist Federation, EAM, ELAS, Guer-
rilla War) 63, 68, 73-74, 78, 80-81,
83, 91, 197-198
Balkan Communist Federation and,
70-71, 73, 74, 77, 78
Bulgarian Communists and, 81, 85,
134, 146, 169, 176-177, 221, 223, 224
Bulgarian Nationalists and, 119-
120, 128, 132-135
Comintern and, 70-71, 73, 74, 78,
81, 83
Congress, Conferences, Plenums of,
78, 81, 82-83, 91, 132, 165, 175,

mittee (Yugoslavia) 113, 114, 115, 116
Macedonian state (see also under People's
Republic of Macedonia) 89, 109, 117,
126, 137, 150
Macedonian Struggle 33-35, 58-60
"Macedonians" (see also under Mace-
donian Bulgarians, "Slav-Macedo-
nians")
in Bulgaria 5, 27 ft. 45, 44, 70, 72,
160-163, 189-192, 211, 215 223-
224, 226
in Yugoslavia 5, 53, 77, 117, 139,
146, 191-192, 218, 219, 225-226
"Macedonization" process 173, 192, 225,
226
MacVeagh, Lincoln 152
Manifesto (1924) 53
Manuiliski 73, 84, 155
Marigović, Foreign Minister 48
Marinov, General Ivan 108
Maritsa river (see Evros)
Markos (see Vafiades, Markos)
Markov, Vele 59
Marcović, Sima 74, 77, 84, 85
Marxism-Leninism (see also under na-
tionalism) 91, 188, 191, 213, 223, 224
Maximos 74, 77, 78
"Megali Idea" 30, 45, 95
Melas, Ambassador L. 180 ft. 93
Melas, Pavlos 34, 35
Melnik (Melenikon) 4, 21
Mesta river (see Nestos)
Metaxas, Ioannis 50, 93, 119
Mihailov, Ivan 53, 61 ft. 9, 94, 109, 145,
173, 194
Milan, Prince 18
Miliokovič, I. 77, 84
Military League 54
Minorities in
Albania 133, 174
Bulgaria 163, 174
Greece 147, 170, 174
Ottoman Empire 61
Rumania 147 ft. 105
Yugoslavia 147 ft. 105, 174
Minority exchanges (see population
exchanges)
Minority rights 38, 46, 47, 49, 82
Minority Treaties 46, 48, 132
Mitrofski, Pascal 123, 183, 187, 201 ft. 26
Mitsaikov, Mito 158
Moldavia 15
"Monarcho-fascists" 175 ft. 78, 178,
186, 206
Monastir 4, 21, 32 ft. 1, 37, 39, 61, 66,
109, 193
Montenegrins 70
Montenegro 39, 64, 86, 117, 141
Moscow Conference (1957) 212
Mount Athos 105

Murzsteg Program 35
Mussolini 95, 96 ft. 5

N

Naltsas, Christ. 134 ft. 69
"Narodno-Osvobotitelen Revolutsionarna
Organizatsia Iliden (see Iliden Orga-
nization)
Narrow socialists 64
Nastev, George 108, 145
Nation (definition) 67
National claims of Greece (see Greek
national claims)
National Committee ₁Bulgarian] for the
Assistance to the Greek Democratic
People 169
National consciousness 12
National Federative Party 61, 62
National Greek Army 184, 185
National Guard 147
National revolutionary movements 66
National Society [Greek] 30
Nationalism
Balkan 14-15, 128, 153, 196
and Communism (see also under
Self-determination) 67-68, 133,
191, 198, 223, 224, 225
and Socialism 59 ft. 4, 60
Nationalism-Socialism 87, 90
NATO 3
Naoussa 10
Neichev, Foreign Minister, 211
Nesković, Blagoe 115 ft. 2
Nestos river 3, 40, 99, 162
Nevrokop 21
"New Lands" 108
Nish 16
NOF 130, 167, 169, 170-173, 175-179, 182-
184, 197, 201, 221
Northern Epirus 133, 155, 165
Northern Greece (see also under Greek
Macedonia, Western Thrace) 177

O

October Revolution 57, 64, 65
Officer's League 51, 71
"Ohrana" (battalions) 106, 119, 125, 130
Ohrid (town) 4, 21, 37, 61
Ohrid lake 3, 37, 162
"Old Greece" 48
Olympus Mountain 3, 10, 162
"Opstestvena Cila" 108
Otho, King 16
Ottoman Empire 15, 16, 27, 61
O.Z.N.A. (Security) 159

248

P

Panitsa, Todor 52, 53, 87
Panslavism 11, 15
Panslavists 15-16, 20
Pan-Western Macedonian Congress 122
P.A.O. 120, 134 ft. 69
Papagos, Field Marshal Alexander 185, 187 ft. 119
Papalazarou, Lazar 123
Papandreou, George 149
Papas, Emmanuel 10
Papatrayannis, Zisis 123
Paris Peace Conference (Treaty) 153, 154-158
Partsalides, M. 165, 197-198
Partisans 111
Patriarchate, Ecumenical 14, 15, 21, 22, 23, 29, 35
"Patriarchists" 28, 34
Peking 218
Peonia 128
People's Daily 203
People's Federal Republic of Yugoslavia (see also under Yugoslavia, Cominform, Communist Party of Yugoslavia, People's Republic of Macedonia)
  Albania 198, 214, 218
  Bulgaria 137, 143, 157, 159-163, 188-192, 194-195, 199, 208, 210-220, 224
  Bulgarian Macedonia 135, 157, 161, 188-191, 194, 210-211, 216, 224
  China 213, 217, 218
  Cominform 169, 173, 174-175, 192, 204, 205, 206, 208, 225
  Foreign relations 137, 140, 150, 175, 192, 209, 224, 225
  Greece 149-152, 167-169, 174,184, 196, 200, 204-209. 226
  Greek Macedonia 135, 146-147, 150-152, 158, 166-169, 181, 184-185, 205-209
  KKE 165, 166, 167, 170, 171, 172 ft. 71, 180-181, 183, 198-199, 200-201, 221-222
  Macedonian unification 117, 127, 136-137, 138, 139, 142-143, 145-146, 150, 152, 171, 175, 180-181, 185, 208, 215-216, 217 ft. 78, 219, 224
  Soviet Union (see also under Cominform) 150, 163-164, 174, 178, 181, 188-189, 192, 210, 211, 212, 213, 214, 216, 217, 218, 219, 222, 224
People's Republic of Macedonia (see also Yugoslav Macedonia) 117-119, 135-137, 138, 158-159, 181, 188, 191-194, 215, 225-226

Bulgarians and, 118, 139-140, 159, 188, 191-194, 198, 211, 214-215, 218, 226
  Soviet Union and, 117, 118, 188, 192-194, 198
People's Republic of Serbia 117, 140, 141
Petrich 4, 52
Petrich Agreement 134, 135
Petrovski 81
Petsopoulos, Yannis 71
Peyov, Naum 121, 123.
Philiki Hetairia 10
Pijade, Moje 141, 180
Pindus Mountains 3
Pipinelis, Panayotis 174 ft. 72, 205 ft. 31
"Pirin" Macedonia (see Bulgarian Macedonia)
Pirinsko Delo 160, 189, 210
Pirovska, Ourania 187
Plastiras, Nicolaos 205, 206
Plebiscites for Macedonia 12, 76
Poland 163
Politika 214
Politis, Ambassador Jean 150, 152 ft. 121, 199 ft. 12
Pop-Arsov, Peter 25
Pop-Hristov, Georgi 60
Pop-Lazarov, Lazo 187
Poptomov, Vladimir 139, 189
Popović, Koca 117, 220 ft. 89
Popular Party of Greece 90
Population exchanges (transfers) 41, 42, 43, 47, 50, 132, 174
Porfyrogenis 172
Pouliopoulos 74, 76, 78, 81, 82
Pravda 163-164, 213
Prespa lake 3
Prilep 37, 109
Protogerov, Alexander 51, 52, 53, 72, 88, 89
"Provisional Government of Free Greece" 172, 186, 187
Provisional Macedonian Committee [Bulgaria] (see also Union of Cultural Macedonian Associations) 190

Q

"Quadalquivir" s/s 32

R

Rabotnitsesko Delo 162
Radić, Stjepan 51
Radio "Free Greece" 182, 204
Radnik 84

V

Vafiades, Markos 170, 172 ft. 71, 178, 179
Vaptsarov, Boris 214
Vardar Banovina 47, 93
"Vardar" Macedonia (see Yugoslav Macedonia)
Vardar (Axios) river 108
Vardar valley 66, 103
Varkiza Agreement 146, 148 ft. 107, 170 ft. 57
Vasiliou, V. 220 ft. 89
Veles (see also Titov Veles) 16, 21, 34, 59
Venizelist coup (1935) 91
Venizelist Party 90
Venizelos, Eleftherios 38, 40 ft. 26, 49
"Verhovists" (see "Supremists")
Veria 21
Vermion 10
Vidin 16
Vienna Reforms (see Macedonia—reforms)
Vitsi 175 ft. 78, 185, 186, 201
Vlachs 23, 24, 25, 35, 61, 76
Vlahov, Dimitar 26 ft. 44, 52, 53, 58, 60, 61, 62, 89, 136 ft. 70, 137, 168 ft. 48, 174, 192
Vlandas 176
Vojvodina 64
Voulgaris, Petros 152
Vukmanović-Tempo, Svetovar 116, 121-122, 135, 138, 152, 158, 166, 181
Vulkov, Colonel 51, 52

W

Wallachia 15
Western Allies 111, 132
Western Macedonia (see under Greek Macedonia)
"Western Regions" 161, 211
Western Thrace (see also Thrace)
Bulgarian claims 98-99, 143 ft. 90, 155-158, 169
Bulgarian occupation 99, 100-101, 124 ft. 37, 132, 133 ft. 91, 144
Refugees in, 72, 101

Soviet Union 155-156, 157
Yugoslavia 156, 157, 160
Women's Anti-Fascist Front (see A.F.Z.)
Workers' Socialist [Communist] Party of Greece (see KKE)
World War I 40, 58, 62, 78

Y

Yalta Conference 150
Yannitsa 128
Young Turks' Revolt 36, 61
Yugoslav Government-in-exile 110-112
Yugoslav Macedonia (see also People's Republic of Macedonia) 3, 4, 5, 46-47, 49, 84-85, 93, 113, 118, 192
Bulgarian occupation (World War I) 41, 52
Bulgarian occupation (World War II) 98-99, 108-110, 113, 114, 115, 144 ft. 91, 194
Bulgarians in 46-47, 49, 51, 85, 93, 94, 108-109, 113, 114, 116
Italian occupation 108
Partisan warfare in, 109, 114-116, 121
Socialists in, 65
Yugoslav peoples 117, 225
Yugoslavia (see also under Serbia, People's Federal Republic of Yugoslavia)
Bulgaria 51, 98, 111
Germany 96-98
Greece 97, 110-112
Macedonia 93, 95-97
"Yugoslavism" 225
Yugov, Anton 141

Z

Zahariades, Nikos 121 ft. 27, 122 ft. 31, 165, 166, 167 ft. 46, 170, 175 ft. 78, 176, 178, 179, 182, 197 ft. 5, 198, 199, 220-221
Zevgos, Yannis 132, 133, 165
Zhivkov, Todor 211 ft. 56, 219 ft. 84, 224
Zinoviev 70
Zveno 54, 159

E R R A T A

Page   4, lines 27-28 : *should read :* ...as Bulgarian "Pirin" Macedonia is the Prefecture of Blagoevgrad

»   4, footnote 4   *read :* detailed, *in lieu of* detail

»   15, footnote 14 and page 20, footnote 24 : *read :* Chirol, *in lieu of :* Chival

»   46, line 16 :   *read :* Treaty of, *in lieu of :* Treaty during

»   76, footnote 57 : *read :* pp. 348-349, *in lieu of :* pp. 3483-49

» 140, lines 19-20 : *read :* Vulko Chervenkov, *in lieu of :* Vasili Chervenkov

» 140, line 31   *add :* Montenegro

» 216, line 20   *read :* heed, *in lieu of :* need

» 224, line 9   *read :* soften, *in lieu of :* harden

THE IMPACT OF THE MACEDONIAN QUESTION ON CIVIL
CONFLICT IN GREECE (1943–1949)

Hardly one single issue had such diverse and longstanding repercussions on the
inception, planning, conduct and perceptions of the Greek Civil War as the
Macedonian question. Imbued with the legacy of nineteenth century conflicting
national visions and interwar destabilizing revisionist schemes, it found itself in the
wartime whirlpool of revolutionary change, activating forces—and passions—that
were to affect developments in three Balkan states.[1]

An examination of the impact of the Macedonian question on the Greek Civil
War can hardly be restricted to the years 1946-1949. Its ramifications in internal
Greek conflicts were discernible even in the early phases of the Occupation and
throughout the Resistance, continued unabated to December 1944 and, despite the
Varkiza settlement, remained active during the interlude of 1945-1946.[2]

Perceptions and realities in Macedonian affairs rarely coincide. Contemporaries
suffered much by lack of dependable information on the aims and policies of adversaries and allies alike. Preconceived notions frequently substituted for intelligent
analyses. As a result, deep-rooted fears and suspicions persisted and created a permanent sense of insecurity, which was further fanned by psychological warfare opera-
tives, tempering with a sensitive national issue for political ends. Meanwhile, dogmatic approaches to rapidly changing situations blurred the vision of leaders and
disoriented public opinion. In the end, actors on the Macedonian stage found
themselves performing in a theater of the absurd.

During the occupation, civil strife in Greek Macedonia between resistance
groups was not limited to a contest for postwar political predominance. In certain
cases it grew into a struggle for national survival. Contenders sought to discredit
each other less in terms of ideology, and more so by references to real or imagined
"antinational," "treacherous" behavior. Followers of the communist-led
EAM/ELAS were labeled "Slavo-communists" (even though most were neither
Slavs nor communists), while their opponents were summarily classified as "collaborationists" (even though most opposed the German, Italian and Bulgarian occupiers
as they did their ideological foes).

The same tactics continued throughout the Civil War. Slogans and labels of
antinational behavior hardened perceptions of each other, fomented fanaticism and

distorted issues. As both contenders turned to foreign ideological relatives to fight their own kin, the respective causes and activities were frequently identified with those of their patrons.

The international aspects of the problem were no less decisive in influencing internal developments. One could easily detect a micro and a macro Macedonian question. While the former referred primarily to the internal social, political and racial issues in each of the three parts of Macedonia, the latter introduced international elements to the problem. These covered Big Power objectives in the Balkan subregion—and their perception of rival policies—as well as the policies of each of the three Balkan states vis-à-vis the Macedonian issue. The recurring crises in Macedonia should accurately be attributed to the interaction of the macro- and the micro- elements of the problem.

Decades after the termination of hostilities, confusion over the Macedonian issue persists. Polemic literature, published memoirs of warriors and politicians, and many monographs on the Resistance and the Civil War, perpetuate wartime distortions, if more prudently they do not evade the issue.[3] In recent years, the availability of new documentary sources—though still unbalanced as to their provenance and fragmentary—offers the opportunity for a new attempt at assessing the impact of the Macedonian question during the 1940s.[4]

II

Wartime and postwar policies and attitudes in Macedonia trace their origins to factors shaped long before 1940. The legacy of the armed clashes of the first decade of the twentieth century—known as *Makedonikos Agonas*—the peace settlements of the second decade, and the mass population movements of the third decade, continued to influence policies (particularly in Bulgaria) and to determine the attitudes of large population groups in Bulgaria, Yugoslavia and Greece. Bulgarian-Macedonian organizations, both of the right and the left, had created strong pressure groups mainly in Bulgaria and southern Yugoslavia, sustaining revolutionary fervency.[5] In Greece, despite a large-scale exodus of the Slavs, during and after World War I, Slav-speakers continued to live in certain border communities of western Macedonia. By the 1930s, there were two mutually opposed factions: a Greek-oriented Slavophone and a Slav-oriented one, (with a pro-Bulgarian tilt), nurturing fratricidal vendettas, going back to the years of the Makedonikos Agonas.[6] The juxtaposition among the pre-liberation Greek-, Vlach-, and Slav-speaking indigenous inhabitants of hundreds of thousands of Christian Orthodox refugees from Asia Minor, the Pontus, Bulgaria and Yugoslavia had established a Greek national character in Greek Macedonia. At the same time, however, this population movement gave rise to a whole range of social and economic problems of mutual adjustment.

A second factor, which grew from Bulgaria's revisionist attitude toward the World War I peace settlements, was the Greeks' threat perception from the north. Impressive defense works were constructed almost exclusively along the Greek-

Bulgarian frontier. But they proved useless when Bulgaria joined the Axis and took possession of parts of Greek Macedonia and Thrace, without fighting for them.

These threat perceptions were augmented, as a result of the revisionist policy of the Bulgarian Communist Party, endorsed and sanctioned by Comintern, calling for a united and independent Macedonia (and Thrace), within a Balkan Communist Federation. The association of the KKE in 1924 with the Comintern's Macedonian policy raised significant objections even within the Party, but a major split was avoided. Outside the Party, the outcry was general, and the KKE's image suffered the onus of "national treachery." In the minds of the Greeks, the status quo in Macedonia was challenged not merely by a single Balkan country , but by a world political alliance, with the Soviet Union at its head. Greek Macedonia could be severed from the Greek state not necessarily by war, but also through a social revolution. As a result, official legislation was introduced in Parliament, equating communism with sedition.[7]

As pressure from outside and from its ranks mounted, the leadership of the Party finally gathered sufficient courage to bypass Comintern directives, and, in 1935, adopted a new resolution. This resolution changed the slogan for "a united and independent Macedonia" with a new one for "complete equality for the minorities." Moreover, the Marxist principle of "self-determination" of national minorities was reaffirmed and the door was left open for a "definite" brotherly solution of the Macedonia question "after the victory of the Soviet power in the Balkans."[8] This new Macedonian platform carried the Party into the 1940s (up to 1949). It was a handicap for the Greek communists that the Metaxas dictatorship prevented them from popularizing their new "equality" principle vs. the old "independence" line. Government propaganda continued to associate the Party with sedition, while certain dissatisfied Slavo-Macedonian communist cadres laid more emphasis on the nebulous "self-determination" principle than on the specific "equality" platform.[9] On the eve of the war, the confusion and disorientation among the Greek- and Slav-speaking groups in Greek Macedonia was complete.

The Greek state, like other Eastern European countries of the interwar period, had pursued a policy of assimilation of ethnic groups. After World War I, and some hesitation in the early 1920s, it had decided to treat the remaining Slav-speakers as Slavophone Greeks. These Slavophones, according to Greek statistics, never passed the 100,000 mark.[10] They were concentrated mainly in the prefectures of Kastoria, Florina and Pella, although certain dispersed Slavophone or mixed villages could also be found in other Macedonian prefectures. The Metaxas' regime, haunted by the specter of Slavism and communism, initiated a policy of accelerated assimilation. Applied by incompetent and short-sighted civil servants, it antagonized even Slavophones of the Greek faction.[11] To peasants of Bulgarian orientation, it served as proof that the Greek state could not offer them a national shelter. In 1941, the occupation of Greece by the Germans and the entrance of Bulgarian troops in eastern Macedonia and Thrace offered the opportunity for accumulated bitterness to reach maturity.

Meanwhile, in Yugoslav Macedonia a more vigorous serbianization campaign had come up against insurmountable difficulties. Local Slavs either remained stubbornly attached to Bulgarian nationalism, or, more prudently, evaded choices, seeking refuge in the regional Macedonian name.[12]

The war and the cession by the Germans to Bulgarian occupation authorities of large parts of Greek and Yugoslav Macedonia reversed the situation. A part of the Slavophone population exhibited their pro-Bulgarian sympathies by taking revenge on their Greek neighbors, particularly those who had settled in Macedonia after their eviction from Turkey. In their zone of occupation, the Bulgarians resorted to genocide-dimension practices, which included the eviction of Greeks and the settlement of Bulgarians.[13]

Among Greeks, opposition to Bulgarian occupation of eastern Macedonia and Thrace and to efforts of extending Bulgarian influence to central and western Macedonia was unanimous. Prior to the development of mass resistance organizations, local community leaders, professionals and intellectuals took it upon themselves to organize Greek opposition to Bulgarian schemes. Even the Athens puppet government found it expedient to ride the popular bandwagon, by dispatching to Macedonian prefectures ex-army officers enjoying a wider political acceptance. The initiative gradually passed, first to the nationalist resistance organizations—*Yperaspistai Voreiou Ellados* (YVE) renamed *Panellinia Apeleftherotiki Organosis* (PAO)—and subsequently to ELAS. Nationalists proceeded from the traditional assumption of the dichotomy of the Slavophones into Greek and Slav factions, and sought to protect and strengthen the resistance of the Greek faction. Slavophones falling prey to Bulgarian propaganda—frequently in exchange for food rations in famine-stricken Macedonia—or distancing themselves from Hellenism as Slavo-Macedonians were considered as enemies of the Greek nation.[14]

Meanwhile, a smaller group of Slavophones began to surface within EAM/ELAS as Slavo-Macedonians. The EAM, having endorsed in practice KKE's post-1935 position on the equality of rights of minorities, accepted in its ranks Slavophones, not only of the Greek faction, but also persons who distanced themselves both from the Greek and the Bulgarian factions.[15] Although this movement had little attraction until the beginning of 1944, it was apparent that the traditional dichotomy of Slavophones gradually grew into a trichotomy.

Thus, on the key issue of the Slavophones, Greek political and resistance groups in Macedonia—particularly prior to the dissolution of the military units of PAO by ELAS in 1943—differed significantly. In the formative years 1941–1943, crossing fences from one faction to the other was a common exercise. Frequently, this was prompted not by ideology or national inclination, but by sheer opportunism and the need for self-preservation. Such constant movements and shifting allegiances bewildered spectators and local actors even in the early stages of the internal Greek struggle for postwar predominance. Unable to follow intelligently radically changing situations they found themselves leaning on their traditional perceptions: a misleading yardstick for assessing developments in occupied Macedonia.

In the perception of Greek nationalists, the acceptance of Slavo-Macedonians (by definition non-Greek and possibly anti-Greek Slavophones) signified that EAM/ELAS pursued the prewar "antinational" Macedonian policy of the KKE. On the other hand, the KKE, through EAM/ELAS, considered that its own policy was in accordance with its declared principles and could undermine more effectively Bulgarian proselytism among the Slavophones. Less widely known at the time was the fact that, even within EAM/ELAS, there was considerable opposition to accepting nationalist-minded Slavo-Macedonians into the Greek resistance.[16]

In their part of Macedonia, the Yugoslavs had to cope with an even more acute problem of Bulgarian nationalism. Even the local communist organization had severed its ties with the Yugoslav Communist Party and had joined the still illegal Bulgarian Party. Faced with a dual challenge by pro-Bulgarian nationalists and communists in Macedonia, the Yugoslav partisan leaders decided not only to reassert control in their own region of Macedonia, but also to find a permanent solution to a problem, which, repeatedly had threatened the sovereignty and territorial integrity of their country. Their main thesis was that Slav-speakers, in all three Macedonian provinces, were ethnic "Macedonians"—a Slavic nation different from the Bulgarians and the Serbs—who, consequently, had the right to self-determination and state unification within the Yugoslav federation.[17]

When Tito succeeded, in August 1941, to gain Stalin's endorsement,[18] it became evident that the center of gravity for the Macedonian question had shifted from Bulgaria to Yugoslavia. Greeks of all political shades, engaged in their own internal struggles in Greek Macedonia, had no idea of these developments. They continued to endeavor, and to fight, on prewar perceptions, having no control to sweeping changes in the Macedonian checkboard that soon would reach their own terrain.

Svetozar Vukmanovic sssemTempo, Tito's emissary to Kossovo and Macedonia, was the man who, in the summer of 1943, outlined to the leaders of KKE and ELAS the Yugoslav plans for wartime collaboration of Balkan communist-controlled partisan armies in Yugoslavia, Albania, Greece and even Bulgaria. He also briefed them on the postwar settlement of the Macedonian question, as seen by the Yugoslav communists.[19] The essence of his proposals provided for a Balkan General Staff to coordinate the activities of the four partisan organizations, not only against the occupying forces but also against the respective nationalist— "reactionary" in his words—organizations, and thus secure a new postwar social order and possibly a Balkan federation. In Macedonia, cooperation would aim at curtailing Bulgarian nationalist influences among the Macedonian Slavs. Free movement of partisan bands across the borders would be allowed, while Yugoslav Macedonian political instructors would be given a free hand to present to Slavophones in Greece the Yugoslav model for the solution of the Macedonian national question. This would entail complete freedom to propagate apparently among all three factions of Slavophones—the idea of the "Macedonian" nation and language, and assurances that the right of self-determination, including the right of secession, would be extended to the Slavo-Macedonians. Moreover, Slavo-

Macedonians would be permitted to form their own political organization and armed units. Tempo avoided an explicit reference to postwar territorial changes in Macedonia. To judge, however, from frequent contemporary Yugoslav Macedonian pronouncements, the Yugoslavs were aiming, as a maximum objective, at a Greater Macedonian state along the Macedonian boundaries of San Stefano Bulgaria, appropriately renamed for the occasion, "Macedonian ethnological boundaries." As a minimum objective, they sought the annexation of adjacent to Yugoslavia Greek Macedonian districts, including, for strategic reasons, the city port of Thessaloniki.[20] Tempo's key argument for putting forward his proposals centered on the need to lure the Bulgarian-oriented Slavophones of all three parts of Macedonia away from the grip of the Bulgarian nationalists and to include them, as Slavo-Macedonians, into the common struggle.

Tempo's proposals opened entirely new perspectives not only for the Greek resistance, but also for the future of Greece. The leaders of the KKE sensed, for the first time, that they had an alternative to British tutelage. For political reasons, however, they rejected the idea for a Balkan General Staff, although they accepted trans-frontier cooperation of their respective partisan units. An initial order by the ELAS General Headquarters provided for the formation of joint Greek-Yugoslav partisan detachments to operate on both sides of the frontier in order to attract to their ranks both the Slavo-Macedonians of Greece and the Greeks of Yugoslavia. Similarly, Yugoslav partisan units were given permission to cross into Greek territory, while Yugoslav Macedonian political instructors were allowed to move freely in Greek Macedonian villages to acquaint Slavophones with the idea of the "Macedonian" nation.[21] More important was the decision to allow the formation of an independent political organization of the Slavo-Macedonians —the *Slavomakedonski Naroden Osvoboditelen Front* (SNOF)—as well as special Slavo-Macedonian armed units. KKE leaders, however, shelved Yugoslav proposals for a postwar renegotiation of the Macedonian question. Pointing to the tremendous cost to their own cause, they appeared determined to remain firm on their 1935 position. They only accepted in rather vague terms, that after the war they would seek solutions to problems between the Balkan peoples, in a spirit of brotherly cooperation and in accordance with the principle of the self-determination of peoples.[22]

In the field some of the decisions (such as the joint Greek-Yugoslav detachments, or the independent Slavo-Macedonian units) were not activated, apparently because of dissenting voices within EAM/ELAS. Certain of the arrangements reached with Tempo took a swing not initially envisaged. Such was the case of the free-roaming Yugoslav-Macedonian activists within Greece, who did not limit themselves to luring Bulgarian-oriented Slavophones into SNOF, but propagated openly the unification of Macedonia. As a result, for a full year—end of 1943 to the end of 1944—Greek western Macedonia became a battleground of antagonistic social forces, opposing ideologies and national hatred; it was a confused situation hardly found in any other region of occupied Greece.[23]

This insufficiently researched aspect of the Macedonian "civil war" bore the cross of all prewar evils. Certainly, on top of the list were the contest for ideological dominance—generally, but not accurately portrayed as communism vs. anticommunism—and the struggle to fill the political vacuum at the moment of liberation. In Macedonia, this dual contest was fought by the anticommunist forces on the basis of national loyalties.

Slavo-Macedonian seditious propaganda in EAM-controlled regions gave credence to suspicions that the KKE had once again "sold" Macedonia to the Slavs. Given the prevailing climate, it is no wonder that texts of alleged agreements of the KKE with either the Bulgarian or the Yugoslav communists were put in circulation. Despite detectable discrepancies, these "agreements" were widely accepted as authentic by nationalist Greeks.[24]

In the military field, EAM/ELAS had, by 1944, gained supremacy over its adversaries, with few notable exceptions in southern and central-eastern Macedonia. As EAM opponents could no more oppose their ideological adversaries, they found themselves leaning more and more heavily for assistance and even guidance either on the Greek government in exile and the British secret agencies, or on the local administrative and security services of the Athens collaborationist government. That such association carried the risk of indirectly—and at times directly—collaborating with the Germans was dismissed on the ground that the risk for Greece of loosing Macedonia to the Slavs, in the event of a communist takeover of the country, was greater than an ephemeral accommodation with the occupier.[25] Perceptions of a Slav and communist menace in Macedonia certainly blurred visions.

Internal dissensions over KKE-directed Macedonian policy were detected also in the central organs of EAM and ELAS, but more so on the local level, in Macedonia, where political and military leaders maintained serious reservations. In certain cases, such reservations caused the reversal of Party orders, or the extermination of dissidents. Already, prior to the summer of 1943, ELAS officers in western Macedonia had led their units against Slavophone partisans and villagers on suspicion of being "Bulgarians." On the opposite side, Party functionaries stood firm by dogmatic interpretations of the Party's "equality" policy, to the point of encouraging Slavo-Macedonian nationalism. Frequently, behind such behavior were Slavo-Macedonian communist cadres who argued that a more liberal attitude toward the Slavophones, including the pro-Bulgarian collaborationists, would bring the Slavophone peasants to EAM. As, however, the allegiance of these cadres was contestable — either because of their former Bulgarian sympathies, or because of their more recent Yugoslav Macedonian connections—the KKE leaders found themselves receiving mixed signals from the Macedonian front. Torn between the strategic requirements of collaborating with the Yugoslav partisans and building a patriotic image at home, they frequently reversed decisions, sending contradictory instructions to the field. As a result, confusion and dissension among the rank and file increased. It is interesting to note that late in the spring of 1944, SNOF was dissolved by Party orders, and some of its influential leaders escaped into Yugoslavia. In less than three months, KKE once again reversed its own decisions, allowed the return of irredentist-prone Slavo-Macedonian cadres, with Naum Pejov at their head, and authorized the formation of pure Slavo-Macedonian armed units within ELAS. In the end, faced with open sedition by these units, ELAS military leaders, both locally and at General Headquarters, overcame hesitant or even resisting Party functionaries, attacked these units and forcefully evicted them from Greek Macedonia, in October 1944. The termination of war in Greece probably prevented a major internal crisis within EAM/ELAS on this issue. The fact that a number of ELAS officers and men under their command, who had played a leading role in subduing the Slavo-Macedonian units, found themselves subsequently in the ranks of the National Army, should be seen as a direct consequence of the wartime internal EAM/ELAS dissensions over Macedonian policy.[26]

Meanwhile, the admittance of Slavophones, as "Slavo-Macedonians" into the ranks of the Resistance, had accentuated, in certain areas, traditional antagonism and even "racial" hatred between autochthones (gigeneis) and Greek Pontic and Asia Minor refugees (prosfyges). Although more research is required into the social aspects of the wartime attitude of Turcophone refugee groups which took up arms to resist ELAS, perceptions of a possible Slav-Macedonian revenge in a postwar communist-ruled Greece are certainly detectable.[27]

Fratricidal conflicts developed also within the trichotomized Slavophone community. The Bulgarian-oriented Slavophone bands that appeared early on the scene, armed and commanded by Bulgarian officers, concentrated their vengeance primarily on members of the Greek Slavophone faction. Carrying on vendettas that went back to the exarchist-patriarchist feuds of Makedonikos Agonas, they labeled their opponents "Grecomans"—maniac Greeks—and set out to exterminate physically their leaders and terrorize into submission the masses.[28] Throughout the occupation, this persecuted section of the population sought either refuge in PAO and ELAS, or the protection of the civil authorities and gendarmerie of the Athens puppet government. Others escaped in the urban centers and in Thessaloniki. In the Kastoria prefecture in the Italian zone of occupation, where the establishment of Greek civil and gendarmerie authorities was delayed, persecution of the Greek Slavophone faction became widespread. The pendulum of revenge in Macedonia had swung against the Greeks.

More intricate were the relations (antagonisms, feuds, alliances) between the initially strong Bulgarian faction and the emerging new contender, the Slavo-Macedonian faction. As both drew from the same pool of anti- (or non-Greek) Slavophones, identification was difficult and easily led to erroneous impressions. Certainly, there had been cases of Slavo-Macedonians within the ranks of EAM/ELAS, who clashed openly with the so-called "Bulgarian comitadjis." Generally, however, these Slavo-Macedonians operated as a lobby within KKE/EAM for the adoption of a lenient attitude toward pro-Bulgarian collaborationists. They were well aware that to secure a popular base for their claims on Greek Macedonian territories, they needed to augment their numbers by the transformation of Bulgarian Slavophones into Slavo-Macedonians. Despite occasional concessions by the KKE and mass indoctrination efforts by local Slavo-Macedonian instructors and agents from Yugoslav Macedonia, progress was slow. As late as spring 1944, there was a resurgence of Bulgarian activity in the Edessa region, where whole villages were armed by Bulgarian officers. It was only in the closing months of 1944, when the departure of the Germans appeared imminent, that most bulgarophiles were eager to exchange the Bulgarian crown for the Slavo-Macedonian red star.[29]

On the other side of the triangle, the disposition of Slavo-Macedonians toward Greek Slavophones was not much better than that of the bulgarophiles, and vice versa. Although both factions could be found in the ranks of EAM/ELAS, it was evident that a collision was unavoidable, as Greek Slavophones could hardly condone the steadily growing orientation of Slavo-Macedonians toward a united Macedonian state within Yugoslavia. Thus, in the closing months of 1944, another fratricidal war was brewing at the local Macedonian level. It exploded immediately after liberation and was carried on during the Civil War.

Trying to maneuver among the Macedonian *symblegades*, the KKE was once again entangled in the web of the Macedonian question. Contradictory instructions and reversible decisions, as a policy for coping with changing or incomprehensible circumstances, did not advance its cause, nor its short- and long-term objectives. KKE leaders appeared extremely conscious of the propaganda cost to the Party for being implicated directly or indirectly in Yugoslav Macedonian aims and activities. They tried to minimize criticism and calm even their own followers in EAM/ELAS, by appealing directly to Tito to restrain the extremist Yugoslav Macedonians. There is also evidence that they even appealed to Dimitrov to restrain Tito.[30] Such frantic efforts could have no lasting effects, as long as the Party demurred from adopting, toward Slavo-Macedonian secessionists, the iron-fist policy it had reserved for its ideological foes.

To opponents, both within and outside EAM, it mattered little whether, in the eyes of KKE leaders, concessions on the Macedonian issue had some justification: that adherence to ideological orthodoxy on the nationalists question was mandatory; that drawing the Slavophones away from the grip of the Bulgarian nationalities strengthened the resistance; that appeasing Tito and securing his support as a counterpoise to British intervention, served the long-term interests of the communist revolution in Greece.

Thus, the image of the Party had been tarnished after all. The stain of treason was certainly unfair to the extent that it was caused by allegations of non-existent wartime agreements ceding Greek Macedonia and Thrace to the Slavs. But it was unavoidable once the Party leadership yielded to Yugoslav pressures and let Yugoslav Macedonians meddle in internal Greek Macedonian affairs, particularly since Yugoslav hegemonistic and expansionist designs in the Balkans could hardly be concealed by 1944.[31]

In summing up, KKE's wartime Macedonian policy should be held accountable for turning ideological contest and even civil strife in Macedonia into a struggle for racial and national survival. The immediate and long-term repercussions became apparent during the post-Varkiza interlude and the Civil War.

On October 30th 1944, Thessaloniki was liberated. Four days later, ELAS military commander for northern Greece, Evripidis Bakirtzis, issued an order to units under his command to man the Greek-Yugoslav frontier with "loyal" troops, i.e., free of Slavo-Macedonian infiltration.[32] Both developments underlined the fact that central and western Macedonia had firmly passed again to Greek hands. Soon, thereafter, in eastern Macedonia, the elimination of the last vestiges of the nationalist forces of Anton Tsaous established indisputably the authority of EAM from one end of Macedonia to the other. Macedonian Cassandras had failed in their prognostications. Greek Macedonia had not been "sold to the Slavs" by the KKE. As for the Slavo-Macedonian activists they had failed to retain even a strip of Greek Macedonian borderland.

III

As Macedonian micro-politics appeared to recede into the background, Macedonian macro-politics, involving the Big Powers and Greece's northern neighbors, entered into the picture. A new phase of the Macedonian question was unfolding outside Greece, as the Greeks themselves were moving to position in the south ready to commence their "Second Round."

British traditional global security perceptions had let the British government formulate a geopolitical approach to war and postwar arrangements that aimed at blocking Soviet presence at the Straits and northern Aegean. Despite the failure to open a Balkan front in 1943, Churchill had succeeded in obtaining Stalin's consent to a free hand in Greece; a tacit understanding that was formalized in the wellknown "percentages agreement." In the concluding months of 1944, developments in Macedonia posed an indirect, though still a very serious challenge to the British position in Greece, gained after painful bargaining.[33] Despite the ascension to power in Bulgaria of the Fatherland Front (9 September), Bulgarian authorities and troops in Greek Macedonia and Thrace had been reluctant to withdraw. They had even concluded separate agreements with both Anton Tsaous and EAM/ELAS for gradually turning over authority to either one, aspiring, in fact, to gain time. It was a desperate move in the hope that the Allies might consider allowing them to retain possession of lands ceded to them by Hitler.[34] On his part, however, Marshal Tolbukhin upheld, scrupulously, Big Power understandings. He refused to cross the border into Greece, even though he was invited to do so by local Greek Communist chiefs.[35] In the end, it was British (and United States) demarches to Moscow that compelled the Bulgarians to withdraw. To British eyes, despite the happy conclusion, the incident indicated that the prospect of a Soviet descent, by proxy, to the Aegean shores, was very much alive.[36]

Soon, however, a second, more complicated problem began to emerge, with direct implications for Macedonia. In the Macedonian Pirin district of Bulgaria,

Yugoslav Macedonian infiltration had come to the open after the government takeover by the Fatherland Front. For almost three months, until the end of November, "Macedonian" national agitation for the immediate incorporation of the Pirin region to the new Yugoslav Macedonian republic developed into a grass-roots campaign, aiming at striking a *fait accompli*. To judge by the writings of Yugoslav and Bulgarian authors, the activity of emissaries from Skopje and of their local supporters in Pirin bears a surprising resemblance to similar activities in Greek Slavophone border areas throughout 1944. In Pirin, the local Bulgarian communist cadres appeared to render full support to the idea of unification, whereas in Greek Macedonia, secessionist-prone Slavo-Macedonians came into open conflict with EAM/ELAS and finally were driven out of the country.[37]

Meanwhile, on the diplomatic level, Belgrade and Sofia had initiated negotiations for a South Slav federation, featuring a unified Macedonian federative state. Unknown at the time was the fact that Stalin himself had encouraged the federation project,[38] apparently in order to secure his hold on the two Balkan states. Despite disclaimers by Yugoslav and Soviet officials, from November 1944 to February 1945 evidence mounted for an imminent Yugoslav-Bulgarian agreement. As a result, the British had not much difficulty in persuading the Americans to join them in putting pressure on the two Balkan capitals—and the Soviet Union—to annul their federation plans. Apart from "ethical" considerations (Bulgaria being an ex-enemy state could not undertake any commitments prior to a peace treaty), the proposed federation threatened to upset the meticulously knit British security planning in the area. The loss of Greek Macedonia—and possibly Thrace—could destroy British strategic aims, much as would the loss of Greece as a whole.[39]

For Tito, the project certainly fitted his wartime ambitious vision of Yugoslavia's predominant role in the Balkans. For different reasons, Georgi Dimitrov, still in Moscow, was in agreement. He advised his comrades in Sofia to conclude a military, economic and political alliance with Yugoslavia, as a first step to the unification of the two countries in a federal state of the Southern Slavs. In his view, such an arrangement would certainly place a protective umbrella over Bulgaria, ensure control of the country by the Communist Party, and absolve the Bulgarian people of the wartime alliance with Germany.[40]

Tito, being the recipient of repeated British warnings, should have been convinced by now that the British meant to hold on to Greece, their last remaining piece of real estate in the Balkans; and that included Greek Macedonia. Meanwhile, the Soviet Union had given proof of its unwillingness to challenge the British in three important cases involving Greece: on the Bulgarian withdrawal from Macedonia and Thrace; on the December British intervention in Athens; and on the Yugoslav-Bulgarian federation scheme. Being a realist, Tito gave assurances that he would wait for the termination of the war to stake his claims for a united Macedonia, "in an orderly fashion," probably at the peace conference.[41]

Deeply involved in Greek internal developments and having a superficial knowledge of rapidly shaping Balkan alignments, the leaders of the KKE sought to appraise Tito's and Dimitrov's views for an armed bid for power. In the light of only fragmentary data, it is still difficult to assess whether the Macedonian question had any direct or indirect influence in determining Yugoslavia's inconsistent reaction to KKE's decision to meet militarily the dual challenge of the Papandreou government and the British.

Secret correspondence reveals that the KKE had repeatedly requested military equipment from the Yugoslav partisans during the concluding months of the war. As late as August 28th 1944, Siantos had sent a dispatch to Tzimas, at Tito's headquarters, to ask of the Yugoslav leader weapons in order to equip a new division. He stressed that "now as never before we have need of war supplies."[42] In October, just a few days after the eviction by ELAS of the armed Slavo-Macedonians, Ranković ordered Tempo, still in Yugoslav Macedonia, that *"for the time being* you should not send our own units into Greece."[43]

These two separate directives indicate, on the one hand, that the KKE was preparing itself for a confrontation after the withdrawal of the Germans, and on the other hand, that the Yugoslav Macedonian partisans were alerted at the possibility of crossing the border into Greek Macedonia. What cannot be established, on the basis of available documentation, is the connection, if any, between these two incidents. But there are still more pieces of information concerning the fate of Greek Macedonia that require careful scrutiny.

At about the same time (October 1944) Vlado Poptomov, a leading Bulgarian communist leader and a native of Macedonia, returning from Moscow, communicated to the Yugoslavs Georgi Dimitrov's views. The Bulgarian leader was in favor of the unification of Macedonia, but preferred to commence with the South Slav federation, while preparing the ground for public acceptance of the idea. As for the accession of Greek Macedonia to a unified Macedonian state, he believed that was "a little more difficult" to achieve, because the inclusion of Thessaloniki would be viewed by the British as a threat to their Mediterranean routes. Therefore, it was necessary to build a case by collecting economic, geographical and national data which would support the claim to Greek Macedonia at the peace conference. In his view, emphasis should be placed on projecting the unjust expulsion of the Slavs from Greek Macedonia after World War I.[44] Apparently, it mattered little to him what kind of government would be in power in Greece at the time of the peace conference.

Such views coming from Dimitrov, still in Moscow, conveyed the impression that they had the endorsement of the Soviets. The Yugoslav communists certainly were not opposed to the approach proposed. Successive public speeches by leading figures, such as Milovan Djilas, Vukmanović-Tempo and Dimitar Vlahov, reaffirmed Yugoslav attachment to the idea of the unification of Macedonia, including Greek Macedonia. In the event, the arguments suggested by Dimitrov were also found in Yugoslav statements.[45]

It was apparent that during the critical weeks between the liberation of Greece and the commencement of the "Second Round," Yugoslavs and Bulgarians were in agreement for detaching, in one way or another, Greek Macedonia from the Greek state. What was still uncertain was whether the Yugoslavs would try to force a solution. Public pronouncements at the time and subsequent writings by Yugoslav authors indicate that at least certain leaders in Yugoslav Macedonia and in the Central Committee of the CPY favored some kind of military action.[46]

It will be recalled that after the withdrawal of the armed Slavo-Macedonians from Greece, early in October, ELAS had sealed the border in order to prevent their return. Meanwhile, the stream of refugees crossing over to Yugoslav Macedonia grew steadily. Among them were persons associated with the Bulgarian occupiers who judged it safer to emerge as "Macedonians" in the newly formed Macedonian state. In the enthusiastic atmosphere prevailing at the time in the border towns of Yugoslavia, particularly in Bitola (Monastir), Slavo-Macedonian refugees were inducted into the "1st Aegean Macedonian Brigade," and began training for eventual duty in Greek Macedonia. Rumors were running wild about the expected entrance into Greece, along with the "Aegean Macedonian Brigade" of two Yugoslav divisions, allegedly to assist ELAS to face the British.[47]

This was the situation when the KKE decided to make its bid to Tito for assistance. Tito was in favor, but there is no concrete evidence to show whether his promise of support entailed anything more than military supplies.[48] Similarly, there are no data to support the idea that the fate or the role of Slavo-Macedonian fighters, then in Yugoslav Macedonia, was discussed. Probably it was not. This is inferred from the refusal of the KKE, early in December, to accept an offer by these Slavo-Macedonians to enter Greece and join in the ELAS operation against EDES. This offer was accompanied by a request for a free indoctrination of Slavophones in the spirit of the "Macedonian nation."[49] Years later, a Greek partisan leader revealed that ELAS attacked EDES in order to prevent an attack by Yugoslav partisans against Zervas.[50] Although the reasons for Aris Velouhiotis' action against EDES are certainly broader than the ones hinted above, nevertheless, the incident reveals that the possibility of an entrance of Yugoslav partisans into Greece preoccupied the leaders of the KKE during the critical days prior and during December 1944.

As the shooting in Athens increased, KKE leaders instructed Tzimas to renew the plea for Tito's support. This time Tito returned a negative reply.[51] Moreover, he sent orders to divert Slavo-Macedonian troops from the Greek border. Thus, instead of liberating Thessaloniki—already in the firm control of EAM/ELAS— Slavo-Macedonian activists found themselves chasing nationalist Albanians in Kossovo.[52]

Tito's reversal of his earlier promise, which coincides with Dimitrov's subsequent similar negative response to a KKE inquiry,[53] indicates that the two Balkan leaders were recipients of similar counsels (or directives) from the same central authority. This is corroborated by the fact that toward the end of December, Tito gave assurances to the British that he did not intend to push forcefully his plans for the annexation of Greek Macedonia, but that he would raise the issue at the peace conference.[54] Thus, after tampering for a short time with the idea of some kind of involvement in Greek Macedonia, the Yugoslav communists quickly backed down when the shooting started in Athens. Safeguarding the revolution at home had first priority. Ambitious plans about Greek Macedonia could wait for a more opportune moment.

For Tito, the rather quick and unexpected capitulation of KKE/ELAS at Varkiza (Feb. 12, 1945) certainly disarrayed his plans for the future of a unified Macedonia. The only card left for keeping alive the flames of the Macedonian question in Greece, while the war against Germany continued, was the Slavo-Macedonian fugitives, who found refuge in Yugoslav Macedonia.

The first step in that direction was the formation, under the control of the Communist Party of Macedonia (CPM), of a new National Liberation Front (NOF) for Greek Macedonia.[55] Already, as early as December 1944, Slavo-Macedonian agitators had infiltrated back into border regions of Greek Macedonia. Working clandestinely, they had succeeded in forming, in the Edessa district, a small "Secret Macedonian Liberation Organization" (T.O.M.O.) to work, ostensibly, for the liberation of Macedonia which ironically had just been liberated from German and Bulgarian occupation and was administered by EAM.[56]

When the Varkiza agreement was signed, the Slavo-Macedonians refused to abide by it. NOF proceeded to form armed bands, to dispatch them across the border, and to commence a small-scale local guerilla war. The key objective was to conduct underground agitation throughout western Macedonia for the eventual "liberation" of Greek Macedonia and its incorporation to Yugoslav Macedonia. Publicly, emphasis was placed on the social and political status of the Slavo-Macedonians within Greece. New data reveal that, at the time, NOF functioned as the "Aegean Macedonian Committee" of the CPM.[57]

Such activity had its victims. The KKE and the whole of EAM/ELAS movement were the first to suffer. Hardly a KKE opponent in Macedonia would accept the sincerity of KKE's disclaimers of any connivance with former ELAS Slavophone fighters attacking in ambushes government and British troops, reaching the border regions in the early months of 1945. Throughout 1945, the KKE stepped up its open condemnation of NOF's activities, as being "provocatory," "chauvinistic" and "autonomist."[58] But to no avail. At the same time, KKE resorted to nationalist rhetorics on Greek national claims, which included northern Epirus — but no more the rectification of the Greek-Bulgarian frontiers—apparently in an effort to dispel accusations of wartime "antinational" behavior on the Macedonian question.[59]

The second victim was the Slavophone population itself. NOF's initiatives, which involved armed activity, offered government forces and irregulars an alibi to take revenge on Slavophones suspected of collaborating with the Bulgarian occupation authorities or with the pro-Yugoslav, Slav-Macedonian organizations. Personal vendettas, however, had also their share of the blame. Although there is no evidence of a specific government plan for the eviction of the

Slavophone population from the country, it is difficult to ascertain the intentions of local officials and nationalist army officers in the field. There was no doubt that the pendulum of revenge had shifted, this time, against the Bulgarian and Slavo-Macedonian factions of the Slavophones. Certainly, the situation in Greek Macedonia in 1945-46 was not dissimilar from cases of countries emerging from foreign occupation where minorities had, for one reason or other, collaborated with the occupiers, only to find themselves, after the war the target of nationalist revenge. Although in Greek Macedonia persecution never reached genocide-like practices, perpetrated, for example, in Yugoslavia against the Germanophone minorities,[60] the climate was hardly tolerable for persons associated directly or indirectly with either one of the two "Slavic menaces": Bulgarian and Slavo-Macedonian. As a result, the number of Slavophones crossing into Yugoslavia in 1945-46 increased to 15,000–20,000.[61]

IV

If we accept the pivotal role of Yugoslavia in Zachariadis' decision to initiate the "Third Round," it is logical to assume that a normalization of relations between KKE and NOF had top priority. There are now reports available of secret meetings of Zachariadis and other members of the Central Committee of the KKE with NOF leaders in Thessaloniki as early as December 1945. These encounters eventually led to Zachariadis' complete reversal of KKE's assessment of NOF's activities and its future role. In the place of open condemnation of NOF, the Greek communist leader, speaking to Party cadres in Thessaloniki in March 1946, referred to NOF as a "democratic," "antifascist" organization working for the common cause.[62] The new position on this crucial issue cleared the road for the late March talks with Tito, who endorsed Zachariadis' decision to commence the armed struggle promising his support.[63]

By May 1946, the first Greek communist armed bands began to cooperate with NOF bands, already in the field, while KKE cadres in the border prefectures of Macedonia entered into discussions with local NOF leaders on matters of common interest. Still, however, both organizations maintained their organizational and operational autonomy.[64]

From May to November 1946, high level negotiations were conducted between KKE, on the one hand, and NOF, CPM and CPY, on the other. Details are fragmentary but sufficient to draw the picture.[65] Many obstacles had to be surmounted and certain misunderstandings cleared before a final agreement could be reached. It is interesting to note that Lazar Kolishevski, head of the CPM, found it necessary to report to Tito, as late as September 7th 1946, that in "Aegean Macedonia," the leaders of the Greek *andartes* "are not willing to carry out decisions in the spirit of the discussions held with Zachariadis, but they try, with every means at their disposal, to disorganize and dissolve the Macedonian units." He added that in Greek Macedonia there were only 70 Greek compared to over 500 "Macedonian" *andartes*, operating under the orders of NOF. Again, on September

24th, Kolishevski, reporting on Markos Vafiadis' arrival in Skopje, informed the
CC of CPY of Vafiadis' request to Slavo-Macedonian leaders to go to Greece. His
instructions, however, to NOF—according to Kolishevski—were not in the spirit
of a previous meeting attended by Vafiadis, Tito, Djilas and Kolishevski. Therefore,
he wished to know whether any changes were made "to the work in Aegean
Macedonia."[66]

Tito's reply, cabled on October 7th, sets out, in a clear way, the ground rules
of cooperation between the CPY and KKE, in reference to the role and position of
the Slavo-Macedonians in the Greek armed struggle. In the first place, Tito pleads
ignorance, (no doubt to Kolishevski's shocked surprise) asking the CPM to explain
what units in Aegean Macedonia "you consider as ours." He then delineates
Yugoslav policy as follows: "We consider that in this situation all units in the territory of Greece should be under the unified direction of Greek commanders with
which you should now be in touch. Your people should not be mixed now with
the organization and direction of the armed struggle in Greece. You should limit
your activity in Aegean Macedonia only to offering specific assistance, as with the
press e.t.c. . . ."[67]

This document reflects the spirit of the KKE-NOF agreement, finally reached
in November 1946. NOF undertook to severe its organizational links with CPM,
to dissolve its political organization and its armed bands, and to fuse into the KKE
and the Democratic Army of Greece (DAG). It must be inferred that NOF assumed
the obligation to desist from conducting any irredentist activity inside Greece.[68]

The decision of the leadership of the KKE to put aside its reservations about
NOF—despite the latter's behavior during 1945, its irredentist pronouncements and
its direct dependence on CPM—was apparently influenced by the following assessments: A great number of Slavo-Macedonians had taken refuge in Yugoslavia, thus
offering a convenient reservoir of manpower. NOF's clandestine network in the
urban and rural districts of Kastoria, Florina and Edessa could be turned to the benefit of the struggle and facilitate a quick takeover of the important border triangle,
adjacent to Yugoslavia and Albania. Furthermore, cooperation with the local CPM
and the agencies of the S.R. of Macedonia would be rendered smoother, particularly for the flow of men and supplies across the border. On the contrary, failure to
reach an understanding with NOF could raise a series of problems with S.R.
Macedonia authorities and make extremely difficult a meaningful cooperation with,
and support from, Yugoslavia. No one could possibly deny that a full-scale uprising
in Greece without Yugoslav support would have been problematic, to say the
least.[69]

There were of course two major drawbacks in reaching an agreement with
NOF. On the one hand, the KKE exposed itself, for a third time, to its adversaries
on the sensitive issue of collaboration with the Slavs. On the other hand, it ran the
risk of a recurrence of Slavo-Macedonian secessionist activity along the lines of
1944. To counter the first, the KKE launched its own campaign against "monarcho-fascism" and "Anglo-American imperialism." To meet the second, it endeav-

ored to maintain a firm grip on Slavo-Macedonian activists without, however, causing rupture or defections.

On the basis of recently released data from the Yugoslav side,[70] KKE proceeded, at least on paper, to accord the Slavo-Macedonians full equality within the Party, with proportional representation in KKE organs and DAG units of various echelons. In prefectures with a sizeable proportion of Slavophone population, NOF cadres would have a leading role in regional Party organizations, while dissemination of the "Macedonian" national idea— but not secessionism—would not be obstructed. Although not identified as such, these concessions appeared to lead to a form of self-rule in the three border prefectures, under the aegis of KKE. However, no special Slavo-Macedonian armed units, or a separate Slavo-Macedonian party organization, would be allowed to function inside Greece.

It is difficult to ascertain the role of the Slavo-Macedonians within DAG. NOF sources tend to classify—erroneously—all Slavophones as Slavo-Macedonians, and, thus, exaggerate their participation and importance in the armed struggle. There have been claims that 50 percent of the DAG fighters, of its casualties and of the refugees were Slavo-Macedonians. Slavo-Macedonian *andartes* by July 1947 numbered about 6000, and by the end of 1948, 14,000, compared to the total DAG force of approximately 40,000.[71] Even if these figures are probably inflated, it is a fact that from the end of 1946 to the end of 1948, Slavophones furnished the KKE with much-needed manpower, disproportionate to their numbers. Inhabiting border regions frequently passing under DAG control, they were more easily exposed to voluntary or compulsory subscription. Their importance, however, increased during the last year of the Civil War, when most large-scale military operations took place in western Macedonia and adjacent Epirus.[72]

Nevertheless, the induction of Slavo-Macedonians into DAG units was also a cause of internal friction, arising from mutual suspicions. When battle ready Slavo-Macedonian bands (estimated at approximately 1000 men) joined, in December 1946, the newly formed KKE-sponsored units, they were immediately sent for duty to central Greece. There, they were disbanded and the men were allocated to new mixed units under trusted KKE commanders. Most of the Slavo-Macedonian cadres found themselves demoted or given secondary posts.[73] Such treatment became a major irritant during the next two years. NOF complained that despite the original agreement, no Slavo-Macedonian cadres reached top positions. Moreover, Slavo-Macedonians of all ranks, who had either been associated in wartime with NOF and the pro-Bulgarian nationalist bands (and later apparently repented), or had taken refuge in Yugoslav Macedonia after 1944, had become suspect of "Macedonian" nationalism. Following KKE's split with the CPY, pro-Tito Slavo-Macedonians, who deserted DAG and KKE, accused KKE of promoting within the Party and DAG commands Slavophones who had no connection with NOF, simply because their "Macedonian" national orientation was "dormant" or worse, yet, they were "Grecomans." In his long letter to the CC KKE, on June 2nd 1949, NOF leader Keramidziev complained that, "we had to struggle against the Great Idea chauvinism of many Greek cadres . . . who were united *with the most fanatic anti-Macedonian elements, i.e. Macedonians from villages who said they were Greeks.*[74]

On its part, the KKE leadership, in its tirades against the pro-Tito faction of NOF, revealed that throughout the two-year struggle, 1947-1948, Slavo-Macedonian activists continued to conduct propaganda within Greece for the unification of Greek Macedonia to the P.R. of Macedonia, to undermine the unity of Greeks and Slavo-Macedonian fugitives in the P.R. of Macedonia and, even, to organize defections from DAG.[75]

In assessing the Slavo-Macedonian factor in KKE's armed struggle, it becomes apparent that until the Tito-Stalin split in mid-1948 the KKE leadership had successfully exploited the Slavo-Macedonians to its own benefit. Contrary to what had happened in 1943-1946—when the Slavo-Macedonians of Greece were under the guidance and patronage of the Yugoslav Macedonian partisans— after 1946, the KKE-CPY agreement allowed the KKE to exercise its authority over the Slavo-Macedonians free of irritating interventions by Skopje emissaries or commissars. What the KKE apparently underestimated was the extent of NOF's ability to spread Slavo-Macedonian nationalism among the Slavophone villagers, taking advantage of opportunities offered by controlling the administration in certain villages, teaching the language and printing Slavo-Macedonian publications. NOF's efforts were similarly aided by KKE's classification as "Slavo-Macedonians"—and later as "Makedones"—of all Slavophones, a fact that automatically ignored the Greek faction of the Slavophones. What mattered to the Party at the time was the classification of Slavophones as either loyal to KKE, or suspect of Yugoslav Macedonian orientation.

Undoubtedly, this situation could not pass unnoticed by the Greek faction of Slavophones who had found themselves on the other side of the fence in the Greek civil strife. Armed by the National Army, they fought their own "national" war. In certain cases, entire Slavophone villages—which have been appropriately called "village-fortresses of Macedonia"[76]—organized their own defense units and, for the duration of the war, stood firm against their national as well as their ideological foes. In those regions fratricidal conflict meant exactly that: brother was fighting brother, as by choice or coercion members of the same family found themselves frequently in opposite camps.

To the other side—which for the sake of convenience is more appropriately identified as the government camp—much of what has only recently been revealed was unknown at the time, or fragmentary and distorted. Government agencies had to depend on public pronouncements by Yugoslavs, NOF and KKE, as well as on information of risky trustworthiness, provided by captured *andartes*. Led by its own perceptions, and ignorant of nuances in the Macedonian aims of the protagonists of the other side, the government camp tended to lump the aims of KKE, Slavo-Macedonians, Yugoslavs, Bulgarians and the Soviet Union into a carefully orchestrated conspiracy for the detachment of Macedonia from Greece.[77] Although such a simplistic view ignored the intricacies of the problem, there was ample justification to substantiate the government's threat perception. The wartime experiences with Yugoslav-supported secessionist activities of the Slavo-Macedonians, which continued in the post-Varkiza interlude, were fresh in the minds of the policymakers and the public. Repeated Yugoslav references, throughout 1945-1947, to the unification of the three parts of Macedonia kept alive and gave a sense of imminence to the threat from the north. Claims to Greek Thrace presented by Bulgaria at the Paris peace conference and supported by the Soviet Union and Yugoslavia added insult to injury, but also increased apprehensions. And, on top of these, came the Tito-Dimitrov Bled agreement, in the summer of 1947, which revealed only a thinly veiled plan for a unified Macedonian federative state within a South Slav Federation.

Internally, the perception for the detachment of Macedonia as a direct consequence of a communist victory in the Civil War was more or less shared by the entire political spectrum of the government camp.[78] Much as it happened in Macedonia during the war years, confrontation with the KKE was removed from the ideological platform of "a bourgeois democracy vs. a proletariat communist state," and developed along the lines of "the nation vs. its enemies."[79] The KKE was identified with Soviet expansionism and, consequently, it was argued, a struggle against it was mandatory for all good patriots who ought to rally to the government camp to stem off the Slavic menace. In short, the fate of Macedonia became the rallying point for government supporters. It matters little whether this policy was the product of a cool assessment of all the parameters of the question (a rather difficult exercise), or the result of the government's own psychological warfare technics. What counted at that moment was that, in the government vs. KKE propaganda contest, the government was scoring points and the KKE was only too conscious of its consequences, but unable to react.[80]

Apart from propaganda strategy, legal measures for the suppression of the rebellion focused also on the threat perception to the northern provinces. Thus the Γ Ψήφισμα enacted in June 1946, provided for court martials, initially, only in northern Greece. Even when these judicial proceedings were extended to the whole of Greece, persons were persecuted and sentenced to life imprisonment or death, on two major counts: the violent overthrow of the existing political system, and the detachment of part or the whole of the state (Compulsory Law 509).[81] The KKE was held by the government camp guilty of secessionist ("autonomist") activities in Macedonia. Prior, however, to 1949, no convincing legal proof could be brought against it to justify direct implication in the annexationist schemes of Greece's northern neighbors—KKE's allies and supporters.

On the international level, the Macedonian question became once again the focal point of the Greek government's case. Greece, it was argued, was faced not with an internal civil war, but with an international conspiracy aiming at turning Greece into a communist state, or a movement aspiring at detaching Macedonia. Both the earlier U.N. Commission of Investigation Concerning Greek Frontier Incidents and its successor, the U.N. Special Committee on the Balkans, were provided with whatever evidence was available on the subject: even wartime agreements that KKE was alleged to have made with neighboring communist parties for the cession of Macedonia to a Balkan communist federation. (These agreements were forged.) There was, of course, ample documentation for the material support offered to the Greek communist insurgents by Yugoslavia and Bulgaria, and for statements by these states on the future unification of Macedonia. But until the latter part of 1947, when the Bled agreement was concluded, it was difficult to build a thoroughly convincing case, particularly for inquisitive third parties.[82]

What counted most, however, was whether the Greek government's threat perceptions were shared in London and Washington.[83] The British government, having already committed itself in retaining Greece to the Western fold, needed little convincing. In the event, it frequently spear-headed anti-Soviet bloc polemics, utilizing the argument of the threat posed to Greece's territorial integrity by Yugolav aspirations on Macedonia. Similarly, the United States, being more and more involved in Greek affairs, found the Macedonian question a valid argument to justify its policy.[84] Yet, at times, more reserved assessments were voiced. Such was the case of Labor Foreign Minister Bevin, in late 1946, who held the view that Yugoslav public statements for the unification of Macedonia were for internal consumption, and in no way could constitute an imminent threat to Greece's territorial integrity. Later, however, when a Soviet threat in the direction of the Straits began to develop, the Foreign Office, and subsequently the State Department, assumed that the case of Macedonia and Thrace, along with the Straits, constituted a well-designed Soviet objective aimed at controlling the Aegean. What appeared to be in doubt was the timing for a Soviet initiative. Thus, the Macedonian question gradually emerged as a peon in the global context of East-West relations.[85]

It is interesting to note that for the same reasons, the Turks also expressed deep concern about rumors for the establishment of a unified Macedonian state that would include Greek Macedonia. In the view of a Turkish diplomat, a Slavo-Macedonian state, with Thessaloniki included, would reduce Greece to impotence and cut off Turkey from Europe. In such a case, he concluded, "if there were no Greece, there would be no Turkey."[86]

Under the circumstances, the State Department took the view that the crux of the Macedonian problem was the maintenance of the territorial integrity of Greece itself. And although the United States could have no saying over a possible unification of the Bulgarian and Yugoslav parts of Macedonia, the preservation of Greece's frontiers against irredentist claims by the northern neighbors justified "all possible and appropriate steps" by the U.S. government.[87]

Such concern was not without some basis. The Macedonian unification scheme that had emerged in the last months of 1944, in the abortive Yugoslav-Bulgarian negotiations for a South Slav Federation, resurfaced with the conclusion of the Tito-Dimitrov agreements at Bled and Evxinograd (August and November

1947, respectively).[88] Despite certain nuances as to the timing and the sequence of the steps necessary to implement the agreements, the fact was that the leader of Bulgaria committed his country to the cession of Pirin Macedonia to Yugoslavia. Along with the last portion of Macedonian land, Dimitrov's Bulgaria was relinquishing all future interest in Macedonian affairs in exchange for a federation arrangement with Yugoslavia and the return of the "western Bulgarian regions," annexed by Yugoslavia after World War I.

There is no doubt that an agreement was reached at Bled on the fate of Greek Macedonia as well. No concrete details were revealed at the time, nor have they become known since. Two years later, however, in 1949, Tito publicly revealed that the case of Greek Macedonia had been examined and that the two leaders had decided to "definitely solve the Macedonian question *as a whole;* the Macedonian people not only in the Vardar, but in Pirin, *and Aegean Macedonia,* would receive their rights and they alone will decide on their future."[89]

Despite the fate of the South Slav Federation, the signing of the agreement was a turning point for the Macedonian question. Yugoslavia had finally secured a contractual agreement from Bulgaria to be the master of the coveted land. But what had been the position of the KKE leaders on this triangular question? There was an inexplicable silence at the time, that has been maintained to this day. Was Zachariadis aware of the Yugoslav-Bulgarian deliberations throughout 1947? Was he consulted by Tito and/or Dimitrov? And if so, what were his reactions, if not his commitments? Opponents suspected the worse: possibly a tacit consent. But they have produced no proof to support their suspicions. The question resurfaced after the publication in 1979 of certain documents from the KKE archives.[90]

On April 14th 1947, Zachariadis, then in Yugoslavia along with part of the Polit Bureau of the KKE, sent to Vafiadis his instructions outlining the strategic objective of the struggle. He wrote:[91]

> Events show that the region that constitutes the weakest and the most important point for the enemy, which offers the people's democratic movement the most favorable politico-social prerequisites, is Macedonia and Thrace, with Thessaloniki at the center. Thus, under these conditions, a basic objective for DAG today is the occupation of Thessaloniki, which would bring a decisive change in the situation and would solve our entire problem.

Zachariadis presented the same views in his memorandum to Tito, following their talks on April 22nd. He added that northern Greece for "monarcho-fascism" was its weakest—and the most important—point from a social, economic, political, *national,* military and geographical viewpoint. Consequently, DAG was planning to concentrate its main strike in this region. The final objective was to secure a territorial base for the establishment of a nucleus for a "Free Greece."[92]

The plan was approved by Tito and subsequently by the Soviet leadership. It was endorsed by the Third Plenum of the CC of KKE in October 1947. Whether this plan, discussed extensively with the leadership of the CPY— which would bear most

of the burden for its logistical support—fitted Tito's perception for a South Slav federation and a unified Macedonian state is still a matter for speculation. The timing,
however, coincides with the Yugoslav-Bulgarian negotiations, which led to the Bled
agreement. Furthermore, reference in Zachariadis' memorandum to Tito, to the
national factor, as one of the points of weakness of the Greek government for keeping
northern Greece—a reference missing in the instructions sent to Vafiadis—should be
interpreted as referring to the question of national minorities. To venture further in
speculation without more concrete evidence is precarious. Nevertheless, the time
coincidence of the discussion of the two projects—the establishment of a "free Greek
state" in northern Greece, and the unified Macedonian state in the context of a South
Slav federation—leaves Zachariadis exposed to the assumption that he might have had
at least some knowledge of the aims of the two Balkan leaders.

Putting aside the military aspects of the Civil War, it appears that the aid furnished to the KKE was not up to the requirements of the initial, grandiose plan for
capturing northern Greece, including Thessaloniki. Meanwhile, the rapid deterioration of Soviet-Yugoslav relations did not augur well for the revolution in Greece.
The crisis that came into the open, late in June 1948, left no choice to Zachariadis
but to side with the Soviet Union.

This time, the spotlight of the Macedonian question shifted in the direction of
Yugoslav Macedonia. Initial statements by Bulgarian leaders denied neither the existence of "Macedonians," nor the ideal of a "united Macedonian state." But, as it
has frequently happened in the history of Macedonia, names assumed different
meanings in the service of different and, at times, contradictory political ends. The
"Macedonians"—in Bulgarian propaganda literature—were now linked to the
Bulgarians, while reference to a "united Macedonian state" in a South Slav federation certainly was not the concept envisaged at Bled; it rather brought recollections
of the 1924 Comintern prototype. In the late months of 1948, however, a long-
term solution to the Macedonian question was not the major preoccupation of the
Bulgarian leaders, who were now hard at work to eradicate four years of
"Macedonian" infiltration in Bulgarian Macedonia, before turning their attention to
reintroducing Bulgarian nationalism among the population of the P.R. of
Macedonia.[93]

Such was the situation in his immediate vicinity when Zachariadis sought to
seize full control of NOF and the Slavo-Macedonians at home. New documents
reveal that in the second half of 1948, KKE, having already sided with Cominform,
lost no time to remove the pro-Tito Slavo-Macedonians from the leadership of
NOF and from important posts in regional KKE organizations. By one stroke, the
KKE leadership freed itself not only of avowed Titoists, but also of extremist
nationalists, maintaining close relations with the P.R. of Macedonia. Nevertheless,
instead of attempting to stamp out "Macedonian" nationalism and consolidate the
Slavophone element within the Greek revolutionary movement, Zachariadis
revealed his weakness by going in the other direction. Having placed trusted
Slavophones at the head of NOF, he initiated a series of measures aimed at raising

the level of indoctrination and education of Slavophone peasants and *andartes* in the concept of the "Macedonian" nation.[94] That was, no doubt, a policy full of contradictions, dictated by international developments and the specific requirements of the armed struggle. Imitating the Bulgarian communists, Zachariadis tried to profit—or at least not to loose—from the turn of Macedonian politics. His own gamble—if it were not dictated from abroad— came late in January 1949.

The announcement of the Fifth Plenum resolution (31.1.1949), particularly its reference to the Macedonia question, created reverberations around the world's chanceries, reappraisal of attitudes towards the KKE of the fence-standing segment of Greek public opinion and politicians, and eventually the hardening of Greek government policy towards the KKE that survived the end of the Civil War for decades. Worse yet, it made collaboration with Tito's Yugoslavia almost impossible. In-Party criticism came into the open immediately after the defeat, and continued until Zachariadis' expulsion from the leadership of the Party.[95]

Briefly stated, the new Party line, as presented in a series of documents and public statements, was the reintroduction of the 1924 platform for an independent Macedonian state, probably within a Balkan communist federation. The difference was that, whereas the 1924 decision was merely a statement of intent, its 1949 reproduction appeared as an action program of a revolution in full swing. Certainly, the full extent of this major policy shift is not, and could not, be reflected in a carefully worded Central Committee resolution. To understand the policy behind it, the historian needs to see all official statements made at the time (including those of KKE-controlled NOF), the measures taken by the KKE leadership to implement the decision, and the criticism voiced from within the Party hierarchy after the defeat, while Zachariadis was still at the helm. Undoubtedly, detailed accounts and documents released in recent years by pro-Tito Slavo-Macedonians give a better perspective, although caution is needed for points of omission. The basic, much-quoted texts are the Resolution of the Fifth Plenum of the CC of KKE (January 31st), the Decision of the Executive Council of NOF (February 4th), KKE and NOF "disclaimers" (broadcasted by Radio Free Greece on March 8th and 9th) and the Resolution of the 2nd Congress of NOF (end of March).[96] These texts clearly indicate that after the successful conclusion of the revolution, the Slavo-Macedonians would be able to establish their own Macedonian state within a Balkan communist federation. The fact that the 2nd Plenum of the Executive Council of NOF, in Zachariadis' presence, stated that the 2nd NOF Congress would announce "the union of Macedonia into a complete, independent and equal Macedonian state within the People's Democratic Federation of the Balkan Peoples," gave the Fifth Plenum's Resolution a sense of immediacy. It was this expectation of an immediate declaration for the establishment of a Macedonian state that caused anxiety in Western capitals and alarm in Athens. Once again, the interaction of perceptions and realities came into play and baffled contemporaries.

Western diplomats saw the KKE resolution in terms of a wider Soviet move aiming primarily at undermining Tito. The reference by the KKE to a Balkan federation, hitherto a popular theme only among Bulgarian and Yugoslav leaders, could mean, in the perception of Western diplomats, that there was a tendency to encircle Tito's Yugoslavia from the south and to drive an edge in the direction of the P.R. of Macedonia. What was difficult to ascertain was whether this scheme, to which more or less Western observers agreed, was not merely a theoretical policy objective, but was meant for immediate application. If that was the case, there was an imminent threat of a direct involvement of the Soviet Union in Balkan affairs.[97] Certainly, there were also more sober appraisals. The international situation offered no indication to justify such Soviet initiative. More probable was the psychological impact on internal Yugoslav politics which the Soviets apparently believed would be sufficient to cause Tito's overthrow.

The Greek government and the Greek media resorted to alarmist assessments. There were reasons for this. To them, the KKE announcement signified, in fact, the public acknowledgement of what the government camp had all the time been suspecting, namely the cession by the KKE of Greek Macedonia to a Slav-dominated Macedonian state. To reach that decision, Zachariadis must have secured solid assurances of increased support from the Soviet Union (which was not the case). Faced with an imminent threat to Macedonia, it was no wonder that Greek media interpreted government anxieties in a sensational way, which, in fact, served two government objectives: the projection of KKE's image as antinational, and the petition for increased economic and military aid from the allies.[98]

On the Yugoslav side, understandably, there was deep concern about KKE's pronounced intentions. The Yugoslav communists had been aware, as early as July 1948, of the KKE's decision to place under its firm control the Slavo-Macedonians. But they kept quiet. Even when the pro-Tito leadership of NOF was removed, there were no public recriminations. Moreover, the decision of the Fifth Plenum was commented favorably for acknowledging the right of self-determination to the Slavo-Macedonians. The only criticism was that it was untimely, since it was linked to the Cominform-inspired Balkan federation. Thus, although the Yugoslavs restrained themselves from publicly condemning KKE's position on the Macedonian question, they too saw it as part of the orchestrated Cominform drive against their Party leadership.[99]

Meanwhile, the Bulgarian government-controlled media gave limited coverage to KKE's decision. There was, however, considerable self-restrain in identifying Greek and Bulgarian views within the context of a more general Soviet plan. Certainly, the Bulgarians viewed in a positive way KKE's position so far as it offered support to their own interpretation of a solution to the Macedonian question.[100]

Of the Soviet involvement in the formulation of KKE's new Macedonian policy, there was little doubt in the West—and certainly in Yugoslavia—that Moscow had been the real instigator of the decision. What was not known at the time, was an important encounter in Bucharest, in March 1949, between Baranov, Cominform's liaison officer with the KKE, and the KKE troika, Ioannidis, Rousos and Partsalidis. Baranov expressed surprise and questioned the wisdom of the KKE in raising the Macedonian question at such an inopportune moment. Partsalidis confronted Zachariadis with Baranov's remarks, during the Seventh Plenum of the Central Committee of the KKE, meeting in exile in 1950. Zachariadis did not dispute Parsalidis' revelations, but sought to defend *his* decision, as a tactical move to keep the Slavo-Macedonians on his side. This debate between the two KKE leaders certainly placed under a different light the alleged Soviet implication in the decisions of the Fifth Plenum. But it was not made public, and remained a privileged communication for members of the Central Committee only.[101]

The worldwide interest in the KKE/NOF declarations created a climate that the Party leaders had probably underestimated. To judge by subsequent statements, it appears that there was a consensus among KKE leaders that Zachariadis had overextended himself in his public pronouncement of his policy. Probably for this reason the 2nd NOF Congress avoided any specific reference to an independent Macedonian state, but reverted to traditional declarations of principle which, with a stress of imagination, could be interpreted either way.[102]

The "retraction" did not mislead anybody at the time. The KKF continued to popularize among Party cadres and the Slavo-Macedonians at large the idea for the eventual self-determination of the Slavo-Macedonians. To inquisitive Greek party cadres the explanation given centered around the meaning of self-determination (including the right of cessation) as a Marxist-Leninist principle, with the addition that the final form and extent of an independent Macedonian state would depend on circumstances and the outcome of a plebiscite.[103]

Meanwhile, a series of specific measures were introduced. Slavo-Macedonians, loyal to the KKE leadership, assumed high posts including a Ministry in the Provisional Government and commanding posts in DAG and the regional Macedonian organizations. More important however, was the fact that by the spring of 1949 a Communist Organization for Aegean Macedonia was formed to operate within KKE, but, in fact, to function as a separate party organization for the Slavo-Macedonians. There was no explanation for this decision other than that it was a first step toward an autonomous Slavo-Macedonian party organization.[104]

The British and Americans, on their part, felt relieved by KKE disclaimers, which removed the immediacy of the crisis. To them this was an indication that the Soviet Union was not contemplating a major new initiative in the Balkans, which would require a reappraisal of their own strategic requirements. Freed from the anguish of February-March, they shifted their attention to creating, carefully, the necessary climate for a rapprochement with Tito. If successful, it could, in an indirect way, relieve the pressure from the Greek government's efforts to crush the revolution.[105]

This was not the case, however, with the Greek government. KKE's verbal "whitewashing" of the initial KKE/NOF declaration was hardly taken into consideration. The incident had created both anguish and exultation. Both, if properly exploited, could be beneficial to the government's aims. On the internal front the condemnation of the KKE policy by former supporters or sympathizers of the KKE's cause—such as Professor Svolos—gave justification to the government's appeal to all Greeks to rally around the government to safeguard not the social system but the country's territorial integrity. It was a call for a panhellenic *djihad*. As such, even the most severe measures against the opponents could be justified. In practice, the government made it a capital offense for any person to even identify himself with the KKE. Such an identification was assumed to carry approval of the Fifth Plenum resolution and consequently the death penalty would mandatory.[106]

On the international level, the Greek government sought to present, in a rather magnified way, the potential threat developing not only to its own territory, but to the entire Balkan area. Early in April, the Coordinating Council of Ministers, presided by King Paul, and in the presence of Commander-in-Chief Alexander Papagos drew up a detailed memorandum that contained the government's assessments. According to this scenario, the avowed intention of the Soviet Union was to step up support for Greek and Slavo-Macedonian guerrillas in Greece and in Yugoslav Macedonia, in order to place the two Balkan countries under its control. With the Balkans under Soviet influence, the threat potential to Turkey and Italy would increase manifold. As a response, the Greek government proposed that in the event of a Soviet attack on Yugoslavia the West should consider occupying Albania in order to hold it as a hostage for exchange; encourage Turkey to contribute more actively in averting the potential threat; finally, provide overwhelming aid to Greece not only for military purposes, but also for facilitating its rapid reconstruction.[107]

It should be added that similar assessments were made at the time by British and American officials, who reached the conclusion that the Greek government and Army should be bolstered materially, in order to face a growing and potentially grave threat. As it proved, this increased threat did not materialize. But the augmented aid came in time to the Greek National Army for its final drive against DAG in the summer of 1949.[108]

A last word for Yugoslavia. Much as Tito tried to keep the bridges open, KKE's handling of the Macedonian question and, more so, its efforts to turn the Slavo-Macedonians in an anti-Tito course, finally raised for the Yugoslavs a clear security problem in their southern province. A problem that had to be met drastically, even against ideological principles and comradely *solidarnost*. How difficult was for the Yugoslavs to stop supporting the Greek communists is evidenced by the fact that for almost a year, despite certain feelers from Western capitals, and even Athens, the Yugoslavs had refrained from reaching any understanding with the Greek government.[109] In July the border was closed to the *andartes*. But whatever has been said about the *pisoplato chtypima* of the Yugoslavs against DAG units in July 1949, it has by now been established that it was entirely inaccurate and unfair.[110]

The armed Civil War ended on the tops of mountains Vitsi and Grammos, in August 1949. From its inception, the Macedonian question, both in its macro- and micro- aspects, had influenced the course of the communist revolution in Greece, at times in a positive way for the communist side. In the end, however, it proved catalytical to its doom.

V

Four decades after the critical 1940s, there are still significant blank spots to our knowledge of events connected with the Macedonian question to permit us an all-round assessment of this important question on Civil War developments. In recent years, certain confused situations have been sufficiently clarified. Among them are: the wartime Yugoslav policy objectives toward Greek Macedonia, the role of the Slavo-Macedonians, and the true extent of KKE attitudes and policies toward both. Some progress has been made in understanding Tito's behavior prior and during the *Dekemvriana*. But our information is still inconclusive on Yugoslav policy-making concerning a possible military intervention in Greek Macedonia during October-November 1944, ostensibly in support of ELAS, but more probably for creating conditions favorable to a future Yugoslav claim on the region.

New data have now revealed, beyond reasonable doubt, NOF's relationship as an appendage to the Communist Party of Macedonia for nearly two years, 1945-1946. Fairly well-established are now the terms which regulated the collaboration of the Slavo-Macedonians with the KKE and DAG, until the split between KKE and CPY. What, however, remains uncertain is Zachariadis' obligations to Tito, at the time of the KKE-NOF agreement, on the future settlement of the Macedonian question.

Similarly, there is uncertainty in connection with the Tito-Dimitrov Bled agreement. There is no doubt that Greek Macedonia had been a subject of the arrangement reached between the two leaders. But no information has been revealed concerning the steps toward its eventual inclusion to a unified Macedonian state. And, more important, it still remains uncertain whether Zachariadis had been consulted, or was aware of, the plans of the two Balkan leaders. There was a strange silence by the KKE on the subject at the time of the conclusion of the agreement. This silence continued even after the split with Tito and has been kept by all sides. Little though it matters for general assessments, this particular moment in the history of the Macedonian question remains a tantalizing blank.

The most criticized turning point of KKE's Macedonian policy—the decision of the Fifth Plenum of the CC in January 1949—has been reviewed and anathematized by all, including in subsequent years by KKE itself. Opponents saw in it the *diktat* of the Kremlin in the context of its efforts to undermine Tito. Supporters, with Zachariadis in the lead, tried to explain it in terms of the armed struggle (attract the Slavo-Macedonians and stamp off Tito's subversion), presenting it, in other words, as their own initiative. Hardly a serious analyst of that period put much credence to these weak arguments for such a major decision. Here again, there is no documentation on the actual Soviet role. Strangely enough, Greek communist leaders, critical of Stalin, have given no convincing evidence either. On the contrary, there is now sufficient evidence that the importance of the Slavo-

Macedonians within DAG had grown during the last year to the point that their continued association and loyalty to KKE's cause were *sine qua non* for its future course. Was it possible that Zachariadis, assessing the overall anti-Tito attitude of the Soviet bloc, the reversal of the Macedonian policy of the Communist Party of Bulgaria and the fact that his Party was anyhow condemned by its adversaries for "treason" on this sensitive issue, miscalculated the psychological reverberation and took it upon himself—not at the request of the Kremlin—to introduce the new policy in the Central Committee Plenum? This is still an assumption that negates the diktat theory. But the attitude of the Soviet Union and Bulgaria during those two critical months—February and March—tends to support the view that Zachariadis was not coerced to align his Party with a general Soviet scheme on Macedonia. Unless further evidence is produced, the responsibility for the decision must fall squarely on the KKE leaders who signed the Fifth Plenum resolution.

Even with such gaps, we have reached a point that our vision is clearer. Our perceptions have come closer to the realities of this intricate and elusive problem, thanks to new available data, and to more sober appraisals of the events of the 1940s. What, then, is our present assessment of the Macedonian question as a factor influencing developments of the Civil War?

Throughout the 1940s the Macedonian question was basically shaped by forces and interests outside Greece. None of the two protagonists of the Greek Civil War—the KKE and the government camp—had any interest in the change of the status quo of the land of Macedonia or of its people. But the dynamics of the Macedonian question pursued an erratic course which the Greek duellists sought to utilize to their own ends. It was unavoidable that the two issues—the fate of Macedonia and the course of the revolution in Greece —converged, interacted, and shaped the destinies of both. When that happened, both sides tried to benefit from it, as best or as suitably they could: militarily, politically, psychologically.

The foreign aspects of the problem were no less intriguing and condusive to Big Power manipulations. Given the fluidity of the situation in the Balkans during the last two years of the war against Germany, the uncertain developments at the time of the liberation and the transitory period until the concretization of spheres of influence, it is no wonder that the Macedonian question seriously affected strategic conceptions and tactical options of the Big Powers.

The real protagonist of the Macedonian question was Yugoslavia. The policies, the power and security perceptions of its leaders and the requirements of that new nation—which was christened, in 1944, "Macedonian"—had a profound effect in wartime and postwar developments in the Balkans. It is an intriguing coincidence that Yugoslavia's Macedonian interests and needs were constantly behind Yugoslav political options vis-à-vis the communist movement in Greece.

Or was it not a coincidence?

NOTES TO APPENDIX I

1. In the heat of the Civil War, William McNeill (*The Greek Dilemma: War and Aftermath*, Philadelphia, 1947, p. 261) reflected a commonly shared perception at the time, when he wrote that, "the future history of the Greek state and people may depend in a large part on the development of the Macedonian issue."

2. The war years and related bibliography are covered in the author's study, "I Valkaniki Diastasi tou Makedonikou Zitimatos sta Chronia tis Katochis kai tis Antistasis" [The Balkan Dimension of the Macedonian Question during the Occupation Years and the Resistance] in H. Fleischer and N. Svoronos (ed.). *I Ellada 1936–1944: Diktatoria, Katochi, Antistasi, Praktika, Á Diethnes Synedrio. Sychronis Istorias* [Greece 1936–1944: Dictatorship, Occupation, Resistance; Annals of the First International Congress of Contemporary History] (Athens, 1989) pp. 418–471 (Hereafter cited as *Valkaniki Diastasi.*) Also, the author's earlier book, *Nationalism and Communism in Macedonia* (Thessaloniki, 1964).

3. Notable exception: Philippos Iliou's serialization of KKE documents in *Agvi* (Dec. 1979 to Jan. 1980), "Ta Archeia tou KKE" [The Archives of the KKE]. Useful references to the Macedonian question in memoirs or works by KKE protagonists: Petros Rousos, *I Megali Pentaetia, 1940–1945* [The Great Five Years], 3rd ed. (Athens, 1982); Giannis Ioannidis, *Anamniseis* [Memoirs], ed. by Alekos Papapanagiotou (Athens, 1979); Thanasis Chatzis, *I Nikifora Epanastasi pou Chathike* [The Victorious Revolution that Was Lost], 3 vols. (Athens, 1977–1979) (the latter with questionable interpretation of documentary KKE sources, published in Skopje). Typical of distorted phraseology and systematic omissions on the Macedonian question are the most recent *Apomnimonevmata* [Memoirs] by Markos Vafeiadis, 3 vols. (Athens, 1984–1985). Compare his oral (taped) reminiscenses to Yugoslav authors: Jovan Popovski, *Zašto me Staljin Nije Streljao?* [Why Stalin Did not Shoot Me?], (Ljubljana, 1982), and Dragan Kljakić, *General Markos*, (Zagreb, 1979). From the pro-government side, the more recent books by journalist Nikos Mertzos, *Svarnout; To Prodomeno Antartiko* [Svarnut; The Betrayed Rebellion], 5th ed., (Thessaloniki, 1983), and *Emeis oi Makedones* [We, the Macedonians], (Thessaloniki, 1986) offer critical appraisal of KKE Macedonian policy through pro-KKE publications. More critical of KKE historiography on the Macedonian issue, are Yugoslav Macedonian authors. Petar Galabov, "Inforbirovski Diskriminacii i Frankolevantinski Insinuacii," [Cominform's Discriminations and Francolevantistic Insinuations], *Iselenicki Kalendar* (Skopje, 1982) pp. 79–85, writes: "As defeated 'generals' they have come to realize that they believed one thing as 'romantic revolutionaries', and now, in their old age, after loosing two revolutions, they believe in another. What is more tragic with these people is that they think they are passing exams as 'more loyal' Greeks, (to prove) that they have always struggled for the national fulfillment of their country (which no one has questioned), and that the Macedonian national question was a cancer caused by others. Vlandas and Gousias, Roussos and Katsoulis, Bartzotas and Blanas, P. Nefeloudis and many others, distort facts in their books in a pharisaic, greater-Greek and anti-Marxist way, and struggle to give an entirely different direction and dimension to the political situation in Greece blaming each other for errors committed. But when the question refers to the Macedonian national question, as in a chorus, they reject or ignore anything Macedonian. There is not a single word in their books about the Macedonians. . . from the viewpoint of "greater-Greek chauvinists and nationalists." For particularly Giorgis Katsoulis (*Istoria tou KKE*, vol. V. 1940–1945, (Athens, 1977)) comes under sharp attack for treating the

Macedonian question from the best bibliographical guide consult: H. Fleicher and S. Bowman, *I Ellada sti Dekaetia 1940–1950* (Athens, 1984), a revised Greek edition from the collective work *Greece in the 1940's: A Bibliographic Companion*, ed. John Iatrides (Hanover and London, 1981).

4. Archiv na Makedonija, *Egejska Makedonija vo NOB* [Aegean Macedonia in the National Liberation War], 7 vols. 1941–1949 (Skopje, 1971–1985) (Hereafter *Eg. M*). Also, *KPG i Makedonskoto Prašanje, 1918–1974* (Skopje, 1982) (Hereafte r *KPG*). Both contain selected documents of EAM/ELAS, KKE and NOF, in possession of Archiv na Makedonija, Skopje. More documents in: Institute for National History, *Izvori na Osloboditelnata Vojna i Revolucijata vo Makedonija, 1941–1945* [Sources of the Liberation War and the Revolution in Macedonia] vol. I, 6 books (Skopje, 1968–1979). Two books by Svetozar Vukmanović–Tempo, *Revolucija koja teče–Memoari* [The Running Revolution; Memoirs], (Zagreb, 1981) and *Borba za Balkan* [Struggle for the Balkans], (Zagreb, 1981; Skopje, 1975), Risto Kirjazovski, *Narodno Osloboditelniot Front i Drugite Organizacii na Makedoncite od Egejska Makedonija, 1945–1949* [The National Liberation Front and the Other Organizations of the Macedonians of Aegean Macedonia], (Skopje, 1985). Also to be used with care, on account of frequent distortions and inaccuracies, Vangel Ajanovski, *Egejski Buri* [Aegean Storms] (Skopje, 1975).

5. Elisabeth Barker, *Macedonia; Its Place in Balkan Power Politics* (London, 1950) pp. 21–29. Kofos, *op. cit.*, pp. 50–54.

6. Understandably Yugoslav Macedonian writers tend to exaggerate interwar Slavo–Macedonian activity in Greek Macedonia. For example, Tošo Popovski, *Makedonskoto Nacionalno Malcinstvo vo Bugarija, Grcija i Albanija* [The Macedonian National Minority in Bulgaria, Greece and Albania], (Skopje, 1981) pp. 64–80. Ajanovski, *op. cit.*, pp. 11–75.

7. George Mavrocordatos, *Stillborn Republic: Social Coalitions and Party Strategies in Greece, 1922–1936* (Berkeley, 1983). Nicos Alivizatos, *Les institutions politiques de la Grèce à travers les crises, 1922–1974* (Paris, 1979). Eleftherios Stavridis, *Ta Paraskinia tou KKE* [The Backstage of the KKE], (Athens, 1953) pp. 285–291, 300–302, 432–447, 459–462.

8. Alekos Papapanagiotou interview in *Anti* (Athens, June 19, 1981) p. 35. Pavlos Nefeloudis, *Stis Piges tis Kakodaimonias* [In the Sources of Misfortune], 2nd ed. (Athens, 1974) pp. 93–97. Texts in: KKE, *Deka Chronia Agones, 1935–1945* [Ten Years of Struggles], (Athens, 1945) pp. 45, 75–76. Kofos, *op. cit.*, pp. 90–92.

9. This is, at least, alleged, *a posteriori*, by Slavo-Macedonian writers, Ajanovski, *op. cit.*, p. 55.

10. Barker, *op. cit.*, p. 31. Kofos, *op. cit.*, pp. 47–48.

11. Kofos, *op. cit.*, p. 50. Similar conclusions are reached in a secret service report, dated 17.12.1949 submitted to Commander-in-Chief Al. Papagos. Text in AYE A/59179/Aut. Mac./G5Ba/1949.

12. Stephen Palmer and Robert King, *Yugoslav Communism and the Macedonian Question* (Hamden, Conn., 1971) pp. 14–15, 56. Evangelos Kofos, *I Makedonia sti Giougoslaviki Istoriografia* [Macedonia in Yugoslav Historiography], (Thessaloniki, 1974) p. 6, ft. 2.

13. Kofos, *op. cit.*, pp. 100–102. Hagen Fleischer, *Im Kreuzschatten der Mächte: Griechenland 1941–1944* (Frankfurt, 1986) pp. 69–72.

14. Details in Kofos, *I Valkaniki Diastasi.* . . *op. cit.*

15. *Ibid.*, quoting EAM and KKE sources published in *Eg. M.*, I, *op. cit.*

16. *Ibid.*

17. Palmer and King, *op. cit.*, pp. 54–55. For a recent detailed review by a Bulgarian author of the CPU's policy on the Macedonian question, Konstantin Palešutski, *Jugoslavskata Komunisticeska Partija i Makedonskijat Văpros, 1919–1945*. [The Yugoslav Communist Party and the Macedonian Question], (Sofia, 1985).

18. Comintern's radiogram in August 1941 directed the Bulgarian and Yugoslav communists that "Macedonia should be attached to Yugoslavia for practical reasons and for the sake of expediency. . . . The two parties should take up the stand of the self-determination of the Macedonian people." Quoted by Tsola Dragoycheva, *Macedonia: Not a Cause of Discord but a Factor of Good Neighbourliness and Cooperation* (Sofia, 1979) pp. 57–58, a rather euphemistic title to a divisive issue.

19. Tempo, *Borba.* . . , *op. cit.*, pp. 79–138, and *Revolucija.* . . III, *op. cit.*, pp. 7–106. Dragoycheva, *op. cit.*, pp. 77–79. Ioannidis, *op. cit.*, pp. 131–135, and particularly comments by Papapanagiotou in pp. 516–520. General appraisal of the above sources: Kofos, *Vlakaniki Diastasi, op. cit.*

20. Quoted in Kofos, *Valkaniki Diastasi, op. cit.*

21. The order, dated 9 July 1943, was signed by Sarafis, Velouchiotis and Tzimas. Published in KPG, *op. cit.*, pp. 177–178.

22. Yugoslav writers, and Tempo in particular, have claimed after the war that EAM/ELAS had consented in 1943–1944 to the ultimate right of self-determination of the Slavo-Macedonians, including the right of secession, but they subsequently did not honor their commitment. See Fitzroy MacLean's report, circ. D 217, 5.2.1945 in FO. Contemporary KKE documents, now in the possession of the Yugoslavs, do not support the allegation about secession. Particularly revealing is Siantos' telegram to Tzimas (14.7.1944), then in Belgrade, which outlines KKE's policy as follows: "The Macedonian question is raising problems with the Yugoslavs. KKE's position is that after victory all peoples would have the right to determine by themselves their position. The brotherly parties (Yugoslav and Bulgarian) pursue an ambiguous line, but KKE's position is correct on the basis of the present ethnological composition of Greek Macedonia." And concludes: "Beware of this delicate issue. Lack of understanding will help Greek reaction in its struggle against the Party and the liberation movement." Copy in the Archives of the Central Committee of the Communist Party of Yugoslavia, Belgrade (hereafter A/CC/CPY), File "Yugoslav-Greek relations."

23. Numerous documents of KKE, EAM/ELAS provenance in *Eg.M., op. cit.*

24. Kofos, *op. cit.*, pp. 128–134.

25. A view expounded in Athanasios Chrysochoou's six volumes under the general

heading, *I Katochi en Makedonia* [Occupation in Macedonia], (Thessaloniki, 1949–1952). A sociological approach in Giorgos Margaritis, "Oi Emfylies diamaches stin Katochi (1941–1944)" [Civil Conflicts during Occupation], *Dekapenthimeros Politis* (Athens, 5.10.1984) pp. 30–33. Also, Fleicher, *op. cit.*, pp. 285–294.

26. Documents from *Eg.M.*, I, *op. cit.*, and *KPG, op. cit.*, cited in Kofos, *Valkaniki Diastasi, op. cit.* Renos Michaleas in Kastoria and "Panos" Evripidis in Edessa are two cases of KKE cadres pursuing pro–Yugoslav line on the question of Slavophones.

27. Margaritis, *op. cit.*

28. Documents in *Eg.M.*, I., *op. cit.* pp. 388–390, 350, reveal that Slavo-Macedonian activists, within the ranks of EAM/ELAS, sought to exterminate the leaders of the pro-Greek faction of the Slavophones. Cited also in Kofos, *Valkaniki Diastasi, op. cit.*

29. *Eg.M.*, I, *op. cit.*, pp. 477, 488, 491–494; *KPG, op. cit.*, pp. 243–245, 255–263, 268, 276–280. Also, Kofos, *op. cit.*, pp. 125–126.

30. A/CC/CPY, "Greece IX-29-IV/2," Kiro Milievski (Sofia) to Tempo and Kolishevski, Oct. 1944.

31. Tempo, *Revolucija. . .* , *op. cit.*, p. 71, his report to the CC CPY, 8.8.1943; also, *Borba za Balkan, op. cit.*, pp. 88, 98, 133. Ioannidis, *op. cit.*, p. 127.

32. *Eg. M.*, I, *op. cit.*, pp. 520–521.

33. The Greek government in exile, unaware of British-Soviet agreements, showed increased nervousness at British-Yugoslav contacts, fearing possible concessions in Macedonia detrimental to Greek interests. Canadian Archives (CA), UK Dominions Secretary to Canadian For. Affairs, D 55, 12.4.1944. A study, however, of the British Foreign Office Research Department, in Oct. 1944, rejected as "not practical" proposed plans for independence, autonomy or federation of Macedonia. It favored the prewar status, with a proposal for free port facilities in Thessaloniki and Kavala for Yugoslav and Bulgarian Macedonia respectively, FO 371/43649/97481, 26.8.1944.

34. Details in Kofos, *Valkaniki Diastasi, op. cit.*

35. On the initiatives of the eastern Macedonia KKE leaders to invite the Soviet Army and allow the Bulgarian army to remain, see G. Erythriadis report: Central Committee KKE, *7 Olomeleia tis KE tou KKE , 14–16 Mai 1950* [The Seventh Plenum of the CC of KKE], Sept. 1950, p. 73. Also his report to the Macedonian Bureau, KKE, 15.10.1944, published in *KPG, op. cit.*, pp. 263–264.

36. It should be recalled that the Churchill-Stalin "percentages agreement" was concluded in Moscow on 9.10.1944. For British pressures on the Bulgarians to withdraw: Stoyan Rachev, *Anglo-Bulgarian Relations during the Second World War (1939–1944)*, (Sofia, 1981) pp. 189–204.

37. *Dragoycheva, op. cit.* pp. 84–85. This is also supported by Yugoslav writers such as Kolishevski, Tempo and Apostolski.

38. CA, Canadian Belgrade Embassy report No. 210, 13.5.1950, quoting Tito's speech to the National Assembly, 27.4.1950. Also US/NA 760H. 74/3.2.1945, State

Dept. to Moscow Embassy, No. 473, 2.5.1945.

39. The British Legation in Sofia had learned "from a most reliable source" that the inclusion of Thessaloniki in the proposed federation "would enjoy Soviet support." FO 371/48181/8533, No. 108, 21.1.1945.

40. Letter by Georgi Dimitrov to Trajko Kostov, Dec. 1, 1944, Dragoycheva, *op. cit.*, p. 86.

41. CA, Secretary of Dominion Affairs (London) to Secretary for External Affairs (Ottawa), No. 1, 1.1.1945.

42. Polychronis Enepekidis, *I Elliniki Antistasis, 1941–1944* [The Greek Resistance], (Athens, 1964) p. 90, quoting German sources for the dispatch of military equipment from Yugoslav partisans to ELAS.

43. Siantos to Tzimas, (Radiogram), 28.8.1944, A/CC/CPY, File, "Greek-Yugoslav Relations 1941–1945."

44. Ranković to Tempo, No. 3, 5.10.1944, A/CC/CPY, File "Greek-Yugoslav Relations, 1941–1945" (emphasis added).

45. Kiro Mitrovski to Tempo and Kolishevski, *op. cit.*

46. Kofos, *op. cit.*, p. 136. Also *Valkaniki Diastasi, op. cit.*

47. FO 371/48181, Brigadier Maclean to FO, 1.2.1945. Ajanovski, *op. cit.*, pp. 139–145.

48. The author has it from a reliable source that in November 1944, two KKE emisaries, Stergios Anastasiadis and Barbalexis, sought to appraise Tito's views for an armed bid for power, and that the Yugoslav leader returned a favorable answer promising all-round support. When the shooting started, however, Tito went back on his earlier promise. In an interview with author Mathiopoulos, Yugoslav historian Vojmir Kljaković confirmed that the KKE had appraised Tito's views prior to the December events, but evaded a reply on Tito's response. He added, however, that when the shooting started, Tito decided to keep his distance, not wishing to offer the British a pretext for intervention in Yugoslavia. Vasos Mathiopoulos, *I Elliniki Antistasi (1941–1944) kai oi "Symmachoi"* [The Greek Resistance and the "Allies"], (Athens, 1976) pp. xvi. Zachariadis revealed later that KKE asked Tito for military aid for the December events, but Tito turned it down and instead prepared partisan units to invade Greek Macedonia. His report, CC KKE. 7 *Olomeleia, op. cit.*, pp. 182, 275. Also speech by Ioannidis, p. 124. Also Stringos to Tzimas (Belgrade), 14.11.1944, in KPG, *op. cit.*, p. 317.

49. Ajanovski, *op. cit.*, pp. 140–145.

50. Andreas Mountrichas—"Orestis"—told Kousoulas that it was Siantos himself who gave him this explanation. George Kousoulas, *Revolution and Defeat; the Story of the Greek Communist Party* (New York, 1969) p. 211.

51. See footnote 48.

52. Ajanovski, *op. cit.*, p. 145, speaks of 4000 Slavo-Macedonians from Greek

Macedonia, who were inducted into the Yugoslav army to take part in operations in Kossovo and other parts of Yugoslavia.

53. V. Kontis, *I Angloamerikaniki Politiki kai to Elliniko Provlima: 1945–1949* [The Anglo-American Policy and the Greek Problem], (Thessaloniki, 1984) pp. 44–46.

54. *Ibid.* pp. 44–45, 107–108.

55. Ajanovski, *op. cit.*, pp. 118–132. Risto Poplazarov, "The National Liberation Movement of Macedonians in Southern Macedonia," reprinted in *Makedonija* (Melbourne), 9.11.1982. Kole Mangov, "Pred 35 godini: Otporot na Makedoncite od Solunske" [35 Years Ago. The Resistance of the Macedonians from the Thessaloniki region"], *Makedonija* (Skopje, Oct. 1981) p. 14. Risto Kirjazovski, *op. cit.*, pp. 106–145. Also US/NA 760H.68/7.2445, report by MacNeil, Athens 24.7.1945.

56. Ajanovski, *op. cit.*, pp. 159–160; Kirjazovski, *op. cit.*, pp. 101–105.

57. Keramitziev and Gotse to CC KKE, 2.6.1949, (published in Slavomacedonian), in EG.M., VI (1949), *op. cit.*, pp. 311–331 (hereafter *Keramitziev–Gotse letter*). This was known to KKE. Zachariadis report, 7 *Olomeleia, op. cit.*, p. 275, stating that the NOFites did not belong to the KKE but to "Kolishevski's Party of Skopje."

58. The pro-KKE Florina newspaper *Agonas* (5.10.1945), following official line, attacked NOF followers as traitors, to which NOF responded by threatening to slaughter pro-EAM/KKE villagers. US/NA 760H.68/12.1845, Athens report 2019, 18.12.1945. Details in Kirjazovski, *op. cit.*, pp. 147–155.

59. On the north Epirus question: CC KKE, *Apofasi tis 12is Olomeleias tis K.E. tou KKE* [Decision of the 12th Plenum of the CC of KKE], (Athens, 1945) p. 48. After the end of the Civil War, that decision came under sharp criticism by all KKE leaders. Details in Kofos, *op. cit.*, pp. 165–166.

60. Following the annihilation, persecution and eviction of the Germanophone minorities, the new Yugoslav government made it absolutely clear to the British and Americans, that it had no intention of receiving back those formerly Yugoslav citizens. See Yugoslav note No. 2183, 27.7.1945, to U.S. Embassy, stating that the German minorities, after cooperating with the occupation authorities, left the country "of their own will" and that "through their option, renounced on their Yugoslav citizenship," quoted in U.S. Embassy dispatch from Belgrade A-105, 3.8.1945 in US/NA 740.60H.114/8-345. And a further Yugoslav request, of 17.5.1946 to the Allies to help Yugoslavia to transfer to Germany the remaining 110,000 members of the German minority, 840.4016/5-2346, Belgrade No. 361, 23.5.1946.

61. US/NA 800.4016DP/11-1445, Belgrade Embassy report No. 165, 14.11.1945. As a permanent solution, the British considered, late in 1944, the transfer of approximately 120,000 Macedonian Slavs north of the Greek frontiers. FO 371/43649/97481, Leeper to Eden No. 57, 24.11.1944.

62. Ajanovski, *op. cit.*, pp. 198–200. Kirjazovski, *op. cit.* pp. 151–152.

63. Late in March 1946, Zachariadis went to Eastern Europe, he secured Gotwald's and subsequently Tito's promise for military assistance, and traveled to Crimea where he

met with Stalin and Molotov, most probably between 3–5 April. The decision for the armed insurrection was taken there and then, and the Greek leader was sent back to Tito to arrange the details. And so he did. These, in the author's privileged knowledge, have been intimated by Zachariadis himself to close colleagues.

64. Kirjazovski, *op. cit.*, pp. 155–169, offers details from Yugoslav and KKE archives.

65. Details in *Keramitziev-Gotse letter, op. cit.*, Kirjazovski, *op. cit.:* Eg. M ., III, *op. cit.; KPG, op. cit.*

66. A/CC/CPY, File "Relations with Greece," Kolishevski to CC CPY , 7.9.1946. For October, same sources put the figure of *andartes* to 2000 Slavo–Macedonians and 700 Greeks.

67. *Ibid.*, Tito to Kolishevski, 7.10.1946.

68. Apart from documents cited by Kirjazovski, *op. cit.*, pp. 155–169, Keramitziev and Gotse, in their letter to the CC of KKE of June 2, 1949 give sufficient details of an agreement, signed on 24.11.1946. Zachariadis denied, in June 1949, the existence of a written agreement, but, in A/CC/CPY, File "Greek-Yugoslav Relations 1941–1945" there is the text of an agreement, between Ioannidis and Karaivanov (on behalf of the KKE and the C.P. of Macedonia respectively), dated 15.10.1946. This text contains most, but not all of the terms quoted by Keramitziev and Gotse, indicating that it was an earlier text. Its substance, however, remains the same. Its most important points are:

a. NOF will be incorporated into KKE, and, more particularly, into its Regional Committee for Macedonia and Thrace, severing its links with the CPM.

b. NOF will set up a central organ under Keramidziev and Mitrovski which will report to the Regional Committee of the KKE for Macedonia and Thrace. NOF will have its own youth organization and press.

c.The *andartes* in Aegean Macedonia and Greece (sic) will have complete organizational and political unity and action. No special "Macedonian" units will function.

d. Dzodze Urdarov, member of the Aegean Committee on the CPM, will be assigned the task to supervise compliance with the (Yugoslav) Party line in the partisan movement in "Aegean Macedonia."

69. After the end of the hostilities, Zachariadis revealed that in his initial agreement with Tito, he had settled also the issue of the Slavo-Macedonians, and the CPY agreed that the "Slavo-Macedonians will struggle alongside with us," and that the "erosion of the Macedonian people (apparently from Skopje) would cease." Zachariadis speech, 7 *Olomeleia, op. cit.*, p. 181–182.

70. Mainly in Eg. M. *op. cit.*, vol. III-VI; KPG, *op. cit.*, and Kirjazovski, *op. cit.*

71. *Keramitziev-Gotse letter, op. cit.*

72. In assessing the causes of defeat, and answering the criticism leveled at him for the change of the Macedonian line of the Party, Zachariadis defended his policy mainly on the need to keep the loyalties of the Slavo-Macedonians to the KKE, because, in the concluding months of the struggle, they provided the main source of reserves. Although

he admitted that the new slogan did not correspond to the wider intersts of the Party, in the particular moment, what counted was a victory in the battle of Vitsi. Zachariadis reports, *6 Olomeleia*, pp. 82, 92 and 7 *Olomeleia, op. cit.*, p. 175.

73. *Keramitziev-Gotse letter, op. cit.*

74. *Ibid.* Similar complaints by Slavo-Macedonian protagonists-turned-authors: Ajanovski, *op. cit.*, pp. 191–231; Naum Pejov, *Makedocite i Gradjanskata Vojna vo Grcija* [The Macedonians and the Civil War in Greece], (Skopje, 1968) pp. 145–151, and Hristo Antonovski in *Glas na Egejskite* (Skopje, 10.2.1952).

75. CC KKE, *6 Olomeleia tis KE tou KKE (9 Ochtovri 1949)* (6th Plenum of CC KKE (9.10.1949)) April 1951, pp. 42, 86, 92. Also 7 *Olomeleia, op. cit.*, p. 125.

76. Georgios Modis, *Choria Frouria tis Makedonias* [Villages Fortresses of Macedonia], (Athens, 1964).

77. Bibliography quoted in Kofos, *op. cit.* In this respect consult two books by Dimitrios Zafeiropoulos, *To KKE kai i Makedonia* [The KKE and Macedonia], (Athens, 1948) and *O Antisymmoriakos Agon* [The Antibandit War], (Athens, 1956).

78. Prior to the 5th Plenum decision (1949) on the Macedonian question, there were certain dissenting voices (Sofianopoulos, Tsirimokos, Svolos). Plastiras appeared to believe that the rebellion did not endanger Greece's territorial integrity, which could be threatened only by war. Letter of "friends" of Plastiras to King Paul, reported by the Athens U.S. Embassy, report No. 1096, 9.11.1948, US/NA 868.00/11-948.

79. K. Tsoukalas, "I Ideologiki Epidrasi tou Emfyliou Polemou" [The Ideological Impact of the Civil War], *I Ellada sti Dekaetia 1940–1950, op. cit.*, p. 575.

80. In its memorandum to the CPSU, in October 1946, requesting assistance to its armed struggle, the KKE referred to the Macedonian question as "one of the most delicate issues which stirs the masses of Greece." Text in *Avgi*, 5.12.1979. This concern with the psychological impact of the problem is reflected in memoirs by KKE leaders, such as Petros Rousos and Giannis Ioannidis.

81. Nikos Alivizatos, "Kathestos Ektaktis Anagkis" ["State of Emergency"], *I Ellada sti Dekaetia 1940–1950, op. cit.*, pp. 397, 388–389, 391.

82. Harry Howard, "The UN Commission of Investigation Concerning Greek Frontier Incidents," *The Department of State Bulletin*, Vol. XVII, No. 418, July 6, 1947, pp. 14–25. The UN Ethridge Report, in May 1947, found little evidence to support Greek allegations. US/NA 501, BC-Greece/4-847. Also, U.S. intelligence agent in Greece Karamesinis reported, late in 1946, that "proofs" gathered that far by the Greek government could not be regarded as "conclusive." US/NA 868.00/8-1046, Athens Embassy report No. 3010, 8.10.1946.

83. G.A. Alexander, *The Prelude to the Truman Doctrine*, pp. 200, 216, 223–224, 230–231.

84. US/NA 868.00/10-1546, State and War Departments memorandum forwarded to the President, 10.10.1946, stressed the need to safeguard Greece's *territorial* and politi-

cal integrity. A State Department assessment, on 6.12.1946, of Soviet objectives vis-à-vis Greece included, overthrow of Greek government *and* detachment of Greek Macedonia, a theme that recurs in many State Department assessments throughout 1947–1948. 760H.68/12-646.

85. Bevin to Marshall, aide-mémoire, 21.7.1946, US/NA 868.00/7-2147. FO 371/72241 X/PO2621, Athens Embassy, No. 139/11/48, 12.3.1948 FO371/72241/ X/P 02621, Belgrade Embassy, No. 217/2/48, 15.3.1948 and No. 195/28.8.1948.

86. Turkish Ambassador to Paris Menemencioglu, in conversation with his British colleague Duff. British aide-mémoire G58/47, 21.7.1947, US/NA 868.00/7-2147. For Turkish apprehensions: 1223/29.11.1946.

87. US/NA FW 868.00/7-2147, memo, 28.7.1947.

88. Kofos, *op. cit.*, pp. 161–163. Texts of the Yugoslav-Bulgarian agreements, signed at Bled and Evxinograd, were published by Slobodan Nešović, *Bledski Sporazumi: Tito-Dimitrov (1947)*, [The Bled Agreements], (Ljubljana, 1979). Nešović claims to have published "all" the agreements, although this author has privileged information, of Bulgarian provenance, about a secret protocol concerning Greek Macedonia.

89. *Borba*, 3.8.1949. Two months prior to the agreements, Dimitrov had told two Western journalists that all three parts of Macedonia would, in due time, be united within the framework of Yugoslavia. FO 371/72192/ X/PO2727, Belgrade Embassy No. 217/22/48, 28.8.1948. During the 10th Plenum of the CC of CPB in August 1946, Dimitrov declared that "it is not right to use the phrases 'Vardarska Makedonija', 'Pirinska Makedonija' and 'Egejska Makedonija'. There are no three Macedonias. There is only on Macedonia." Quoted by Nešović, *op. cit.* p. 55.

90. *Avgi*, Dec. 1979–Jan. 1980.

91. *Avgi*, 11.12.1979.

92. *Avgi*, 9.12.1979.

93. Kofos, *op. cit.*, pp. 188–191.

94. *Keramitziev-Gotse letter, op. cit.*

95. Strong criticism during the 6th and 7th Plenums, *op. cit.*

96. Kofos, *op. cit.*, pp. 177–184. Text of the 5th Plenum and relevant discussion in CC KKE, *5 Olomeleia tis KE tou KKE , 30-31 Genari 1949* [Fifth Plenum of the CC of KKE, 30–31 January 1949], June 1949, text p. 16, Zachariadis report pp. 29–31, 37–38, Porfyrogenis' qualified approval, pp. 58–59. Most texts and extensive commentary published in newspaper *Pros ti Niki* (from March to August 1949).

97. Typical of British concerns was a FO minute: "The creation of an autonomous/independent Macedonian state would solve Soviet problems. Salonica would be offered to Tito's successors and Bulgaria would get E. Macedonia and W. Thrace. It is clear, therefore that we must do all possible to prevent Macedonian autonomy," FO 371/78396/18, 17.3.1949.

98. This is clearly depicted in the report of the Chief of the Imperial Staff William Slim after his visit to Greece (9–10 March). To quote: ". . . it may be part of the 1949 Cominform policy in Greece to resurrect the idea of an 'Independent Macedonia', comprising. . . a large part of Northern Greece including Salonica." That would result in "an increased movement of Communist trained forces across the frontier from Bulgaria." Thus the need to offer additional aid to the Greek National Army was the logical conclusion. FO 371/7834/26, "Report on Greece," 16.3.1949.

99. Moje Pijade, "On the Question of a Balkan Federation," quoted by Kofos, *op. cit.*, pp. 180–181. The article was originally published in *Borba,* 6.3.1949.

100. The Bulgarians were extremely reserved in their commentary of KKE's Macedonian decision, Kofos, *op. cit.*, p. 180.

101. Statement by Partsalidis, 7 *Olomeleia, op. cit.*, p. 38.

102. Kofos, *op. cit.*, p. 182.

103. Popularization of the Party policy through the pages of *Gia ti Niki* (March to August 1949). In his strong criticism of Zachariadis' Macedonia policy, Partsalidis revealed that, following the 5th Plenum, the Slavo-Macedonians disseminated rumors that "the borders of the independent Macedonian state would start from Mount Olympus, with Thessaloniki as capital, while we remained silent, thus increasing confusion." 7 *Olomeleia,* p. 38.

104. Kofos, *op. cit.*, p. 182. Ajanovski, *op. cit.*, pp. 378–389. Kirjazovski, *op. cit.*, pp. 303–312. Barker, *op. cit.*, p. 123.

105. Elisabeth Barker, "Yugoslav Policy towards Greece, 1947–1949," in *Studies in the History of the Greek Civil War, 1945–1949* (Copenhagen, 1987), pp. 286–294: and Jože Pirjevec, "The Tito-Stalin Split and the End of the Civil War in Greece," *ibid,* pp. 312–315.

106. FO 371/7834/35. Report, "Brighter Prospects for Greece," 29.3.1949. US/NA 868.00/3.3049, Athens Embassy report 30.3.1949. On the reaction of Northern Greeks FO 371/78366/36, Thessaloniki Consulate report, March-April 1949. Greek press reaction: FO 371/78396/10. Rendis' statement: FO 371/78398/4, 3.4.1949.

107. Full text published by Kontis, *op. cit.*, pp. 465–472.

108. *Ibid.* pp. 389–390.

109. On initial Yugoslav reaction: Moje Pijade, *op. cit.*, quoted in Kofos, *op. cit.* pp. 180-181.

110. Decisions of *6th Olomeleia, op. cit.*, p. 92, adopted Zachariadis' contention that Yugoslav troops, along with Greek army units attacked DAG units during the Kaimaktsalan operations, early in August 1949. All available sources have refuted these allegations. N. Zachariadis, "To Stileto tou Tito Chtypa Pisoplata ti Laiko-Dimokratiki Ellada" [Tito's Dagger Stabs in the Back People's Democratic Greece] *Syllogi Ergon,* April 1953, reprinted from Cominform's *For a Lasting Peace for the People's Democracy,* 1.8.1949.

THE MACEDONIAN QUESTION: THE POLITICS OF MUTATION

Twenty years ago, I was concluding my book, *Nationalism and Communism in Macedonia*, with the phrase: "The Macedonian Question can and should be considered a subject for the student of history rather than an issue for the policymaker."[1] Since that time, much water has run under the bridges of the Vardar/Axios River. The problem has not withered away. It has kept politicians, as well as historians, fairly well preoccupied, and in all probability, it is likely to do so for years to come.

It is generally accepted that the emergence of this problem on the political scene during the last decades of the nineteenth century came about as a result of the hoped for withdrawal, or eviction of the Ottomans from their European possessions. The rush to fill the vacuum brought to the foreground the question of succession in Macedonia and Thrace, two regions of mixed ethnic composition.

Early scenarios called for the incorporation of the entire region of Macedonia to one of the Balkan states; Greece, first, then Bulgaria. Later, however, when conflicting Balkan nationalisms converged on the region, it became evident that one-sided solutions were unrealistic. Partition began to appear as a more feasible option, although realism hardly characterized the initiatives of Balkan nationalists at the time. Numerous schemes and demarcation lines were discussed and drawn on maps for almost a century. Unable to reach consensus, the aspiring suitors of Macedonia, as well as certain European Powers, canvassed the idea of autonomy. In the minds of the suitors, however, autonomy was not an end in itself, but a roundabout approach to annexation.[2] Much later, after the First World War, the proposal for the establishment of an autonomous Macedonian state, within a Balkan federation, gained some popularity with certain socialist groups and was adopted as a policy platform by the Comintern, and the Balkan communist parties. At about the same time, certain extreme nationalists of the interwar Internal Macedonian Revolutionary Organization (IMRO) advocated the erection of a totally independent Macedonia, in the form of a "Switzerland in the Balkans."[3]

Such conflicting schemes and aspirations unleashed national as well as social movements, sparked liberation as well as imperialist wars, and resulted in holy but sometimes in unholy alliances. The tenacity of the struggles for Macedonia may well be explained on the grounds of geopolitics, nationalism, ethnological complexities and conflicting historical interpretations. Those were struggles of liberation by peoples striving for the overthrow of a five century-old, socially oppressive and nationally alien regime. At the same time, they were manifestations of clashing strategic interests of the emerging Balkan states, which sought to promote maximalist objectives, not only in the Macedonian region, but throughout the Balkan peninsula. Disputes over the interpretation of the ancient and medieval history of Macedonia further accentuated the debate over ethnological issues.

The Greeks, for instance, considered, *sine qua non,* the holding at least of the southern part of Macedonia, including the littoral of Thrace, in order to keep the road open to Constantinople. On their part, the Bulgarians, as well as the Serbs, aspired at gaining hold of most of Macedonia, in order to secure an outlet to the Aegean Sea. Furthermore, the European Powers, with conflicting interests in the Balkans, found in Macedonia fertile ground for intrigue, thus, rendering the fortune of that Ottoman province a matter of European concern.

Of the three contenders—and heirs—of Macedonia, Serbia (later Yugoslavia) had the weakest historical and ethnological titles to claim Macedonia. Yet, as a result of the peace settlements of the Balkan wars and the First World War, she obtained control of approximately 39 percent of Macedonia, compared to 51 percent for Greece and 10 percent for Bulgaria. As expected, Bulgaria hardly consoled herself with this arrangement, and awaited a more opportune moment to state once again her claims on Macedonia. During the Second World War she sensed that the opportunity had finally come, and she sided with Germany. But her gains in Macedonia (Yugoslav as well as Greek) proved ephemeral.

With the termination of the war, the initiative in dictating the course of Macedonian developments passed from the Bulgarians to the Yugoslavs. Under Tito, it was Yugoslavia's turn to strike for a one-sided solution to the Macedonian problem. Certainly, a major obstacle in this direction, were the pro-Bulgarian sympathies and orientation of a large segment of the population in the Yugoslav and the Bulgarian parts of Macedonia. In Greek Macedonia, the ethnological problem— acute at the time of its liberation from Ottoman rule because of the admixture of Greeks, Slavs, Moslems and Jews—had been considerably resolved during the inter-war and war years as a result of population exchanges, transfers and evictions. In Yugoslav Macedonia, a similar solution was out of the question. The expulsion of the Bulgarians would weaken dangerously the Slav majority vis-à-vis the rapidly growing Moslem Albanian population, living rather compactly in the western districts. Instead, a novel approach was chosen: a surgical-type operation for the mutation of the indigenous Slavonic inhabitants and their transformation into ethnic "Macedonians."

To transform nationally an entire population was hardly an overnight undertaking. It required imagination, talent, tenacity, and above all unquestionable authority over the region and the masses. Happily for the policymakers, these were available in abundance among the young partisans who took over the reigns of postwar federal Yugoslavia. As a starting point, they set up the framework of a state—the People's (later Socialist) Republic of Macedonia (S.R.M.)—albeit of a federative status. This was a prerequisite, in order to attain parity for the new nation with the other nations of federal Yugoslavia, and to discourage secessionist inclinations or annexationist aspirations.[4]

Next in line was the transformation of the local spoken language—usually described as a western Bulgarian dialect[5]—into a "Macedonian" literary language. This process aimed at drawing an edge and loosening the linguistic ties of the Slav-Macedonians with the Bulgarians. In a way, it resembled a similar approach introduced, in an admittedly rude way, by the interwar Yugoslav governments, which aimed not only at alienating the population of Yugoslav Macedonia from the Bulgarians, but also at opening the road to its "serbianization."[6]

The third objective was a bit embarrassing: a newly formed communist regime was called upon to sanction the establishment of a new Church. The "Autocephalous Macedonian Orthodox Church" was established by state decree over the objections of the Serbian Orthodox Patriarchate, which was the head of all the orthodox dioceses in Yugoslavia. The ecclesiastical coup broke all the canons of the Eastern Orthodox Church, and as a consequence, the "Macedonian" Church was never recognized, not only by the Serbian Patriarchate but also by all the other Orthodox Churches, including the Patriarchates of Constantinople and Moscow. Nevertheless, on the credit/debit sheet figured more prominently the fact that an independent Slav-Macedonian Church functioned and its services could be enlisted in exporting the mutation experiment among the Macedonian diaspora, where the religious feelings were particularly strong.[7]

The fourth objective was a most vital one. It aimed at a complete reinterpretation and recasting of the historical past of Macedonia. By a proper manipulation of historical facts and personages, it was expected that the material foundations of the new nation would be cemented, giving credence to the argument that the new nation did not emerge arbitrarily in 1944, but that it had a past of its own, well over 13 centuries, back to the time of the descent of the Slavic tribes on Macedonia.[8]

Finally, in order to sustain the new nation in its uphill drive, it was endowed with a messianic mission, a kind of a "great idea," similar to those that shook the Balkan nations in their nineteenth century emancipation struggles. The Slav-Macedonians' mission envisaged the future unification of the three Macedonian regions and the establishment of a Macedonian state within the Yugoslav federation.[9] In the years since the inception of the Socialist Republic of Macedonia that vision became the unifying and guiding force of Slav-Macedonian neo-nationalism. It was based primarily on the firm solidarity with the other Yugoslav peoples—in order to forestall any thought of future cessation—and it was veered to a collision course with the Bulgarians—in order to prevent a recurrence of bulgarophilism among the Slavs of the S.R. of Macedonia.[10]

The whole process was carried out with extreme care, maintaining the necessary balances. Bulgarian influences were eradicated but without stirring social upheavals or psychological traumas. The aim was to transform peacefully and, if possibly, voluntarily, all former "Bulgarians" into "Macedonians," to induct them into the family of Yugoslav nations, to keep the options open for a "final" solution of the Macedonian question, and, at the same time, to avoid armed conflicts with neighboring Bulgaria.[11]

While the mutation process went on in the interior of Yugoslavia, policymakers sought to obtain international recognition for an experiment which appeared unique for Europe. During the first postwar years—particularly during the Soviet-Yugoslav crisis—the recognition of the S.R. of Macedonia as an equal partner of the Yugoslav federation received top priority. The next step was the recognition of the Slav-Macedonian nation in its totality, including segments of it living as minorities in neighboring countries or in the diaspora. When, during the mid-1950s, relations with the Soviet Union returned back to normal and Yugoslavia gravitated toward nonalignment, the territorial integrity of federal Yugoslavia was acknowledged by the West, as well as by the Soviet bloc, and along with it, the status of the S.R. of Macedonia as an integral part of the Yugoslav federation was confirmed. This led to a *de facto* recognition of the "Macedonian" nation and language, as provided in the Yugoslav constitution. *De jure* acceptance of the "Macedonian" nation, in the wider historical and geographical context claimed by Yugoslavs, was hardly automatic.[12]

It was well understood that merely political endorsement of the mutation experiment by itself was not enough. Political expediences could well prove to be reversible. The concurrence of the international scientific community was an essential prerequisite. The novel theories, however, for the ethnogenesis of the Macedonian people, coming out of the laboratories of historical and linguistic institutes in the S.R. of Macedonia, could probably serve adequately the needs of the natives, but they were hardly convincing to impartial foreign scholars.[13]

Gradually, policymakers in Skopje began to shift their attention to faraway countries, such as Canada, U.S.A. and Australia, where large numbers of immigrants from Macedonia had settled prior and after the Second World War. They had emigrated from all three parts of Macedonia. Among them were Greek-speakers, Slav-speakers and even some Vlach-speakers. In the pre-World War II years, they had settled mostly in the United States, where they formed either Greek-Macedonian or Bulgarian-Macedonian associations and joined, respectively, the wider Greek and Bulgarian communities. No "Macedonian" communities—in the ethnic sense of the word—were recorded at the time. In the post-World War II period, new waves of immigrants, both from Greek Macedonia and the S.R. of Macedonia began to land in North America and Australia. Among those originating from Greek Macedonia were a few thousands of Slav-speakers. In terms of national affiliation they were split into Greeks and Slav-Macedonians. In the latter category were persons involved, in one way or other, in the Greek armed civil strife of the 1940s who had found it expedient to seek refuge abroad. In subsequent years, economic and/or political reasons led along the same road fortune-seekers from the S.R. of

Macedonia. There were no more immigrants from Bulgarian Macedonia. Most of the newcomers chose to dissolve into the melting pot of the countries of their adoption. Others found the new "Macedonian" national identity a rather convenient and legitimate umbrella. For the old Bulgarian-Macedonian communities the new arrivals had little liking. Although personal and financial reasons did lure a few, association with the Bulgarian name, particularly during the Cold War period, was hardly an attractive reference.[14]

It was precisely at this point—around the mid-1960s,—that the "Macedonization" process began to make its appearance felt, particularly in Canada and Australia, where the newcomers began to outnumber the prewar Bulgarian-Macedonian immigrants. To expedite and strengthen this process, authorities in the S.R. of Macedonia set out the necessary machinery for exporting to Macedonian immigrant communities the well-tried mutation experiment. A well-provided central agency for immigrants, under the name "Matitsa," was established in Skopje to coordinate all relevant activities. Priests and teachers were sent out from Skopje to administer churches and school classes conducted in the Slav-Macedonian language. In cities with large Macedonian population, the Yugoslav consuls were usually nominees of the local government in Skopje. Certainly, this patronizing by official emissaries from Yugoslavia was not without its risks. A large percentage of Slav-Macedonians, particularly among those originating from Greek Macedonia, reacted negatively to a streamlined and even enforced mutation policy. Living in multicultural societies they chose their own way, forming their own independent organizations and even churches. They considered inadequate the goal for a united Macedonian state within the Yugoslav federation. From the comfort of their adopted new countries, they could afford to dwell in illusionary grandiose schemes for a future united and independent Macedonia; independent even from Yugoslavia.[15] The mutation experiment abroad began to show signs of malfunction. The possibility of a boomerang at the foundations of the S.R. of Macedonia could not be taken lightly.

In more recent years, efforts have once again shifted internally. This time attention was focused on the Moslem inhabitants of the S.R. of Macedonia who have appropriately been named "Moslem Macedonians." These Moslems have traditionally associated themselves with either the Albanian or the Turkish ethnic communities. Over the decades, thousands of them emigrated to Turkey, affirming in a rather poignant way, their national orientation. Nevertheless, notwithstanding insurmountable difficulties, mutation policy experts in Skopje—copying ironically the bulgarization process of Moslems in Bulgaria—sought to reestablish national links between the Moslems and the Slavs of the S.R. Macedonia. They argued that today's Moslems were Slav-Macedonians converted forcibly to Islam during the first centuries of Ottoman rule. If these Moslems could be enticed to rediscover their forgotten roots, the numbers of "Macedonians" in the S.R. of Macedonia would be augmented. Certainly this new phase of the mutation policy has nothing to do with the fear of a revival of Bulgarian nationalism among the population of the republic.

Rather, it was conceived for the purpose of curtailing the menacing numerical growth of the Moslem Albanians vis-à-vis the Slavic element of the population. Whether the conversion to Macedonianism of the Moslems would meet with a similar success as the conversion of prewar Bulgarians is still very much a matter of speculation. It appears, however, that the worldwide rise of Islam, which has also affected Moslem communities in Yugoslavia, would be a tougher challenge to the mutation process than postwar discredited Bulgarian nationalism.[16]

Turning, now, to the examination of Bulgaria's reaction to the mutation process in the S.R. of Macedonia, and to Yugoslav attempts at exporting the experiment across the Yugoslav-Bulgarian border, one is struck by the fact that the Bulgarians still bend under the weight of the cross of Dimitrov's Macedonian policy. Much as the Bulgarians wish to forget it, the Yugoslavs loose no opportunity to remind them and the world, that Bulgaria's venerable leader had succeeded in compelling his Party and government to endorse Tito's solution to the Macedonian question. By that endorsement, Dimitrov had agreed not only to the transformation of the Bulgarian Macedonians into ethnic "Macedonians," but he had also consented to the unification of Bulgarian Macedonia with the S.R. of Macedonia. Today, the Bulgarians, in their effort to keep their distances from that policy without unduly marring the image of the founder of new Bulgaria, argue that the Bulgarian policy on Macedonia in 1944-1948 had been dictated by unfortunate circumstances, as Bulgaria had just come out of the war a weak, defeated country. As such, she was ruthlessly pressed by a strong Yugoslavia, pursuing at a time a hegemonistic policy in the Balkans. Nevertheless—argue the Bulgarians—even that policy had left somehow the door open for the establishment in the future of a unified Macedonian state within a South Slavic federation. Within that context and under more equitable conditions, the new state could turn gradually into a second Bulgarian state, given the Bulgarian orientation of the majority of its inhabitants.[17]

Later in the 1950s the Bulgarian policy on the Macedonian question followed rather faithfully the ups and downs of Soviet-Yugoslav relations. From the mid-1960s, however, Bulgaria pursued, with remarkable firmness, a policy which tacitly accepted the mutation experiment within the S.R. of Macedonia; rejected outright pressures for the introduction of the same experiment in Bulgarian Macedonia—and by inference in Greek Macedonia—and opposed any claims for the reinterpretation of Macedonian history in a way to justify the existence of historical roots for the "Macedonian" nation, prior to 1940.[18]

Under Todor Zhivkov, the Bulgarians opted for a policy of strict adherence to the status quo in Macedonia. In the past two decades, they turned with increased enthusiasm to developing internally a strong patriotic mentality among the Bulgarian people. Although certain manifestations of this process may bring to the Yugoslavs unpleasant reminiscenses of prewar nationalist exhaltations,[19] the shift may well be interpreted as a diversion from traditional Macedonian aspirations. Patriotic pride in ancient roots and the historical and cultural achievements of the Bulgarian people are the novel substitutes. Roots are now being searched in the glory of the ancient Thracians. According to current Bulgarian ethnogenetic dogma, the long-forgotten Thracians are considered to be one of the three constituent elements of the Bulgarian people; the other two being the Slavic and Fino-Tataric tribes, which settled the "Bulgarian lands" between the sixth and the eighth centuries A.D. For the Bulgarian historians, these "Bulgarian lands" are the regions of Moesia (north of the Balkan mountains), Thrace and Macedonia. It is interesting to note that the historical or cultural presence of the Bulgarians in the wider Macedonian region over the centuries is a popular subject not only in Bulgarian scientific treatises, but also in popular writings, radio, film productions and school textbooks. In recent years, prewar Bulgarian historiography has been enlisted to provide additional data or arguments to fit the current line.[20] Historical references to the regions or the peoples of Greek and Yugoslav Macedonia, however, are limited to the period prior to the outbreak of the Second World War. On the side, the process of the integration of all ethnic groups, or minorities, in the Bulgarian nationality has been accelerated.

To conclude, the Bulgarians, having abandoned territorial aspirations on either the Macedonian or the Thracian regions of their neighbors, have turned internally to build their defenses on two fronts: The first against the contamination of their Pirin district of Macedonia from the mutation experiment of neighboring S.R. of Macedonia; the second, against the possibility of a future emergence of Turkish nationalism among the sizeable Moslem minority.[21] So long as the internal structures in Bulgaria remain motionless, the emergence of Kossovo-type phenomena are hardly likely on either the two fronts.

Greek attitudes vis-à-vis the Yugoslav mutation experiment resemble somehow those of Bulgaria, with certain marked differences. It is well known that since the conclusion of the First World War treaties, Greece has ceased to lay claims on regions or on ethnic minorities in either Yugoslavia or Bulgaria. Following the interwar exchanges of populations with Turkey and Bulgaria, and the mass exodus of the remaining Slavs at the end of the bitter internal strifes of 1943-1949, Greece has ceased to be a protagonist in the Macedonian theater, and has contended herself to playing second fiddle. Still, Greek attitudes toward Macedonian developments are so emotional that Greeks tend either to magnify well out of proportion events or situations connected with Macedonia, or keep a discreet silence. There are reasons for this: historical, political and social.

On the historical side, wars, revolutions, foreign occupations have succeeded each other on the soil of Greek Macedonia for well over a century. A feeling of constant insecurity from the north has conditioned Greek foreign policy options for well over the first half of the twentieth century. In two world wars, parts of Greek Macedonia were overrun by the Bulgarian army, while a civil war was fought under the spectre of a possible loss of Macedonia and its annexation to a unified Macedonian state, either within federal Yugoslavia, or in a Balkan communist federation. As historical memories die hard in the Balkans, it is no wonder that large segments of the Greek public, particularly in the north, still appear oversensitive to developments concerning Macedonia.

A second, political reason affecting the attitudes of the Greek communists is a kind of "guilt complex" toward the Macedonian question. The prewar endorsement by the Greek Communist Party of Comintern's policy for a united Macedonian state within a Balkan communist federation and the adoption of a similar line again in 1949 have caused wounds within the Greek communist movement, and alienated the Party from large segments of the Greek public. Those platforms have long been abandoned and sharply criticized.[22] Nevertheless, it appears that they still haunt the Party and compel it to maneuver on a course of aloofness in Macedonian matters. This attitude seems to have the support of Party members. Moreover, it has appeased certain traditional critics on the other side of the political spectrum.[23] But this same line has come under sharp attack by Yugoslav Macedonian nationalists who would like to compromise the leadership of the KKE with the publication of documents, memoirs and treatises focusing on the Greek Party's former positions on the Macedonian question.[24]

A third reason should be sought in the Greeks' sensitivity with their conception of their historical continuity and their links with the Greeks of classical times and the medieval Byzantines. Tempering with this image is bound to stimulate almost biological reflexes. Such was, for instance, their reaction when, in the early decades of the nineteenth century, the German historian Jacob Philip Fallmerayer bluntly declared that the Greek race had disappeared from Europe and that "not a single drop of authentic and pure Greek blood ran in the veins of the Christian population of Greece."[25] Putting hematological theories aside, the Greeks reply that they have survived three multiethnic, multilingual empires (Roman, Byzantine and Ottoman), that culturally, if not physically, they succeeded in fusing into a Helleno-byzantine and Orthodox Christian cultural community of Greek- as well as alien-speaking groups which shared a common destiny and, finally, a common national identity. This thesis came under sharp challenge by emerging Balkan nationalisms in the nineteenth century. Nevertheless, wars and population migrations for well over a century, and well into the 1950s, have sufficiently cleared the picture. On the one hand, non-integrated, alien-speaking population groups, which found themselves automatically outside the newly drawn Greek state frontiers, merged with kin nationalities in Turkey, Bulgaria, Yugoslavia and Albania. On the other hand, other Christian non-Greek linguistic groups—Albanian, Slavonic, Vlach and Turkish (mainly newcomers Orthodox Christians from Asia Minor)—integrated smoothly into the Greek-speaking Orthodox Christian society which took its present form only after the Second World War and the Civil War of the 1940s. Any challenge to this dual concept (i.e. the historical continuity of the Greek nation and the actual national homogeneity of the Greek state) is bound to raise sharp reactions by almost all segments of Greek society.

Undoubtedly a fourth element which shapes Greek attitudes toward the Macedonian question is the high degree of misinformation and even ignorance of the Greeks about an issue that frequently stirs up emotions. A significant segment of the educated Greek public, including politicians, professionals, clergy and even scholars, have no accurate knowledge of developments in neighboring countries during the past forty years. The limited intercourse with Bulgaria and Yugoslavia—at least until the early 1960s and again during the military dictatorship, 1967-1974—as well as lack of knowledge of Balkan Slav languages are some of the reasons for this situation. Equally accountable, however, is the constant flow of misinformation reaching the Greek public in the form of official statements and "scholarly" publications.[26] The policy of "silence" adopted by successive postwar Greek governments, apparently in the interest of maintaining good neighborly relations, particularly with Yugoslavia, has similarly disorientated the Greek public. As a result, certain Yugoslav initiatives, aimed at disputing basic tenets of Greek Macedonian policy, have elicited cryptic statements of the type "there is no Macedonian question," or panic cries about a "permanent Slavic conspiracy against [Greek] Macedonia."[27] Both are hardly enlightening to a bewildered public.

With some detachment from press headlines, one can argue, without a great margin for error, that for Greece, the age-old Macedonian question has ceased to be an open question. National homogeneity in the region is very much a fact, not only on account of the recurring mass exoduses of the Slavic population in the course of fifty years, but also because of large-scale emigration and urbanization. Current economic, social and political conditions in Greece—and in Greek Macedonia in particular—including the state of human rights, compare favorably with those in the S.R. of Macedonia. Remarkably, Greek political parties, which differed so sharply in the past on this issue, show an unprecedented degree of concurrence vis-à-vis the Macedonian question. Greece's initiatives for Balkan cooperation and the record of friendly relations with Bulgaria for well over twenty years—the longest period in modern times for the two traditionally quarreling neighbors—have eliminated territorial or minority claims in their mutual relations. In this direction (on the elimination of territorial claims), Yugoslavia's nonaligned policy, as well as the Helsinki agreements, reaffirming the status quo of European frontiers, have equally contributed.

Having controlled their own problem, the Greeks are hardly disinterested onlookers of the Yugoslav-Bulgarian dispute, or of the Yugoslav mutation experiment. Their position on these issues, however, is rather obscure, even from a close range. Laconic official statements from time to time throw only dim light on Greek perceptions of the labyrinth of Macedonian complexities. Equally baffling are various treatises coming from the pen of journalists or historians. In the absence of an authoritative source, one could only attempt to sketch what may appear as the consensus of Greek views on the present Macedonian problem.[28]

At the outset, it appears that the Greeks reject outright the existence of a "Macedonian nation," a "Macedonian language" and even a "Macedonian republic." A more careful study of Greek views, however, would reveal that the Greeks do not dispute the existence of a nation, a language or a republic after 1944, but they rather refute the legitimacy of the appropriation of the Macedonian name for defining a Slavic population in the Balkans. For the Greeks—as for the Bulgarians—the name "Macedonian" is merely a geographical term that applies equally to any native of the wider Macedonian region, irrespective of his or her national identity. Unlike the Bulgarians, for the Greeks the name by itself is a cherished historical feature, an inseparable element of Greek cultural heritage for well over two and a half millennia. Understandably, it is highly unlikely to expect them to consent to the arbitrary appropriation of the Macedonian name by a Slavic people across their frontiers.

The controversy over the name is not limited to the literary, historical, cultural and even sentimental value attached to it by the Greeks. There are political undertones, as well. Certainly, the choice of the Macedonian name by the postwar Yugoslav regime was not coincidental. It was employed to act as a catalyst in the mutation process. By a masterful interplay of the geographical and national concepts of the term, these two concepts fused into one. In the ensuing confusion, the newly established "Macedonian" nation could rightfully stake a claim to everything *Macedonian*: i.e. everything of, or pertaining to the region of Macedonia and its inhabitants. Manipulation of historical events became easier and the history and cultural heritage of all the nationalities which passed through or still live in the wider region of Macedonia were automatically declared "Macedonian," of the Yugoslav type. Thus, Greeks, Bulgarians, Vlachs, Turks, Albanians, Jews were divested of elements of their heritage, and their presence in Macedonia—past or present—was disputed.[29]

Faced with such extreme theories, some Greeks take the view that the only true Macedonians are the Greek inhabitants of Macedonia, who are the only people entitled to bear the name. Others adopt a more conciliatory approach. They suggest that a way out of the vortex of the Macedonian name controversy could be found if all the Macedonians—i.e. all the inhabitants of Macedonia—are clearly identified as either Slav- or Yugoslav-Macedonians, Greek-Macedonians or Bulgarian-Macedonians. Thus, the name will retain its old geographical context, the ethnicity of each group of Macedonia will be more accurately identified, and misunderstandings—coincidental or intentional—will be eliminated. Once this issue is solved, conflicting views might converge. With the Yugoslavs pursuing a policy of noninterference, under any pretext, in the internal affairs of neighboring countries, and disclaiming territorial pretensions, the Greeks might find it easier to understand the mutation experiment pursued in the S.R. of Macedonia for the past forty years. On the other hand, if extremist views for transplanting the experiment across the borders or for tempering with the history and cultural heritage of neighboring peoples reflect official Yugoslav policy, the chances are that the problem, will not be easily resolved.

★ ★ ★

In summing up, the Macedonian question in our times appears to have retained the elements of a political dispute, mainly in Yugoslav-Bulgarian relations.

Nevertheless, mutual recriminations for territorial claims on the respective Macedonian provinces of the two countries are not based on an imminent or even visible danger. They rather persist because of mutual suspicions entrenched in bitter experiences of non too distant conflicts, and the awareness of Big Power rivalries which imperil carefully built balances in the Balkans. In all probability disputes over the ethnic origins and the national identity of the Slavs of Macedonia will continue.

In the course of the past forty years, Yugoslav Macedonia has witnessed—and to some extent is still witnessing—internal pressures typical of all neo-nationalistic movements, such as those of the recently emancipated peoples of Africa. In the diaspora, the "macedonianization" process did make some progress among small groups of Slav emigrants from Macedonia. Although the S.R. of Macedonia spares no efforts to keep this process under its own control and guidance, certain manifestations among Slav-Macedonian organizations, mainly in Canada and Australia, indicate that the course outlined in Skopje is not followed piously. A third road to macedonianhood calls not for federative status within Yugoslavia but for a united Macedonian state, independent even of Belgrade guardianship. The adherents of this "third road" are experimenting with their own mutation process, claiming their roots not only to the Slavic tribes of the sixth and seventh centuries A.D., but even to the "non-Greek" Macedonians of antiquity, to kings Philip and Alexander the Great, Aristotle *et al.*[30]

Looking into the future and excluding unforeseen international complications, one is tempted to argue that the future shape of the Macedonian question will mainly depend on the ability of the Yugoslav leaders—including those in Skopje—to mellow gradually the messianic effervescence and desiderata of the neo-nationalist activists within the S.R. of Macedonia, and to restrain their desire to attempt to transplant the mutation experiment across the border into Bulgarian Macedonia. Developments, however, will proceed at a pace corresponding to the degree of genuine acceptance of the mutation experiment within the S.R. Macedonia, not only by the other Yugoslav peoples, but mainly by Bulgaria.

NOTES TO APPENDIX II

1. Evangelos Kofos, *Nationalism and Communism in Macedonia* (Thessaloniki, 1964), p. 226.

2. *Makedonia, 4000 Chronia Ellinikis Istorias kai Politismou* (Ekdotiki Athinon, 1982), Chapter "Agones gia tin Apeleftherosi tis Makedonias, 1830–1912," pp. 444–484. L. S. Stavrianos, *The Balkans since 1453* (Holt, Rinehart and Winston, N.Y, 1963), pp. 517–524.

3. Ivan Mihailov, *Macedonia: A Switzerland of the Balkans* (St. Louis, 1950).

4. Evangelos Kofos, "The Making of the People's Republic of Macedonia," *Balkan Studies*, III (Thessaloniki, 1962), pp. 375–396. Also, Evangelos Kofos, *I Makedonia stin Yugoslaviki Istoriografia* (Thessaloniki, 1974), pp. 5–13.

5. Nicholas Andriotis, *The Federative Republic of Skopje and its Language*, 2nd ed. (Athens, 1966), pp. 12–18, citing various authorities on slavic languages, most of whom stress the similarities of Bulgarian and the Slav-Macedonian spoken idiom.

6. Elizabeth Barker, *Macedonia; Its Place in Balkan Power Politics* (Royal Institute of International Affairs, London, 1950), pp. 22–23. Stephen Palmer and Robert King, *Yugoslav Communism and the Macedonian Question* (Archon, Hamden, Conn., 1971), p. 12.

7. Ch. Papastathis, "L'autocéphalie de l'Eglise de la Macédoine Yugoslave," *Balkan Studies* VII, 1968, pp. 151–154. Ath. Angelopoulos, *To Aftokefalon tis "Makedonikis" Orthodoxou Ekklisias epi ti Vasei ton Apofaseon tis Ektaktou Synodou tis Ierarchias tis Servikis Orthodoxou Ekklisias* (Thessaloniki, 1968). Also, Palmer and King, *op. cit.*, pp. 165–173.

8. Dragan Taškovski, *Radjanjeto na Makedonskata Nacija* (Skopje, 1967) and Kon, *Etnogenezeta na Makedonskiot Narod* (Skopje, 1974). For a Bulgarian critical appraisal: Dimitar Kosev, "Revisionističeski Falsifikacii na Balgarska Istorija v Skopskite Istorici," *Istoričeski Pregled* (Sofia, 1959), pp. 15–44. For a Greek appraisal: Kofos, *I Makedonia. . ., op. cit.*, and by the same author, paper on "O Makedonikos Agonas sti Yugoslaviki Istoriografia," in the *Annals* of a Symposium on the Macedonian Struggle, held in Thessaloniki, in Nov. 1984. A penetrating analysis in Stefan Troebst, *Die bulgarisch-jugoslawische Kontroverse um Makedonien, 1967–1982* (München, 1983), pp. 41–92 and 151–182.

9. In a speech at Skopje on October 11, 1945, Tito declared: "We have never refused the right of the Macedonian people to be united. We will never renounce this right. This is our principle"; Kofos, *Nationalism. . . , op. cit.*, p. 152. Text was republished in a 1986 collection of documents of Yugoslav diplomatic archives and reprinted in *Borba* (6.11.1986). This principle has been echoed in various Yugoslav publications, as for example in the state publication, *Vision de la Macédoine* (Belgrade, 1973), p. 147, which refers to Greek and Bulgarian Macedonia, as "non encore libérées".

10. The Bulgarians have repeatedly complained about the anti-Bulgarian elements of the mutation policy applied in the S.R. Macedonia. See the publication of the Bulgarian Academy of Sciences, *Makedonskiot Vâpros* (Sofia, 1968) and the pamphlet of the Bulgarian Ministry of Foreign Affairs, *For All-round Development of Bulgaro-Yugoslav Relations* (Sofia, 1978).

11. Details in Palmer and King, *op. cit.*, chapter "Macedonian Nationalism under Yugoslav Communism", pp. 133–183.

12. See for example the works by Palmer and King, and Troebst already quoted.

13. An excellent analysis of this phenomenon in Troebst, *op. cit.*, chapter VI "International Historiographic Views," pp. 195–206. The author observes that while the views of Skopje are partly accepted by Western European slavists, historians are cautious towards the interpretation of history as presented by nationalist-minded Skopje historians.

14. There is a rich reservoir of literature, mainly journals and periodicals, published by various immigrant groups, or aimed at immigrants from Macedonia. One, however, should approach this material with caution given its unconcealed partiality. For the views of Bulgaro-Macedonians of North America: *Makedonska Tribuna* (an Indianapolis, Ind., newspaper). For the Bulgarian views: the journal *Rodoljubje*, formerly *Slaviani* (Sofia). Among the numerous pro-Skopje publications: the newspaper *Makedonija* (Toronto) and the journal *Iskra* (Adelaide, Australia). Also the monthly journal *Makedonija* (Skopje). Among supporters of an independent and united Macedonia are the magazines, *Makedonska Nacia* (Göteborg, Sweden) and *Glas na Makedoncite* (Kogarah, NSW, Australia). For Greek-Macedonian views: the monthly journal *Makedoniki Zoi* (Thessaloniki), and various newspapers published by Greek-Macedonian groups and organizations abroad, such as *Makedoniki Icho*, and *Patrides* (Toronto), and the *Makedonikos Logos* (Melbourne). Also various publications about the Greeks in the United States of America, Canada and Australia have valuable data for immigrants from Macedonia. Slav-Macedonians in Canada have also sponsored certain publications, such as *Brief History of the Canadian Macedonian Immigrants and their Background* (Toronto, 1980). See also the highly controversial article about "Macedonians" in the *Harvard Encyclopaedia of American Ethnic Groups* (Cambridge, Mass., 1980).

15. Articles in *Makedonska Nacia* and *Glas na Makedoncite, op. cit.*, and the Melbourne newspaper *Makedonija*.

16. *Impact International* (28.11.1986) wrote that "the aim obviously is to wean away Macedonian Muslims from their Albanian co-religionists."

17. Cola Dragojceva, "Na Klasovi i internationalisticeski pozicii," *Septemvri* (Sofia, 1979), pp. 5–80. A French version: Tsola Dragoitcheva, *La Macédoine-facteur de bon voisinage et de coopération et non de discorde; Souvenirs et réflexions* (Sofia Presse, 1979), pp. 1–108.

18. Best example illustrating this point was the publication of the Bulgarian Academy of Sciences, *Macedonia, Documents and Material* (Sofia, 1978).

19. The commemoration of historical events, particularly of the Treaty of San Stefano, gave rise to much patriotic rhetoric and, as a result, to harsh polemics from Skopje. Bulgarian marxist historians defend the San Stefano and First World War Bulgarian policies, labeling them "progressive nationalism." Troebst, *op. cit.*, pp. 166 and 183.

20. The Bulgarian views on the ancient Thracians: *Istorija na Balgarija,* I (Bulgarian Academy of Sciences, Sofia, 1979), pp. 110–273. References to the rehabilitation of pre-war bourgeois Bulgarian historians in Troebst, *op. cit.*, p. 159, 161, 179-180.

21. Amnesty International, *Bulgaria: Imprisonment of Ethnic Turks* (London, April, 1986).

22. Kofos, *Nationalism. . . , op. cit.*, pp. 197–198.

23. See: Michalis Papaconstantinou, *I Makedonia meta ton Makedoniko Agona* (Athens, 1985), pp. 17–19, 23–24, where a leading politician of the New Democracy Party departs from traditional criticsm of the KKE for "treason" on the Macedonian Question.

24. Among a number of publications: Archiv na Makedonia, *KPG i Makedonskoto Nacionalno Prashanje, 1918–1974* (Skopje, 1982.) Also *Egejska Makedonija vo Antifashističnata Vojna, 1941–1943 godina* (Skopje, 1985).

25. Recent Greek translation and comments by Constantine Romanos: Jacob Philip Fallmerayer, *Peri tis Katagogis ton Ellinon* (Athens, 1984).

26. During a flare-up of public statements and press polemics, exchanged between Yugoslavs and Greeks, in 1985–1986, certain Greek authors and journalists, writing on the subject, revealed considerable lack of insight on current affairs and policy-making in Yugoslavia, which have a direct bearing on the Macedonian controversy.

27. Frequent Greek statements that "there is no Macedonian question" indicate that there is no more basis—historical, legal, ethnological—to dispute the *status quo* in Greek Macedonia. Naturally, exaggerated claims by Skopje writers do raise an issue that has a bearing on the climate of traditionally good Greek-Yugoslav relations. On the other hand, the projection of phobias of times past to present circumstances are out of tune with reality. A former Greek Minister of northern Greece, Nicolaos Martis, in his book, *The Falsification of Macedonian History* (Athens, 1984), p. 113–114, comments: "I cannot pass in silence the complete ignorance of our people; and in particular of the intellectual, political and other leaders of our country, regarding what is happening against our historical and cultural heritage. . . .The responsible politicians and intellectuals, who had the possibility to know what is happening across the border, faced the situation phlegmatically and I would say with a certain modicum of arrogance. For the intellectuals, all these are but gross concoctions, unable to influence the most naive of humans. Why must they occupy themselves with a worthless fabrication?"

28. An enlightening short booklet by the Center for Macedonians Abroad, Society for Macedonian Studies, *Macedonia and the Macedonian Question; A Brief Survey* (Thessaloniki, 1983), pp. 1–45, presents, in a concise way, Greek views on various aspects of the Macedonian controversy.

29. *Ibid.*, pp. 42–43, and Kofos, *I Makedonia. . . , op. cit.*, pp. 14–18. For Yugoslav views on the question of the Macedonian name see: D. Taškovski, *Radjanjeto. . . , op cit.*, pp. 20, 31–32 (page references to a Greek mimeographed translation by the Institute for Balkan Studies).

30. Numerous articles in *Glas na Makedoncite, op. cit.*, and various pamphlets of self-styled organizations like "National Macedonian Revolutionary Organization," or "National Liberation Front of Macedonia" tracing the roots of the "Macedonian nation" far beyond kings Alexander and Philip to "124 years after the cataclysm," and spreading the boundaries of Macedonia all the way to Thrace and parts of Anatolia, with Constantinople—not Thessaloniki—the capital of the future Macedonian State.

NATIONAL HERITAGE AND NATIONAL IDENTITY
IN NINETEENTH- AND TWENTIETH-CENTURY MACEDONIA

Perhaps nowhere else in Europe has the heritage of the past so triggered and stimulated political developments as in the Balkans. During the period of the 'national awakening' and emancipation of the Balkan peoples, from the last decades of the eighteenth century to the early decades of the twentieth, historical legacies helped create national awareness and shape national ideology. They also sustained nations in their uphill drive toward state-building, national unification and, possibly, the reincarnation of long extinct empires.

Historical legacies constituted one of the chief factors moulding national consciousness. In the peasant societies of the Ottoman Empire, religion and language still constituted the basic ingredients for self-identification. Historical legacy, an exoteric element, had been preserved in ecclesiastical or monastic institutions and in the diaspora, and gradually emerged in urban and semi-urban centers of the Empire. Once, however, it was diffused among the masses, it caught the imagination of the people, lifted the morale of the *rayas* (subject population) and generated a messianic zeal to attain the goals of the 'imagined'[1] national mission ordained by the legacy—or glory—of the past.

As one after the other the subject peoples of the Balkans began to acquire the nucleus of their future national states—which hardly encompassed the lands and peoples claimed by each nation—the respective national ideologies, precursors of political and even armed activity, began to spread from the national state to the Ottoman provinces.[2] Soon the respective national ideologies began to converge on regions of mixed ethnological composition and, more important, of overlapping historical claims. Under such conditions, antagonistic national programs hardened attitudes and rendered impossible the drawing of future state demarcation lines by consent. Probably the most complicated case was presented by Macedonia. Located on the convergent point of four conflicting national programs—Greek, Bulgarian, Serbian and Albanian—it provided a microcosm of Balkan complexities. Its geographical delimitation was uncertain and, at best, arbitrary; its ethnological composition ambiguous; and its historical legacies open to controversial and conflicting interpretations.

Prior to the 1870s, religion and, to a lesser degree, language still determined the identity of most of the inhabitants of Macedonia. The Muslims formed roughly one third of the population but were far from being a homogeneous ethnic entity. Broadly speaking, there were three categories of Muslims. The first included the descendants of Turkish and Asiatic tribes that settled in Macedonia at the time of the conquest and subsequently; the second were Muslim Albanians; and the third were various Muslim minorities of Christian (Greek, Slav, Vlach) or Jewish origin.[3] As the Muslim religion carried power and social privileges, it dominated completely all other individual characteristics of the various Islamized groups (language, customs, historical collective memory). Only the Albanian Muslims, forming a compact group and, to a certain degree, enjoying at times considerable self-rule, were able, by the time of the Congress of Berlin in 1878, to manifest their own, distinct national orientations within the confines of the Muslim society. But their influence on Macedonian affairs was peripheral, because throughout the nineteenth century they tended to associate themselves with the Ottoman state.[4] On their part, the Islamized Balkan minorities, identified by their non-Turkish vernacular, continued to the end to remain loyal to Ottoman authority. Common historical legacies with their linguistic relatives and neighbors had faded away and been erased from the collective memory under the blanket of the teachings of the Koran. More important, the spreading of national ideologies, based as they largely were on the real or imagined historical legacies of the respective ethnic groups, could not penetrate the religious barriers among neighbors belonging to the same linguistic group.

Trying to classify the Christians of Macedonia by their national orientation was a demanding exercise. Despite the variety of languages and dialects spoken, religion continued, well after the Crimean War, to be considered the main determinant of identity. A large segment of the Christian peasant population of Macedonia owed allegiance to the Ecumenical Patriarchate of Constantinople, a religious institution which, despite its ecumenical role and its status as an institution of the Ottoman state, had not ceased to be a bearer of the Greek language and Greek Byzantine traditions. Such allegiance conveyed the impression that non-Greek-speaking groups—Slav, Vlach, Albanian—were automatically identifiable as Greek. Thus, when the institutions of the newly formed modern Greek state (consuls, schools, army) assumed the initiative to spread the Greek national ideology to Greek- and non-Greek-speaking inhabitants of Macedonia, they found fertile ground, cultivated by the institutions of the Church. Another positive agent was the vivid memory of the fairly recent participation of polyglot communities of Macedonian Christians in the Greek War of Independence. Their involvement in the Greek liberation movement—both during the War of Independence and in subsequent Greek secret revolutionary preparations and actual uprisings (1839-40, 1856, 1868 and 1878)—had enhanced the solidarity of the multilingual communities of Macedonia with the goals of Greek national ideology.[5]

Meanwhile, in the Greek kingdom, where nationalism and the vaguely defined 'Great Idea' assumed the form of mass psychosis, the ethnological peculiarities of Macedonia were simplistically appraised in terms of Church affiliation and active participation in the Greek liberation struggles. Thus, almost all the Christian populations were grouped within the context of a broadly defined multilingual Greek nationality. Although there were valid grounds for such classification in southern Macedonian regions and urban centers, or among certain linguistic groups (most clearly the Vlachs), in the interior and particularly in the mostly Slavonic northern third of Macedonia, the penetration of Greek national ideology was a slow and uncertain process.

By the 1860s, however, new influences, which ran counter to Greek aspirations, began to sweep the province. For one, the reforms introduced in the Ottoman Empire after the Crimean War *(tanzimat)* extended the opportunity for self-assertion to other ethnic groups not necessarily content with being represented by institutions of the Ecumenical Patriarchate. In the Macedonian countryside reaction to economic and social injustices turned the Slavophone peasants against not only the Ottoman administrators but, at times, against the higher clergy. Since in most Macedonian dioceses the latter were usually Greek, social cleavages also assumed an ethnic content. Undoubtedly, this trend, more pronounced in the Bulgarian provinces on both sides of the Balkan mountain range, gradually filtered into the predominantly Slavonic northern zone of Macedonia. In this it was assisted by the shift of Russian patronage, after the Crimean War, from Christian Orthodoxy to the Slav Christians.[6]

When the Greek–Bulgarian ecclesiastical dispute broke out in the 1860s, leading to the establishment of a Bulgarian national church in 1870, in the mixed regions of Macedonia it was transformed into a national confrontation between Greeks and Bulgarians. Here, again, this confrontation, despite its severity in certain localities, was a slow process. It took almost a generation for the new Bulgarian national ideology to spread, over pre-existing layers of church affiliation, language and undigested national ideologies, through the northern and central zones of Macedonia.

The content of Bulgarian national ideology and, for that matter, the mechanism for its dissemination showed similar patterns with Greek nationalism and, indeed, with that of the other Balkan national creeds. There were also certain remarkable differences. In all cases, however, a common denominator for building and strengthening national ideology was the 'myth', or perception, of the respective nation's historical heritage.

With the establishment of the modern Greek state in 1830, Greek national ideology developed on the basis of national continuity. It stressed classical Greek roots but also traced, from Byzantium, through *Turkokratia,* to Independence, the survival of the Greek nation, the Greek language, Greek customs and, of course, the Greek Orthodox religion.[7] In Macedonia, however, emphasis was focused on two important, specific points. The first centered on the grandeur of ancient Macedonia and the saga of Alexander the Great. The magnetism of the great king, his achievements and the name of the Macedonians had been stimulants of Greek national ideology in Macedonia even before the Greek War of Independence;[8] during the period of the Enlightenment, Greeks of Macedonia, both locally and in the diaspora, carried the Macedonian name as an additional testimony of their Greekness.[9] As yet there was no challenge to the view that the ancient Macedonians were Greeks, and that the Greek inhabitants of Ottoman-held Macedonia were the only bona fide ethnic group entitled to bear the Macedonian name. These modern *Makedones* took pride in claiming descent from kings Philip and Alexander, just as eighteenth-century Athenian villagers traced their 'imagined' lineage from Themistocles and Pericles.

The extraordinary revival of Hellenic names, particularly those of ancient Macedonian origin, which were given to children, to cultural clubs and even to towns (Edessa in lieu of Vodena, Monastir in lieu of Bitola) indicates how strongly the heritage of the past conditioned nationalist manifestations.[10] Interest in archaeological research in Macedonia was not limited to trained archaeologists or historians, but caught the imagination of local teachers, priests and professional people. In 1896 the monumental work by M. Dimitsas, an Ohrid philologist, appeared under the appropriate title *I Makedonia en Lithois Fthengomenois kai Mnimeiois Sozomenois* [Macedonia in Speaking Stones and Surviving Monuments].[11] The product of years of laborious library and field work from one end of Macedonia to the other, this book stimulated among Greeks interest and pride in their national roots, as well as a sense of legal ownership of the land with the hidden testimonies of its Greekness. It is no wonder that nationalist literature of the period made repeated references to ancient ruins and Greek inscriptions to prove the Hellenic origins of Macedonians.[12]

As education spread further into non-Greek-speaking communities, the Alexander saga captivated their imagination too. Seeking to identify themselves with the glory of the ancient Macedonians, they associated themselves with classical Hellas. It is not surprising that in the latter part of the nineteenth century, when, mainly in the central zone of Macedonia, Greek and Bulgarian ideologies competed for the loyalties of Slav-speaking communities, Greek educators and propagandists published and circulated the popular story of Alexander's life in the local Slav dialect, but in Greek script.[13]

Historical geography was similarly employed to determine ethnological boundaries as perceived by the competing national ideologies. Macedonia, a land of ill-defined and rather arbitrary geographical delimitation, was easy prey to manipulation by geographers, historians and politicians. Until the 1870s it was customary among Greeks to claim, on historical grounds, the entire geographical region of Macedonia as far north as the Shar Mountains. Subsequently, the emergence of the Bulgarian national movement—and to a lesser extent Serbian activities—made necessary a more realistic approach. Indeed, Macedonian ethnography differed remarkably from region to region. Excluding the Muslims, three zones could be roughly identified. The northern zone, bordering on Serbia and the Bulgarian principality, extended over one third of the entire geographical area of Macedonia and was inhabited by Slav-speaking populations of either Bulgarian or Serbian orientation. The southern zone, bordering on Thessaly (annexed to the

Greek kingdom after 1881), had a distinct Greek-speaking population. The central zone, however, was an ethnically mixed region of Greek, Slav and, to a lesser extent, Vlach-speaking Christians. Their national orientation varied from one locality to another. In terms of national identity, Slav speakers could invariably be split into Greek, Bulgarian or Serb factions, even within the same village community.[14]

Such political realities curtailed earlier, excessive Greek claims to the northern zone. Greek historians came forward with more plausible theories concerning the historical boundaries of ancient Macedonia. Conveniently, these boundaries followed a west-east line from Lake Ohrid - Prilep - north of Monastir - Strumnitsa - Nevrokop - Nestos (Mesta) River. By coincidence or design, these northern limits corresponded almost perfectly with the northern boundary of the central zone.[15] The Greeks could thus argue that the political and cultural heritage of Macedonia, the historical geography of the region, and the Macedonian name all justified their aspirations to both the southern and the central zone.

The second pillar of Greek national ideology was the legacy of the Byzantine Empire. Quite apart from the traditional view of the advocates of the 'Great Idea' that the modern Greek state was destined to act as a nucleus for a resurrected Byzantium, in Macedonia the medieval multiethnic, multilingual empire had a particular attraction. Prior to the appearance of Bulgarian, Serb and even Romanian national ideologies in Macedonia, the Byzantine tradition of multiethnic societies and empires had been popular among Balkan Greeks. It had found its expression in Rigas Ferraios's dream of a Balkan federation. It was no coincidence that a significant number of Rigas's disciples were Macedonian Greeks of the central European diaspora. Understandably, the Greeks expected to play the leading role in their visionary federation or empire. Much as Alexander's campaigns had resulted in the multinational Hellenistic states of the *diadochoi,* spreading Greek culture and language over most of the Balkans and the Near East, and much as the Eastern Roman empire had evolved into a Greek Byzantine society, so their visionary state was able to embrace other ethnic groups who were willing to share Greek language and culture. These romantic visions of the late eighteenth century and the early decades of the nineteenth gave way to more practical considerations as national states emerged in the Balkans. Nevertheless, in Macedonia, Greek national ideology continued to be preoccupied with such considerations down to the early years of the twentieth century. The fact that a significant number of Slav speakers in the central zone of Macedonia, most of the Vlach-speaking communities, and the scattered Christian Albanian villages had opted for the Greek Orthodox Patriarchate and Greek education was an encouraging sign to the Greeks that Greek national ideology stood a good chance of being adopted by the majority of the Christian population of central and southern Macedonia.[16]

A third historical weapon in the arsenal of Greek ideology emerged after the Bulgarian ecclesiastical schism. It related exclusively to Macedonia and, to a lesser extent, southern Thrace. For almost a quarter of a century since 1870, the contest between Greeks and Bulgarians in Macedonia over the Slav-speaking inhabitants had developed on the basis of ecclesiastical loyalties. Opting for the Bulgarian Exarchate, particularly in the absence of physical coercion by armed bands, was sufficient evidence of Bulgarian national identity. Greek nationalists, fearing that the neutral, ecumenical and non-racist approach of the Ecumenical Patriarchate could not serve their needs for national polarization, sought to Hellenize the institution of the Church. To them it was not enough that the language of the liturgy was Greek and the clergy Greek speakers. The Orthodox faith—the only 'true' faith—and the Church—with all its saints—must acquire a distinct and convincing Greek identity. The peasants of Macedonia, by remaining loyal to the Patriarchate, would accordingly continue to be listed as 'true' believers, while simultaneously being ushered into the 'cherished' world of Greek national ideology.[17]

Thus the legacies of Hellenic—and Hellenistic—Macedonia, of the medieval Byzantine Empire and the traditions of the Greek Orthodox Church, all contributed to rendering Greek national ideology adaptable to the unique requirements of nineteenth-century Macedonia. In order to spread this ideology and at the same time cope with the Bulgarian challenge (and to a lesser extent with that of Serbian and Romanian ideologies), the Greeks employed all traditional means at their disposal: schools, cultural associations, the press, and distinguished personalities. In doing so, however, they were exposed to contradictory signals emanating from the two centers of Hellenism: the irredentist, revolutionary nationalism of the capital of the independent Greek state, and the conservative, evolutionary ecumenicism of the Constantinople-based hierarchy of the subject Greeks. This strain was clearly manifested in the uneasy, and at times polemical, relations between Greek consuls and bishops in the dioceses of Macedonia. Consular dispatches to the Athens government and bishops' reports to the Constantinople Patriarchate provide ample evidence of the two different approaches. It was only at the turn of the century, when the ecclesiastico-educational contest between Greeks and Bulgarians developed into armed struggle between opposing bands, that the Church's evolutionary approach was subjected to the requirements of militant national ideology.[18]

Bulgarian national ideology, a latecomer in Macedonia, had to strive against difficult odds in its effort to implant in the Slav-speaking inhabitants of Macedonia a Bulgarian historical legacy over a well-embedded Greek layer. Father Paisii's appeal to Bulgarians, late in the eighteenth century, to be proud of their name, of their kings and patriarchs and, in short, to stop falling prey to Greek cultural 'imperialism', did not spread to Macedonia before the 1870s.[19] Even then, the process was slow. As a result Bulgarian national ideology tried to utilize the linguistic affinities and the social and economic grievances of the Slav speakers of Macedonia in order to lead, under the Bulgarian flag, the oppressed and backward peasant masses against the Ottoman regime. Bulgarian national ideology would be transplanted—or 'revived'—more effectively within the context of a popular social mobilization than by indigestible theories about the Bulgarian historical heritage of the Macedonian Slavs.

There were strong voices dissenting from this approach. The leaders of the

Bulgarian Exarchate in particular, lay and clergy alike, much as they had struggled, mainly on national grounds, to attain their independence from the Ecumenical Patriarchate, were reluctant to opt for revolutionary initiatives. Whilst true disciples of Bulgarian national ideology, they favored an evolutionary process on the grounds that if the Slav-speaking population of Macedonia embraced Bulgarian national ideology, then Bulgaria could rightfully claim, and obtain, Macedonia at an opportune moment without risking an armed struggle. Consequently, in their minds, education and the Church were the most appropriate vehicles for instilling a Bulgarian national consciousness in the uninitiated or 'derailed' Macedonian Slavs. If that course were adopted, then a strong case for the Bulgarian historical presence and heritage in Macedonia could be made.[20]

The historical element, in the context of the Bulgarian national ideology, served a double purpose: it strengthened racial pride and cohesiveness, and rallied opposition to the Greeks. The Greeks, as well as the oppressive Turks, were viewed as enemies of the Bulgarians. Macedonia was portrayed as the cradle, from medieval times, of the Bulgarian nation and culture. Emphasis was placed on the fact that Tsar Samuel's empire had its capital in Ohrid. Since Bulgarian, like Greek, national ideology fostered a vision of the reincarnation of medieval imperial legacies, Macedonia rightfully held a pivotal role in the realization of this dream. The Greeks were seen in the traditional role of oppressors of the Bulgarian people. Starting from the premise that the Byzantine Empire belonged to the heritage of the Greeks, Bulgarian nationalists sought to ignite a sense of revenge for evils suffered centuries earlier; references to Emperor Basil II, the 'Bulgar slayer', were particularly poignant.[21]

In the sphere of cultural legacies, Bulgarian national ideology held that the Byzantine apostles to the Slavs, Constantine (Cyril) and Methodius—the two Greek brothers from Thessaloniki sent by the Byzantine emperor to Moravia to spread Christianity, and who in the process invented the Slavic 'Cyrillic' script—were Bulgarians. Disregarding the civilizing mission of Byzantium to the Slav world, Bulgarian national ideology sought to appropriate not only the nationality of the two brothers but also their achievements.[22] Thus, the nineteenth-century Bulgarian *vâzrazdanje* (renaissance) could trace glorious roots to medieval times. That these roots were found in Thessaloniki, first city of Macedonia, added more strength to Bulgarian claims on the region.

The delicate issue of the ecclesiastical schism raised considerable obstacles to the spreading of Bulgarian national ideology among the conservative Slav-speaking Christian peasants. Indeed, until the appearance of armed Bulgarian bands in Macedonia late in the nineteenth century, the Bulgarian Exarchate met with considerable difficulty in convincing the masses to abandon their allegiance of many centuries to the Patriarchate and shift their loyalties to the Exarchate. As a result, exarchists had to resort to historical arguments to sustain the legality of their initiative to form an independent church. The Bulgarian Exarchate was presented not simply as a state church of the Bulgarian principality, but as the successor to the

Archdiocese of Ohrid, which had been abolished in 1767. Its semi-independent jurisdiction over most of the dioceses of Macedonia rendered it—in the eyes of Bulgarian nationalists—a Bulgarian ecclesiastical institution. Therefore, they argued, the Exarchate which emerged in 1870, far from being schismatic and anticanonical, was an institution which affirmed the continuity of the presence of the Bulgarian nation in Macedonia.[23]

In the Greek-Bulgarian contest over the validity of their respective historical titles to Macedonia, the Greek claim to the heritage of the ancient Macedonians was the most difficult for the Bulgarians to counter. Propagandists, taking certain liberties with history, even sought to establish a Bulgarian connection with Alexander the Great.[24] More important, however, was the controversy over the Macedonian name. The Greeks bore it with pride, fancying themselves the direct descendants of Alexander's generals. Later in the nineteenth century, the name *Makedontsi* was used to distinguish the Bulgarians of Macedonia from those of the Bulgarian principality and the Adrianople *vilayet*. The Macedonian name acquired a distinct geographical connotation, defining all the inhabitants of Macedonia. The Greeks called themselves *Makedones,* the Bulgarians *Makedontsi,* and the Vlachs *Macedoneni.* Gladstone's much-quoted phrase, "Macedonia to the Macedonians," clearly referred to all the inhabitants of Macedonia irrespective of creed or ethnic origin, not to an imagined 'Macedonian' ethnic group.[25]

Gradually, the emergence of the 'Macedonian Question' as a problem of European concern drew the attention of diplomats and journalists to the plight of *Macedonians,* the name by which foreigners came increasingly to identify native-born Bulgarians of Macedonia in order to distinguish them from Bulgarians of the Bulgarian state. Such identification became particularly necessary when the Bulgarian Macedonian revolutionaries openly opposed schemes for direct annexation of Macedonia to Bulgaria and proceeded to develop their own political program for an autonomous Macedonian state. This Macedonian autonomist movement had been prompted by political and social considerations and in no way involved a reappraisal of national ideology. A few years later, during the Balkan wars of 1912-1913 and World War I, the Bulgarian Macedonian revolutionaries put aside their autonomist slogans and actively joined the ranks of the Bulgarian army to fight for the liberation of Macedonia from Ottoman rule and its unification with the Bulgarian 'fatherland'.[26] However, the legacy of the Macedonian name was destined to play an important role in Balkan politics when the Macedonian question reemerged, during World War II, in an entirely different form.

The turn-of-the-century Macedonian imbroglio was not simply a Greek-Bulgarian feud, for Bulgarian and Greek aspirations were challenged by two outsiders: the Serbian and Romanian national ideologies. Their presence in Macedonian affairs was felt mainly after the Congress of Berlin (1878) although early manifestations were visible in the preceding decade.

The Serbian challenge to the Bulgarian national ideology was directed at the Slavonic population of the northern zone of Macedonia. Like the Bulgarians, the

Serbs resorted to medieval historical legacies. Projecting the rather vague geographical name of 'Old Serbia', they sought to substantiate their territorial claims—to Kossovo, the Sanjak of Novi Bazar and the central and northern zones of Macedonia—by reference to Stefan Dušan's medieval empire. Intellectuals and scholars were engaged in tracing the Serbian origins of historical figures and institutions hitherto claimed by the Bulgarians as their own. The Slav-speaking inhabitants of Macedonia were summarily classified as Serbs. By the end of the century, the diffusion of Serbian national ideology among the Slavonic peasant masses of northern Macedonia had met with only limited success. As a result, Serbian nationalists changed their tactics by propounding the novel theory that the inhabitants of Macedonia were not Bulgarians but Macedonian Slavs related to the Serbs. Whatever the political merits of this maneuver, the 'imagined' new nationality was nothing more than the product of academic and political laboratories, with little, if any, support in the field.[27] Although the Serbs quickly reverted to more traditional theories concerning the 'pure' Serbian ancestry of the Slav speakers of Macedonia, the short-lived tinkering with a nebulous Macedonian Slav national identity proved, in a sense, a precursor of similar theories which emerged during World War II.

The Romanian involvement in Macedonian affairs was even more complex. The Latin connection between the Romanian language and the dialect spoken by the Vlachs of Macedonia, Epirus and Thessaly had generated lively interest among scholars and politicians in the ethnic affinities between these Balkan nomads and the Latinophone populations north of the Danube. When the proponents of Romanian national ideology sought new avenues for cultural and even territorial expansion, the Vlachs appeared a logical outlet, despite the absence of geographical proximity.

It is beyond the scope of this study to trace the various theories about the origins of the Vlachs and their alleged connection with the Romanian nation. What matters is the fact that during the last three decades of the nineteenth century Romanian nationalists vigorously endeavored to challenge the long-entrenched association of the Vlachs with the Greek national ideology. This association had developed over the centuries, as a result of common religion, education and suffering, and had been cemented by the Vlachs' active participation in the Greek national liberation movement. Urbanized and semi-urbanized Vlachs had been the vanguards of Hellenism in their communities, particularly in areas where the Slavonic element was dominant. Nomadic Vlachs were counted upon to provide the backbone of Greek insurrectionary movements in Macedonia.[28]

Nevertheless there did exist certain marked exceptions. Just as Bulgarian national ideology had succeeded in eroding and finally transforming the formerly Greek orientation of a segment of the Slav-speaking population of Macedonia, so Romanian national ideology penetrated certain Vlach communities of Macedonia, Epirus and Thessaly. Following paths well trodden by Greeks, Bulgarians and Serbs, Romanian nationalist activity in Vlach settlements employed techniques and institutions such as schools, churches, political activities and guerrilla bands. Proponents of Romanian ideology naturally sought to create a counterpoise to the Greek theory of the Vlachs' Greek origin by insisting upon the common origins, and stressing the linguistic affinities, of Romanians and Vlachs. As a result, the Greek-Romanian contest over the Vlach population of Macedonia developed on the basis of histori-cal/cultural heritage versus linguistic affinities. Given the relatively high level of social and cultural development of most Vlach communities, the success of the Romanian national ideology among the Macedonian Vlachs remained marginal. By the turn of the century, Vlach communities, converted to the Romanian national ideology, were granted by the Ottoman government official recognition as a sepa-rate ethnic group (millet).[29] The decision was prompted by political considerations, particularly the Ottoman government's need to curtail Greek nationalist activity in Macedonia and keep the Balkan Christians divided.

The first decade of this century was for Macedonia the testing period for the conflicting national ideologies of the nineteenth century. Political, cultural and reli-gious rivalries gave way to armed conflicts between rival nationalities (Greeks against Bulgarians, Bulgarians against Serbs, Romanian-oriented Vlachs against Greeks). The five-year 'Macedonian Struggle' (1903-1908), much as it undermined Ottoman authority in Macedonia, was primarily a fratricidal struggle among the subject Balkan Christians. In conditions of extreme violence, physical survival fre-quently took precedence over national ideology, particularly in the ethnologically mixed central zone. Under threat of imminent extermination by rival armed bands, entire village communities rapidly changed national allegiances which had been shaped, painstakingly, over decades. The long, laborious process of nation-building had given way to the show of arms, which proved to be a more efficient method for serving Greek, Bulgarian and Serbian state-building needs. The Balkan wars of 1912-1913 led to the eviction of the Turks from Macedonia and confirmed the superiority of force over ideological conversion.

Greece annexed a little over 50 percent of the Macedonian region, including the southern and most of the central zones. This roughly corresponded to the assumed territory of ancient Macedonia. Consequently, the Greeks were able to pose not only as legitimate heirs to the heritage and name of the ancient Macedonians, but also as the legal possessors of their ancient land (except for a nar-row zone north of the new Greek-Serbian and Greek-Bulgarian frontier). Greek territorial aspirations were thus fulfilled, while the tenets which, throughout the nineteenth century, had shaped Greek national identity in Macedonia appeared to have been justified.

This was not the case with the Bulgarians. The northern, mainly Slavonic half of Macedonia was partitioned among the Slavic contenders, Serbia and Bulgaria, in a proportion of four to one: that is, in inverse ratio to their actual ethnological strength. Bulgarian claims to the whole of Macedonia had been shattered by their defeat in the Second Balkan War (1913). Bitterness at the loss of the coveted province was accentuated by the amputation of the 'imagined' historical heritage. Not only had they failed to resurrect the medieval Bulgarian empire, but they were obliged to accept the passing of Ohrid, Tsar Samuel's capital, under the sceptre of the king of the Serbs.

Following the sharing out of Macedonia during and after the Balkan wars, World War I and its aftermath initiated revolutionary changes that reshaped the ethnological pattern in the three Macedonian provinces. In Greek Macedonia, the mass exchange of populations with Turkey resulted in the exodus of all the Muslim inhabitants, and their replacement by an even larger number of Greeks from Asia Minor, Serbian Macedonia and Bulgaria. In Serbian Macedonia, old theories about a separate Slav Macedonian ethnic group had been forgotten. The Macedonian name now disappeared, while an influx of Serbian settlers assisted the spread of state national ideology. Finally, in Bulgarian Macedonia, the Bulgarian Macedonian population was increased by the arrival of Slav refugees from Greece.[30]

In contrast to the Ottoman period, when all subject Christians were exposed to competing national ideologies, during the interwar years each of the three parts of Macedonia followed the destiny of the relevant Balkan country. The dominance of state national ideology was complete, expediting integration of all population elements into its respective society. In Serbian (subsequently Yugoslav) Macedonia, integration met serious problems. The 'Serbianizing' process aimed not at a small alien minority but at the majority of the population; as a result, peaceful conversion through reeducation frequently gave way to more coercive practices. In Greek Macedonia, the small number of Slav speakers who remained (approximately 100,000, i.e. under 10 percent of the Greek native and refugee population) were treated as Greek Slavophones and offered no resistance to their integration into Greek society. As noted above, a sizeable segment of this population group had identified itself with Greek national ideology during the formative decades of the nineteenth century. The introduction of compulsory methods of assimilation by the Metaxas dictatorship, just prior to World War II, merely alienated non-assimilated Slavophones from the Greek state. At the same time, in the Pirin Macedonian district of Bulgaria, interwar Bulgarian governments found themselves repeatedly compelled to resort to punitive measures in order to control the increasingly restless Bulgarian Macedonians. Unlike, however, in Serbian Macedonia, national identity caused no problem in Bulgarian Macedonia. Agitation was motivated mainly by political desiderata such as the annexation of the Greek and Serbian parts of Macedonia to Bulgaria, or the establishment of an autonomous (Bulgarian) Macedonian state.[31]

During the closing years of the interwar period, Bulgarian identity became a liability in Serbian Macedonia. To avoid unnecessary harassment, those affected took refuge in an ethnically 'neutral' Macedonian identity. This was also true in certain marginal cases in Greek Macedonia. In Bulgarian Macedonia, autonomist opponents of the Sofia government similarly projected their regional, Macedonian identity over their Bulgarian, national one.[32] This tendency towards regional self-identification was further assisted by the newly introduced Macedonian policy of the Comintern. The platform adopted by the international communist movement, and endorsed by the Balkan communist parties, called for the establishment of a united and independent Macedonian state within the framework of a Balkan communist federation. Initially, reference in Comintern documents to 'Macedonians', i.e. to citizens of the future Macedonian republic, had merely a geographical content. Gradually, however, the name acquired a national meaning that applied to Slav speakers.[33] Thus, in communist jargon, the Macedonian name began, for the first time, to identify a specific ethnic group. The Greek Communist party, however, aware of the Greek legacy of the term *Makedones,* chose the more suitable term of *Slav-Macedonians,* in order to differentiate the Slavophones from the rest of the *Makedones,* namely the Greeks of Macedonia.[34] It was evident that the choice of this compound appellation defined, by its first component, a national affinity, and by its second, the regional origin of the inhabitants of Macedonia. Thus, on the eve of World War II, the Macedonian name once again came into prominence.

During the war, Bulgaria was allowed by Nazi Germany to occupy and administer most of Yugoslav Macedonia, as well as Greek Eastern Macedonia and Thrace. A resurgence of pro-Bulgarian sympathies among the inhabitants of Yugoslav Macedonia (and a segment of Slavophones in Greece) was short-lived. The burden of occupation, despite the initial euphoria, proved counterproductive to the survival of Bulgarian national ideology in the occupied regions.[35] With the termination of the war, the initiative in dictating the course of Macedonian developments passed from the Bulgarians to the Yugoslavs. A major obstacle in enforcing a one-sided Yugoslav solution was the pro-Bulgarian feeling and orientation of a large segment of the population of Yugoslav Macedonia. An expulsion of Bulgarian Macedonians to Bulgaria, however, would weaken the Slav majority of the region vis-à-vis the rapidly growing Muslim Albanian population. The chosen solution was a 'surgical' operation, or more accurately a 'mutation': the transformation of the native Slavonic inhabitants, whatever their national orientations, into ethnic 'Macedonians'.[36]

The mutation process was no easy undertaking. It required imagination, talent, tenacity and, above all, the unquestionable authority of the state. Happily for the nation-builders, these elements were available in abundance among the young partisans who took up the reins of postwar federal Yugoslavia. To turn vision into reality, they endeavored to endow their creation, the 'Macedonian' nation, with the necessary ingredients: an easily identifiable name; a federative 'Macedonian' state; a separate 'Macedonian' language; an autocephalous 'Macedonian' church; a unique 'Macedonian' history; and a messianic 'Macedonian' mission or 'Great Idea'.[37]

As already shown, the Macedonian *name* (Makedontsi) had been widely used by the Slavs of Macedonia to denote their regional identity. Given the political conditions at the time—a defeated and discredited Bulgaria and an emerging Yugoslav federation of equal nationalities—the transformation from 'region' to 'nation' was received locally with minimal opposition. Family names with Bulgarian -ev or -ov endings, or Serbian -ic endings, were converted to the purer 'Macedonian' -ovski or -evski. Members of other non-Slavonic groups, such as the Vlachs, also found it prudent to 'Macedonize' their names.[38]

The People's (later Socialist) Republic of Macedonia, one of the six republics of Federal Yugoslavia, emerged as an equal partner in the company of formerly dominant Serbia and Croatia. The republican state organs, despite their limitations, provided sufficient leverage and authority for the growth of a separate 'Macedonian' bureaucracy, an essential element for the legitimacy of any state entity. Historical legitimacy was sought in the legacy not of Alexander's Macedonian state but in Tsar Samuel's medieval empire, which was projected as the precursor of the People's Republic of Macedonia. The 'Macedonian' language was constitutionally elevated to the rank of one of the federation's three official languages, even though the process of its purification from Bulgarian connections was not yet complete. The transformation of a spoken, Bulgarian-related, dialect into a separate Slav-Macedonian literary language was not an overnight operation. Although linguists may argue endlessly as to the merits and success of this linguistic mutation, the officially decreed change, and the prestigious status of the new language within the federation, expedited the process whereby ties were severed with Bulgarian-speaking people. Here again, historical legacies were evoked to provide the new language with legitimacy. Old Church Slavonic, allegedly based on Slavonic dialects spoken by Slavic tribes in the Thessaloniki region, was christened 'Old Macedonian'. Thus, the newly constructed literary language of the People's Republic of Macedonia acquired, at a stroke, historical roots and unequalled prestige as the basis for the first Slavonic script.[39]

On another level, the uncanonical establishment of an autocephalous 'Macedonian' Orthodox Church, again by government decree and over the objections of the Serbian Patriarchate, helped break the spiritual ties that connected the Slavs of Macedonia with the Serbian nation. The government was certainly not aiming to better serve the spiritual needs of believers in a newly established communist state. However, a separate church, despite its marginal role in domestic developments, proved a successful carrier of the mutation process abroad, among the Macedonian diaspora. The roots of the 'Autocephalous Macedonian Orthodox Church' were traced to the former Archdiocese of Ohrid, properly acclaimed progenitor of the newly independent Church of Skopje.[40]

The 'Great Idea' of the new nation was patterned on the Italian Risorgimento. It emerged as a belated twentieth-century version of similar visionary schemes concocted by all Balkan peoples during their nineteenth-century national liberation struggles. It envisaged the future unification of the three Macedonian regions—irrespective of their actual ethnological composition—in a single Macedonian state within the Yugoslav federation. Despite its romantic overtones in a epoch characterized by hard realism, this messianic idea aimed to sustain the newly sanctioned nation in its uphill drive towards self-assertion and world recognition.[41] The most delicate operation, vital for the success of the experiment, was the reinterpretation and recasting of Macedonia's history in a way that would give credence to the new nationality and provide viable foundations to face the challenge that lay ahead.[42]

The moulding of the 'Macedonian' nation in the Socialist Republic of

Macedonia involved combining features of the nineteenth-century national revival of the Serbs, Bulgarians, Greeks and Albanians with aspects of the Marxist interpretation of history. Twentieth-century Yugoslav Macedonian historians, educators and politicians were asked to cope with the reversal of established interpretations of Macedonian heritage among the existing Balkan nationalities: Greeks, Bulgarians, Serbs and, marginally, Albanians and Romanians. Yugoslav historians, far from working in a vacuum, were accordingly compelled from the outset to create an entirely novel historical framework. Within it, they searched for a scientific justification of the newly emerged nation which bore the renowned Macedonian name.

Whatever scientific credentials were missing from such an enterprise were more than compensated for by the political and social conditions prevailing in Yugoslavia and the Balkans after the end of World War II. In the first place, the formerly pro-Bulgarian inhabitants of Yugoslavia had already distanced themselves from Bulgaria as a reaction against Bulgarian repression during the Occupation. Secondly, both defeated Bulgaria and strife-torn Greece lacked the power and prestige to challenge the Macedonian initiatives of Tito's Yugoslavia. The iron fist authority exercised by the Communist party of Yugoslavia over the Socialist Republic of Macedonia gave a free hand to Yugoslav Macedonian historiographers, who could labor with equal ease in the annals of history and the world of fantasies. Their task was to formulate, a posteriori, the historical justification for the political edifice of the 'Macedonian' nation, and the sustaining inspiration for future generations of 'Macedonians'.

It is possible to identify three main purposes in Yugoslav Macedonian revisionist historiography: first, to purge the history of Macedonia and its peoples of their Bulgarian association and their Greek, Serbian, Turkish and Albanian connections; second, to apply a 'Macedonian' coating to thirteen centuries of political, social and cultural history, thereby legitimizing a claim to direct descent from the early Slavic tribes which settled in Macedonia during the sixth and seventh centuries; and third, to secure, exclusively for the Slavs of Macedonia, the Macedonian name.

Yugoslav Macedonian historians were careful to avoid the temptation to claim continuity from the Macedonians of antiquity. The danger of allowing an illustrious period of Macedonian history to remain Greece's heritage spurred them, however, to contest the Greek affiliation of the ancient Macedonians. Instead they experimented with various theories, identifying the ancient Macedonians with the Illyrians, or presenting them as a separate, autochthonous race somewhere between the Illyrians and the Thracians. Recorded Greek influences were interpreted as importations from the Greek city-states of the south or the Greek colonies of Chalkidiki. The Macedonian monarchs and their entourage were seen as Hellenic converts, with the population at large remaining Macedonian, i.e. non-Greek. Nevertheless, Yugoslav Macedonian historiographers saw the need for their own 'Macedonian' nation to acquire bonds with antiquity. They engineered the theory that the Slav arrivals, a full millenium after the 'golden' period of Macedonia, exterminated part of the native population and subsequently mixed with the survivors. In this somewhat oversimplified ethnogenetic process, the *Macedonian Slavs,* by their intermarriage with the relics of the *Ancient Macedonians,* offered twentieth-century *Yugoslav 'Macedonians'* the missing link in the lineage from kings Philip and Alexander and the Macedonian-born philosopher Aristotle.[43]

The main aim of Yugoslav Macedonian historiography, however, was the reduction, if not the eclipse, of the Bulgarian presence in Macedonian history, and the portrayal of whatever Bulgarian activity *was* recorded in Macedonia as hostile to the Macedonian people. Starting with the 'Macedonianization' of Tsar Samuel and his empire, all those political, cultural and even military achievements in Macedonia which hitherto had been associated with the Bulgarians were claimed as 'Macedonian'.

In recent years, the Ottoman period has been more extensively researched for further evidence in support of the origins of the 'Macedonian' nation. The emphasis, however, remains focused on the nineteenth century, when the Bulgarian renaissance began to infiltrate into Macedonia. Within a generation it matured into a national liberation movement aimed at the overthrow of Ottoman rule and the destruction of rival Greek and Serbian national movements in the region. Yugoslav Macedonian ethnogenetic specialists do not deny the initial Bulgarian nature of the cultural-spiritual awakening of the Macedonian Slavs and the political-military ramifications of their movement. They insist, however, that the layer of Bulgarian national ideology which was spread over the Macedonian Slavs—just like the Greek national ideology that had preceded it—was circumstantial and incapable of standing the test of time. The main reason for the initial Bulgarian successes was the absence of a 'Macedonian' bourgeoisie, which left the field open to the Greek and, subsequently, the Bulgarian bourgeoisies to project among the Macedonian Slavs their respective national images and aspirations. Another reason was the fact that the Orthodox Slav peasants of Macedonia were caught up in the Greek-Bulgarian feud, locally fought between the Ecumenical Patriarchate and the Bulgarian Exarchate. They had only two choices: to remain loyal to the Patriarchate and thus be labelled Greeks, or to opt for the Exarchate and become Bulgarians. Local antagonisms soon grew into fratricidal conflicts, solidifying national identities. Nevertheless, Yugoslav Macedonian historians contend, admittedly not very convincingly, that towards the end of the nineteenth century a 'Macedonian' bourgeoisie did finally emerge in Macedonia. With extraordinary speed, it developed a 'Macedonian' national identity, which caught the imagination of the Macedonian masses. They, in turn, cast off their temporary Bulgarian—and Greek—national identity, and raised their own national liberation struggle under the guidance of the Internal Macedonian Revolutionary Organization. Under such revolutionary conditions, the hitherto 'misguided' Macedonian *narod* (people) was transformed, almost overnight, into the Macedonian *nacia* (nation). Thus, the armed conflict of Greeks, Bulgarians and Serbs in Ottoman-held Macedonia during the first decade of the twentieth century was not a contest for predominance among the three Balkan nationalities which inhabited Macedonia, but a struggle of 'Macedonians' against intruding foreign national ideologies. The Balkan wars of 1912-1913, which terminated Ottoman rule in Macedonia, are viewed in Yugoslav Macedonian historiography as involving a new subjugation of the 'Macedonians' to the imperialist bourgeoisies of Greece, Serbia (Yugoslavia) and Bulgaria.[44]

In relation to the second target of Yugoslav historiography, namely the application of the 'Macedonian' label to almost all human activity in Macedonia over a span of thirteen centuries, the breadth and depth of the operation are impressive. The catalyst was the Macedonian name. To Yugoslav policymakers of the early 1940s, it mattered little whether the name bore an ancient Greek legacy, or had been reintroduced since the Enlightenment as a regional name that was gradually shared by all the nationalities inhabiting the region. The advantages offered by the name 'Macedonia' to the ethnogenetic process were too many and too effective to be ignored. It was already familiar to the masses as a regional label, and therefore convenient for rapid adoption. It was clearly distinguishable from the Bulgarian, Greek or Serbian names, and was thus expected to lure Slav speakers away from whatever connections they maintained with these three nations. Most important, it offered the opportunity, through the interplay of its regional and national meanings, to create confusion, to muddle issues, facts, personalities, institutions and everything connected with Macedonia from antiquity to modern times. The alternating use of the regional and national meanings confused even specialists and swept the masses into an imagined world where anything *Macedonian* was automatically transformed in their minds to 'Macedonian'.

Social scientists in general, and historians in particular, felt free to exploit this confusion to strengthen the foundations of the new national ideology and to expand the physical and theoretical limits of the 'Macedonian' nation and its cultural heritage. In the Ottoman period the admixture of cultures in Macedonia allowed all its suitors to stake claims to local customs and folk culture. The tendency was either to associate them with the culture of adjacent regions where a given national group enjoyed undisputed dominance, or to trace them to common medieval or ancient origins. In the heat of the national antagonisms of the nineteenth century, excesses and exaggerations were frequent.

In the mid-twentieth century the issue reemerged, as Yugoslav Macedonians pursued well-trodden paths formerly explored—and exploited—by Greeks, Bulgarians and Serbs. There were, however, important differences. Whereas earlier disputants had sought to associate Macedonian cultural phenomena with neighboring regions and nationalities or with their ancient civilizations, the new suitors stressed the wholly autochthonous character of these phenomena. Once again, by the interplay of the national and the geographical interpretations of the Macedonian name, they sought to justify the appropriation of almost all cultural activity in Macedonia for the new 'Macedonian' nationality.[45]

In the field of political history, Yugoslav Macedonian historiography focuses on two important recent phases: the national liberation struggles of the end of the nineteenth and the beginning of the twentieth centuries; and World War II.

Sufficient reference has already been made to the first phase, which has been projected as a purely 'Macedonian' one, minus certain unpleasant manifestations conveniently attributed to the Bulgarians, Serbs or Greeks. Yugoslav Macedonian historians consider it the period of the self-assertion of the 'Macedonian' nation, while also viewing the liberation of Macedonia from Ottoman rule as a new, 'triple subjugation' to the three 'bourgeoisies' of Greece, Bulgaria and Serbia.[46]

The second phase, i.e. World War II, is projected as the 'second Iliden' which led to the official recognition of the 'Macedonian' nation and the establishment of the first Macedonian state. Yugoslav historians, however, are aware of the pro-Bulgarian manifestations of a large segment of the people of Yugoslav Macedonia—and of a section of the Slav speakers of Greece—during the German and Bulgarian occupation. The interpretation of this phenomenon is not easy. Indeed, if pro-Bulgarian manifestations are not seen as an expression of Bulgarian national identity, the alternative is to explain them in terms of collaborationism. The onus would be unbearable because it would involve even personalities who emerged at the end of the war as leading 'Macedonians'. As a result, a face-lift operation was undertaken to eradicate past Bulgarian connections and to glorify 'Macedonian' resistance beyond any realistic proportions. Despite the awkward position of knowledgeable contemporaries, an extraordinary volume of published works set the framework of new historical legacies for future 'Macedonian' generations. Already these have left their mark on the two generations which have grown up in the Socialist Republic of Macedonia—and the diaspora—since the end of World War II.

In the circumstances it is no surprise that a race is underway among Yugoslav Macedonian historiographers to claim the contemporary ground. Thus it has been argued that the first Allied victory against fascism in Europe was achieved by the 'Macedonians'. This refers to the Greek army's victorious repulsion of the Italian invasion of October 1940. Since some Greek army divisions drew their manpower partly from Macedonia, Yugoslav Macedonian authors labelled them 'Macedonian' in order to appropriate the credit for the first Allied victory. Similarly, the fact that Slav Macedonians joined, or were drafted into, the Greek communist forces during the Greek Civil War of 1946-1949 has been exaggerated in Yugoslav Macedonian historiography to such an extent that the conflict appears almost as a struggle of 'Macedonian' Greeks for the autonomy of Macedonia.[47]

To sum up postwar developments in the Socialist Republic of Macedonia: observers agree that the mutation process has progressed fairly well and has become entrenched, particularly among the new generations. It is difficult—and, indeed, immaterial—to apportion the respective roles of political developments, social structures and historical legacies in the success of this experiment. The fact, however, that Yugoslav Macedonians—politicians, historians and the media—react with extreme nervousness to historical interpretations other than those delineated by the revisionist historians of Skopje indicates that the historical edifice built over the past forty years continues to inspire considerable uncertainty.

New challenges, not of a historical nature, are emerging for the Socialist

Republic of Macedonia from another quarter. As Serbs, Greeks and even Bulgarians have more or less acquiesced in the solution applied to Yugoslavia's internal Macedonian problem, the rapid numerical growth of the Albanian minority poses a serious future challenge to the Republic's 'Macedonian' character. As a result, a new mutation process for turning various Muslim groups into 'Macedonians' has been initiated. It has already been shown that during the Ottoman period the Muslim religion had completely overshadowed linguistic or ethnic peculiarities. Thus, Slav-speaking Muslims identified themselves with Turkish- or Albanian-speaking co-religionists rather than with their fellow Slav-speaking Christians. The present regime in Skopje has launched a new initiative to sever Muslim groups from their ties with the Albanians and to transplant common historical legacies with the 'Macedonians'. Other, similar initiatives appear to involve Turkish- and Albanian-speaking groups, the hope being to expand the target area for new mutation processes in the future. Reaction has been violent from the Albanian side, however, with Tirana's atheist regime strongly criticizing the tinkering with the religious–ethnic affiliations of the Muslims of the Socialist Republic of Macedonia.[48] It remains to be seen whether historical legacies, real or imagined, can overcome the barriers of nationalist religion.

In Bulgarian Macedonia the inhabitants—who were kin to the Slav speakers of Yugoslav Macedonia—were exposed, following independence, to the same Bulgarian national ideology they had been receiving via Bulgarian activists and revolutionaries during the Ottoman period. Nevertheless, throughout most of the interwar period the region became a hotbed for political, not national, antagonisms among the various factions of Bulgarian Macedonian irredentism. During World War II, especially after the rise to power of the Fatherland Front, the Bulgarian Communist party, under Dimitrov, endorsed the Yugoslav solution to the Macedonian question. For three years the Bulgarian communists allowed 'Macedonian' activists from the Socialist Republic of Macedonia to carry their mutation experiment among the inhabitants of Bulgarian (Pirin) Macedonia.[49]

There were similarities, but also certain differences, between the Socialist Republic of Macedonia mutation model and that of the Pirin district. In both cases, state authority gave full support to the experiment. Nevertheless, whereas in the former the emergence of a Macedonian state generated support for the new nation as the local inhabitants realized that they were gaining equal status with the nationalities of the Yugoslav federation, in the latter the 'Macedonianization' process led directly to the secession of the Pirin district from Bulgaria. To Bulgarian Macedonian autonomists of the interwar period, a federative Macedonian state within federal Yugoslavia could hardly appeal as the justification of their struggles.

The determination of Georgi Dimitrov to honor his political commitments to Tito, made in the Bled agreements of 1947, was highlighted in 1948 by the transfer of Goce Delcev's remains from Sofia to Skopje.[50] It was a symbolic gesture signifying the decision of Dimitrov's Bulgaria to abdicate part of what had hitherto been considered her historical legacy in Macedonia. With Delcev's remains departed the

Bulgarian identity of a national liberation struggle fought in Macedonia for almost half a century (1870-1913).

Given the prevailing political conditions in Bulgaria immediately after the end of World War II, it was hardly surprising that the 1946 census gave the resounding number of 252,908 'Macedonians' in Bulgaria as a whole. In the Pirin district the percentage of 'Macedonians' was 70.[51] Shortly thereafter, in July 1948, Tito's expulsion from the Cominform offered the Bulgarians a way out of their predicament. Yugoslav Macedonian educators, political theorists and agents were expelled from Bulgarian Macedonia, and a reverse process of rehabilitation began. In subsequent years, despite fluctuations dictated by the course of Soviet-Yugoslav relations, the short-lived 'Macedonian' identity of the Pirin inhabitants was exchanged for the traditional Bulgarian one. Delcev's remains were kept in Skopje, but his 'rediscovered' Bulgarian identity secured him, once again, a venerable place in the Bulgarian pantheon.

In later years the Yugoslav-Bulgarian controversy over Macedonia was expressed not in terms of territorial claims, but through arguments over the national identity of the Slavonic people of Macedonia at large, as testified by the legacies of the past. Despite frequent fluctuations, Bulgarian official interpretation of Macedonian affairs has, more or less, acknowledged that the prevailing social and political conditions in the Socialist Republic of Macedonia have led, over a forty-year period, to the growth of a new national identity among the inhabitants of that part of Macedonia. Yugoslav Macedonians are no longer identified as Bulgarians, but rather as 'of Bulgarian extraction'. Yet even that tacit recognition is rejected by nationalist Yugoslav Macedonians, who view the claim to the Bulgarian origins of the 'Macedonians' as the negation of the foundation of the 'Macedonian' nation.[52]

Thus, despite the political formula advanced by Sofia, the Yugoslav-Bulgarian debate has remained unresolved. Neither side appears willing—or sufficiently imprudent—to make a concession on the cardinal issue of the historical origins of the Slavonic people of Macedonia. For the Yugoslav Macedonians, to retreat from their entrenched positions could well trigger a chain reaction that would challenge the very foundations of the edifice of their new nation. Likewise, for the Bulgarians to place in question their historical presence in Macedonia would deprive the Bulgarian people of their patrimony, and could well signal Bulgaria's total withdrawal from Macedonia, past, present and future, including from their own Pirin district.

Nevertheless, in a compromise move rare in Balkan politics, the Bulgarians in 1978 offered the Yugoslavs an ingenious proposal aimed at breaking the vicious circle of recriminations over the interpretation of the historical past of the Slavonic people of Macedonia. They suggested that the two sides should undertake joint study and find "generally acceptable and scientifically grounded stands on the disputed questions, and on the holding of coordinated or joint celebrations of *common remarkable events and personalities* in the history of the Bulgarian and Yugoslav peoples."[53] This Solomonic solution offered the two parties equal opportunity to interpret the legacy of the past in the most suitable way for each side. The Yugoslavs chose to turn down the proposal. It appeared that the theory of one history, of two nations, in three countries, was too daring or too risky for the young Socialist Republic of Macedonia to accept. Thus, the Yugoslav-Bulgarian debate over the interpretation of historical legacies in Macedonia continued unresolved into the 1980s.

Unexpectedly, at about the same time, the Greeks reentered the arena of the Macedonian controversy. Their involvement was not associated with any territorial or ethnological disputes, as had been the case in the past. With the termination of the Greek Civil War in 1949, the last vestiges of the Slav minority—earlier identified as Bulgarian and subsequently as Slav-Macedonian—had left the country en masse. The political rapprochement with Yugoslavia in the early 1950s, and the amelioration of relations with Bulgaria in the mid-1960s, had freed the Greeks from foreign aspirations and claims on Greek Macedonia. Belatedly, however, the Greeks began to realize that the mutation process, which had been going on in the Socialist Republic of Macedonia for almost four decades, had been unobtrusively undermining not only the Bulgarian but also the Greek heritage in Macedonia. Greek indifference towards developments in the Socialist Republic was due to the reluctance of successive Greek governments to let anything weaken their close relationship with Belgrade. On its part, the Greek left, bearing the onus of tragic mistakes in the handling of the Macedonian question during the Civil War, remained silent even when Yugoslav Macedonian historiographers directly challenged the Greek Communist party with its Civil War Macedonian record. Similarly, Greek intellectuals and scholars, with certain exceptions, tended to adopt a contemptuous attitude summed up in the statement: "everybody knows that Alexander the Great was Greek."[54]

Meanwhile, the death of Marshal Tito in 1980 removed a balancing element in Yugoslavia's internal national conflicts that had restrained nationalist excesses throughout the postwar era.

With the advent to positions of influence and leadership of the second generation of 'Macedonians'—a generation without the inhibitions of a former Bulgarian orientation—'Macedonian' neonationalism felt confident enough to expand in other directions. In rapid succession, a growing number of historical treatises, publications, movies and television series shifted their attention to Greek Macedonia and even to Albania. Yugoslav Macedonian historiography sought to establish the existence of 'Macedonian' minorities in all three neighboring countries.[55] It also tried to explore, and subsequently to appropriate as 'Macedonian', new vistas of cultural creativity or political history hitherto identified with the Greeks.

This second generation historiography is not directed at internal targets, since the mutation process within the Socialist Republic of Macedonia appears to have reached a satisfactory level. It is rather aimed at foreign audiences in an effort to gain international acceptance. Certainly a de facto recognition of the 'Macedonian' nation as a political reality since 1944 has been tacitly gained. What is sought is a kind of de jure recognition of a 'Macedonian' nation in all its dimensions, including the historical dimension, and which traces the origins of the new nation back at least thirteen centuries. To achieve this goal, the Socialist Republic of Macedonia has initiated a major cultural campaign abroad, taking advantage of Yugoslavia's favorable international position as a buffer between East and West and as protagonist in the nonaligned movement. Yugoslav bilateral cultural agreements invariably include a 'Macedonian' clause. Annual international conferences are held to acquaint foreign scholars with 'Macedonian' history, language and culture, while scholarships are offered in abundance to those willing to acquaint themselves with the past and present of the new nation. To break the linguistic isolation, a major translation program has been put into operation in order to make available in major foreign languages the basic works of Yugoslav Macedonian authors. It is as yet difficult to assess the impact of this activity. Neutral observers, however, believe that unlike politicians, who are motivated by subjective factors, scholars remain at the very least sceptical regarding the conclusions of revisionist 'Macedonian' historiography.[56]

In recent years, the policy of carrying the mutation process across the border to the Bulgarian province of Blagoevgrad (Pirin) has been extended to Greek Macedonia. Aware that the Slav-Macedonians, namely the Slav-oriented Slavophones, had left Greece in the 1950s as a result of the Civil War, Yugoslav Macedonians have directed their efforts mainly at Greek-speaking audiences in Greek Macedonia. Realizing that such traditional tools for conveying national ideology as schools, churches or the press are not available, or not suitable for existing conditions, they have instead opted for the services of the electronic media, television and radio. The approach could well be termed a 'tele-mutation process', inasmuch as it attempts to convey a novel national ideology across borders without direct physical contact between sender and receiver.[57]

Greek-language broadcasts from Radio Skopje have substantially increased the coverage of historical and cultural themes dealing with Greek Macedonia and the 'Aegean Macedonians'.[58] An analysis of these broadcasts reveals a pattern similar to that introduced in the Socialist Republic of Macedonia in the early phases of the mutation process. There are, however, certain marked differences. Whereas in the 1940s and 1950s the primary aim was to eradicate the Bulgarian connection, in the Greek-language broadcasts of the 1980s the emphasis is on challenging traditional Greek perceptions of Macedonian history and culture. Greek Macedonia is portrayed as the cradle which nurtured the 'Macedonian' national ideology. References to events and personalities of the medieval and Ottoman periods are not rare. Emphasis, however, is centered on the 'Macedonian' character of twentieth-century personalities and developments. Thus, various leaders of the 'Macedonian Struggle', known to Greeks as Bulgarians, are acclaimed by Radio Skopje as 'Macedonians' and are projected as local heroes. Similarly, Slav-Macedonians, who had participated during the Occupation and the Civil War in communist-led organizations, are singled out as 'Macedonian' fighters who died for the 'liberation' of Macedonia. Thus, a barely concealed plan to create and popularize a pantheon of 'Aegean Macedonian' personalities emerges over a series of broadcasts, TV serials, round-table discussions and even folk songs. Indeed, World War II, the Resistance and the Civil War are the subjects of extensive discussion and coverage. It is evident that 'Macedonian' historiography in recent years has diverted its effort so as to induct into modern 'Macedonian' history part of the Greek resistance in Macedonia as well as a significant portion of the Greek Civil War.[59] Radio and television programs from Skopje aim subliminally to convey a sense of pride for deeds—real or imag-ined—of 'Aegean Macedonians', and to connect them to the overall 'Macedonian' heritage. It is interesting to note that these historiographical experiments are pro-cessed along strongly anti-Greek lines, aimed apparently at rekindling the passions of the war years and particularly of the Civil War. It is a method reminiscent of the 1940s and 1950s, when the strongly anti-Bulgarian platform of the mutation process in the Socialist Republic of Macedonia was employed as shock treatment aimed at stripping Bulgarian identity from a considerable part of the local population.

Greek reaction to such developments, low-key just a decade ago, has acquired momentum in recent years, in the form of a campaign to 'defend' Greek national heritage. This reaction is far from resembling the mass psychosis caused in the nine-teenth century by Fallmerayer's denial of the continuity of the Greek nation. Nevertheless, it is clear that sections of the Greek press, the intelligentsia and some political figures have been alerted to the problem.[60]

Compared to other epochs—the armed struggles of the nineteenth century, the World War II occupation, and the Civil War—Greek Macedonia is today no longer a battleground for conflicting national ideologies. This helps explain the lack of any visible Greek government reaction to the broadcasts and opinions of Skopje radio and television. Concern has been registered, however, over the probable impact abroad of revisionist 'Macedonian' historiography. The appropriation of the Macedonian name by the Slavs has conveyed the impression to the Greeks that a significant portion of their heritage is in danger of being misrepresented before an ignorant international public. The initiatives of individual scholars or institutes, mainly in Greek Macedonia, are no match for the state machine of Skopje and its dissemination of 'Macedonianism'. By a strange coincidence, archaeological excava-tions in Greek Macedonia during the last decade have brought rich dividends. Not only has human knowledge about the little-known world of the ancient Macedonians widened, but new evidence of their Hellenic identity has been pro-vided in abundance.[61] Greek government financial assistance to archaeologists, tra-ditionally meagre, has become suddenly generous. Impressive exhibitions of the new findings have been organized and sent abroad, indirectly reasserting the links of Macedonia with Hellenism over three millennia. To the educated public, at least, the connection is self-evident. During recent decades, however, the worldwide contraction in classical studies has caused the ranks of knowledgeable audiences to shrink, and has increased vulnerability to controversial interpretations of historical phenomena.

Gradually, the Balkan controversy over the historical heritage of Macedonia began to take on an international dimension. This was particularly evident in countries such as Canada and Australia, and to a lesser extent the United States, with strong immigrant communities originating from all three parts of Macedonia. These immigrants had left their land of origin both before and after World War II. As a result they had become bearers of a variety of national orientations which they, or their families, had developed at specific historical moments. At the risk of oversimplification, it is possible to detect a strong Bulgarian national identity among prewar Slav-speaking immigrants to the United States, and a 'Macedonian' identity, of the Yugoslav type, among mainly postwar immigrants from Yugoslav Macedonia, and Slav-speaking immigrants from Greek Macedonia who had left their villages owing to the Greek Civil War. To complete the picture, larger numbers of Greek Macedonians, from Greece, who emigrated to the same countries, formed their own regional Macedonian associations within the wider context of the Greek communities, and proudly projected their Macedonian name as a historical and regional, not as a national, feature.[62]

Multicultural societies such as Canada and Australia offered unlimited opportunities to ethnic groups to cultivate and assert their respective ethnic characteristics. Grasping the opportunity, the various Macedonian groups found themselves competing over their origin, the Macedonian name and Macedonian heritage.[63] In a sense the situation resembled that of the last decades of Ottoman-ruled Macedonia, when the terrain was wide open for competing nationalities to assert themselves by undermining the historical titles, real or 'imagined', of their opponents. The policy of multiculturalism in Canada and Australia, and the general trend for 'roots-searching' in the United States, have stimulated competition among the traditional ethnic groups deriving from Macedonia. Moreover, they have generated new debates, this time among Slav-Macedonian groups who differ sharply regarding the extent and the nature of the historical basis of their national ideology.

Undoubtedly the bulk of new emigrants from the Socialist Republic of Macedonia were effectively immunized with 'Macedonian' national ideology, acquired through the educational process in their native land. Gradually, however, a slow process of mutation, originating from Greek or Bulgarian Macedonia, began to affect Slav-speaking immigrant groups. Despite certain gains, the new process came up abruptly against an unexpected situation: the development of a new brand of 'Macedonianism', which one might be tempted to identify as 'Macedono-Australian' or 'Macedono-Canadian'. It is an interesting phenomenon, which attests the influence of the historical factor in the shaping of national ideologies, particularly among people with inadequately formed perceptions of identity.

The case of Slav-Macedonian migrants who left Greek Macedonia with traumatic wartime and Civil War experiences is particularly revealing. Most were acutely conscious of their own family histories, dating from the years of the 'Macedonian Struggle' at the turn of the century when many families were divided, with some members joining the Greek and the others the Bulgarian side. After liberation, during the interwar period, they acquired Greek citizenship, received a Greek education and were treated as Greek Slavophones. Historical legacies, based on the 'continuity theory' of the Greek nation which was taught in Greek schools, bound Grecophone and Slavophone school children together through their 'imagined' descent from Alexander the Great. In wartime-occupied Macedonia, Slavophones were once again divided by conflicting national ideologies. Pressure was exerted, first by the Bulgarian occupation authorities and subsequently by Yugoslav Macedonian partisans, on behalf of their respective national ideologies. The situation bore a striking resemblance to that of the 'Macedonian Struggle', when opting for one or other identity was often not a voluntary process but the result of physical coercion, the need for survival, or particular circumstances. In a sense, similar conditions also prevailed during the Greek Civil War. Slavophones joining the Greek communist guerrilla forces were identified and treated as 'Slav-Macedonians' both by the KKE (Communist party of Greece) and by the government, while those joining the national army and fighting on the government side were accepted as Greeks. Emerging from the ashes of fratricidal conflict, the national identities of the two groups of Slavophones had been fossilized, not only by the fortunes of the war but also by the blending of political orientations with national ideologies.

With the conclusion of the Civil War, those Slavophones who took refuge in the Socialist Republic of Macedonia—estimated at roughly 40,000—were immediately subjected by the local authorities to the mutation process, then in full bloom. Eventually, a generation later, they appeared substantially integrated into the new social and national environment as 'Macedonians', and more precisely as 'Aegean Macedonians'. The rest found themselves in various Eastern European countries or in the Soviet Union itself, where they were exposed in KKE-operated Greek schools to a rather different blend of 'Macedonian' ideology. Its basic essentials were borrowed from the mutation experiment of the Socialist Republic of Macedonia. Owing, however, to tensions existing in the 1950s between Tito's Yugoslavia and the Soviet bloc, the KKE tried, initially at least, to maintain a distance between Slav-Macedonians within its jurisdiction—mainly young children—and the Macedonian Socialist Republic, while cultivating a sense of fraternity with the rest of the Greeks. A confused mixture of Greek and 'Macedonian' historical legacies was thus embedded in the minds of these young people. Years later, many of them, and their families, found their way to multicultural societies such as Canada and Australia, still searching for a suitable identity.

Although the Skopje brand of 'Macedonianism' appeared closer to these immigrants than the Greek or Bulgarian identity shared by other Slavophone immigrants, frequently from the same Greek Macedonian village, they felt reluctant to join the various Yugoslav-run 'Macedonian' organizations. Instead, they formed their own 'Macedonian' clubs, established their own 'Macedonian' churches, and published their own ethnic journals. Although, frequently, they crossed lines, they maintained their own political program, and manifested a unique perception of their historical heritage which clearly distinguished them from the Yugoslav 'Macedonians'. Their political program called for nothing less than a truly independent and united Macedonian state, free not only from Greece and Bulgaria but also from Yugoslavia. Their national ideology deviated also from the Yugoslav 'Macedonian' ethnogenetic theories, particularly in its insistence upon preserving an 'imagined' connection with the heritage of ancient Macedonia and the grandeur of its kings Philip and Alexander. Strongly denying the Greek identity of the ancient Macedonians, these 'Aegean Macedonians' sought, and seek, to expand their heritage in time, measuring it in millennia (in lieu of the thirteen centuries claimed by Yugoslav 'Macedonians') and in space, to encompass most of the eastern Balkan peninsula and parts of Asia Minor.[64]

Such grandiose perceptions were not uncommon in the eighteenth and early nineteenth centuries, among nationalists in an era of nation-building. The reemergence of such visions in multicultural states, at the end of the twentieth century, could probably be explained in terms of conditions prevailing in such pluralistic societies. 'Roots-searching' is not a panacea for an identity lost or for a challenged identity, but a social status symbol for survival and acceptance.

Back in the 'old countries', however, half a century after the wartime emergence of 'Macedonianism', national identities appear to have more or less crystallized. Different social, political and ethnological conditions in the three Macedonian regions have shaped different patterns. In the Yugoslavian Socialist Republic of Macedonia, the emerging second generation of 'Macedonians' appears to have accepted fully the new 'Macedonian' national ideology, founded on a revisionist appraisal of Macedonian history. Polemic literature or scholarly treatises challenging this appraisal, be they of Bulgarian, Greek or non-Balkan provenance, are deeply resented and sharply attacked. The debate is hardly theoretical. Whereas Bulgarians and Greeks oppose 'Macedonian' revisionist historiography as a negation of their own heritage, Yugoslav 'Macedonians' defend it because they view it as a basic prerequisite for their national survival.

For Greece, the acute problem caused by the interwar large-scale population exchanges and the civil struggles of the 1940s was the social, not the national integration of various groups within Greek Macedonia. Greek national identity among the various autochthonous and refugee elements was shared. Despite their different provenance (Macedonia, Asia Minor, neighboring Balkan states) all these Greek groups had been recipients of the same national ideology during the formative decades of the eighteenth and nineteenth centuries. At the threshold of the twenty-first century, from the former refugee elements a third generation is gradually emerging. While displaying a strong desire to preserve the cultural heritage of the 'lost countries', its members are fully integrated into the society they helped build in Macedonia. Urbanization, mobility and intermarriage have shaped a society in Greek Macedonia that scarcely resembles any longer the 'salade macédoine' of the first decade of this century. Macedonian regionalism in Greece is no different from Cretan, Epirotic or Peloponnesian regionalism. Today's Greek Macedonians take pride in their regional Macedonian name under such stimulants as the impressive new archaeological finds in Vergina, Pella, Dion and elsewhere, or new historical assessments of the contribution of their fathers to the overall Greek national liberation movement of the nineteenth century, which led to the formation of the modern unified Greek state.

During the nation-building process of almost two centuries, originally in the ethnologically mixed Ottoman region of Macedonia and subsequently in the Macedonian districts of Greece, Yugoslavia and Bulgaria, three distinct national identities have emerged, based on three different perceptions of the history of Macedonia. Historical legacies are less and less being used as tools for shaping new national ideologies. They are, rather, perceived as cherished monuments that sustain the respective peoples in their real or 'imagined' identities. As such, they are defended against foreign attempts to appropriate them or to falsify them. This seems to be the core of the contemporary debate over Macedonia.

NOTES TO APPENDIX III

1. In this text the term 'imagined' is used to define the subjective or visionary perception of groups or communities of their own national identity, heritage or 'mission'. For a detailed discussion, see the contributions to this issue by P. Kitromilides and T. Veremis, as well as Benedict Anderson's *Imagined Communities* (London, 1986).

2. Paschalis Kitromilides, "To Elliniko Kratos os Ethniko Kentro" [The Greek State as National Center], in *Ellinismos-Ellinokratia* (Athens, 1983), pp. 143–164.

3. On the Greek-speaking Muslims of south-west Macedonia, popularly known as Valaades, see Apostolos Vakalopoulos, *History of Macedonia, 1354–1833* (Thessaloniki, 1973), pp. 346–357.

4. On the Albanians, see H.N. Brailsford, *Macedonia: Its Races and their Future* (London, 1906), pp. 88–91 and 221–277; Archiv Kosova, *The Albanian League of Prizrend in the English Documents (1878–1881)*, 2 vols. (Priština, 1978); Stefanaq Pollo and Arben Puto, *Histoire de l'Albanie des origines à nos jours* (Roanne, France, 1974), pp. 125–155.

5. E. Kofos, "Struggles for Liberation", in M.B. Sakellariou, ed., *Macedonia: 4000 Years of Greek History and Civilization* (Athens, 1982) (hereafter *Macedonia: 4000 Years*), pp. 444–484.

6. Veselin Trajkov, *Rakovski i Balkanskite Narodi* [Rakovski and the Balkan Peoples] (Sofia, 1971), p. 503.

7. Konstantinos Paparigopoulos's monumental work *Istoria tou Ellinikou Ethnous apo ton Archaiotaton Chronon mechri ton Neoteron* [History of the Greek Nation from Ancient to Modern Times], 4 vols. (Athens, 1865–1874), is based on the continuity perception of Greek history. The same principle is shared by contemporary historians; see Apostolos Vakalopoulos, *Istoria tou Neou Ellinismou*, 6 vols. (Athens, 1961–1987); Nikos Svoronos, *Episkopisi tis Neoellinikis Istorias* (Athens, 1976); and the 16-volume collective work *Istoria tou Ellinikou Ethnous* (Athens, 1971–1978) (hereafter *I.E.E.*)

8. Among Rigas's revolutionary propaganda material were prints of Alexander's portrait, with appropriate commentary, a fact that attests to the popularity of the ancient Macedonian king. Apostolos Daskalakis, *Meletai peri Riga Velestinli* [Studies on Rigas Velestinlis] (Athens, 1964), pp. 315–316.

9. A significant number of Rigas's collaborators were Macedonian Greeks of the central European diaspora. I.K. Vasdravellis, *Oi Makedones kata tin Epanastasin tou 1821* [The Macedonians during the Revolution of 1821] (Thessaloniki, 1967), pp. 55–67.

10. The extensive use of Greek geographical names coincides with the peak of the Greek-Bulgarian national conflict in Macedonia during the last decade of the nineteenth and the first decade of the twentieth century. For example see document in K. Stalidis, "O Ellinismos tis Edessas prin kai kata ton Makedoniko Agona" [The Hellenism of Edessa prior and during the Macedonian Struggle], in *O Makedonikos Agonas - Symposium* (Thessaloniki 1987). p. 395.

11. The book was reissued in two volumes, in 1980: M. Dimitsas, *Sylloge Inscriptionum Graecarum et Latinarum Macedoniae* (Chicago, 1980).

12. Greek folk tradition in Macedonia preserved the memory of ancient Macedonia throughout the Ottoman period, albeit not always accurately. See A. Vakalopoulos, "O Makedonikos Agonas, koryfaia fasi ton agonon gia ti Makedonia" [The Macedonian Struggle as the Supreme Phase of the Struggles for Macedonia], in *O Makedonikos Agonas - Symposium*, p. 2.

13. *Preskazanie na Golem Alexadr* [Story of Alexander the Great] (Venetia [sic], no date), p. 18.

14. *Macedonia: 4000 Years*, p. 452.

15. E. Kofos, "Dilemmas and Orientations of Greek Policy in Macedonia: 1878–1886," *Balkan Studies*, Vol. 21, No. 1 (1980), pp. 48–49; and *I.E.E.*, Vol. XIII, pp. 379–381.

16. For contemporary definitions of Greek, see E. Kofos, *I Epanastasis tis Makedonias kata to 1878* [The Macedonian Revolution of 1878] (Thessaloniki, 1969), p. 13, n.1, and E. Kofos, *Greece and the Eastern Crisis, 1875–1878* (Thessaloniki, 1975), p. 25, n. 1.

17. On Greek state–Ecumenical Patriarchate relations, see E. Kofos, "Patriarch Joachim III (1878–1884) and the Irredentist Policy of the Greek State," *Journal of Modern Greek Studies*, Vol. 4, No. 2 (1986), pp. 107–120. It is worth noting that in the heat of the 'Macedonian Struggle', Greek Macedonian bands were supplied with a 'question-and-answer' sheet containing in simple words the basic arguments of Greek national ideology. Text in the Archive of the Foreign Ministry [Archeio Ypourgeiou Exoterikon: AYE], File 1907/aak, Θ.

18. Charalampos Papastathis, "I Ekklisia kai o Makedonikos Agonas" [The Church and the Macedonian Struggle], in *O Makedonikos Agonas–Symposium*, pp. 63–70.

19. Michael Laskaris, *To Anatoliko Zitima* [The Eastern Question], A (Athens, 1948), p. 247. E. Kofos, *O Ellinismos stin Periodo 1869–1881* [Hellenism in the Period 1869–81] (Athens, 1981), pp. 15–18.

20. On the Bulgarian Exarchate see Kyril, Patriarkh Bălgarski, *Bălgarskata Eksarkhia v Odrinsko i Makedonija sled Osvoboditelnata Vojna, 1877–1878* [The Bulgarian Exarchate in the Region of Adrianople and Macedonia after the War of Liberation, 1877–78], I, a (Sofia, 1969).

21. Veselin Trajkov, *Ideologičeski Tečenija i Programi v Nacionalno-Osvoboditelnite Dviženija na Balkanite do 1878 godina* [Ideological Tendencies and Programs in the National-liberation Movements of the Balkans up to 1878] (Sofia, 1978), p. 439. Representative works of interwar national Bulgarian bibliography are: Petar Nikov, *Văzrazdanie na Bălgarskija Narod; Cerkovno-Nacionalni Borbi i Postiženija* [Renaissance of the Bulgarian People; Ecclesiastico-national Struggles and Achievements] (Sofia, 1929), and C. Siljanov, *Osvoboditelnite Borbi v Makedonija* [The Liberation Struggles in Macedonia] (Sofia, 1933).

22. There are still Bulgarian historians who argue that the two brothers were Slavs, but the argument is refuted by a short Greek study: Basil Laourdas, *Kyrillos kai Methodios, Oi Ierapostoloi ton Slavon* [Cyril and Methodius, the Apostles of the Slavs] (Thessaloniki,

1966), pp. 23–30.

23. A general and detailed critique of the anti-Greek aspects of the Bulgarian national ideology appears in V. Colocotronis, *La Macédoine et l'Hellénisme* (Paris, 1919), pp. 517–541.

24. *Ibid.*, pp. 525, 528–529. Brailsford, *op. cit.*, p. 103, wrote after visiting the region at the peak of the Greek-Bulgarian band activity in the Macedonian villages that "The legend that Alexander the Great was a Greek goes out by one road and the rival myth that Alexander was a Bulgarian comes in by the other."

25. Francis Stevenson, *The Macedonian Question* (London, 1902), p. 9. For a critique of contemporary misinterpretation of Gladstone's views, see E. Kofos, *O Makedonikos Agonas sti Giougoslaviki Istoriografia* [The Macedonian Struggle in Yugoslav Historiography] (Thessaloniki, 1987), p. 5 n. 10.

26. Krste Bitoski, *Dejnosta na Pelagoniskata Mitropolija, 1878–1912* [The Activity of the Pelagonia Diocese] (Skopje, 1968), pp. 270–271.

27. D. Djordjević, *Istoria tis Servias, 1800–1918* [History of Serbia 1800–1918], (Thessaloniki, 1970), pp. 270–273; K. Džambazovski, *Kulturni-obštestvenite vrski na Makedoncite so Srbija kon krajot na XIX vek* [The Cultural and Social Relations of the Macedonians with Serbia toward the End of the Nineteenth Century] (Skopje, 1960); Ljubiša Doklestić, *Srpsko-Makedonskite Odnosi vo 19 vek* [Serbian-Macedonian Relations in the Nineteenth Century] (Skopje, 1973), pp. 93–99, 173–194, 211–214, 289–296.

28. Colocotronis, *op. cit.*, pp. 457–462. Brailsford, *op. cit.*, pp. 179–181, 184.

29. Nikolaos Vlachos, *To Makedonikon os Fasis tou Anatolikou Zitimatos, 1879–1908* (Athens, 1935), pp. 425–429.

30. For the Greek-Turkish and Greek-Bulgarian exchanges of populations, see Stephen Ladas, *The Exchange of Minorities, Bulgaria, Greece, Turkey* (New York, 1932); D. Pentzopulos, *The Balkan Exchange of Minorities and its Impact upon Greece* (Paris, 1965).

31. Elizabeth Barker, *Macedonia: Its Place in Balkan Power Politics* (London, 1950), pp. 21–29; E. Kofos, *Nationalism and Communism in Macedonia* (Thessaloniki, 1964), pp. 47–50.

32. Stephen Palmer and Robert King, *Yugoslav Communism and the Macedonian Question* (Hamden, 1971), pp. 12–14.

33. Konstantin Palešutski, *Jugoslavskata Komunistíčeska Partija i Makedonskijat Văpros, 1919–1945* [The Yugoslav Communist Party and the Macedonian Question] (Sofia, 1985).

34. Initially, the KKE used the terms *Makedones* and *Slavomakedones* interchangeably, but during the war years and in the resistance movement of the National Liberation Front (EAM) it more frequently chose the latter, in order not to offend the Greek masses of Macedonia who also used the name *Makedones* as a geographic term; details in E. Kofos, "I Valkaniki Diastasi tou Makedonikou sta Chronia tis Katochis kai stin Antistasi" [The Balkan Dimension of the Macedonian Question during the Occupation and in the

Resistance], in *Annals, Conference on Dictatorship, Occupation, Resistance, 1936–1944,* (Athens, 25–29 April 1984) pp. 418–471.

35. Barker, *op. cit.*, pp. 80, 83.

36. E. Kofos, "The Macedonian Question: The Politics of Mutation" (hereafter "Mutation"), in this volume *supra.*

37. 'Macedonian'- in inverted commas - is used in this text to distinguish the new national content attached to a traditionally *geographical* name. A first approach to the mutation process is attempted in E. Kofos, *I Makedonia stin Giougoslaviki Istoriografia* [Macedonia in Yugoslav Historiography] (Thessaloniki, 1974).

38. Palmer and King, *op. cit.*

39. *Ibid.*, pp. 154–159. Nicholas Andriotis, *The Federative Republic of Skopje and its Language* (2nd ed. Athens, 1966), pp. 12–18, cites numerous sources on the Bulgarian connection of the 'Macedonian' language.

40. C. Papastathis, "L'autocéphalie de l'Église de la Macédoine Yougoslave," *Balkan Studies*, Vol. 7 (1968), pp. 151–154.

41. The movement for unification was particularly strong during the war years and until Tito was expelled from the Cominform in 1948. It has since been abandoned as official dogma, but has survived in 'Macedonian' literature and historical treatises, and has been adopted by certain 'Macedonian' groups in the diaspora.

42. A critique of 'Macedonian' historiography is covered in two studies in Greek by this author: *I Makedonia stin Giougoslaviki Istoriografia* and *O Makedonikos Agonas sti Giougoslaviki Istoriografia* (both cited above).

43. *Istorija na Makedonskiot Narod* (Skopje, 1969), Vol. I, pp. 79–99.

44. Dragan Taškovski, *Radjanjeto na Makedonskata Nacija* [The Birth of the Macedonian Nation] (Skopje, 1967); by the same author, *Kon Etnogenezata na Makedonskiot Narod* [On the Ethnogenesis of the Macedonian People] (Skopje, 1974); and in English, *The Macedonian Nation* (Skopje, 1976).

45. Angelos Procopiou, *The Macedonian Question in Byzantine Painting* (Athens, 1962), pp. 13–27.

46. During a public debate in Yugoslavia in the summer of 1987, the 'Macedonians' defeated a Serbian proposal to inscribe in the calendar of important Yugoslav anniversaries for 1988 the 75th anniversary of the Treaty of Bucharest (1913) which had terminated the Second Balkan War and recognized the annexation by Serbia of over 30 percent of Macedonia, coveted at the time by Bulgaria.

47. In a text about the 'Macedonians' of Australia, prepared by Peter Hill, mainly from 'Macedonian' sources, it is contended that "during the Greek Civil War, the Slav Macedonians made up the bulk of the left-wing forces and hoped for an autonomous greater Macedonian State within a Balkan Federation." Text in *Makedonija* (Melbourne), 30 April–7 May 1987.

48. *Zeri i Popullit* (Tirana), 27 December 1987, accused 'leading circles' in the Socialist Republic of Macedonia of putting pressure on the Albanians, adding that "it is illogical and stupid to believe that in Macedonia a nation can be established by decree, and that a nationality, such as the Albanians, can disappear."

49. Kofos, *Nationalism, op. cit.,* pp. 143–146; Palmer and King, *op. cit.,* pp. 120-121.

50. Kofos, *Nationalism, op. cit.,* p. 160.

51. Tošo Popovski, *Makedonskoto Nacionalno Malcinstvo vo Bulgarija, Grcija i Albanija* [The Macedonian National Minority in Bulgaria, Greece and Albania] (Skopje, 1981), p. 131.

52. Bulgarian Academy of Sciences, *Macedonia: Documents and Material* (Sofia, 1978), pp. 14–15, states that "up to the Second World War the majority of the Slav population [in Yugoslav Macedonia] was Bulgarian". There is no assertion that it still is.

53. Bulgarian Ministry of Foreign Affairs, *For All-round Development of Bulgaro-Yugoslav Relations* (Sofia, 24 July 1978), p. 14.

54. Nicolaos Martis, *The Falsification of Macedonian History* (Athens, 1984), p. 114.

55. Typical is T. Popovski's book, cited above.

56. Stefan Troebst, *Die bulgarisch-jugoslawische Kontroverse um Makedonien, 1967–1982* (Munich, 1983), p. 200.

57. The method is not novel. Anderson (*op. cit.,* p. 127) writes that "multilingual broadcasting can conjure up the imagined community to illiterates and populations with different mother-tongues."

58. Transcripts of broadcasts in the possession of the author.

59. An eight-volume series of documents, dealing with events in Greek Macedonia during the Occupation and the Civil War, appeared in Skopje under the title *Egejska Makedonija vo NOB* [Aegean Macedonia in the National Liberation Struggle]. The title clearly signifies that events in Greek Macedonia at the time are held to form part of the recent history of the 'Macedonian' nation.

60. Some data are given by N. Martis, a former Minister of northern Greece, *op. cit.,* pp. 114–117.

61. Manolis Andronikos, *Vergina: The Royal Tombs* (Athens, 1984).

62. Two Federations of Greek Macedonian associations exist, bearing the Macedonian name the 'Pan-Macedonian Association of the United States and Canada' and the 'Pan-Macedonian Federation of Australia'. The latter is composed of the Pan-Macedonian associations on state level.

63. The analysis of 'Macedonian' nationalism in multicultural states is based on the study of a wide range of immigrant material, representing all trends of 'Macedonianism' abroad as well as Greek-Macedonian and Bulgarian-Macedonian views (material in the possession of the author). See also Kofos, "Mutation."

64. A few years ago a *Kratka Istorija na Makedonija* [Short History of Macedonia] appeared in Australia summarizing the perceptions of the followers of this movement. Denying that 'Macedonians' are, or have ever been, either Slavs or Greeks, it revealed that the Macedonians—a separate people— appeared 124 years after the cataclysm and spread from Macedonia to Bulgaria and Asia Minor. Not only was Alexander's empire 'Macedonian', but also the Byzantine Empire. Thus, Constantinople, not Thessaloniki should be the capital of a resurrected Macedonian empire. The ancient Macedonians and the present 'Macedonians' spoke and continue to speak a *Macedonian* language which is neither Greek nor Slavonic. In their pantheon of heroes and saints are Alexander, Aristotle and Democritus, Cyril and Methodius, Tsar Samuel, Goce Delcev, and the leaders of the Slav-Macedonian organizations which participated in the Greek Resistance and the Greek Civil War. A similar treatise was published in *Makedonija* (Melbourne), 30 July-21 August 1986, reprinted from *Glas na Makedoncite*. The following excerpts are particularly revealing: "For almost three hundred years we have been taught under cruel circumstances that we are Sloveni—Macedonians are dead and we are different people— 'Macedonian Slavians'. . . . Slavianism for us Macedonians is a deadly destructive political, moral and national force which aims to eradicate Macedonianism completely. . . . Politically, once we become Slavs we automatically lose any significance as descendants of the ancient Macedonians. . . . By calling ourselves Slavs we legalize this robbery by the Greeks [of the ancient Macedonians]. . . . For us, Macedonian revolutionaries, Macedonianism gives wholeness to our being, past, present and future. It is inner liberation from foreign imposed ideas, and confidence in our ability to be what we have been and will again be. . . . If we remain silent, we will remain Slavs, and as Slavs we have no legal right to anything Macedonian. . . . "